ESSAYS OF

ARTHUR SCHOPENHAUER

SELECTED AND TRANSLATED

By T. BAILEY SAUNDERS, M.A.

Vitam impendere vero.—JUVENAL.

A. L. BURT COMPANY, ❧ ❧ ❧ ❧ ❧
❧ ❧ ❧ ❧ PUBLISHERS, NEW YORK

TRANSLATOR'S PREFACE.

SCHOPENHAUER is one of the few philosophers who can be generally understood without a commentary. All his theories claim to be drawn direct from facts, to be suggested by observation, and to interpret the world as it is; and whatever view he takes, he is constant in his appeal to the experience of common life. This characteristic endows his style with a freshness and vigor which would be difficult to match in the philosophical writing of any country, and impossible in that of Germany. If it were asked whether there were any circumstances, apart from heredity, to which he owed his mental habit, the answer might be found in the abnormal character of his early education, his acquaintance with the world rather than with books, the extensive travels of his boyhood, his ardent pursuit of knowledge for its own sake and without regard to the emoluments and endowments of learning. He was trained in realities even more than in ideas; and hence he is original, forcible, clear, an enemy of all philosophic indefiniteness and obscurity; so that it may well be said of him, in the words of a writer in the "Revue Contemporaine," *ce n'est pas un philosophe comme les autres, c'est un philosophe qui a vu le monde.*

It is not my purpose, nor would it be possible within the limits of a prefatory note, to attempt an account of Schopenhauer's philosophy, to indicate its sources, or to suggest or rebut the objections which may be taken to it. M. Ribot, in his excellent little book,* has done all that

---

* "La Philosophie de Schopenhauer," par Th. Ribot.

is necessary in this direction. But the essays here presented need a word of explanation. It should be observed,
and Schopenhauer himself is at pains to point out, that
his system is like a citadel with a hundred gates: at whatever point you take it up, wherever you make your
entrance, you are on the road to the center. In this
respect his writings resemble a series of essays composed
in support of a single thesis; a circumstance which led
him to insist, more emphatically even than most philosophers, that for a proper understanding of his system it
was necessary to read every line he had written. Perhaps
it would be more correct to describe " Die Welt als Wille
und Vorstellung" as his main thesis, and his other
treatises as merely corollary to it. The essays in these
volumes form part of the corollary; they are taken from
a collection published toward the close of Schopenhauer's
life, and by him entitled " Parerga und Paralipomena,"
as being in the nature of surplusage and illustrative of his
main position. They are by far the most popular of his
works, and since their first publication in 1851 they
have done much to build up his fame. Written so as to
be intelligible enough in themselves, the tendency of many
of them is toward the fundamental idea on which his
system is based. It may therefore be convenient to
summarize that idea in a couple of sentences; more especially as Schopenhauer sometimes writes as if his advice
had been followed and his readers were acquainted with
the whole of his work.

All philosophy is in some sense the endeavor to find a
unifying principle, to discover the most general conception
underlying the whole field of nature and of knowledge.
By one of those bold generalizations which occasionally
mark a real advance in science, Schopenhauer conceived
this unifying principle, this underlying unity, to consist
in something analogous to that will which self-conscious-

ness reveals to us. Will is, according to him, the fundamental reality of the world, the thing-in-itself; and its objectivation is what is presented in phenomena. The struggle of the will to realize itself evolves the organism, which in its turn evolves intelligence as the servant of the will. And in practical life the antagonism between the will and the intellect arises from the fact that the former is the metaphysical substance, the latter something accidental and secondary. And further, will is desire, that is to say, need of something; hence need and pain are what is positive in the world, and the only possible happiness is a negation, a renunciation of the will to live.

It is instructive to note, as M. Ribot points out, that in finding the origin of all things, not in intelligence, as some of his predecessors in philosophy had done, but in will, or the force of nature, from which all phenomena have developed, Schopenhauer was anticipating something of the scientific spirit of the nineteenth century. To this it may be added that in combating the method of Fichte and Hegel, who spun a system out of abstract ideas, and in discarding it for one based on observation and experience, Schopenhauer can be said to have brought down philosophy from heaven to earth.

In Schopenhauer's view the various forms of religion are no less a product of human ingenuity than Art or Science. He holds, in effect, that all religions take their rise in the desire to explain the world; and that, in regard to truth and error, they differ, in the main, not by preaching monotheism, polytheism or pantheism, but in so far as they recognize pessimism or optimism as the true description of life. Hence any religion which looked upon the world as being radically evil appealed to him as containing an indestructible element of truth. I have endeavored to present his view of two of the great reli-

gions of the world in the extract to which I have given
the title of "The Christian System." The tenor of it is
to show that, however little he may have been in
sympathy with the supernatural element, he owed much
to the moral doctrines of Christianity and of Buddhism,
between which he traced great resemblance.

Of Schopenhauer, as of many another writer, it may be
said that he has been misunderstood and depreciated just
in the degree in which he is thought to be new; and that,
in treating of the conduct of life, he is, in reality, valuable only in so far as he brings old truths to remembrance.
His name used to arouse, and in certain quarters still
arouses, a vague sense of alarm; as though he had come
to subvert all the rules of right thinking and all the
principles of good conduct, rather than to proclaim once
again and give a new meaning to truths with which the
world has long been familiar. Of his philosophy in its
more technical aspects, as matter upon which enough,
perhaps, has been written, no account need be taken here,
except as it affects the form in which he embodies these
truths or supplies the fresh light in which he sees them.
For whatever claims to originality his metaphysical theory
may possess, the chief interest to be found in his views
of life is an affair of form rather than of substance; and
he stands in a sphere of his own, not because he sets new
problems or opens up undiscovered truths, but in the
manner in which he approaches what has been already
revealed.

He is not on that account less important; for the great
mass of men at all times requires to have old truths imparted as if they were new—formulated, as it were,
directly for them as individuals, and of special application
to their own circumstances in life. A discussion of human
happiness and the way to obtain it is never either unnecessary or uncalled for, if one looks to the extent to

which the lives of most men fall short of even a poor
ideal, or, again, to the difficulty of reaching any definite
and secure conclusion. For to such a momentous inquiry
as this, the vast majority of mankind gives nothing more
than a nominal consideration, accepting the current
belief, whatever it may be, on authority, and taking as
little thought of the grounds on which it rests as a man
walking takes of the motion of the earth. But for those
who are not indifferent—for those whose desire to fathom
the mystery of existence gives them the right to be called
thinking beings—it is just here, in regard to the conclusion to be reached, that a difficulty arises, a difficulty
affecting the conduct of life: for while the great facts of
existence are alike for all, they are variously appreciated,
and conclusions differ, chiefly from innate diversity of
temperament in those who draw them. It is innate temperament, acting on a view of the facts necessarily in-
complete, that has inspired so many different teachers.
The tendencies of a man's own mind—the idols of the
cave before which he bows—interpret the facts in accordance with his own nature: he elaborates a system containing, perhaps, a grain of truth, to which the whole of life
is then made to conform; the facts purporting to be the
foundation of the theory, and theory in its turn giving
its own color to the facts.

Nor is this error, the manipulation of facts to suit a
theory, avoided in the views of life which are presented
by Schopenhauer. It is true that he aimed especially at
freeing himself from the trammels of previous systems;
but he was caught in those of his own. His natural
desire was to resist the common appeal to anything ex-
tramundane—anything outside or beyond life—as the basis
of either hope or fear. He tried to look at life as it is;
but the metaphysical theory on which his whole philosophy
rests made it necessary for him, as he thought, to regard

it as an unmixed evil. He calls our present existence an infinitesimal moment between two eternities, the past and the future, a moment—like the life of Plato's "Dwellers in the Cave"—filled with the pursuit of shadows; where everything is relative, phenomenal, illusory, and man is bound in the servitude of ignorance, struggle and need, in the endless round of effort and failure. If you confine yourself, says Schopenhauer, only to some of its small details, life may indeed appear to be a comedy, because of the one or two bright spots of happy circumstance to be found in it here and there; but when you reach a higher point of view and a broader outlook, these soon become invisible, and life, seen from the distance which brings out the true proportion of all its parts, is revealed as a tragedy—a long record of struggle and pain, with the death of the hero as the final certainty. How then, he asks, can a man make the best of his brief hour under the hard conditions of his destiny? What is the true Wisdom of Life?

Schopenhauer has no pre-conceived divine plan to vindicate; no religious or moral enthusiasm to give a roseate hue to some far-off event, obliging us in the end to think that all things work together for good. Let poets and theologians give play to imagination! he, at any rate, will profess no knowledge of anything beyond our ken. If our existence does not entirely fail of its aim, it must, he says, be suffering; for this is what meets us everywhere in the world, and it is absurd to look upon it as the result of chance. Still, in the face of all this suffering, and in spite of the fact that the uncertainty of life destroys its value as an end in itself, every man's natural desire is to preserve his existence; so that life is a blind, unreasoning force, hurrying us we know not whither. From his high metaphysical standpoint, Schopenhauer is ready to admit that there are many things in life which give a short satisfaction and blind us for the moment to the realities of existence—pleasures as they may be called, in so far as they are a mode of relief; but that pleasure is not positive in its nature nor anything more than the negation of suffering, is proved by the fact that, if pleasures come in abundance, pain soon returns in the form of satiety; so that the sense of illusion is all that has been gained. Hence, the most a man can achieve in the way of welfare is a measure of relief from this suffering; and, if people were prudent, it is at this they would aim, instead of trying to secure a happiness which always flies from them.

It is a trite saying that happiness is a delusion, a chimera, the *fata morgana* of the heart; but here is a writer who will bring our whole conduct into line with that, as a matter of practice; making pain the positive groundwork of life, and a desire to escape it the spur of all effort. While most of those who treat of the conduct of life come at last to the conclusion, more or less vaguely expressed, that religion and morality form a positive source of true happiness, Schopenhauer does not professedly take this view; though it is quite true that the practical outcome of his remarks tends, as will be seen, in support of it; with this difference, however—he does not direct the imagination to anything outside this present life as making it worth while to live at all; his object is to state the facts of existence as they immediately appear, and to draw conclusions as to what a wise man will do in the face of them.

In the practical outcome of Schopenhauer's ethics—the end and aim of those maxims of conduct which he recommends, there is nothing that is not substantially akin to theories of life which, in different forms, the greater part of mankind is presumed to hold in reverence. It is the premises rather than the conclusion of his argument which interest us as something new. The whole world, he says, with all its phenomena of change, growth and development, is ultimately the manifestation of will—*Wille und Vorstellung*—a blind force conscious of itself only when it reaches the stage of intellect. And life is a constant self-assertion of this will; a long desire which is never fulfilled; disillusion inevitably following upon attainment, because the will, the thing-in-itself—in philosophical language, the *noumenon*—always remains as the permanent element; and with this persistent exercise of its claim, it can never be satisfied. So life is essentially suffering; and the only remedy for it is the freedom of the intellect from the servitude imposed by its master, the will.

The happiness a man can attain, is thus, in Schopenhauer's view, negative only; but how is it to be acquired ? Some temporary relief, he says, may be obtained through the medium of Art, for in the apprehension of Art we are raised out of our bondage, contemplating objects of thought as they are in themselves, apart from their relations to our own ephemeral existence and free from any taint of the will. This contemplation of pure thought is destroyed when Art is degraded from its lofty sphere, and made an instrument in the bondage of the will. How few of those who feel that the pleasure of Art transcends all others could give such a striking explanation of their feeling !

But the highest ethical duty, and consequently the supreme endeavor after happiness, is to withdraw from the struggle of life, and so obtain release from the misery which that struggle imposes upon all, even upon those who are for the moment successful. For as will is the inmost kernel of everything, so it is identical under all its manifestations; and through the mirror of the world a man may arrive at the knowledge of himself. The recognition of the identity of our own nature with that of others is the beginning and foundation of all true morality. For once a man clearly perceives this solidarity of the will, there is aroused in him a feeling of sympathy which is the main-spring of ethical conduct. This feeling of sympathy must, in any true moral system, prevent our obtaining success at the price of others' loss. Justice, in this theory, comes to be a noble, enlightened self-interest; it will forbid our doing wrong to our fellow-man, because, in injuring him, we are injuring ourselves—our own nature, which is identical with his. On the other hand, the recognition of this identity of the will must lead to commiseration—a feeling of sympathy with our fellow-sufferers—to acts of kindness and benevolence, to the manifestation of what Kant, in the "Metaphysic of Ethics," calls the only absolute good, the good will. In Schopenhauer's phraseology, the human will, in other words, ἔρως, the love of life, is in itself the root of all evil, and goodness lies in renouncing it. Theoretically, his ethical doctrine is the extreme of socialism, in a large sense; a recognition of the inner identity and equal claims, of all men with ourselves; a recognition issuing in ἀγάπη, universal benevolence, and a stifling of particular desires.

It may come as a surprise to those who affect to hold Schopenhauer in abhorrence, without, perhaps, really knowing the nature of his views, that, in this theory of the essential evil of the human will—ἔρως, the common selfish idea of life—he is reflecting and indeed probably borrowing what he describes as the fundamental tenet of Christian theology, that "the whole creation groaneth and travaileth in pain,* standing in need of redemption. Though Schopenhauer was no friend to Christian theology in its ordinary tendencies, he was very much in sympathy with some of the doctrines which have been connected with it. In his opinion the foremost truth which Christianity pro-

---

* Romans viii. 22.

claimed to the world lay in its recognition of pessimism, its view that the world was essentially corrupt, and that the devil was its prince or ruler.* It would be out of place here to inquire into the exact meaning of this statement, or to determine the precise form of compensation provided for the ills of life under any scheme of doctrine which passes for Christian: and even if it were in place, the task would be an extremely difficult one; for probably no system of belief has ever undergone, at various periods, more radical changes than Christianity. But whatever prospect of happiness it may have held out, at an early date of its history, it soon came to teach that the necessary preparation for happiness, as a positive spiritual state, is renunciation, resignation, a looking away from external life to the inner life of the soul—a kingdom not of this world. So far, at least, as concerns its view of the world itself, and the main lesson and duty which life teaches, there is nothing in the theory of pessimism which does not accord with that religion which is looked up to as the guide of life over a great part of the civilized world.

What Schopenhauer does is to attempt a metaphysical explanation of the evil of life, without any reference to anything outside it. Philosophy, he urges, should be cosmology, not theology; an explanation of the world, not a scheme of divine knowledge: it should leave the gods alone—to use an ancient phrase—and claim to be left alone in return. Schopenhauer was not concerned, as the apostles and fathers of the Church were concerned, to formulate a scheme by which the ills of this life should be remedied in another—an appeal to the poor and oppressed, conveyed often in a material form, as, for instance, in the story of Dives and Lazarus. In his theory of life as the self-assertion of will, he endeavors to account for the sin,

---

* John xii.31

misery and iniquity of the world, and to point to the way of escape—the denial of the will to live.

Though Schopenhauer's views of life have this much in common with certain aspects of Christian doctrine, they are in decided antagonism with another theory, which, though, comparatively speaking, the birth of yesterday, has already been dignified by the name of a religion, and has, no doubt, a certain number of followers. It is the theory which looks upon the life of mankind as a continual progress toward a state of perfection, and humanity in its nobler tendencies as itself worthy of worship. To those who embrace this theory, it will seem that because Schopenhauer does not hesitate to declare the evil in the life of mankind to be far in excess of the good, and that, as long as the human will remains what it is, there can be no radical change for the better, he is therefore outside the pale of civilization, an alien from the commonwealth of ordered knowledge and progress. But it has yet to be seen whether the religion of humanity will fare better, as a theory of conduct or as a guide of life, than either Christianity or Buddhism. If any one doctrine may be named which has distinguished Christianity wherever it has been a living force among its adherents, it is the doctrine of renunciation; the same doctrine which in a different shape and with other surroundings, forms the spirit of Buddhism. With those great religions of the world which mankind has hitherto professed to revere as the most ennobling of all influences. Schopenhauer's theories, not perhaps in their details, but in the principle which informs them, are in close alliance.

Renunciation, according to Schopenhauer, is the truest wisdom of life, from the higher ethical standpoint. His heroes are the Christian ascetics of the Middle Age, and the followers of Buddha who turn away from the Sansara to the Nirvana. But our modern habits of thought are

different. We look askance at the doctrines, and we have
no great enthusiasm for the heroes. The system which is
in vogue among us just now objects to the identification
of nature with evil, and in fact, abandons ethical dualism
altogether. And if nature is not evil, where, it will be
asked, is the necessity or the benefit of renunciation
—a question which may even come to be generally
raised, in a not very distant future, on behalf of some new
conception of Christianity.

And from another point of view, let it be frankly
admitted that renunciation is incompatible with ordinary
practice, with the rules of life as we are compelled to
formulate them; and that, to the vast majority, the doctrine seems little but a mockery, a hopelessly unworkable
plan, inapplicable to the conditions under which men
have to exist.

In spite of the fact that he is theoretically in sympathy
with truths which lie at the foundation of certain widely
revered systems, the world has not yet accepted Schopenhauer for what he proclaimed himself to be, a great
teacher: and probably for the reason that hope is not an
element in his wisdom of life, and that he attenuates love
into something that is not a real, living force—a shadowy
recognition of the identity of the will. For men are disinclined to welcome a theory which neither flatters their
present position nor holds out any prospect of better things
to come. Optimism—the belief that in the end everything
will be for the best—is the natural creed of mankind; and
a writer who of set purpose seeks to undermine it by an
appeal to facts is regarded as one who tries to rob humanity of its rights. How seldom an appeal to the facts
within our reach is really made! Whether the evil of life
actually out-weighs the good—or, if we should look for
better things, what is the possibility or the nature of a
future life, either for ourselves as individuals, or as part

of some great whole, or, again, as contributing to a coming state of perfection?—such inquiries claim an amount of attention which the mass of men everywhere is unwilling to give. But, in any case whether it is a vague assent to current beliefs, or a blind reliance on a baseless certainty, or an impartial attempt to put away what is false—hope remains as the deepest foundation of every faith in a happy future.

But it should be observed that this looking to the future as a complement for the present is dictated mainly by the desire to remedy existing ills; and that the great hold which religion has on mankind, as an incentive to present happiness, is the promise it makes of coming perfection. Hope for the future is a tacit admission of evil in the present; for if a man is completely happy in this life, and looks upon happiness as the prevailing order, he will not think so much of another. So a discussion of the nature of happiness is not thought complete if it takes account only of our present life, and unless it connects what we are now and what we do here with what we may be hereafter. Schopenhauer's theory does not profess to do this; it promises no positive good to the individual; at most, only relief: he breaks the idol of the world, and sets up nothing in its place; and like many another iconoclast, he has long been condemned by those whose temples he has desecrated. If there are optimistic theories of life, it is not life itself, he would argue, which gives color to them; it is rather the reflection of some great final cause which humanity has created as the last hope of its redemption:

> " Heaven but the vision of fulfilled desire,
> And hell the shadow from a soul on fire,
> Cast on the darkness into which ourselves,
> So late emerged from, shall so soon expire. " *

---

* Omar Khayyam ; translated by E. Fitzgerald.

Still, hope, it may be said, is not knowledge, nor a real answer to any question; at most, a makeshift, a moral support for intellectual weakness. The truth is that, as theories, both optimism and pessimism are failures; because they are extreme views where only a very partial judgment is possible. And in view of the great uncertainty of all answers, most of those who do not accept a stereotyped system leave the question alone, as being either of little interest, or of no bearing on the welfare of their lives, which are commonly satisfied with low aims; tacitly ridiculing those who demand an answer as the most pressing affair of existence. But the fact that the final problems of the world are still open, makes in favor of an honest attempt to think them out, in spite of all previous failure or still existing difficulty; and however old these problems may be, the endeavor to solve them is one which it is always worth while to encourage afresh. For the individual advantages which attend an effort to find the true path accrue quite apart from any success in reaching the goal; and even though the height we strive to climb be inaccessible, we can still see and understand more than those who never leave the plain. The sphere, it is true, is enormous—the study of human life and destiny as a whole; and our mental vision is so ill-adapted to a range of this extent that to aim at forming a complete scheme is to attempt the impossible. It must be recognized that the data are insufficient for large views, and that we ought not to go beyond the facts we have, the facts of ordinary life, interpreted by the common experience of every day. These form our only material. The views we take must of necessity be fragmentary—a mere collection of *aperçus*, rough guesses at the undiscovered; of the same nature, indeed, as all our possessions in the way of knowledge—little tracts of solid land reclaimed from the mysterious ocean of the unknown.

But if we do not admit Schopenhauer to be a great teacher—because he is out of sympathy with the highest aspirations of mankind, and too ready to dogmatize from partial views—he is a very suggestive writer, and eminently readable. His style is brilliant, animated, forcible, pungent; although it is also discursive, irresponsible, and with a tendency to superficial generalization. He brings in the most unexpected topics without any very sure sense of their relative place; everything, in fact, seems to be fair game, once he has taken up his pen. His irony is noteworthy; for it extends beyond mere isolated sentences, and sometimes applies to whole passages, which must be read *cum grano salis*. And if he has grave faults as well as excellences of literary treatment, he is at least always witty and amusing, and that, too, in dealing with subjects—as here, for instance, with the Conduct of Life—on which many others have been at once severe and dull. It is easy to complain that though he is witty and amusing, he is often at the same time bitter and ill-natured. This is in some measure the unpleasant side of his uncompromising devotion to truth, his resolute eagerness to dispel illusion at any cost—those defects of his qualities which were intensified by a solitary and, until his last years, unappreciated life. He was naturally more disposed to coerce than to flatter the world into accepting his views; he was above all things *un esprit fort,* and at times brutal in the use of his strength. If it should be urged that, however great his literary qualities, he is not worth reading because he takes a narrow view of life and is blind to some of its greatest blessings, it will be well to remember the profound truth of that line which a friend inscribed on his earliest biography: *" Si non errasset fecerat ille minus,"* * a truth which is seldom without application, whatever be the form of human effort. Schopenhauer cannot be neglected because

---

* Slightly altered from Martial. Epigram : I, xxii.

he takes an unpleasant view of existence, for it is a view which must present itself, at some time, to every thoughtful person. To be outraged by Schopenhauer means to be ignorant of many of the facts of life.

In this one of his smaller works, "Aphorismen zur Lebensweisheit," Schopenhauer abandons his high metaphysical standpoint, and discusses, with the same zest and appreciation as in fact marked his enjoyment of them, some of the pleasures which a wise man will seek to obtain —health, moderate possessions, intellectual riches. And when, as in this little work, he comes to speak of the wisdom of life as the practical art of living, the pessimist view of human destiny is obtruded as little as possible. His remarks profess to be the result of a compromise—an attempt to treat life from the common standpoint. He is content to call these witty and instructive pages a series of aphorisms; thereby indicating that he makes no claim to expound a complete theory of conduct. It will doubtless occur to any intelligent reader that his observations are but fragmentary thoughts on various phases of life; and, in reality, mere *aphorisms*—in the old, Greek sense of the word—pithy distinctions, definitions of facts, a marking-off, as it were, of the true from the false in some of our ordinary notions of life and prosperity. Here there is little that is not in complete harmony with precepts to which the world has long been accustomed; and in this respect, also, Schopenhauer offers a suggestive comparison rather than a contrast with most writers on happiness.

The philosopher in his study is conscious that the world is never likely to embrace his higher metaphysical or ethical standpoint, and annihilate the will to live; nor did Schopenhauer himself do so except so far as he, in common with most serious students of life, avoided the ordinary aims of mankind. The theory which recommended universal benevolence as the highest ethical

duty, came, as a matter of practice, to mean a formal
standing-aloof—the *ne plus ultra* of individualism. The
Wisdom of Life, as the practical art of living, is a compromise. We are here not by any choice of our own; and
while we strive to make the best of it, we must not let
ourselves be deceived. If you want to be happy, he says,
it will not do to cherish illusions. Schopenhauer would
have found nothing admirable in the conclusion at which
the late M. Edmond Scherer, for instance, arrived.
"*L'art de vivre,*" he wrote in his preface to Amiel's
"Journal," "*c'est de se faire une raison, de souscrire au
compromis, de se prêter aux fictions.*" Schopenhauer
conceives his mission to be, rather, to dispel illusion, to
tear the mask from life; a violent operation, not always
productive of good. Some illusion, he urges, may
profitably be dispelled by recognizing that no amount of
external aid will make up for inward deficiency; and that
if a man has not got the elements of happiness in himself,
all the pride, pleasure, beauty and interest of the world
will not give it to him. Success in life, as gauged by the
ordinary material standard, means to place faith wholly in
externals as the source of happiness; to assert and emphasize the common will to live, in a word to be vulgar.
He protests against this search for happiness—something
subjective—in the world of our surroundings, or anywhere
but in a man's own self; a protest the sincerity of which
might well be imitated by some professed advocates of
spiritual claims.

It would be interesting to place his utterances on this
point side by side with those of a distinguished interpreter
of nature in this country, who has recently attracted
thousands of readers by describing "The Pleasures of
Life;" in other words, the blessings which the world holds
out to all who can enjoy them—health, books, friends,
travel, education, art. On the common ground of their

regard for these pleasures there is no disagreement between the optimist and the pessimist. But a characteristic difference of view may be found in the application of a rule of life which Schopenhauer seems never to tire of repeating; namely, that happiness consists for the most part in what a man is in himself, and that the pleasure he derives from these blessings will depend entirely upon the extent to which his personality really allows him to appreciate them. This is a rule which runs some risk of being overlooked when a writer tries to dazzle the mind's eye by describing all the possible sources of pleasure in the world of our surroundings; but Sir John Lubbock, in common with every one who attempts a fundamental answer to the question of happiness, cannot afford to overlook it. The truth of the rule is perhaps taken for granted in his account of life's pleasures; but it is significant that it is only when he comes to speak of life's troubles that he freely admits the force of it. "Happiness," he says, in this latter connection, "depends much more on what is within than without us." Yet a rigid application of this truth might perhaps discount the effect of those pleasures with which the world is said to abound. That happiness as well as unhappiness depends mainly upon what is within, is more clearly recognized in the case of trouble; for when troubles come upon a man, they influence him, as a rule, much more deeply than pleasures. How few, even among the millions to whom these blessings are open—health, books, travel, art—really find any true or permanent happiness in them!

While Schopenhauer's view of the pleasures of life may be elucidated by comparing it with that of a popular writer like Sir John Lubbock, and by contrasting the appeals they severally make to the outer and the inner world as a source of happiness; Schopenhauer's view of life itself will stand out more clearly if we remember the opinion so boldly expressed by the same English writer. "If we resolutely look," observes Sir John Lubbock, "I do not say at the bright side of things, but at things as they really are; if we avail ourselves of the manifold blessings which surround us, we cannot but feel that life is indeed a glorious inheritance."* There is a splendid excess of optimism about this statement which well fits it to show up the darker picture drawn by the German philosopher.

Finally, it should be remembered that though Schopenhauer's picture of the world is gloomy and somber, there is nothing weak or unmanly in his attitude. If a happy existence, he says—not merely an existence free from pain—is denied us, we can at least be heroes and face life with courage: *das höchste was der Mensch erlangen kann ist ein heroischer Lebenslauf.* A noble character will never complain at misfortune; for if a man looks round him at other manifestations of that which is his own inner nature, the will, he finds sorrows happening to his fellow-men harder to bear than any that have come upon himself. And the ideal of nobility is to deserve the praise which Hamlet—in Shakespeare's Tragedy of Pessimism—gave to his friend:

> "Thou hast been
> As one, in suffering all, that suffers nothing."

But perhaps Schopenhauer's theory carries with it its own correction. He describes existence as a more or less violent oscillation between pain and boredom. If this were really the sum of life, and we had to reason from such a partial view, it is obvious that happiness would lie in action; and that life would be so constituted as to supply two natural and inevitable incentives to action; and thus to contain in itself the very conditions of happiness. Life itself reveals our destiny. It is not the

---

* "The Pleasures of Life. Part I. p. 5."

struggle which produces misery, it is the mistaken aims
and the low ideals—*was uns alle bändigt, das Gemeine!*

That Schopenhauer conceives life as an evil is a
deduction, and possibly a mistaken deduction, from his
metaphysical theory. Whether his scheme of things is
correct or not—and it shares the common fate of all
metaphysical systems in being unverifiable, and to that
extent unprofitable—he will in the last resort have made
good his claim to be read by his insight into the varied
needs of human life. It may be that a future age will
consign his metaphysics to the philosophical lumber-room;
but he is a literary artist as well as a philosopher, and he
can make a bid for fame in either capacity.   T. B. S.

CONTENTS.

THE WISDOM OF LIFE.

COUNSELS AND MAXIMS.

RELIGION AND OTHER ESSAYS.

THE WISDOM OF LIFE.

"Le bonheur n'est pas chose aisée: il est trèsdifficile de le trouver en nous, et impossible de le trouver ailleurs."— CHAMFORT.

THE WISDOM OF LIFE.

INTRODUCTION.

IN THESE pages I shall speak of "The Wisdom of Life" in the common meaning of the term, as the art, namely, of ordering our lives so as to obtain the greatest possible amount of pleasure and success; an art the theory of which may be called *Eudæmonology*, for it teaches us how to lead a happy existence. Such an existence might perhaps be defined as one which, looked at from a purely objective point of view, or, rather, after cool and mature reflection—for the question necessarily involves subjective considerations—would be decidedly preferable to non-existence; implying that we should cling to it for its own sake, and not merely from the fear of death; and further, that we should never like it to come to an end.

Now whether human life corresponds, or could possibly correspond, to this conception of existence, is a question to which, as is well-known, my philosophical system returns a negative answer. On the eudæmonistic hypothesis, however, the question must be answered in the affirmative; and I have shown, in the second volume of my chief work (ch. 49), that this hypothesis is based upon a fundamental mistake. Accordingly, in elaborating the scheme of a happy existence, I have had to make a complete surrender of the higher metaphysical and ethical standpoint to which my own theories lead; and everything I shall say here will to some extent rest upon a compromise; in so far, that is, as I take the common standpoint of every day, and embrace the error which is at the bottom of it. My remarks, therefore, will possess only a qualified value, for the very word *eudæmonology* is a euphemism. Further, I make no claims to completeness; partly because the subject is inexhaustible, and partly because I should otherwise have to say over again what has been already said by others.

The only book composed, as far as I remember, with a like purpose to that which animates this collection of aphorisms, is Cardan's *De utilitate ex adversis capienda,* which is well worth reading, and may be used to supplement the present work. Aristotle, it is true, has a few words on eudæmonology in the fifth chapter of the first book of his " Rhetoric ;" but what he says does not come to very much. As compilation is not my business, I have made no use of these predecessors ; more especially because in the process of compiling individuality of view is lost, and individuality of view is the kernel of works of this kind. In general, indeed, the wise in all ages have always said the same thing, and the fools, who at all times form the immense majority, have in their way too acted alike, and done just the opposite ; and so it will continue. For, as Voltaire says, " we shall leave this world as foolish and as wicked as we found it on our arrival."

CHAPTER I.

DIVISION OF THE SUBJECT.

ARISTOTLE* divides the blessings of life into three classes—those which come to us from without, those of the soul, and those of the body. Keeping nothing of this division but the number, I observe that the fundamental differences in human lot may be reduced to three distinct classes :

(1) What a man is : that is to say, personality, in the widest sense of the word ; under which are included health, strength, beauty, temperament, moral character, intelligence and education.

(2) What a man has : that is, property and possessions of every kind.

(3) How a man stands in the estimation of others : by which is to be understood, as everybody knows, what a man is in the eyes of his fellow-men, or, more strictly, the light in which they regard him. This is shown by their opinion

---

* "Eth. Nichom.," I. 8.

of him ; and their opinion is in its turn manifested by the honor in which he is held, and by his rank and reputation.

The differences which come under the first head are those which Nature herself has set between man and man ; and from this fact alone we may at once infer that they influence the happiness or unhappiness of mankind in a much more vital and radical way than those contained under the two following heads, which are merely the effect of human arrangements. Compared with genuine personal advantages, such as a great mind or a great heart, all the privileges of rank or birth, even of royal birth, are but as kings on the stage to kings in real life. The same thing was said long ago by Metrodorus, the earliest disciple of Epicurus, who wrote as the title of one of his chapters, "The happiness we receive from ourselves is greater than that which we obtain from our surroundings."* And it is an obvious fact, which cannot be called in question, that the principal element in a man's well-being—indeed, in the whole tenor of his existence—is what he is made of, his inner constitution. For this is the immediate source of that inward satisfaction or dissatisfaction resulting from the sum total of his sensations, desires and thoughts ; while his surroundings, on the other hand, exert only a mediate or indirect influence upon him. This is why the same external events or circumstances affect no two people alike ; even with perfectly similar surroundings every one lives in a world of his own. For a man has immediate apprehension only of his own ideas, feelings and volitions ; the outer world can influence him only in so far as it brings these to life. The world in which a man lives shapes itself chiefly by the way in which he looks at it, and so it proves different to different men ; to one it is barren, dull, and superficial ; to another rich, interesting, and full of meaning. On hearing of the interesting events which have happened in the course of a man's experience, many people will wish that similar things had happened in their lives too, completely forgetting that they should be envious rather of the mental aptitude which lent those events the significance they possess when he describes them ; to a man of genius they were interesting adventures ; but to the dull perceptions

---

* Cf. Clemens Alex. Strom. II., 21.

of an ordinary individual they would have been stale, everyday occurrences. This is in the highest degree the case with many of Goethe's and Byron's poems, which are obviously founded upon actual facts ; where it is open to a foolish reader to envy the poet because so many delightful things happened to him, instead of envying that mighty power of phantasy which was capable of turning a fairly common experience into something so great and beautiful.

In the same way, a person of melancholy temperament will make a scene in a tragedy out of what appears to the sanguine man only in the light of an interesting conflict, and to a phlegmatic soul as something without any meaning—all of which rests upon the fact that every event, in order to be realized and appreciated, requires the co-operation of two factors : namely, a subject and an object ; although these are as closely and necessarily connected as oxygen and hydrogen in water. When therefore the objective or external factor in an experience is actually the same, but the subjective or personal appreciation of it varies, the event is just as much a different one in the eyes of different persons as if the objective factors had not been alike ; for to a blunt intelligence the fairest and best object in the world presents only a poor reality, and is therefore only poorly appreciated—like a fine landscape in dull weather, or in the reflection of a bad *camera obscura*. In plain language, every man is pent up within the limits of his own consciousness, and cannot directly get beyond those limits any more than he can get beyond his own skin ; so external aid is not of much use to him. On the stage, one man is a prince, another a minister, a third a servant or a soldier or a general, and so on—mere external differences : the inner reality, the kernel of all these appearances is the same—a poor player, with all the anxieties of his lot. In life it is just the same. Differences of rank and wealth give every man his part to play, but this by no means implies a difference of inward happiness and pleasure ; here, too, there is the same being in all—a poor mortal, with his hardships and troubles. Though these may, indeed, in every case proceed from dissimilar causes, they are in their essential nature much the same in all their forms, with degrees of intensity which vary, no doubt, but in no wise correspond to the part a man has to play, to the presence or absence of position and wealth. Since everything which exists or happens for a man exists only in his consciousness and happens for it alone, the most essential thing for a man is the constitution of this consciousness, which is in most cases far more important than the circumstances which go to form its contents. All the pride and pleasure of the world, mirrored in the dull consciousness of a fool, is poor indeed compared with the imagination of Cervantes writing his "Don Quixote" in a miserable prison. The objective half of life and reality is in the hand of fate, and accordingly takes various forms in different cases : the subjective half is ourself, and in essentials it always remains the same.

Hence the life of every man is stamped with the same character throughout, however much his external circumstances may alter ; it is like a series of variations on a single theme. No one can get beyond his own individuality. An animal, under whatever circumstances it is placed, remains within the narrow limits to which nature has irrevocably consigned it ; so that our endeavors to make a pet happy must always keep within the compass of its nature, and be restricted to what it can feel. So it is with man ; the measure of the happiness he can attain is determined beforehand by his individuality. More especially is this the case with the mental powers which fix once for all his capacity for the higher kinds of pleasure. If these powers are small, no efforts from without, nothing that his fellowmen or that fortune can do for him, will suffice to raise him above the ordinary degree of human happiness and pleasure, half animal though it be ; his only resources are his sensual appetite—a cozy and cheerful family life at the most—low company and vulgar pastime ; even education, on the whole, can avail little, if anything, for the enlargement of his horizon. For the highest, most varied and lasting pleasures are those of the mind, however much our youth may deceive us on this point ; and the pleasures of the mind turned chiefly on the powers of the mind. It is clear, then, that our happiness depends in a great degree upon what we are, upon our individuality, while lot or destiny is generally taken to mean only what we have, or our reputation. Our lot in this sense, may improve ; but we do not ask much of it if we are inwardly rich : on the other hand, a fool remains a fool, a dull blockhead, to his last hour, even though he were surrounded by houris in paradise. This is why Goethe, in the

West-östlicher Divan, says that every man, whether he
occupy a low position in life, or emerges as its victor,
testifies to personality as the greatest factor in happiness :

> "Volk und Knecht und Ueberwinder
> Sie gestehen, zu jeder Zeit,
> Höchstes Glück der Erdenkinder
> Sei nur die Persönlichkeit."

Everything confirms the fact that the subjective element
in life is incomparably more important for our happiness
and pleasure than the objective, from such sayings as
"Hunger is the best sauce," and "Youth and age cannot live
together," up to the life of the genius and the saint.
Health outweighs all other blessings so much that one may
really say that a healthy beggar is happier than an ailing
king. A quiet and cheerful temperament, happy in the
enjoyment of a perfectly sound physique, an intellect
clear, lively, penetrating and seeing things as they are, a
moderate and gentle will, and therefore a good conscience
—these are privileges which no rank or wealth can make
up for or replace. For what a man is in himself, what
accompanies him when he is alone, what no one can give
or take away, is obviously more essential to him than
everything he has in the way of possessions, or even what
he may be in the eyes of the world. An intellectual man
in complete solitude has excellent entertainment in his own
thoughts and fancies, while no amount or diversity of
social pleasure, theaters, excursions and amusements, can
ward off boredom from a dullard. A good, temperate,
gentle character can be happy in needy circumstances,
while a covetous, envious and malicious man, even if he
be the richest in the world, goes miserable. Nay more ;
to one who has the constant delight of a special individuality, with a high degree of intellect, most of the
pleasures which are run after by mankind are perfectly
superfluous ; they are even a trouble and a burden. And
so Horace says of himself, that, however many are deprived
of the fancy goods of life, there is one at least who can
live without them :

> "Gemmas, marmor, ebur, Tyrrhena sigilla, tabellas,
> Argentum, vestes Gætulo murice tinctas
> Sunt qui non habeant, est qui non curat habere;"

and when Socrates saw various articles of luxury spread out for sale, he exclaimed : "How much there is in the world that I do not want."

So the first and most essential element in our life's happiness is what we are, our personality, if for no other reason than that it is a constant factor coming into play under all circumstances; besides, unlike the blessings which are described under the other two heads, it is not the sport of destiny and cannot be wrested from us ; and, so far, it is endowed with an absolute value in contrast to the merely relative worth of the other two. The consequence of this is that it is much more difficult than people commonly suppose to get a hold on a man from without. But here the all-powerful agent, Time, comes in and claims its rights, and before its influence physical and mental advantages gradually waste away. Moral character alone remains inaccessible to it. In view of the destructive effect of time, it seems, indeed, as if the blessings named under the other two heads, of which time cannot directly rob us, were superior to those of the first. Another advantage might be claimed for them, namely, that being in their very nature objective and external, they are attainable, and every one is presented with the possibility, at least, of coming into possession of them ; while what is subjective is not open to us to acquire, but making its entry by a kind of divine right, it remains for life, immutable, inalienable, an inexorable doom. Let me quote those lines in which Goethe describes how an unalterable destiny is assigned to every man at the hour of his birth, so that he can develop only in the lines laid down for him, as it were, by the conjunctions of the stars ; and how the Sibyl and the prophets declare that himself a man can never escape, nor any power of time avail to change the path on which his life is cast :

> " Wie an dem Tag, der dich der Welt verliehen,
> Die Sonne stand zum Grusse der Planeten,
> Bist alsobald und fort und fort gediehen,
> Nach dem Gesetz, wonach du angetreten.
> So musst du sein, dir kannst du nicht entfliehen.
> So sagten schon Sibyllen und Propheten;
> Und keine Zeit und keine Macht zerstückelt
> Geprägte Form, die lebend sich entwickelt."

The only thing that stands in our power to achieve, is

to make the most advantageous use possible of the personal qualities we possess, and accordingly to follow such pursuits only as will call them into play, to strive after the kind of perfection of which they admit and to avoid every other ; consequently, to choose the position, occupation and manner of life which are most suitable for their development.

Imagine a man endowed with Herculean strength who is compelled by circumstances to follow a sedentary occupation, some minute exquisite work of the hands, for example, or to engage in study and mental labor demanding quite other powers, and just those which he has not got, compelled, that is, to leave unused the powers in which he is pre-eminently strong ; a man placed like this will never feel happy all his life through. Even more miserable will be the lot of the man with intellectual powers of a very high order, who has to leave them undeveloped and unemployed, in the pursuit of a calling which does not require them, some bodily labor, perhaps, for which his strength is insufficient. Still, in a case of this kind, it should be our care, especially in youth, to avoid the precipice of presumption, and not ascribe to ourselves a superfluity of power which is not there.

Since the blessings described under the first head decidedly outweigh those contained under the other two, it is manifestly a wiser course to aim at the maintenance of our health and the cultivation of our faculties, than at the amassing of wealth ; but this must not be mistaken as meaning that we should neglect to acquire an adequate supply of the necessaries of life. Wealth, in the strict sense of the word, that is, great superfluity, can do little for our happiness ; and many rich people feel unhappy just because they are without any true mental culture or knowledge, and consequently have no objective interests which would qualify them for intellectual occupations. For beyond the satisfaction of some real and natural necessities, all that the possession of wealth can achieve has a very small influence upon our happiness, in the proper sense of the word ; indeed, wealth rather disturbs it, because the preservation of property entails a great many unavoidable anxieties. And still men are a thousand times more intent on becoming rich than on acquiring culture, though it is quite certain that what a man is contributes much more to his happiness than what he has. So you may see many a man, as industrious as an ant, ceaselessly occupied from morning to night in the endeavor to increase his heap of gold. Beyond the narrow horizon of means to this end, he knows nothing; his mind is a blank, and consequently unsusceptible to any other influence. The highest pleasures, those of the intellect, are to him inaccessible, and he tries in vain to replace them by the fleeting pleasures of sense in which he indulges, lasting but a brief hour and at tremendous cost. And if he is lucky, his struggles result in his having a really great pile of gold, which he leaves to his heir, either to make it still larger, or to squander it in extravagance. A life like this, though pursued with a sense of earnestness and an air of importance, is just as silly as many another which has a fool's cap for its symbol.

What a man has in himself is, then, the chief element in his happiness. Because this is, as a rule, so very little, most of those who are placed beyond the struggle with penury, feel at bottom quite as unhappy as those who are still engaged in it. Their minds are vacant, their imagination dull, their spirits poor, and so they are driven to the company of those like them—for *similis simili gaudet*—where they make common pursuit of pastime and entertainment, consisting for the most part in sensual pleasure, amusement of every kind, and finally, in excess and libertinism. A young man of rich family enters upon life with a large patrimony, and often runs through it in an incredibly short space of time, in vicious extravagance; and why? Simply because, here too, the mind is empty and void, and so the man is bored with existence. He was sent forth into the world outwardly rich but inwardly poor, and his vain endeavor was to make his external wealth compensate for his inner poverty, by trying to obtain everything from without, like an old man who seeks to strengthen himself as King David or Marechal de Retz tried to do. And so in the end one who is inwardly poor comes to be also poor outwardly.

I need not insist upon the importance of the other two kinds of blessings which make up the happiness of human life; nowadays the value of possessing them is too well known to require advertisement. The third class, it is true, may seem, compared with the second, of a very ethereal character, as it consists only of other people's opinions. Still every one has to strive for reputation, that is to say, a good name. Rank, on the other hand, should be aspired to only by those who serve the state, and fame by very few indeed. In any case, reputation is looked upon as a priceless treasure, and fame as the most precious of all the blessings a man can attain—the Golden Fleece, as it were, of the elect : while only fools will prefer rank to property. The second and third classes, moreover, are reciprocally cause and effect ; so far that is, as Petronius' maxim, *habes habeberis*, is true ; and conversely, the favor of others, in all its forms, often puts us in the way of getting what we want.

CHAPTER II.

PERSONALITY, OR WHAT A MAN IS.

WE HAVE already seen, in general, that what a man is contributes much more to his happiness than what he has or how he is regarded by others. What a man is, and so what he has in his own person, is always the chief thing to consider; for his individuality accompanies him always and everywhere, and gives its color to all his experiences. In every kind of enjoyment for instance, the pleasure depends principally upon the man himself. Every one admits this in regard to physical, and how much truer it is of intellectual pleasure. When we use that English expression, " to enjoy one's self," we are employing a very striking and appropriate phrase; for observe—one says, not " he enjoys Paris," but " he enjoys himself in Paris." To a man possessed of an ill-conditioned individuality, all pleasure is like delicate wine in a mouth made bitter with gall. Therefore, in the blessings as well as in the ills of life, less depends upon what befalls us than upon the way in which it is met, that is, upon the kind and degree of our general susceptibility. What a man is and has in himself—in a word, personality, with all it entails, is the only immediate and direct factor in his happiness and welfare. All else is mediate and indirect, and its influence can be neutralized and frustrated ; but the influence of personality never. This is why the envy which personal qualities excite is the most implacable of all—as it is also the most carefully dissembled.

Further, the constitution of our consciousness is the ever present and lasting element in all we do or suffer ; our individuality is persistently at work, more or less, at every moment of our life : all other influences are temporal, incidental, fleeting, and subject to every kind of chance and change. This is why Aristotle says : " It is not wealth but character that lasts." * And just for the same reason we can more easily bear a misfortune which comes to us entirely from without, than one which we have drawn upon ourselves ; for fortune may always change, but not character. Therefore, subjective blessings—a noble nature, a capable head, a joyful temperament, bright spirits, a well-constituted, perfectly sound physique, in a word, *mens sana in corpore sano*, are the first and most important elements in happiness ; so that we should be more intent cn promoting and preserving such qualities than on the possession of external wealth and external honor.

And of all these, the one which makes us the most directly happy is a genial flow of good spirits ; for this excellent quality is its own immediate reward. The man who is cheerful and merry has always a good reason for being so—the fact, namely, that he is so. There is nothing which, like this quality, can so completely replace the loss of every other blessing. If you know any one who is young, handsome, rich and esteemed, and you want to know, further, if he is happy, ask, Is he cheerful and genial ?—and if he is, what does it matter whether he is young or old, straight or humpbacked, poor or rich ?—he is happy. In my early days I once opened an old book and found these words : " If you laugh a great deal, you are happy ; if you cry a great deal, you are unhappy "—a very simple remark, no doubt ; but just because it is so simple I have never been able to forget it, even though it is in the last degree a truism. So if cheerfulness knocks at our door, we should throw it wide open, for it never comes inopportunely ; instead of that, we often make scruples about letting it in. We want to be quite sure that we have every reason to be contented, then we are afraid that cheerful-

* Eth. Eud., vii. 2. 37 :—

ή γὰρ φύσις βέβαιον, οὐ τὰ χρήματα.

ness of spirits may interfere with serious reflections or weighty cares. Cheerfulness is a direct and immediate gain—the very coin, as it were, of happines, and not, like all else, merely a check upon the bank ; for it alone makes us immediately happy in the present moment, and that is the highest blessing for beings like us, whose existence is but an infinitesimal moment between two eternities. To s cure and promote this feeling of cheerfulness should be the supreme aim of all our endeavors after happiness.

Now it is certain that nothing contributes so little to cheerfulness as riches, or so much, as health. Is it not in the lower classes, the so-called working classes, more especially those of them who live in the country, that we see cheerful and contented faces? and is it not among the rich, the upper classes, that we find faces full of ill-humor and vexation? Consequently we should try as much as possible to maintain a high degree of health ; for cheerfulness is the very flower of it. I need hardly say what one must do to be healthy—avoid every kind of excess, all violent and unpleasant emotion, all mental overstrain, take daily exercise in the open air, cold baths and such like hygienic measures. For without a proper amount of daily exercise no one can remain healthy ; all the processes of life demand exercise for the due performance of their functions, exercise not only of the parts more immediately concerned, but also of the whole body. For, as Aristotle rightly says, " Life is movement ;" it is its very essence. Ceaseless and rapid motion goes on in every part of the organism. The heart, with its complicated double systole and diastole, beats strongly and untiringly ; with twenty-eight beats it has to drive the whole of the blood through arteries, veins and capillaries ; the lungs pump like a steam-engine, without intermission ; the intestines are always in peristaltic action ; the glands are all constantly absorbing and secreting ; even the brain has a double motion of its own, with every beat of the pulse and every breath we draw. When people can get no exercise at all, as is the case with the countless numbers who are condemned to a sedentary life, there is a glaring and fatal disproportion between outward inactivity and inner tumult. For this ceaseless internal motion requires some external counterpart, and the want of it produces effects like those of emotion which we are obliged to suppress. Even trees must be shaken by

the wind, if they are to thrive. The rule which finds
its application here may be most briefly expressed in Latin ;
omnis motus, quo celerior, eo magis motus.

How much our happiness depends upon our spirits, and
these again upon our state of health, may be seen by comparing the influence which the same external circumstances
or events have upon us when we are well and strong with
the effect which they have when we are depressed and
troubled with ill-health. It is not what things are
objectively and in themselves, but what they are for us, in
our way of looking at them, that makes us happy or the
reverse. As Epictetus says, " Men are not influenced by
things but by their thoughts about things." And, in general, nine-tenths of our happiness depends upon health
alone. With health, everything is a source of pleasure ;
without it, nothing else, whatever it may be, is enjoyable ;
even the other personal blessings—a great mind, a happy
temperament—are degraded and dwarfed for want of it.
So it is really with good reason that, when two people
meet, the first thing they do is to inquire after each other's
health, and to express the hope that it is good ; for good
health is by far the most important element in human
happiness. It follows from all this that the greatest of
follies is to sacrifice health for any other kind of happiness,
whatever it may be, for gain, advancement, learning or
fame, let alone, then, for fleeting sensual pleasures.
Everything else should rather be postponed to it.

But however much health may contribute to that flow of
good spirits which is so essential to our happiness, good
spirits do not entirely depend upon health ; for a man may
be perfectly sound in his physique and still possess a
melancholy temperament and be generally given up to sad
thoughts. The ultimate cause of this is undoubtedly to be
found in innate, and therefore unalterable, physical constitution, especially in the more or less normal relation
of a man's sensitiveness to his muscular and vital energy.
Abnormal sensitiveness produces inequality of spirits, a
predominating melancholy, with periodical fits of unrestrained liveliness. A genius is one whose nervous power
or sensitiveness is largely in excess ; as Aristotle* has very
correctly observed, " Men distinguished in philosophy,

---

* Probl. xxx. ep. 1.

politics, poetry or art, appear to be all of a melancholy temperament." This is doubtless the passage which Cicero has in his mind when he says, as he often does, *"Aristoteles ait omnes ingeniosos melancholicos esse."** Shakespeare has very neatly expressed this radical and innate diversity of temperament in those lines in "The Merchant of Venice :"

> " Nature has framed strange fellows in her time ;
> Some that will evermore peep through their eyes
> And laugh, like parrots at a bag-piper ;
> And others of such vinegar aspect,
> That they'll not show their teeth in way of smile,
> Though Nestor swear the jest be laughable."

This is the difference which Plato draws between εὔκολος and δύσκολος—the man of easy, and the man of difficult disposition—in proof of which he refers to the varying degrees of susceptibility which different people show to pleasurable and painful impressions ; so that one man will laugh at what makes another despair. As a rule, the stronger the susceptibility to unpleasant impressions, the weaker is the susceptibility to pleasant ones, and *vice versâ.* If it is equally possible for an event to turn out well or ill, the δύσκολος will be annoyed or grieved if the issue is unfavorable, and will not rejoice, should it be happy. On the other hand, the εὔκολος, will neither worry nor fret over an unfavorable issue, but rejoice if it turns out well. If the one is successful in nine out of ten undertakings, he will not be pleased, but rather annoyed that one has miscarried ; while the other, if only a single one succeeds, will manage to find consolation in the fact and remain cheerful. But here is another instance of the truth, that hardly any evil is entirely without its compensation ; for the misfortunes and sufferings which the δύσκολοι, that is, people of gloomy and anxious character, have to overcome, are, on the whole, more imaginary and therefore less real than those which befall the gay and careless ; for a man who paints everything black, who constantly fears the worst and takes measures accordingly, will not be disappointed so often in this world, as one who always looks upon the bright side of things. And when a morbid affection of the nerves, or a derangement of the

* Tusc. i., 33.

digestive organs, plays into the hand of an innate tendency to gloom, this tendency may reach such a height that permanent discomfort produces a weariness of life. So arises an inclination to suicide, which even the most trivial unpleasantness may actually bring about; nay, when the tendency attains its worst form, it may be occasioned by nothing in particular, but a man may resolve to put an end to his existence, simply because he is permanently unhappy, and then coolly and firmly carry out his determination; as may be seen by the way in which the sufferer, when placed under supervision, as he usually is, eagerly waits to seize the first unguarded moment, when, without a shudder, without a struggle or recoil, he may use the now natural and welcome means of effecting his release.* Even the healthiest, perhaps even the most cheerful man, may resolve upon death under certain circumstances; when, for instance, his sufferings, or his fears of some inevitable misfortune, reach such a pitch as to outweigh the terrors of death. The only difference lies in the degree of suffering necessary to bring about the fatal act, a degree which will be high in the case of a cheerful, and low in that of a gloomy man. The greater the melancholy, the lower need the degree be: in the end, it may even sink to zero. But if a man is cheerful, and his spirits are supported by good health, it requires a high degree of suffering to make him lay hands upon himself. There are countless steps in the scale between the two extremes of suicide, the suicide which springs merely from a morbid intensification of innate gloom, and the suicide of the healthy and cheerful man, who has entirely objective grounds for putting an end to his existence.

Beauty is partly an affair of health. It may be reckoned as a personal advantage; though it does not, properly speaking, contribute directly to our happiness. It does so indirectly, by impressing other people; and it is no unimportant advantage, even in man. Beauty is an open letter of recommendation, predisposing the heart to favor the person who presents it. As is well said in those lines of Homer, the gift of beauty is not lightly to be

---

* For a detailed description of this condition of mind *cf.* Esquirol Des maladies mentales.

thrown away, that glorious gift which none can bestow save the gods alone—

> οὖτοι ἀπόβλητ᾽ ἐστὶ θεῶν ἐρικυδέα δῶρα,
> ὅσσα κεν αὐτοὶ δῶσιν, ἐκὼν δ᾽οὐκ ἄν τις ἔλοιτο.*

The most general survey shows us that the two foes of human happiness are pain and boredom. We may go further, and say that in the degree in which we are fortunate enough to get away from the one, we approach the other. Life presents, in fact, a more or less violent oscillation between the two. The reason of this is that each of these two poles stands in a double antagonism to the other, external or objective, and inner or subjective. Needy surroundings and poverty produce pain ; while, if a man is more than well off, he is bored. Accordingly, while the lower classes are engaged in a ceaseless struggle with need, in other words, with pain, the upper carry on a constant and often desperate battle with boredom.† The inner or subjective antagonism arises from the fact that, in the individual, susceptibility to pain varies inversely with susceptibility to boredom, because susceptibility is directly proportionate to mental power. Let me explain. A dull mind is, as a rule associated with dull sensibilities, nerves which no stimulus can affect, a temperament, in short, which does not feel pain or anxiety very much, however great or terrible it may be. Now, intellectual dullness is at the bottom of that vacuity of soul which is stamped on so many faces, a state of mind which betrays itself by a constant and lively attention to all the trivial circumstances in the external world. This is the true source of boredom —a continual panting after excitement, in order to have a pretext for giving the mind and spirits something to occupy them. The kind of things people choose for this purpose shows that they are not very particular, as witness the miserable pastimes they have recourse to, and their ideas of social pleasure and conversation ; or, again, the number of people who gossip on the doorstep or gape out of the

---

* " Iliad " 3, 65.

† And the extremes meet ; for the lowest state of civilization, a nomad or wandering life, finds its counterpart in the highest, where every one is at times a tourist. The earlier stage was a case of necessity ; the latter is a remedy for boredom.

window. It is mainly because of this inner vacuity of soul that people go in quest of society, diversion, amusement, luxury of every sort, which lead many to extravagance and misery. Nothing is so good a protection against such misery as inward wealth, the wealth of the mind, because the greater it grows, the less room it leaves for boredom. The inexhaustible activity of thought! finding ever new material to work upon in the multifarious phenomena of self and nature, and able and ready to form new combinations of them—there you have something that invigorates the mind, and apart from moments of relaxation, sets it far above the reach of boredom.

But, on the other hand, this high degree of intelligence is rooted in a high degree of susceptibility, greater strength of will, greater passionateness; and from the union of these qualities comes an increased capacity for emotion, an enhanced sensibility to all mental and even bodily pain, greater impatience of obstacles, greater resentment of interruption—all of which tendencies are augmented by the power of the imagination, the vivid character of the whole range of thought, including what is disagreeable. This applies, in varying degrees, to every step in the long scale of mental power, from the veriest dunce to the greatest genius that ever lived. Therefore the nearer any one is, either from a subjective or from an objective point of view, to one of these sources of suffering in human life, the farther he is from the other. And so a man's natural bent will lead him to make his objective world conform to his subjective as much as possible; that is to say, he will take the greatest measures against that form of suffering to which he is most liable. The wise man will, above all, strive after freedom from pain and annoyance, quiet and leisure, consequently a tranquil, modest life, with as few encounters as may be ; and so, after a little experience of his so-called fellow-men, he will elect to live in retirement, or even, if he is a man of great intellect, in solitude. For the more a man has in himself, the less he will want from other people, the less, indeed, other people can be to him. This is why a high degree of intellect tends to make a man unsocial. True, if quality of intellect could be made up for by quantity, it might be worth while to live even in the great world ; but, unfortunately, a hundred fools together will not make one wise man.

But the individual who stands at the other end of the scale is no sooner free from the pangs of need than he endeavors to get pastime and society at any cost, taking up with the first person he meets, and avoiding nothing so much as himself. For in solitude, where every one is thrown upon his own resources, what a man has in himself comes to light; the fool in fine raiment groans under the burden of his miserable personality, a burden which he can never throw off, while the man of talent peoples the waste places with his animating thoughts. Seneca declares that folly is its own burden—*omnis stultitia laborat fastidio sui*—a very true saying, with which may be compared the words of Jesus, the son of Sirach, "The life of a fool is worse than death."* And, as a rule, it will be found that a man is sociable just in the degree in which he is intellectually poor and generally vulgar. For one's choice in this world does not go much beyond solitude on one side and vulgarity on the other. It is said that the most sociable of all people are the negroes; and they are at the bottom of the scale in intellect. I remember reading once in a French paper† that the blacks in North America, whether free or unslaved, are fond of shutting themselves up in large numbers in the smallest space, because they cannot have too much of one another's snub-nosed company.

The brain may be regarded as a kind of parasite of the organism, a pensioner, as it were, who dwells with the body: and leisure, that is, the time one has for the free enjoyment of one's consciousness or individuality, is the fruit or produce of the rest of existence, which is in general only labor and effort. But what does most people's leisure yield?—boredom and dullness; except of course, when it is occupied with sensual pleasure or folly. How little such leisure is worth may be seen in the way in which it is spent: and, as Ariosto observes, how miserable are the idle hours of ignorant men!—*ozio lungo d'uomini ignoranti.* Ordinary people think merely how they shall spend their time; a man of any talent tries to use it. The reason why people of limited intellect are apt to be bored is that their intellect is absolutely nothing more than the

---

*Ecclesiasticus, xxii. 11.   †*Le Commerce*, Oct. 19th, 1837.

means by which the motive power of the will is put into
force: and whenever there is nothing particular to set the
will in motion, it rests, and their intellect takes a holiday,
because, equally with the will, it requires something external to bring it into play. The result is an awful
stagnation of whatever power a man has—in a word,
boredom. To counteract this miserable feeling, men run
to trivialities which please for the moment they are taken
up, hoping thus to engage the will in order to rouse it to
action, and so set the intellect in motion; for it is the
latter which has to give effect to these motives of the will.
Compared with real and natural motives, these are but as
paper money to coin; for their value is only arbitrary—
card games and the like, which have been invented for
this very purpose. · And if there is nothing else to be done,
a man will twirl his thumbs or beat the devil's tattoo; or
a cigar may be a welcome substitute for exercising his
brains. Hence, in all countries the chief occupation of
society is card-playing,* and it is the gauge of its value,
and an outward sign that it is bankrupt in thought.
Because people have no thoughts to deal in, they deal
cards, and try and win one another's money. Idiots! But
I do not wish to be unjust; so let me remark that it may
certainly be said in defense of card-playing that it is a
preparation for the world and for business life, because
one learns thereby how to make a clever use of fortuitous
but unalterable circumstances (cards, in this case), and
to get as much out of them as one can: and to do this a
man must learn a little dissimulation, and how to put a
good face upon a bad business. But, on the other hand,
it is exactly for this reason that card-playing is so demoralizing, since the whole object of it is to employ every kind
of trick and machination in order to win what belongs to
another. And a habit of this sort, learned at the card-table,
strikes root and pushes its way into practical life; and in
the affairs of every day a man gradually comes to regard
meum and *tuum* in much the same light as cards, and to
consider that he may use to the utmost whatever

---

*Translator's Note.—Card-playing to this extent is now, no doubt,
a thing of the past, at any rate among the nations of northern
Europe. The present fashion is rather in favor of a dilettante interest in art or literature.

advantages he possesses, so long as he does not come within the arm of the law. Examples of what I mean are of daily occurrence in mercantile life. Since, then, leisure is the flower, or rather the fruit, of existence, as it puts a man into possession of himself, those are happy indeed who possess something real in themselves. But what do you get from most people's leisure?—only a good-for-nothing fellow, who is terribly bored and a burden to himself. Let us, therefore, rejoice, dear brethren, for " we are not children of the bondwoman, but of the free."

Further, as no land is so well off as that which requires few imports, or none at all, so the happiest man is one who has enough in his own inner wealth, and requires little or nothing from outside for his maintenance, for imports are expensive things, reveal dependence, entail danger, occasion trouble, and, when all is said and done, are a poor substitute for home produce. No man ought to expect much from others, or, in general, from the external world. What one human being can be to another is not a very great deal : in the end every one stands alone, and the important thing is who it is that stands alone. Here, then, is another application of the general truth which Goethe recognizes in " Dichtung und Wahrheit " (Bk. III.), that in everything a man has ultimately to appeal to himself ; or, as Goldsmith puts it in " The Traveller :"

> " Still to ourselves in every place consign'd
> Our own felicity we make or find."

Himself is the source of the best and most a man can be or achieve. The more this is so—the more a man finds his sources of pleasure in himself—the happier he will be. Therefore, it is with great truth that Aristotle* says, " To be happy means to be self-sufficient." For all other sources of happiness are in their nature most uncertain, precarious, fleeting, the sport of chance ; and so even under the most favorable circumstances they can easily be exhausted ; nay, this is unavoidable, because they are not always within reach. And in old age these sources of happiness must necessarily dry up : love leaves us then, and wit, desire to travel, delight in horses, aptitude for social intercourse ;

---

* Eth. Eud., vii. 2.

friends and relations, too, are taken from us by death. Then more than ever, it depends upon what a man has in himself ; for this will stick to him longest and at any period of life it is the only genuine and lasting source of happiness.   There is not much to be got anywhere in the world.   It is filled with misery and pain ; and if a man escapes these, boredom lies in wait for him at every corner. Nay more ; it is evil which generally has the upper hand, and folly makes the most noise.   Fate is cruel, and mankind pitiable.   In such a world as this, a man who is rich in himself is like a bright, warm, happy room at Christmastide, while without are the frost and snow of a December night.   Therefore, without doubt, the happiest destiny on earth is to have the rare gift of a rich individuality, and, more especially, to be possessed of a good endowment of intellect ; this is the happiest destiny, though it may not be, after all, a very brilliant one.   There was great wisdom in that remark which Queen Christina of Sweden made, in her nineteenth year, about Descartes, who had then lived for twenty years in the deepest solitude in Holland, and, apart from report, was known to her only by a single essay : " M. Descartes," she said, " is the happiest of men, and his condition seems to me much to be envied."* Of course, as was the case with Descartes, external circumstances must be favorable enough to allow a man to be master of his life and happiness ; or, as we read in Ecclesiastes†—" Wisdom is good together with an inheritance, and profitable unto them that see the sun." The man to whom nature and fate have granted the blessing of wisdom, will be most anxious and careful to keep open the fountains of happiness which he has in himself ; and for this, independence and leisure are necessary.   To obtain them, he will be willing to moderate his desires and harbor his resources, all the more because he is not, like others, restricted to the external world for his pleasures.   So he will not be misled by expectations of office, or money, or the favor and applause of his fellow-men, into surrendering himself in order to conform to low desires and vulgar tastes ; nay, in such a case he will follow the advice that Horace gives in his epistle

---

* "Vie de Descartes," par Baillet.   Liv. vii., ch. 10.

† vii. 12.

to Mæcenas.* It is a great piece of folly to sacrifice the inner for the outer man, to give the whole or the greater part of one's quiet leisure and independence for splendor, rank, pomp, titles and honor. This is what Goethe did. My good luck drew me quite in the other direction.

The truth which I am insisting upon here, the truth, namely, that the chief source of human happiness is internal, is confirmed by that most accurate observation of Aristotle in the "Nichomchen Ethics,"† that every pleasure presupposes some sort of activity, the application of some sort of power, without which it cannot exist. The doctrine of Aristotle's, that a man's happiness consists in the free exercise of his highest faculties, is also enunciated by Stobæus in his exposition of the Peripatetic philosophy :‡ "happiness," he says, "means vigorous and successful activity in all your undertakings;" and he explains that by vigour (ἀρέτη) he means mastery in any thing, whatever it be. Now, the original purpose of those forces with which nature has endowed man is to enable him to struggle against the difficulties which beset him on all sides. But if this struggle comes to an end, his unemployed forces become a burden to him ; and he has to set to work and play with them—use them, I mean, for no purpose at all, beyond avoiding the other source of human suffering, boredom, to which he is at once exposed. It is the upper classes, people of wealth, who are the greatest victims of boredom. Lucretius long ago described their miserable state, and the truth of his description may be still recognized to-day, in the life of every great capital—where the rich man is seldom in his own halls, because it bores him to be there and still he returns thither because he is no better off outside—or else he is away in post-haste to his house in the country, as if it were on fire ; and he is no sooner arrived there, than he is bored again, and seeks to forget everything in sleep, or else hurries back to town once more.

> " Exit saepe foras magnis ex ædibus ille,
>   Esse domi quem pertaesum est, subitoque reventat ;
>   Quippe foris nihilo melius qui sentiat esse.

---

* Lib. 1., ep. 7.
  Nec somnum plebis laudo, satur altilium, nec
  Otia divitiis Arabum liborrima muto.

† i. 7 and vii. 13, 14.   ‡ Ecl. eth. ii., ch. 7.

Currit, agens mannos, ad villam precipitanter,
Auxilium tectis quasi ferre ardentibus instans :
Oscitat extemplo, tetigit quum limina villae ;
Aut abit in somnum gravis, atque oblivia quaerit ;
Aut etiam properans urbem petit atque revisit." *

In their youth, such people must have had a superfluity
of muscular and vital energy—powers which unlike those
of the mind, cannot maintain their full degree of vigor
very long; and in later years they either have no mental
powers at all, or cannot develop any for want of employment which would bring them into play; so that they are
in a wretched plight. *Will*, however, they still possess,
for this is the only power that is inexhaustible; and they
try to stimulate their will by passionate excitement, such as
games of chance for high stakes—undoubtedly a most degrading form of vice. And one may say generally that if
a man finds himself with nothing to do, he is sure to choose
some amusement suited to the kind of power in which he
excels—bowls, it may be, or chess; hunting or painting;
horse-racing or music; cards, or poetry, heraldry, philosophy,
or some other dilettante interest. We might classify these
interests methodically, by reducing them to expressions of
the three fundamental powers, the factors, that is to say,
which go to make up the physiological constitution of man;
and further, by considering these powers by themselves,
and apart from any of the definite aims which they may subserve, and simply as affording three sources of possible
pleasure, out of which every man will choose what suits him,
according as he excels in one direction or another.

First of all come the pleasures of vital energy, of food,
drink, digestion, rest and sleep; and there are parts of the
world where it can be said that these are characteristic and
national pleasures. Secondly, there are the pleasures of
muscular energy, such as walking, running, wrestling,
dancing, fencing, riding and similar athletic pursuits,
which sometimes take the form of sport, and sometimes of
a military life, and real warfare. Thirdly, there are the
pleasures of sensibility, such as observation, thought, feeling, or a taste for poetry or culture, music, learning, reading,
meditation, invention, philosophy and the like. As regards
the value, relative worth and duration of each of these
kinds of pleasure, a great deal might be said, which, how-

* 111. 1073.

ever, I leave the reader to supply. But every one will see that the nobler the power which is brought into play, the greater will be the pleasure which it gives; for pleasure always involves the use of one's own powers, and happiness consists in a frequent repetition of pleasure. No one will deny that in this respect the pleasures of sensibility occupy a higher place than either of the other two fundamental kinds; which exist in an equal, nay, in a greater degree in brutes; it is his preponderating amount of sensibility which distinguishes man from other animals. Now, our mental powers are forms of sensibility, and therefore a preponderating amount of it makes us capable of that kind of pleasure which has to do with mind, so-called intellectual pleasure; and the more sensibility predominates, the greater the pleasure will be. *

---

*Nature exhibits a continual progress, starting from the mechanical and chemical activity of the inorganic world, proceeding to the vegetable, with its dull enjoyment of self, from that to the animal world, where intelligence and consciousness begin, at first very weak, and only after many intermediate stages attaining its last great development in man, whose intellect is Nature's crowning point; the goal of all her efforts, the most perfect and difficult of all her works. And even within the range of the human intellect, there are a great many observable differences of degree, and it is very seldom that intellect reaches its highest point, intelligence properly so-called, which in this narrow and strict sense of the word, is nature's most consummate product, and so the rarest and most precious thing of which the world can boast. The highest product of Nature is the clearest degree of consciousness, in which the world mirrors itself more plainly and completely than anywhere else. A man endowed with this form of intelligence is in possession of what is noblest and best on earth; and accordingly, he has a source of pleasure in comparison with which all others are small. From his surroundings he asks nothing but leisure for the free enjoyment of what he has got, time, as it were, to polish his diamond. All other pleasures that are not of the intellect are of a lower kind; for they are, one and all, movements of will—desires, hopes, fears and ambitions, no matter to what directed: they are always satisfied at the cost of pain, and in the case of ambition, generally with more or less of illusion. With intellectual pleasure, on the other hand, truth becomes clearer and clearer. In the realm of intelligence pain has no power. Knowledge is all in all. Further, intellectual pleasures are accessible entirely and only through the medium of the intelligence and are limited by its capacity. For all the wit there is in the world is useless to him who has none. Still this advantage is accompanied by a substantial disadvantage; for the whole of Nature shows that with the growth of intelligence comes increased capacity for pain, and it is only with the highest degree of intelligence that suffering reaches its supreme point.

The normal, ordinary man takes a vivid interest in anything only in so far as it excites his will, that is to say, is a matter of personal interest to him. But constant excitement of the will is never an unmixed good, to say the least; in other words, it involves pain. Card-playing, that universal occupation of "good society" everywhere, is a device for providing this kind of excitement, and that, too, by means of interests so small as to produce slight and momentary, instead of real and permanent, pain. Card-playing is, in fact, a mere tickling of the will.*

On the other hand, a man of powerful intellect is capable of taking a vivid interest in things in the way of mere knowledge, with no admixture of will; nay, such an interest is a necessity to him. It places him in a sphere where pain is an alien, a diviner air where the gods live serene:

θεοὶ ῥεῖα ζώοντες.†

Look on these two pictures—the life of the masses, one long, dull record of struggle and effort entirely devoted to the petty interests of personal welfare, to misery in all its forms, a life beset by intolerable boredom as soon as ever those aims are satisfied and the man is thrown back upon himself, whence he can be roused again to some sort of movement only by the wild fire of passion. On the other side you

---

*Vulgarity is, at bottom, the kind of consciousness in which the will completely predominates over the intellect, where the latter does nothing more than perform the service of its master, the will. Therefore, when the will makes no demands, supplies no motives, strong or weak, the intellect entirely loses its power, and the result is complete vacancy of mind. Now will without intellect is the most vulgar and common thing in the world, possessed by every blockhead, who, in the gratification of his passions, shows the stuff of which he is made. This is the condition of mind called vulgarity, in which the only active elements are the organs of sense, and that small amount of intellect which is necessary for apprehending the data of sense. Accordingly, the vulgar man is constantly open to all sorts of impressions, and immediately perceives all the little trifling things that go on in his environment: the lightest whisper, the most trivial circumstance, is sufficient to rouse his attention; he is just like an animal. Such a man's mental condition reveals itself in his face, in his whole exterior; and hence that vulgar, repulsive appearance, which is all the more offensive, if as is usually the case, his will—the only factor in his consciousness—is a base, selfish and altogether bad one.

†Odyssey IV., 805.

have a man endowed with a high degree of mental power, leading an existence rich in thought and full of life and meaning, occupied by worthy and interesting objects as soon as ever he is free to give himself to them, bearing in himself a source of the noblest pleasure. What external promptings he wants come from the works of nature, and from the contemplation of human affairs and the achievements of the great of all ages and countries, which are thoroughly appreciated by a man of this type alone, as being the only one who can quite understand and feel with them. And so it is for him alone that those great ones have really lived ; it is to him that they make their appeal ; the rest are but casual hearers who only half understand either them or their followers. Of course, this characteristic of the intellectual man implies that he has one more need than the others, the need of reading, observing, studying, meditating, practicing, the need, in short, of undisturbed leisure. For, as Voltaire has very rightly said, " there are no real pleasures without real needs ;" and the need of them is why to such a man pleasures are accessible which are denied to others—the varied beauties of nature and art and literature. To heap these round people who do not want them and cannot appreciate them, is like expecting gray hairs to fall in love. A man who is privileged in this respect leads two lives, a personal and an intellectual life ; and the latter gradually comes to be looked upon as the true one, and the former as merely a means to it. Other people make this shallow, empty and troubled existence an end in itself. To the life of the intellect such a man will give the preference over all his other occupations : by the constant growth of insight and knowledge, this intellectual life, like a slowly-forming work of art, will acquire a consistency, a permanent intensity, a unity which becomes ever more and more complete ; compared with which a life devoted to the attainment of personal comfort, a life that may broaden indeed, but can never be deepened, makes but a poor show : and yet, as I have said, people make this baser sort of existence an end in itself.

The ordinary life of every day, so far as it is not moved by passion, is tedious and insipid ; and if it is so moved, it soon becomes painful. Those alone are happy whom nature has favored with some superfluity of intellect, something beyond what is just necessary to carry out the behests of their will ; for it enables them to lead an intellectual life as well, a life unattended by pain and full of vivid interests. Mere leisure, that is to say, intellect unoccupied in the service of the will, is not of itself sufficient : there must be a real superfluity of power, set free from the service of the will and devoted to that of the intellect ; for, as Seneca says, *otium sine litteris mors est et vivi hominis sepultura*—illiterate leisure is a form of death, a living tomb. Varying with the amount of the superfluity, there will be countless developments in this second life, the life of the mind ; it may be the mere collection and labeling of insects, birds, minerals, coins, or the highest achievements of poetry and philosophy. The life of the mind is not only a protection, against boredom, it also wards off the pernicious effects of boredom ; it keeps us from bad company, from the many dangers, misfortunes, losses and extravagances which the man who places his happiness entirely in the objective world is sure to encounter. My philosophy, for instance, has never brought me in a sixpence ; but it has spared me many an expense.

The ordinary man places his life's happiness in things external to him, in property, rank, wife and children, friends, society, and the like, so that when he loses them or finds them disappointing, the foundation of his happiness is destroyed. In other words, his center of gravity is not in himself ; it is constantly changing its place, with every wish and whim. If he is a man of means, one day it will be his house in the country, another buying horses, or entertaining friends, or traveling—a life, in short, of general luxury, the reason being that he seeks his pleasure in things outside him. Like one whose health and strength are gone, he tries to regain by the use of jellies and drugs, instead of by developing his own vital power, the true source of what he has lost. Before proceeding to the opposite, let us compare with this common type the man who comes midway between the two, endowed, it may be, not exactly with distinguished powers of mind, but with somewhat more than the ordinary amount of intellect. He will take a dilettante interest in art, or devote his attention to some branch of science—botany, for example, or physics, astronomy, history, and find a great deal of pleasure in such studies, and amuse himself with them when external sources of happiness are exhausted or fail to satisfy him any more. Of a man like this it may be said that his center of gravity is partly in himself. But a dilettante interest in art is a very different thing from creative activity; and an amateur pursuit of science is apt to be superficial and not to penetrate to the heart of the matter. A man cannot entirely identify himself with such pursuits, or have his whole existence so completely filled and permeated with them that he loses all interest in everything else. It is only the highest intellectual power, what we call genius, that attains to this degree of intensity, making all time and existence its theme, and striving to express its peculiar conception of the world, whether it contemplates life as the subject of poetry or of philosophy. Hence, undisturbed occupation with himself, his own thoughts and works, is a matter of urgent necessity to such a man; solitude is welcome, leisure is the highest good, and everything else is unnecessary, nay, even burdensome.

This is the only type of man of whom it can be said that his center of gravity is entirely in himself; which explains why it is that people of this sort—and they are very rare—no matter how excellent their character may be, do not show that warm and unlimited interest in friends, family, and the community in general, of which others are so often capable; for if they have only themselves they are not inconsolable for the loss of everything else. This gives an isolation to their character, which is all the more effective since other people never really quite satisfy them, as being, on the whole, of a different nature: nay more, since this difference is constantly forcing itself upon their notice, they get accustomed to move about among mankind as alien beings, and in thinking of humanity in general, to say *they* instead of *we*.

So the conclusion we come to is that the man whom nature has endowed with intellectual wealth is the happiest; so true it is that the subjective concerns us more than the objective; for whatever the latter may be, it can work only indirectly, secondarily, and through the medium of the former—a truth finely expressed by Lucian:

Πλοῦτος ὁ τῆς ψυχῆς πλοῦτος μόνος ἐστὶν ἀληθής
Τἆλλα δ'ἔχει ἄτην πλείονα τῶν κτεάνων *

---

* Epigrammata, 12.

—the wealth of the soul is the only true wealth, for with all other riches comes a bane even greater than they. The man of inner wealth wants nothing from outside but the negative gift of undisturbed leisure, to develop and mature his intellectual faculties, that is, to enjoy his wealth ; in short, he wants permission to be himself, his whole life long, every day and every hour. If he is destined to impress the character of his mind upon the whole race, he has only one measure of happiness or unhappiness—to succeed or fail in perfecting his powers and completing his work. All else is of small consequence. Accordingly the greatest minds of all ages have set the highest value upon undisturbed leisure, as worth, exactly as much as the man himself. "Happiness appears to consist in leisure," says Aristotle ;* and Diogenes Laertius reports that "Socrates praised leisure as the fairest of all possessions." So, in the "Nichomachean Ethics," Aristotle concludes that a life devoted to philosophy is the happiest ; or, as he says in the "Politics,"† "the free exercise of any power, whatever it may be, is happiness." This, again, tallies with what Goethe says in "Wilhelm Meister:" "the man who is born with a talent which he is meant to use, finds his greatest happiness in using it."

But to be in possession of undisturbed leisure, is far from being the common lot ; nay, it is something alien to human nature, for the ordinary man's destiny is to spend life in procuring what is necessary for the subsistence of himself and his family ; he is a son of struggle and need, not a free intelligence. So people as a rule soon get tired of undisturbed leisure, and it becomes burdensome if there are no fictitious and forced aims to occupy it, play, pastime and hobbies of every kind. For this very reason it is full of possible danger, and *difficilis in otio quies* is a true saying—it is difficult to keep quiet if you have nothing to do. On the other hand, a measure of intellect far surpassing the ordinary, is as unnatural as it is abnormal. But if it exists, and the man endowed with it is to be happy, he will want precisely that undisturbed leisure which the others find burdensome or pernicious ; for without it he is a Pegasus in harness, and consequently unhappy. If these two unnatural circumstances, external and internal,

---

* Eth. Nichom. x. 7   † iv. 11.

undisturbed leisure and great intellect, happen to coincide in the same person, it is a great piece of fortune ; and if fate is so far favorable, a man can lead the higher life, the life protected from the two opposite sources of human suffering, pain and boredom, from the painful struggle for existence, and the incapacity for enduring leisure (which is free existence itself) evils which may be escaped only by being mutually neutralized.

But there is something to be said in opposition to this view. Great intellectual gifts mean an activity pre-eminently nervous in its character, and consequently a very high degree of susceptibility to pain in every form. Further, such gifts imply an intense temperament, larger and more vivid ideas, which, as the inseparable accompaniment of great intellectual power, entail on its possessor a corresponding intensity of the emotions, making them incomparably more violent than those to which the ordinary man is a prey. Now, there are more things in the world productive of pain than of pleasure. Again, a large endowment of intellect tends to estrange the man who has it from other people and their doings ; for the more a man has in himself, the less he will be able to find in them ; and the hundred things in which they take delight, he will think shallow and insipid. Here, then, perhaps, is another instance of that law of compensation which makes itself felt everywhere. How often one hears it said, and said, too, with some plausibility, that the narrow-minded man is at bottom the happiest, even though his fortune is unenviable. I shall make no attempt to forestall the reader's own judgment on this point ; more especially as Sophocles himself has given utterance to two diametrically opposite opinions :

> Πολλῷ τὸ φρονεῖν εὐδαιμονίας
> πρῶτον ὑπάρχει.*

He says in one place—wisdom is the greatest part of happiness ; and again, in another passage, he declares that the life of the thoughtless is the most pleasant of all :

> Ἐν τῷ φρονεῖν γὰρ μηδὲν ἥδιστος βίος.†

---

* Antigone, 1347–8.   † Ajax, 554.

The philosophers of the Old Testament find themselves in a like contradiction.

"The life of a fool is worse than death" *

and—

"In much wisdom is much grief ;
And he that increaseth knowledge increaseth sorrow." {

I may remark, however, that a man who has no mental needs, because his intellect is of the narrow and normal amount, is, in the strict sense of the word, what is called a philistine—an expression at first peculiar to the German language, a kind of slang term at the universities, afterward used, by analogy, in a higher sense, though still in its original meaning, as denoting one who is not a "Son of the Muses." A philistine is and remains ἄμουσος ἄνηρ. I should prefer to take a higher point of view, and apply the term philistine to people who are always seriously occupied with realities which are no realities ; but as such a definition would be a transcendental one, and therefore not generally intelligible, it would hardly be in place in the present treatise, which aims at being popular. The other definition can be more easily elucidated, indicating, as it does, satisfactorily enough, the essential nature of all those qualities which distinguish the philistine. He is defined to be "a man without mental needs." From this it follows, firstly, in relation to himself, that he has no intellectual pleasures ; for, as was remarked before, there are no real pleasures without real needs. The philistine's life is animated by no desire to gain knowledge and insight for their own sake, or to experience that true æsthetic pleasure which is so nearly akin to them. If pleasures of this kind are fashionable, and the philistine finds himself compelled to pay attention to them, he will force himself to do so, but he will take as little interest in them as possible. His only real pleasures are of a sensual kind, and he thinks that these indemnify him for the loss of the others. To him oysters and champagne are the height of existence ; the aim of his life is to procure what will contribute to his bodily welfare, and he is indeed in a happy way if

* Ecclesiasticus, xxii. 11.　　　　+ Ecclesiastes, i. 18.

this causes him some trouble. If the luxuries of life are
heaped upon him, he will inevitably be bored, and against
boredom he has a great many fancied remedies, balls,
theaters, parties, cards, gambling, horses, women, drinking,
traveling and so on; all of which cannot protect a man
from being bored, for where there are no intellectual
needs, no intellectual pleasures are possible. The peculiar
characteristic of the philistine is a dull, dry kind of gravity,
akin to that of animals. Nothing really pleases, or excites,
or interests him, for sensual pleasure is quickly exhausted,
and the society of philistines soon becomes burdensome,
and one may even get tired of playing cards. True, the
pleasures of vanity are left, pleasures which he enjoys in
his own way, either by feeling himself superior in point of
wealth, or rank, or influence and power to other people,
who thereupon pay him honor ; or at any rate, by going
about with those who have a superfluity of these blessings,
sunning himself in the reflection of their splendor—what
the English call a snob.

From the essential nature of the philistine it follows,
secondly, in regard to others, that, as he possesses no intellectual, but only physical needs, he will seek the society
of those who can satisfy the latter, but not the
former. The last thing he will expect from his friends is
the possession of any sort of intellectual capacity ; nay, if
he chances to meet with it, it will rouse his antipathy and
even hatred ; simply because in addition to an unpleasant
sense of inferiority, he experiences, in his heart, a dull
kind of envy, which has to be carefully concealed even
from himself. Nevertheless, it sometimes grows into a
secret feeling of rancor. But for all that, it will never
occur to him to make his own ideas of worth or value conform to the standard of such qualities ; he will continue
to give the preference to rank and riches, power and influence, which in his eyes seem to be the only genuine advantage, in the world ; and his wish will be to excel
in them himself. All this is the consequence of his
being a man without intellectual needs. The great
affliction of all philistines is that they have no interest in
ideas, and that, to escape being bored, they are in constant
need of realities. Now realities are either unsatisfactory
or dangerous ; when they lose their interest, they become
fatiguing. But the ideal world is illimitable and calm,

" Something afar
From the sphere of our sorrow."

Note.—In these remarks on the personal qualities which go to make happiness, I have been mainly concerned with the physical and intellectual nature of man. For an account of the direct and immediate influence of morality upon happiness, let me refer to my prize essay on "The Foundation of Morals" (Sec. 22).

CHAPTER III.

PROPERTY, OR WHAT A MAN HAS.

EPICURUS divides the needs of mankind into three classes, and the division made by this great professor of happiness is a true and a fine one. First come natural and necessary needs, such as, when not satisfied, produce pain—food and clothing, *victus et amictus*, needs which can easily be satisfied. Secondly, there are those needs which, though natural, are not necessary, such as the gratification of certain of the senses. I may add, however, that in the report given by Diogenes Laertius, Epicurus does not mention which of the senses he means; so that on this point my account of his doctrine is somewhat more definite and exact than the original. These are needs rather more difficult to satisfy. The third class consists of needs which are neither natural nor necessary, the need of luxury and prodigality, show and splendor, which never come to an end, and are very hard to satisfy.*

It is difficult, if not impossible, to define the limits which reason should impose on the desire for wealth; for there is no absolute or definite amount of wealth which will satisfy a man. The amount is always relative, that is to say, just so much as will maintain the proportion between what he wants and what he gets; for to measure a man's happiness only by what he gets, and not also by what he expects to get, is as futile as to try and express a fraction which shall have a numerator but no denominator. A man never feels the loss of things which it never occurs to him to ask for;

---

* Cf. Diogenes Laertius, Bk. x., ch. xxvii., pp. 127 and 149; also Cicero *de finibus*, i. 13.

he is just as happy without them; while another, who may have a hundred times as much, feels miserable because he has not got the one thing which he wants. In fact, here too, every man has an horizon of his own, and he will expect just as much as he thinks it possible for him to get. If an object within his horizon looks as though he could confidently reckon on getting it, he is happy; but if difficulties come in the way, he is miserable. What lies beyond his horizon has no effect at all upon him. So it is that the vast possessions of the rich do not agitate the poor, and conversely, that a wealthy man is not consoled by all his wealth for the failure of his hopes. Riches, one may say, are like sea-water; the more you drink, the thirstier you become: and the same is true of fame. The loss of wealth and prosperity leaves a man, as soon as the first pangs of grief are over, in very much the same habitual temper as before; and the reason of this is, that as soon as fate diminishes the amount of his possessions, he himself immediately reduces the amount of his claims. But when misfortune comes upon us, to reduce the amount of our claims is just what is most painful; once that we have done so, the pain becomes less and less, and is felt no more; like an old wound which has healed. Conversely, when a piece of good fortune befalls us, our claims mount higher and higher as there is nothing to regulate them; it is in this feeling of expansion that the delight of it lies. But it lasts no longer than the process itself, and when the expansion is complete, the delight ceases; we have become accustomed to the increase in our claims, and consequently indifferent to the amount of wealth which satisfies them. There is a passage in the "Odyssey"* illustrating this truth, of which I may quote the last two lines:

Τοῖος γὰρ νόος ἐστὶ ἐπιχθονίων ἀνθρώπων
Οἷον ἐφ᾽ ἦμαρ ἄγει πατὴρ ἀνδρῶν τε θεῶν τε.

—the thoughts of man that dwells on the earth are as the day granted him by the father of gods and men. Discontent springs from a constant endeavor to increase the amount of our claims, when we are powerless to increase the amount which will satisfy them.

When we consider how full of needs the human race is,

---

* x viii. 130-7.

how its whole existence is based upon them, it is not a matter for surprise that wealth is held in more sincere esteem, nay, in greater honor, than anything else in the world; nor ought we to wonder that gain is made the only goal of life and everything that does not lead to it pushed aside or thrown overboard—philosophy, for instance, by those who profess it. People are often reproached for wishing for money above all things, and for loving it more than anything else; but it is natural and even inevitable for people to love that which, like an unwearied Proteus, is always ready to turn itself into whatever object their wandering wishes or manifold desires may for the moment fix upon. Everything else can satisfy only one wish, one need; food is good only if you are hungry: wine, if you are able to enjoy it; drugs, if you are sick; fur for the winter; love for youth, and so on. These are all only relatively good ἀγαθὰ πρός τι. Money alone is absolutely good, because it is not only a concrete satisfaction of one need in particular; it is an abstract satisfaction of all.

If a man has an independent fortune, he should regard it as a bulwark against the many evils and misfortunes which he may encounter ; he should not look upon it as giving him leave to get what pleasure he can out of the world, or as rendering it incumbent upon him to spend it in this way. People who are not born with a fortune, but end by making a large one through the exercise of whatever talents they possess, almost always come to think that their talents are their capital, and that the money they have gained is merely the interest upon it ; they do not lay by a part of their earnings to form permanent capital, but spend their money much as they have earned it. Accordingly, they often fall into poverty ; their earnings decrease, or come to an end altogether, either because their talent is exhausted by becoming antiquated—as, for instance, very often happens in the case of fine art ; or else it was valid only under a special conjunction of circumstances which has now passed away. There is nothing to prevent those who live on the common labor of their hands from treating their earnings in that way if they like ; because their kind of skill is not likely to disappear, or, if it does, it can be replaced by that of their fellow-workmen ; morever, the kind of work they do is always in demand ; so that what the proverb says is quite true, "a useful trade is a mine of gold." But with artists and professionals of of every kind the case is quite different, and that is the reason why they are well paid. They ought to build up a capital out of their earnings; but they recklessly look upon them as merely interest, and end in ruin. On the other hand, people who inherit money know, at least, how to distinguish between capital and interest, and most of them try to make their capital secure and not encroach upon it; nay if they can, they put by at least an eighth of their interest in order to meet future contingencies. So most of them maintain their position. These few remarks about capital and interest are not applicable to commercial life, for merchants look upon money only as a means of further gain, just as a workman regards his tools; so even if their capital has been entirely the result of their own efforts, they try to preserve and increase it by using it. Accordingly, wealth is nowhere so much at home as in the merchant class.

It will generally be found that those who know what it is to have been in need and destitution are very much less afraid of it, and consequently more inclined to extravagance, than those who know poverty only by hearsay. People who have been born and bred in good circumstances, are as a rule, much more careful about the future, more economical, in fact, than those who by a piece of good luck, have suddenly passed from poverty to wealth. This looks as if poverty were not really such a very wretched thing as it appears from a distance. The true reason, however, is rather the fact that the man who has been born into a position of wealth comes to look upon it as something without which he could no more live than he could live without air; he guards it as he does his very life; and so he is generally a lover of order, prudent and economical. But the man who has been born into a poor position looks upon it as the natural one, and if by any chance he comes in for a fortune, he regards it as a superfluity, something to be enjoyed or wasted, because if it comes to an end, he can get on just as well as before, with one anxiety the less; or, as Shakespeare says in Henry VI*.,

> " . . . . the adage must be verified
> That beggars mounted run their horse to death."

---

* Part III., Act 1, Sc. 4.

But it should be said that people of this kind have a firm and excessive trust, partly in fate, partly in the peculiar means which have already raised them out of need and poverty—a trust not only of the head, but of the heart also ; and so they do not, like the man born rich, look upon the shallows of poverty as bottomless, but console themselves with the thought that once they have touched ground again, they can take another upward flight. It is this trait in human character which explains the fact that women who were poor before their marriage often make greater claims, and are more extravagant, than those who have brought their husbands a rich dowry ; because as a rule, rich girls bring with them, not only a fortune, but also more eagerness, nay, more of the inherited in-stinct, to preserve it, than poor girls do. If any one doubts the truth of this, and thinks that it is just the opposite, he will find authority for his view in Ariosto's first satire ; but, on the other hand, Dr. Johnson agrees with my opinion. "A woman of fortune," he says, "being used to the handling of money, spends it judiciously ; but a woman who gets the command of money for the first time upon her marriage, has such a gusto in spending it, that she throws it away with great profusion."* And in any case let me advise any one who marries a poor girl not to leave her the capital but only the interest, and to take especial care that she has not the management of the children's fortune.

I do not by any means think that I am touching upon a subject which is not worth my while to mention when I recommend people to be careful to preserve what they have earned or inherited. For to start life with just as much as will make one independent, that is, allow one to live comfortably without having to work—even if one has only just enough for one's self, not to speak of a family—is an advantage which cannot be over-estimated ; for it means exemption and immunity from that chronic disease of penury, which fastens on the life of man like a plague ; it is emancipation from that forced labor which is the natural lot of every mortal. Only under a favorable fate like this can a man be said to be born free, to be, in the proper sense of the word, *sui juris*, master of his

---

* Boswell's "Life of Johnson" : ann : 1776, ætat : 67.

own time and powers, and able to say every morning, "This day is my own." And just for the same reason the difference between the man who has a hundred a year and the man who has a thousand, is infinitely smaller than the difference between the former and a man who has nothing at all. But inherited wealth reaches its utmost value when it falls to the individual endowed with mental powers of a high order, who is resolved to pursue a line of life not compatible with the making of money; for he is then doubly endowed by fate and can live for his genius; and he will pay his debt to mankind a hundred times, by achieving what no other could achieve, by producing some work which contributes to the general good, and redounds to the honor of humanity at large. Another, again, may use his wealth to further philanthropic schemes, and make himself well-deserving of his fellow-men. But a man who does none of these things, who does not even try to do them, who never attempts to study thoroughly some one branch of knowledge so that he may at least do what he can toward promoting it—such a one, born as he is into riches, is a mere idler and thief of time, a contemptible fellow. He will not even be happy, because, in his ease, exemption from need delivers him up to the other extreme of human suffering, boredom, which is such martyrdom to him, that he would have been better off if poverty had given him something to do. And as he is bored he is apt to be extravagant, and so lose the advantage of which he showed himself unworthy. Countless numbers of people find themselves in want, simply because, when they had money, they spent it only to get momentary relief from the feeling of boredom which oppressed them. It is quite another matter if one's object is success in political life, where favor, friends and connections are all-important, in order to mount by their aid step by step on the ladder of promotion, and perhaps gain the topmost rung. In this kind of life, it is much better to be cast on the world without a penny : and if the aspirant is not of noble family, but is a man of some talent, it will redound to his advantage to be an absolute pauper. For what every one most aims at in ordinary contact with his fellows is to prove them inferior to himself; and how much more is this the case in politics. Now, it is only an absolute pauper who has such a thorough conviction of his own complete, profound and positive inferiority from every point of view, of his own utter insignificance and worthlessness, that he can take his place quietly in the political machine.* He is the only one who can keep on bowing low enough, and even go right down upon his face if necessary; he alone can submit to everything and laugh at it; he alone knows the entire worthlessness of merit; he alone uses his loudest voice and his boldest type whenever he has to speak or write of those who are placed over his head, or occupy any position of influence; and if they do a little scribbling, he is ready to applaud it as a master-work. He alone understands how to beg, and so betimes, when he is hardly out of his boyhood, he becomes a high priest of that hidden mystery which Goethe brings to light:

> " Ueber's Niederträchtige
> Niemand sich beklage :
> Denn es ist das Mächtige
> Was man dir auchsage :"

—it is no use to complain of low aims; for, whatever people may say, they rule the world.

On the other hand, the man who is born with enough to live upon is generally of a somewhat independent turn of mind; he is accustomed to keep his head up; he has not learned all the arts of the beggar; perhaps he even presumes a little upon the possession of talents which, as he ought to know, can never compete with cringing mediocrity; in the long run he comes to recognize the inferiority of those who are placed over his head, and when they try to put insults upon him, he becomes refractory and shy. This is not the way to get on in the world. Nay, such a man may at last incline to the opinion freely expressed by Voltaire: "We have only two days to live; it is not worth our while to spend them in cringing to contemptible rascals." But alas! let me observe by the way, that " contemptible rascal " is an attribute which may be predicated of an abominable number of

---

* *Translator's Note.*—Schopenhauer is probably here making one of his many virulent attacks upon Hegel; in this case on account of what he thought to be the philosopher's abject servility to the government of his day. Though the Hegelian sytem has been the fruitful mother of many liberal ideas, there can be no doubt that Hegel's influence in his own lifetime, was an effective support of Prussian bureaucracy.

people. What Juvenal says—it is difficult to rise if youɪ poverty is greater than your talent—

> " Haud facile emergunt quorum virtutibus obstat
> Res angusta domi "—

is more applicable to a career of art and literature than to political and social ambition.

Wife and children I have not reckoned among a man's possessions; he is rather in their possession. It would be easier to include friends under that head; but a man's friends belong to him not a whit more than he belongs to them.

CHAPTER IV.

POSITION, OR A MAN'S PLACE IN THE ESTIMATION OF OTHERS.

Section 1.—Reputation.

BY A peculiar weakness of human nature, people generally think too much about the opinion which others form of them; although the slightest reflection will show that this opinion, whatever it may be, is not in itself essential to happiness. Therefore it is hard to understand why everybody feels so very pleased when he sees that other people have a good opinion of him, or say anything flattering to his vanity. If you stroke a cat, it will purr; and as inevitably, if you praise a man, a sweet expression of delight will appear on his face; and even though the praise is a palpable lie, it will be welcome, if the matter is one on which he prides himself. If only other people will applaud him, a man may console himself for downright misfortune, or for the pittance he gets from the two sources of human happiness already discussed: and conversely, it is astonishing how infallibly a man will be annoyed, and in some cases deeply pained, by any wrong done to his feeling of self-importance, whatever be the nature, degree, or circumstances of the injury, or by any depreciation, slight, or disregard.

If the feeling of honor rests upon this peculiarity of human nature, it may have a very salutary effect upon the

welfare of a great many people, as a substitute for morality:
but upon their happiness, more especially upon that peace
of mind and independence which are so essential to happiness, its effect will be disturbing and prejudicial rather
than salutary. Therefore it is advisable, from our point
of view, to set limits to this weakness, and duly to consider and rightly to estimate the relative value of advantages, and thus temper, as far as possible, this great
susceptibility to other people's opinion, whether the opinion
be one flattering to our vanity, or whether it causes us
pain; for in either case it is the same feeling which is
touched. Otherwise, a man is the slave of what other
people are pleased to think—and how little it requires to
disconcert or soothe the mind that is greedy of praise:

> " Sic leve, sic parvum est, animum quod laudis avarum
>   Subruit ac reficit."*

Therefore it will very much conduce to our happiness
if we duly compare the value of what a man is in and for
himself with what he is in the eyes of others. Under the
former comes everything that fills up the span of our existence and makes it what it is, in short, all the advantages
already considered and summed up under the heads of
personality and property; and the sphere in which all this
takes place is the man's own consciousness. On the other
hand, the sphere of what we are for other people is their
consciousness, not ours; it is the kind of figure we make in
their eyes, together with the thoughts which this arouses.†
But this is something which has no direct and immediate
existence for us, but can effect us only mediately and indirectly, so far, that is, as other people's behavior toward us is directed by it; and even then it ought to affect us
only in so far as it can move us to modify what we are in
and for ourselves. Apart from this, what goes on in other
people's consciousness is, as such, a matter of indifference
to us; and in time we get really indifferent to it, when we
come to see how superficial and futile are most people's

---

* Horace, Epist: II, 1, 180.

† Let me remark that people in the highest positions in life, with
all their brilliance, pomp, display, magnificence and general show,
may well say: Our happiness lies entirely outside us, for it exists
only in the heads of others.

thoughts, how narrow their ideas, how mean their sentiments, how perverse their opinions, and how much of error there is in most of them: when we learn by experience with what depreciation a man will speak of his fellow, when he is not obliged to fear him, or thinks that what he says will not come to his ears. And if ever we have had an opportunity of seeing how the greatest of men will meet with nothing but slight from half-a-dozen blockheads, we shall understand that to lay great value upon what other people say is to pay them too much honor.

At all events, a man is in a very bad way, who finds no source of happiness in the first two classes of blessings already treated of, but has to seek it in the third, in other words, not in what he is in himself, but in what he is in the opinion of others. For, after all, the foundation of our whole nature, and, therefore, of our happiness, is our physique, and the most essential factor in happiness is health, and, next in importance after health, the ability to maintain ourselves in independence and freedom from care. There can be no competiton or compensation between these essential factors or the one side, and honor, pomp, rank and reputation on the other, however much value we may set upon the latter. No one would hesitate to sacrifice the latter for the former, if it were necessary. We should add very much to our happiness by a timely recognition of the simple truth that every man's chief and real existence is in his own skin, and not in other people's opinions; and, consequently, that the actual conditions of our personal life—health temperament, capacity, income, wife, children, friends, home, are a hundred times more important for our happiness than what other people are pleased to think of us: otherwise we shall be miserable. And if people insist that honor is dearer than life itself, what they really mean is that existence and well-being are as nothing compared with other people's opinions. Of course, this may be only an exaggerated way of stating the prosaic truth that reputation, that is, the opinion others have of us, is indispensable if we are to make any progress in the world: but I shall come back to that presently. When we see that almost everything men devote their lives to attain, sparing no effort and encountering a thousand toils and dangers in the process, has, in the end, no further object than to raise themselves in the estimation of others; when we see that not only offices, titles, decorations, but also wealth, nay, even knowledge* and art, are striven for only to obtain, as the ultimate goal of all effort, greater respect from one's fellow men—is not this a lamentable proof of the extent to which human folly can go? To set much too high a value on other people's opinion is a common error everywhere; an error, it may be, rooted in human nature itself, or the result of civilization and social arrangements generally; but, whatever its source, it exercises a very immoderate influence on all we do, and is very prejudicial to our happiness. We can trace it from a timorous and slavish regard for what other people will say, up to the feeling which made Virginius plunge the dagger into his daughter's heart, or induces many a man to sacrifice quiet, riches, health and even life itself, for posthumous glory. Undoubtedly this feeling is a very convenient instrument in the hands of those who have the control or direction of their fellow-men; and accordingly we find that in every scheme for training up humanity in the way it should go, the maintenance and strengthening of the feeling of honor occupies an important place. But it is quite a different matter in its effect on human happiness, of which it is here our object to treat; and we should rather be careful to dissuade people from setting too much store by what others think of them. Daily experience shows us, however, that this is just the mistake people persist in making; most men set the utmost value precisely on what other people think, and are more concerned about it than about what goes on in their own consciousness, which is the thing most immediately and directly present to them. They reverse the natural order—regarding the opinions of others as real existence and their own consciousness as something shadowy; making the derivative and secondary into the principal, and considering the picture they present to the world of more importance than their own selves. By thus trying to get a direct and immediate result out of what has no really direct or immediate existence, they fall into the kind of folly which is called vanity—the appropriate term for that which has no solid or intrinsic value. Like a miser, such people forget the end in their eagerness to obtain the means.

Scire tuum nihil est nisi te scire hoc sciat alter (Persius i. 27) —knowledge is no use unless others know that you have it.

The truth is that the value we set upon the opinion of others, and our constant endeavor in respect of it, are each quite out of proportion to any result we may reasonably hope to attain; so that this attention to other people's attitude may be regarded as a kind of universal mania which every one inherits. In all we do, almost the first thing we think about is, what will people say; and nearly half the troubles and bothers of life may be traced to our anxiety on this score; it is the anxiety which is at the bottom of all that feeling of self-importance, which is so often mortified because it is so very morbidly sensitive. It is solicitude about what others will say that underlies all our vanity and pretension, yes, and all our show and swagger too. Without it, there would not be a tenth part of the luxury which exists. Pride in every form, *point d'honneur* and *punctilio,* however varied their kind or sphere, are at bottom nothing but this—anxiety about what others will say—and what sacrifices it often costs! One can see it even in a child; and though it exists at every period of life, it is strongest in age; because, when the capacity for sensual pleasure fails, vanity and pride have only avarice to share their dominion. Frenchmen, perhaps, afford the best example of this feeling, and among them it is a regular epidemic, appearing sometimes in the most absurd ambition, or in a ridiculous kind of national vanity and the most shameless boasting. However, they frustrate their own aims, for other people make fun of them and call them *la grande nation.*

By way of specially illustrating this perverse and exuberant respect for other people's opinion, let me take a passage from the *Times* of March 31st, 1846, giving a detailed account of the execution of one Thomas Wix, an apprentice who, from motives of vengeance, had murdered his master. Here we have very unusual circumstances and an extraordinary character, though one very suitable for our purpose; and these combine to give a striking picture of this folly, which is so deeply rooted in human nature, and allow us to form an accurate notion of the extent to which it will go. On the morning of the execution, says the report, "the rev. ordinary was early in attendance upon him, but Wix, beyond a quiet demeanor, betrayed no interest in his ministrations, appearing to feel anxious only to acquit himself 'bravely' before the spectators of his ignominious end. . . . . In the procession Wix fell into his proper place with alacrity, and, as he entered the Chapel-yard, remarked, sufficiently loud to be heard by several persons near him, ' Now, then, as Dr. Dodd said, I shall soon know the grand secret.' On reaching the scaffold, the miserable wretch mounted the drop without the slightest assistance, and, when he got to the center, he bowed to the spectators twice, a proceeding which called forth a tremendous cheer from the degraded crowd beneath."

This is an admirable example of the way in which a man, with death in the most dreadful form before his very eyes, and eternity beyond it, will care for nothing but the impression he makes upon a crowd of gapers, and the opinion he leaves behind him in their heads. There was much the same kind of thing in the case of Lecomte, who was executed at Frankfurt, also in 1846, for an attempt on the king's life. At the trial he was very much annoyed that he was not allowed to appear, in decent attire, before the Upper House ; and on the day of the execution it was a special grief to him that he was not permitted to shave. It is not only in recent times that this kind of thing has been known to happen. Mateo Aleman tells us, in the Introduction to his celebrated romance, "Guzman de Alfarache," that many infatuated criminals, instead of devoting their last hours to the welfare of their souls, as they ought to have done, neglect this duty for the purpose of preparing and committing to memory a speech to be made from the scaffold.

I take these extreme cases as being the best illustrations of what I mean : for they give us a magnified reflection of our own nature. The anxieties of all of us, our worries, vexations, bothers, troubles, uneasy apprehensions and strenuous efforts are due, in perhaps the large majority of instances, to what other people will say ; and we are just as foolish in this respect as those miserable criminals. Envy and hatred are very often traceable to a similar source.

Now, it is obvious that happiness, which consists for the most part in peace of mind and contentment, would be served by nothing so much as by reducing this impulse of human nature within reasonable limits—which would perhaps make it one-fiftieth part of what it is now. By doing so, we should get rid of a thorn in the flesh which is always causing us pain. But it is a very difficult task, because the impulse in question is a natural and innate perversity of human nature. Tacitus, says, "The lust of fame is the last that a wise man shakes off." * The only way of putting an end to this universal folly is to see clearly that it is a folly; and this may be done by recognizing the fact that most of the opinions in men's heads are apt to be false, perverse, erroneous and absurd, and so in themselves unworthy of any attention; further, that other people's opinions can have very little real and positive influence upon us in most of the circumstances and affairs of life. Again, this opinion is generally of such an unfavorable character that it would worry a man to death to hear everything that was said of him, or the tone in which he was spoken of. And finally, among other things, we should be clear about the fact that honor itself has no really direct, but only an indirect, value. If people were generally converted from this universal folly, the result would be such an addition to our peace of mind and cheerfulness as at present seems inconceivable; people would present a firmer and more confident front to the world, and generally behave with less embarrassment and restraint. It is observable that a retired mode of life has an exceedingly beneficial influence on our peace of mind, and this is mainly because we thus escape having to live constantly in the sight of others, and pay everlasting regard to their casual opinions; in a word, we are able to return upon ourselves. At the same time a good deal of positive misfortune might be avoided, which we are now drawn into by striving after shadows, or, to speak more correctly, by indulging a mischievous piece of folly; and we should consequently have more attention to give to solid realities and enjoy them with less interruption than at present. But χαλεπὰ τὰ καλὰ—what is worth doing is hard to do.

Section 2.—Pride.

The folly of our nature which we are discussing puts forth three shoots, ambition, vanity and pride. The difference between the last two is this: pride is an established conviction of one's own paramount worth in some particular respect, while vanity is the desire of rousing such a

---

* Hist., iv., 6.

conviction in others, and it is generally accompanied by the secret hope of ultimately coming to the same conviction one's self. Pride works from within; it is the direct appreciation of one's self. Vanity is the desire to arrive at this appreciation indirectly, from without. So we find that vain people are talkative, and proud, taciturn. But the vain person ought to be aware that the good opinion of others, which he strives for, may be obtained much more easily and certainly by persistent silence than by speech, even though he has very good things to say. Any one who wishes to affect pride is not therefore a proud man; but he will soon have to drop this, as every other assumed character.

It is only a firm, unshakable conviction of pre-eminent worth and special value which makes a man proud in the true sense of the word—a conviction which may, no doubt, be a mistaken one or rest on advantages which are of an adventitious and conventional character : still pride is not the less pride for all that, so long as it be present in real earnest. And since pride is thus rooted in conviction, it resembles every other form of knowledge in not being within our own arbitrament. Pride's worst foe—I mean its greatest obstacle—is vanity, which courts the applause of the world in order to gain the necessary foundation for a high opinion of one's own worth, while pride is based upon a pre-existing conviction of it.

It is quite true that pride is something which is generally found fault with, and cried down ; but usually, I imagine, by those who have nothing upon which they can pride themselves. In view of the impudence and foolhardiness of most people, any one who possesses any kind of superiority or merit will do well to keep his eyes fixed on it, if he does not want it to be entirely forgotten ; for if a man is good-natured enough to ignore his own privileges, and hob-nob with the generality of other people, as if he were quite on their level, they will be sure to treat him, frankly and candidly, as one of themselves. This is a piece of advice I would specially offer to those whose superiority is of the highest kind—real superiority, I mean, of a purely personal nature—which cannot, like orders and titles, appeal to the eye or ear at every moment ; as otherwise, they will find that familiarity breeds contempt or, as the Romans used to say, *sus Minervam.* " Joke with a

slave, and he'll soon show his heels," is an excellent Arabian
proverb; nor ought we to despise what Horace says,

" Sume superbiam
Quæsitam meritis "—

usurp the fame you have deserved. No doubt, when
modesty was made a virtue, it was a very advantageous
thing for the fools; for everybody is expected to speak of
himself as if he were one. This is leveling down indeed!
for it comes to look as if there were nothing but fools in
the world.

The cheapest sort of pride is national pride; for if a
man is proud of his own nation, it argues that he has no
qualities of his own of which he can be proud; otherwise,
he would not have recourse to those which he shares with
so many millions of his fellow-men. The man who is
endowed with important personal qualities will be only too
ready to see clearly in what respects his own nation falls
short, since their failings will be constantly before his eyes.
But every miserable fool who has nothing at all of which he
can be proud adopts, as a last resource, pride in the nation
to which he belongs; he is ready and glad to defend all
its faults and follies, tooth and nail, thus re-imbursing
himself for his own inferiority. For example, if you
speak of the stupid and degrading bigotry of the English
nation with the contempt it deserves, you will hardly find one
Englishman in fifty to agree with you; but if there should
be one, he will generally happen to be an intelligent man.

The Germans have no national pride, which shows how
honest they are, as everybody knows and how dishonest are
those who, by a piece of ridiculous affectation, pretend that
they are proud of their country—the *Deutsche Brüder* and
the demagogues who flatter the mob in order to mislead it.
I have heard it said that gunpowder was invented by a
German. I doubt it. Lichtenberg asks, "Why is it that a
man who is not a German does not care about pretending
that he is one; and that if he makes any pretense at all, it
is to be a Frenchman or an Englishman?"*

---

* *Translator's Note.*—It should be remembered that these remarks
were written in the earlier part of the present century, and that a
German philosopher nowadays, even though he were as apt to say
bitter things as Schopenhauer, could hardly write in a simliar
strain.

However that may be, individuality is a far more important thing than nationality, and in any given man deserves a thousand-fold more consideration. And since you cannot speak of national character without referring to large masses of people, it is impossible to be loud in your praises and at the same time honest. National character is only another name for the particular form which the littleness, perversity and baseness of mankind take in every country. If we become disgusted with one, we praise another, until we get disgusted with this too. Every nation mocks at other nations, and all are right.

The contents of this chapter, which treats. as I have said, of what we represent in the world, or what we are in the eyes of others, may be further distributed under three heads; honor, rank and fame.

Section 3.—Rank.

Let us take rank first, as it may be dismissed in a few words, although it plays an important part in the eyes of the masses and of the philistines, and is a most useful wheel in the machinery of the state.

It has a purely conventional value. Strictly speaking, it is a sham; its method is to exact an artificial respect, and, as a matter of fact, the whole thing is a mere farce.

Orders, it may be said, are bills of exchange drawn on public opinion, and the measure of their value is the credit of the drawer. Of course, as a substitute for pensions, they save the state a good deal of money; and besides, they serve a very useful purpose, if they are distributed with discrimination and judgment. For people in general have eyes and ears, it is true: but not much else, very little judgment indeed, or even memory. There are many services to the state quite beyond the range of their understanding: others again, are appreciated and made much of for a time, and then soon forgotten. It seems to me, therefore, very proper, that a cross or a star should proclaim to the mass of people always and everywhere, "This man is not like you; he has done something." But orders lose their value when they are distributed unjustly, or without due selection, or in too great numbers: a prince should be as careful in conferring them as a man of business is in signing a bill. It is a pleonasm to inscribe on any order for distinguished service; for every order ought to be for distinguished service. That stands to reason.

Section 4.—Honor.

Honor is a much larger question than rank, and more difficult to discuss. Let us begin by trying to define it.

If I were to say honor is external conscience, and conscience is inward honor, no doubt a good many people would assent; but there would be more show than reality about such a definition, and it would hardly go to the root of the matter. I prefer to say, honor is, on its objective side, other people's opinion of what we are worth; on its subjective side, it is the respect we pay to this opinion. From the latter point of view, to be a man of honor is to exercise what is often a very wholesome, but by no means a purely moral, influence.

The feelings of honor and shame exist in every man who is not utterly depraved, and honor is everywhere recognized as something particularly valuable. The reason of this is as follows. By and in himself a man can accomplish very little; he is like Robinson Crusoe on a desert island. It is only in society that a man's powers can be called into full activity. He very soon finds this out when his consciousness begins to develop, and there arises in him the desire to be looked upon as a useful member of society, as one, that is, who is capable of playing his part as a man—*pro parte virili*—thereby acquiring a right to the benefits of social life. Now, to be a useful member of society, one must do two things; firstly, what every one is expected to do everywhere, and, secondly, what one's own particular position in the world demands and requires.

But a man soon discovers that everything depends upon his being useful, not in his own opinion, but in the opinion of others; and so he tries his best to make that favorable impression upon the world, to which he attaches such a high value. Hence, this primitive and innate characteristic of human nature, which is called the feeling of honor, or, under another aspect, the feeling of shame—*verecundia*. It is this which brings a blush to his cheek at the thought of having suddenly to fall in the estimation of others, even when he knows that he is innocent, nay, even if his remissness extends to no absolute obligation, but only to one which he has taken upon himself of his own free will.

Conversely, nothing in life gives a man so much courage as the attainment or renewal of the conviction that other people regard him with favor; because it means that every one joins to give him help and protection, which is an infinitely stronger bulwark against the ills of life than anything he can do himself.

The variety of relations in which a man can stand to other people so as to obtain their confidence, that is their good opinion, gives rise to a distinction between several kinds of honor, resting chiefly on the different bearings that *meum* may take to *tuum ;* or, again, on the performance of various pledges ; or finally, on the relation of the sexes. Hence, there are three main kinds of honor, each of which takes various forms—civic honor, official honor, and sexual honor.

Civic honor has the widest sphere of all. It consists in the assumption that we shall pay unconditional respect to the rights of others, and, therefore, never use any unjust or unlawful means of getting what we want. It is the condition of all peaceable intercourse between man and man ; and it is destroyed by anything that openly and manifestly militates against this peaceable intercourse, anything, accordingly, which entails punishment at the hands of the law, always supposing that the punishment is a just one.

The ultimate foundation of honor is the conviction that moral character is unalterable : a single bad action implies that future actions of the same kind will, under similar circumstances, also be bad. This is well expressed by the English use of the word character as meaning credit, reputation, honor. Hence honor, once lost, can never be recovered ; unless the loss rested on some mistake, such as may occur if a man is slandered or his actions viewed in a false light. So the law provides remedies against slander, libel, and even insult : for insult, though it amount to no more than mere abuse, is a kind of summary slander with a suppression of the reasons. What I mean may be well put in the Greek phrase—not quoted from any author—ἔστιν ἡ λοιδορία διαβολὴ σύντομος. It is true that if a man abuses another, he is simply showing that he has no real or true causes of complaint against him ; as, otherwise, he would bring these forward as the premises, and rely upon his hearers to draw the conclusion themselves : instead of which, he gives the conclusion and leaves out the premises, trusting that people will suppose that he has done so only for the sake of being brief.

Civic honor draws its existence and name from the middle classes ; but it applies equally to all, not excepting the highest. No man can disregard it, and it is a very serious thing, of which every one should be careful not to make light. The man who breaks confidence has forever forfeited confidence, whatever he may do, and whoever he may be ; and the bitter consequences of the loss of confidence can never be averted.

There is a sense in which honor may be said to have a negative character in opposition to the positive character of fame. For honor is not the opinion people have of particular qualities which a man may happen to possess exclusively : it is rather the opinion they have of the qualities which a man may be expected to exhibit, and to which he should not prove false. Honor, therefore, means that a man is not exceptional; fame, that he is. Fame is something which must be won ; honor only something which must not be lost. The absence of fame is obscurity, which is only a negative ; but loss of honor is shame, which is a positive quality. This negative character of honor must not be confused with anything passive ; for honor is above all things active in its working. It is the only quality which proceeds directly from the man who exhibits it : it is concerned entirely with what he does and leaves undone, and has nothing to do with the actions of others or the obstacles they place in his way. It is something entirely in our own power—τῶν ἐφ'ἡμῶν. This distinction, as we shall see presently, marks off true honor from the sham honor of chivalry.

Slander is the only weapon by which honor can be attacked from without: and the only way to repel the attack is to confute the slander with the proper amount of publicity, and a due unmasking of him who utters it.

The reason why respect is paid to age is that old people have necessarily shown in the course of their lives whether or not they have been able to maintain their honor unblemished; while that of young people has not yet been put to the proof, though they are credited with the possession of it. For neither length of years—equaled, as it is, and even excelled, in the case of some of the lower animals—

nor, again, experience, which is only a closer knowledge of the world's ways, can be any sufficient reason for the respect which the young are everywhere required to show toward the old; for if it were merely a matter of years, the weakness which attends on age would call rather for consideration than for respect. It is, however, a remarkable fact that white hair always commands reverence—a reverence really innate and instinctive. Wrinkles—a much surer sign of old age—command no reverence at all; you never hear any one speak of "venerable wrinkles;" but "venerable white hair" is a common expression.

Honor has only an indirect value. For, as I explained at the beginning of this chapter, what other people think of us, if it affects us at all, can affect us only in so far as it governs their behavior toward us, and only just so long as we live with, or have to do with, them. But it is to society alone that we owe that safety which we and our possessions enjoy in a state of civilization; in all we do we need the help of others, and they, in their turn, must have confidence in us before they can have anything to do with us. Accordingly, their opinion of us is, indirectly, a matter of great importance; though I cannot see how it can have a direct or immediate value. This is an opinion also held by Cicero. "I quite agree," he writes, "with what Chrysippus and Diogenes used to say, that a good reputation is not worth raising a finger to obtain, if it were not that it is so useful."* This truth has been insisted upon at great length by Helvetius in his chief work De l'Esprit,† the conclusion of which is that we love esteem not for its own sake, but solely for the advantages which it brings. And as the means can never be more than the end, that saying, of which so much is made, "honor is dearer than life itself" is, as I have remarked, a very exaggerated statement. So much, then, for civic honor.

Official honor is the general opinion of other people that a man who fills any office really has the necessary qualities for the proper discharge of all the duties which appertain to it. The greater and more important the duties a man has to discharge in the state, and the higher and more influential the office which he fills, the stronger must be the opinion which people have of the moral and intellect-

---

* "De finibus" iii., 17.   † "Disc:" iii., 13.

ual qualities which render him fit for his post. Therefore, the higher his position, the greater must be the
degree of honor paid to him, expressed, as it is, in titles,
orders and the generally subservient behavior of others
toward him. As a rule, a man's official rank implies the
particular degree of honor which ought to be paid to him,
however much this degree may be modified by the capacity
of the masses to form any motion of its importance.
Still, as a matter of fact, greater honor is paid to a man
who fulfills special duties than to the common citizen,
whose honor mainly consists in keeping clear of dishonor.

Official honor demands, further, that the man who
occupies an office must maintain respect for it, for the
sake both of his colleagues and of those who will come
after him. This respect an official can maintain by a
proper observance of his duties, and by repelling any
attack that may be made upon the office itself or upon
its occupant: he must not, for instance, pass over unheeded any statement to the effect that the duties of the
office are not properly discharged, or that the office itself
does not conduce to the public welfare. He must prove
the unwarrantable nature of such attacks by enforcing the
legal penalty for them.

Subordinate to the honor of official personages comes
that of those who serve the state in any other capacity, as
doctors, lawyers, teachers, any one, in short, who by gradu-
ating in any subject, or by any other public declaration
that he is qualified to exercise some special skill, claims to
practice it; in a word, the honor of all those who take any
public pledges whatever. Under this head comes military
honor, in the true sense of the word, the opinion that
people who have bound themselves to defend their country
really possess the requisite qualities which will enable them
to do so, especially courage, personal bravery and strength,
and that they are perfectly ready to defend their country
to the death, and never and under no circumstances desert
the flag to which they have once sworn allegiance. I have
here taken official honor in a wider sense than that in which
it is generally used, namely, the respect due by citizens to
an office itself.

In treating of sexual honor and the principles on which
it rests, a little more attention and analysis are necessary;
and what I shall say will support my contention that all

honor really rests upon a utilitarian basis. There are two natural divisions of the subject—the honor of women and the honor of men, in either side issuing in a well-understood *esprit de corps.* The former is by far the more important of the two, because the most essential feature in woman's life is her relation to man.

Female honor is the general opinion in regard to a girl that she is pure, and in regard to a wife that she is faithful. The importance of this opinion rests upon the following considerations. Women depend upon men in all the relations of life ; men upon women it might be said, in one only. So an arrangement is made for mutual interdependence—man undertaking responsibility for all woman's needs and also for the children that spring from their union—an arrangement on which is based the welfare of the whole female race. To carry out this plan, women have to band together with a show of *esprit de corps,* and present one undivided front to their common enemy, man —who possesses all the good things of the earth, in virtue of his superior physical and intellectual power—in order to lay siege to and conquer him, and so get possession of him and a share of those good things. To this end the honor of all women depends upon the enforcement of the rule that no woman should give herself to a man except in marriage, in order that every man may be forced, as it were, to surrender and ally himself with a woman ; by this arrangement provision is made for the whole of the female race. This is a result, however which can be obtained only by a strict observance of the rule ; and, accordingly, women everywhere show true *esprit de corps,* in carefully insisting upon its maintenance. Any girl who commits a breach of the rule betrays the whole female race, because its welfare would be destroyed if every woman were to do likewise ; so she is cast out with shame as one who has lost her honor. No woman will have anything more to do with her ; she is avoided like the plague. The same doom is awarded to a woman who breaks the marriage tie ; for in so doing she is false to the terms upon which the man capitulated : and as her conduct is such as to frighten other men from making a similar surrender, it imperils the welfare of all her sisters. Nay more ; this deception and coarse breach of troth is a crime punishable by the loss, not only of personal, but also of civic honor. This is why we minimize the shame of a girl, but not of a wife; because, in the former case, marriage can restore honor, while in the latter, no atonement can be made for the breach of contract.

Once this *esprit de corps* is acknowledged to be the foundation of female honor, and is seen to be a wholesome, nay, a necessary arrangement, as at bottom a matter of prudence and interest, its extreme importance for the welfare of women will be recognized. But it does not possess anything more than a relative value. It is no absolute end, lying beyond all other aim of existence and valued above life itself. In this view, there will be nothing to applaud in the forced and extravagant conduct of a Lucretia or a Virginius—conduct which can easily degenerate into tragic farce, and produce a terrible feeling of revulsion. The conclusion of *Emilia Galotti,* for instance, makes one leave the theater completely ill at ease; and, on the other hand, all the rules of female honor cannot prevent a certain sympathy with Clara in *Egmont.* To carry this principle of female honor too far is to forget the end in thinking of the means—and this is just what people often do; for such exaggeration suggests that the value of sexual honor is absolute; while the truth is that it is more relative than any other kind. One might go so far as to say that its value is purely conventional, when one sees from Thomasius how in all ages and countries, up to the time of the Reformation, irregularities were permitted and recognized by law, with no derogation to female honor—not to speak of the temple of Mylitta at Babylon.*

There are also of course, certain circumstances in civil life which make external forms of marriage impossible, especially in Catholic countries, where there is no such thing as divorce. Ruling princes everywhere, would, in my opinion, do much better, from a moral point of view, to dispense with forms altogether rather than contract a morganatic marriage, the descendants of which might raise claims to the throne if the legitimate stock happened to die out: so that there is a possibility, though perhaps, a remote one, that a morganatic marriage might produce a civil war. And, besides, such a marriage, concluded in defiance of all outward ceremony, is a concession made to women and priests—two classes of persons to whom one should be most careful to give as little

---

* Herodotus, i. 199.

tether as possible. It is further to be remarked that every man in a country can marry the woman of his choice, except one poor individual, namely the prince. His hand belongs to his country, and can be given in marriage only for reasons of state, that is, for the good of the country. Still, for all that, he is a man; and, as a man, he likes to follow whither his heart leads. It is an unjust, ungrateful and priggish thing to forbid, or to desire to forbid, a prince from following his inclinations in this matter; of course, as long as the lady has no influence upon the government of the country. From her point of view she occupies an exceptional position, and does not come under the ordinary rules of sexual honor: for she has merely given herself to a man who loves her, and whom she loves but cannot marry. And in general, the fact that the principle of female honor has no origin in nature, is shown by the many bloody sacrifices which have been offered to it—the murder of children and the mother's suicide. No doubt a girl who contravenes the code commits a breach of faith against her whole sex: but this faith is one which is only secretly taken for granted, and not sworn to. And since, in most cases, her own prospects suffer most immediately, her folly is infinitely greater than her crime.

The corresponding virtue in men is a product of the one I have been discussing. It is their *esprit de corps*, which demands that, once a man has made that surrender of himself in marriage which is so advantageous to his conqueror, he shall take care that the terms of the treaty are maintained both in order that the agreement itself may lose none of its force by the permission of any laxity in its observance, and that men, having given up everything, may, at least, be assured of their bargain, namely, exclusive possession. Accordingly, it is part of a man's honor to resent a breach of the marriage tie on the part of his wife, and to punish it, at the very least by separating from her. If he condones the offense, his fellow-men cry shame upon him: but the shame in this case is not nearly so foul as that of the woman who has lost her honor: the stain is by no means of so deep a dye—*levioris notae macula*—because a man's relation to woman is subordinate to many other and more important affairs in his life. The two great dramatic poets of modern times have each taken man's honor as the theme of two plays; Shakespeare in "Othello" and "The Winter's Tale," and Calderon in "El medico de su honra" (the "Physician of his Honor)," and "Asecreto agravios ecreta vengeanza" ("for Secret Insult Secret Vengeance)." It should be said, however that honor demands the punishment of the wife only; to punish her paramour too, is a work of superogation. This confirms the view I have taken, that a man's honor originates in *esprit de corps*.

The kind of honor which I have been discussing hitherto has always existed in its various forms and principles among all nations and at all times ; although the history of female honor shows that its principles have undergone certain local modifications at different periods. But there is another species of honor which differs from this entirely, a species of honor of which the Greeks and Romans had no conception, and up to this day it is perfectly unknown among Chinese, Hindoos or Mohammedans. It is a kind of honor which arose only in the Middle Age, and is indigenous only to Christian Europe, nay, only to an extremely small portion of the population, that is to say, the higher classes of society and those who ape them. It is knightly honor, or *point d'honneur*. Its principles are quite different from those which underlie the kind of honor I have been treating until now, and in some respects are even opposed to them. The sort I am referring to produces the cavalier ; while the other kind creates the man of honor. As this is so, I shall proceed to give an explanation of its principles, as a kind of code or mirror of knightly courtesy.

(1.) To begin with, honor of this sort consists, not in other people's opinion of what we are worth, but wholly and entirely in whether they express it or not, no matter whether they really have any opinion at all, let alone whether they know of reasons for having one. Other people may entertain the worst opinion of us in consequence of what we do, and may despise us as much as they like ; so long as no one dares to give expression to his opinion, our honor remains untarnished. So if our actions and qualities compel the highest respect from other people, and, they have no option but to give this respect —as soon as any one, no matter how wicked or foolish he may be, utters something depreciatory of us, our honor is offended, nay, gone forever, unless we can manage to restore it. A superfluous proof of what I say, namely, that knightly honor depends, not upon what people think, but upon what they say, is furnished by the fact that insults can be withdrawn, or, if necessary, from the subject of an apology, which makes them as though they had never been uttered. Whether the opinion which underlay the expression has also been rectified, and why the expression should ever have been used, are questions which are perfectly unimportant: so long as the statement is withdrawn, all is well. The truth is that conduct of this kind aims, not at earning respect, but at extorting it.

(2.) In the second place, this sort of honor rests, not on what a man does, but on what he suffers, the obstacles he encounters; differing from the honor which prevails in all else, in consisting, not in what he says or does himself, but in what another man says or does. His honor is thus at the mercy of every man who can talk it away on the tip of his tongue; and if he attacks it, in a moment it is gone forever—unless the man who is attacked manages to wrest it back again by a process which I shall mention presently, a process which involves danger to his life, health, freedom, property and peace of mind. A man's whole conduct may be in accordance with the most righteous and noble principles, his spirit may be the purest that ever breathed, his intellect of the very highest order; and yet his honor may disappear the moment that any one is pleased to insult him, any one at all who has not offended against this code of honor himself, let him be the most worthless rascal or the most stupid beast, an idler, gambler, debtor, a man, in short, of no account at all. It is usually this sort of fellow who likes to insult people; for, as Seneca* rightly remarks, "*ut quisque contemtissimus et ludibrio est it a solutissimæ linguæ est*"—the more contemptible and ridiculous a man is, the readier he is with his tongue. His insults are most likely to be directed against the very kind of man I have described, because people of different tastes can never be friends, and the sight of pre-eminent merit is apt to raise the secret ire of a ne'er-do-well. What Goethe says in the "West-östlicher Divan," is quite true, that it is uselesss to complain against your enemies; for they can never become your friends, if your whole being is a standing reproach to them:

---

* " De Constantia." 11.

> "Was klagst du über Feinde?
> Sollten Solche je werden Freunde
> Denen das Wesen, wie du bist,
> Im stillen ein ewiger Vorwurf ist?"

It is obvious that people of this worthless description have good cause to be thankful to the principle of honor, because it puts them on a level with people who in every other respect stand far above them. If a fellow likes to insult any one, attribute to him, for example, some bad quality, this is taken as *prima facie* a well-founded opinion true in fact; a decree, as it were, with all the force of law; nay, if it is not at once wiped out in blood, it is a judgment which holds good and valid to all time. In other words, the man who is insulted remains—in the eyes of all honorable people—what the man who uttered the insult—even though he were the greatest wretch on earth—was pleased to call him; for he has "put up with" the insult—the technical term, I believe. Accordingly, all honorable people will have nothing more to do with him, and treat him like a leper, and, it may be, refuse to go into any company where he may be found, and so on.

This wise proceeding may, I think, be traced back to the fact that in the Middle Age, up to the fifteenth century, it was not the accuser in any criminal process who had to prove the guilt of the accused, but the accused who had to prove his innocence.[*] This he could do by swearing he was not guilty; and his backers—*consacramentales*—had to come and swear that in their opinion he was incapable of perjury. If he could find no one to help him in this way, or the accuser took objection to his backers, recourse was had to trial "by the judgment of God," which generally meant a duel. For the accused was now in disgrace,[†] and had to clear himself. Here then is the origin of the notion of disgrace, and of that whole system which prevails nowadays among honorable people—only that the oath is omitted. This is also the explanation of that deep feeling of indignation which honorable people are called upon to show if they

---

[*] See C. G. von Wachter's "Beitrage zur deutschen Geschichte," especially the chapter on criminal law.

[†] *Translator's Note.*—It is true that this expression has another and special meaning in the technical terminology of chivalry, but it is the nearest English equivalent which I can find for the German—*ein Bescholtener.*

are given the lie: it is a reproach which they say must be wiped out in blood. It seldom comes to this pass, however, though lies are of common occurrence: but in England, more than elsewhere, it is a superstition which has taken very deep root. As a matter of order, a man who threatens to kill another for telling a lie should never have told one himself. The fact is, that the criminal trial of the Middle Age also admitted of a shorter form. In reply to the charge, the accused answered: "That is a lie;" whereupon it was left to be decided by "the judgment of God." Hence, the code of knightly honor prescribes that, when the lie is given, an appeal to arms follows as a matter of course. So much, then for the theory of insult.

But there is something even worse than insult, something so dreadful that I must beg pardon of all "honorable people" for so much as mentioning it in this code of knightly honor for I know they will shiver, and their hair will stand on end, at the very thought of it—the *summum malum* the greatest evil on earth, worse than death and damnation. A man may give another—*horribile dictu!*—a slap or a blow. This is such an awful thing, and so utterly fatal to all honor, that, while any other species of insult may be healed by blood-letting, this can be cured only by the *coup-de-grâce*.

(3.) In the third place, this kind of honor has absolutely nothing to do with what a man may be in and for himself; or, again, with the question whether his moral character can ever become better or worse, and all such pedantic inquiries. If your honor happens to be attacked, or to all appearances gone, it can very soon be restored in its entirety if you are only quick enough in having recourse to the one universal remedy—a duel. But if the aggressor does not belong to the classes which recognize the code of knightly honor, or has himself once offended against it, there is a safer way of meeting any attack upon your honor, whether it consists in blows, or merely in words. If you are armed, you can strike down your opponent on the spot, or perhaps an hour later. This will restore your honor.

But if you wish to avoid such an extreme step, from fear of any unpleasant consequences arising therefrom, or from uncertainty as to whether the aggressor is subject to the laws of knightly honor or not, there is another means of making your position good, namely, the *Avantage*. This consists in returning rudeness with still greater rudeness, and if insults are no use, you can try a blow, which forms a sort of climax in the redemption of your honor; for instance a box on the ear may be cured by a blow with a stick, and a blow with a stick by a thrashing with a horsewhip; and as the approved remedy for this last, some people recommend you to spit at your opponent. * If all these means are of no avail, you must not shrink from drawing blood. And the reason for these methods of wiping out insult is, in this code, as follows:

(4.) To receive an insult is disgraceful; to give one, honorable. Let me take an example. My opponent has truth, right and reason on his side. Very well. I insult him. Thereupon right and honor leave him and come to me, and for the time being, he has lost them—until he gets them back, not by the exercise of right or reason, but by shooting and sticking me. Accordingly, rudeness is a quality which, in point of honor, is a substitute for any other and outweighs them all. The rudest is always right. What more do you want? However stupid, bad or wicked a man may have been, if he is only rude into the bargain, he condones and legitimizes all his faults. If in any discussion or conversation, another man shows more knowledge, greater love of truth, a sounder judgment, better understanding than we or generally exhibits intellectual qualities which cast ours into the shade, we can at once annul his superiority and our own shallowness, and in our turn be superior to him, by being insulting and offensive. For rudeness is better than any argument; it totally eclipses intellect. If our opponent does not care for our mode of attack, and will not answer still more rudely, so as to plunge us into the ignoble rivalry of the *Avantage*, we are the victors and honor is on our side. Truth, knowledge, understanding, intellect, wit, must beat a retreat and leave the field to this almighty insolence.

"Honorable people" immediately make a show of mounting their war-horse, if any one utters an opinion adverse to theirs, or shows more intelligence than they can muster; and if in any controversy they are at a loss for a reply, they

---

* *Translator's Note.*—It must be remembered that Schopenhauer is here describing, or perhaps caricaturing, the manners and customs of the German aristocracy of half a century ago. Now, of course, *nous avons change tout cela!*

look about for some weapon of rudeness, which will serve as well and come readier to hand; so they retire masters of the position. It must now be obvious that people are quite right in applauding this principle of honor as having ennobled the tone of society. This principle springs from another, which forms the heart and soul of the entire code.

(5.) Fifthly, the code implies that the highest court to which a man can appeal in any differences he may have with another on a point of honor is the court of physical force, that is, of brutality. Every piece of rudeness is, strictly speaking, an appeal to brutality: for it is a declaration that intellectual strength and moral insight are incompetent to decide, and that the battle must be fought out by physical force—a struggle which, in the case of man, whom Franklin defines as a tool-making animal, is decided by the weapons peculiar to the species; and the decision is irrevocable. This is the well-known principle of the right of might—irony, of course, like the wit of a fool, a parallel phrase. The honor of a knight may be called the glory of might.

(6.) Lastly, if, as we saw above, civic honor is very scrupulous in the matter of *meum* and *tuum*, paying great respect to obligations and a promise once made, the code we are here discussing displays, on the other hand, the noblest liberality. There is only one word which may not be broken, the word of honor—"upon my honor," as people say—the presumption being, of course, that every other form of promise may be broken. Nay, if the worst comes to the worst, it is easy to break even one's word of honor, and still remain honorable—again by adopting that universal remedy, the duel, and fighting with those who maintain that we pledged our word. Further, there is one debt, and one alone, that under no circumstances must be left unpaid—a gambling debt, which has accordingly been called a debt of honor. In all other kinds of debt you may cheat Jews and Christians as much as you like; and your knightly honor remains without a stain.

The unprejudiced reader will see at once that such a strange, savage and ridiculous code of honor as this has no foundation in human nature, nor any warrant in a healthy view of human affairs. The extremely narrow sphere of its operation serves only to intensify the feeling, which is exclusively confined to Europe since the Middle Age, and then only to the upper classes, officers and soldiers, and people who imitate them. Neither Greeks nor Romans knew anything of this code of honor or of its principles ; nor the highly civilized nations of Asia, ancient or modern. Among them no other kind of honor is recognized but that which I discussed first, in virtue of which a man is what he shows himself to be by his actions, not what any wagging tongue is pleased to say of him. They thought that what a man said or did might perhaps affect his own honor, but not any other man's. To them, a blow was but a blow —and any horse or donkey could give a harder one—a blow which under certain circumstances might make a man angry and demand immediate vengeance ; but it had nothing to do with honor. No one kept account of blows or insulting words, or of the satisfaction which was demanded or omitted to be demanded. Yet in personal bravery and contempt of death, the ancients were certainly not inferior to the nations of Christian Europe. The Greeks and Romans were thorough heroes, if you like ; but they knew nothing about *point d'honneur*. If they had any idea of a duel, it was totally unconnected with the life of the nobles ; it was merely the exhibition of mercenary gladiators, slaves devoted to slaughter, condemned criminals, who, alternately with wild beasts, were set to butcher one another to make a Roman holiday. When Christianity was introduced, gladiatorial shows were done away with, and their place taken, in Christian times, by the duel, which was a way of settling difficulties by "the judgment of God." If the gladiatorial fight was a cruel sacrifice to the prevailing desire for great spectacles, dueling is a cruel sacrifice to existing prejudices ; a sacrifice, not of criminals, slaves and prisoners, but of the noble and the free.*

There are a great many traits in the character of the ancients which show that they were entirely free from these prejudices. When for instance, Marius was summoned to a duel by a Teutonic chief, he returned answer to the effect that, if the chief were tired of his life, he might go

---

* *Translator's Note.* These and other remarks on dueling will no doubt wear a belated look to English readers ; but they are hardly yet antiquated for most parts of the Continent.

and hang himself; at the same time he offered him a veteran gladiator for a round or two. Plutarch relates in his life of Themistocles that Eurybiades, who was in command of the fleet, once raised his stick to strike him; whereupon Themistocles, instead of drawing his sword, simply said : " Strike, but hear me." How sorry the reader must be, if he is an honorable man, to find that we have no information that the Athenian officers refused in a body to serve any longer under Themistocles, if he acted like that! There is a modern French writer who declares that if any one considers Demosthenes a man of honor, his ignorance will excite a smile of pity, and that Cicero was not a man of honor either! * In a certain passage in Plato's " Laws,"† the philosopher speaks at length of αἰκία or assault, showing us clearly enough that the ancients had no notion of any feeling of honor in connection with such matters. Socrates' frequent discussions were often followed by his being severely handled, and he bore it all mildly. Once, for instance, when somebody kicked him, the patience with which he took the insult surprised one of his friends. " Do you think," said Socrates, " that if an ass happened to kick me, I should resent it ?"‡ On another occasion, when he was asked, " Has not that fellow abused and insulted you ?" "No," was his answer, " what he says is not addressed to me."§ Stobæus has preserved a long passage from Musonius, from which we can see how the ancients treated insults. They knew no other form of satisfaction than that which the law provided, and wise people despised even this. If a Greek received a box on the ear, he could get satisfaction by the aid of the law : as is evident from Plato's "Gorgias," where Socrates' opinion may be found. The same thing may be seen in the account given by Gellius of one Lucius Veratius, who had the audacity to give some Roman citizens whom he met on the road a box on the ear, without any provocation whatever; but to avoid any ulterior consequences, he told a slave to bring a bag of small money, and on the spot paid the trivial legal penalty to the men whom he had astonished by his conduct.

---

* *Soirées littéraires* : par C. Durand. Rouen, 1828.   † Bk. ix.

‡ Diogenes Laertius, ii. 21.   § Ibid. 36.

Crates, the celebrated cynic philosopher, got such a box on the ear from Nicodromus, the musician, that his face swelled up and became black and blue; whereupon he put a label on his forehead, with the inscription, *Nicodromus fecit*, which brought much disgrace to the fluteplayer who had committed such a piece of brutality upon the man whom all Athens honored as a household god.* And in a letter to Melesippus, Diogenes of Sinope tells us that he got a beating from the drunken sons of the Athenians ; but he adds that it was a matter of no importance.† And Seneca devotes the last few chapters of his " De Constantia " to a lengthy discussion on insult—*contumelia ;* in order to show that a wise man will take no notice of it. In Chapter XIV. he says, " What shall a wise man do, if he is given a blow ? What Cato did, when some one struck him on the mouth ; not fire up or avenge the insult, or even return the blow, but simply ignore it."

"Yes," you say, "but these men were philosophers."—And you are fools, eh? Precisely.

It is clear that the whole code of knightly honor was utterly unknown to the ancients; for the simple reason that they always took a natural and unprejudiced view of human affairs, and did not allow themselves to be influenced by any such vicious and abominable folly. A blow in the face was to them a blow and nothing more, a trivial physical injury; wheras the moderns make a catastrophe out of it, a theme for a tragedy: as, for instance, in the *Cid* of Corneille, or in a recent German comedy of middle class life, called "The Power of Circumstance," which should have been entitled "The Power of Prejudice." If a member of the national assembly at Paris got a blow on the ear, it would resound from one end of Europe to the other. The examples which I have given of the way in which such an occurrence would have been treated in classic times may not suit the ideas of "honorable people;" so let me recommend to their notice, as a kind of antidote, the story of Monsieur Desglands in Diderot's masterpiece, "Jacques le fataliste." It is an excellent specimen of modern knightly honor, which, no doubt they will find enjoyable and edifying.‡

---

* Diogenes Laertius, vi. 87, and Apul : Flor : p. 126.

† Cf. Casaubon's Note, ad Diog. Laert., vi. 33.

‡ *Translator's Note.*—The story to which Schopenhauer here refers

From what I have said it must be quite evident that the principle of knightly honor has no essential and spontaneous origin in human nature. It is an artificial product, and its source is not hard to find. Its existence obviously dates from the time when people used their fists more than their heads, when priestcraft had enchained the human intellect, the much bepraised Middle Age, with its system of chivalry. That was the time when people let the Almighty not only care for them but judge for them too: when difficult cases were decided by an ordeal, a "judgment of God;" which, with few exceptions, meant a duel, not only where nobles were concerned, but in the case of ordinary citizens as well. There is a neat illustration of this in Shakespeare's "Henry VI."* Every judicial sentence was subject to an appeal to arms—a court, as it were of higher instance, namely "the judgment of God;" and this really meant that physical strength and activity, that is, our animal nature, usurped the place of reason on the judgment seat, deciding in matters of right and wrong, not by what a man had done, but by the force with which he was opposed, the same system, in fact as prevails to-day under the principles of knightly honor. If any one doubts that such is really the origin of our modern duel, let him read an excellent work by J. B. Millingen, "The History of Dueling." † Nay, you may still find among the supporters of the system—who, by the way, are not usually the most educated or thoughtful of men— some who look upon the result of a duel as really constituting a divine judgment in the matter in dispute: no doubt in consequence of the traditional feeling on the subject.

---

is briefly as follows: Two gentlemen, one of whom was named Desglands, were paying court to the same lady. As they sat at table side by side, with the lady opposite, Desglands did his best to charm her with his conversation; but she pretended not to hear him, and kept looking at his rival. In the agony of jealousy, Desglands, as he was holding a fresh egg in his hand, involuntarily crushed it; the shell broke, and its contents bespattered his rival's face. Seeing him raise his hand, Desglands seized it and whispered: "Sir, I take it as given." The next day Desglands appeared with a large piece of black sticking-plaster upon his right cheek. In the duel which followed, Desglands severely wounded his rival; upon which he reduced the size of the plaster. When his rival recovered, they had another duel; Desglands drew blood again, and again made his plaster a little smaller; and so on for five or six times. After every duel Desglands' plaster grew less and less, until at last his rival was killed.

* Part II., Act 2, Sc. 3.   † Published in 1849.

But leaving aside the question of origin, it must now be clear to us that the main tendency of the principle is to use physical menace for the purpose of extorting an appearance of respect which is deemed too difficult or superfluous to acquire in reality; a proceeding which comes to much the same thing as if you were to prove the warmth of your room by holding your hand on the thermometer and so make it rise. In fact, the kernel of the matter is this: whereas civic honor aims at peaceable intercourse, and consists in the opinion of other people that we deserve full confidence, because we pay unconditional respect to their rights; knightly honor, on the other hand, lays down that we are to be feared, as being determined at all costs to maintain our own.

As not much reliance can be placed upon human integrity, the principle that it is more essential to arouse fear than to invite confidence would not, perhaps, be a false one, if we were living in a state of nature, where every man would have to protect himself and directly maintain his own rights. But in civilized life, when the state undertakes the protection of our person and property, the principle is no longer applicable: it stands, like the castles and watch-towers of the age when might was right, a useless and forlorn object, amid well-tilled fields and frequented roads, or even railways.

Accordingly, the application of knightly honor, which still recognizes this principle, is confined to those small cases of personal assault which meet with but slight punishment at the hands of the law, or even none at all, for *de minimis non*—mere trivial wrongs, committed sometimes only in jest. The consequence of this limited application of the principle is that it has forced itself into an exaggerated respect for the value of the person—a respect utterly alien to the nature, constitution or destiny of man—which it has elevated into a species of sanctity: and as it considers that the state has imposed a very insufficient penalty on the commission of such trivial injuries, it takes upon itself to punish them by attacking the aggressor in life or limb. The whole thing manifestly rests upon an excessive degree of arrogant pride, which, completely forgetting what man really is, claims that he shall be absolutely free from all attack or even censure. Those who determine to carry out this principle by main force, and announce, as their rule of action, "whoever insults or strikes me shall die!" ought for their pains to be banished the country.*

As a palliative to this rash arrogance, people are in the habit of giving way on everything. If two intrepid persons meet, and neither will give way, the slightest difference may cause a shower of abuse, then fisticuffs, and, finally, a fatal blow: so that it would really be a more decorous proceeding to omit the intermediate steps and appeal to arms at once. An appeal to arms has its own special formalities; and these have developed into a rigid and precise system of laws and regulations, together forming the most solemn farce there is—a regular temple of honor dedicated to folly! For if two intrepid persons dispute over some trivial matter (more important affairs are dealt with by law), one of them, the cleverer of the two, will of course yield; and they will agree to differ. That this is so is proved by the fact that common people—or, rather, the numerous classes of the community who do not acknowledge the principle of knightly honor, let any dispute run its natural course. Among these classes homicide is a hundred-fold rarer than among those—and they amount perhaps, in all, to hardly one in a thousand—who pay homage to the principle : and even blows are of no very frequent occurrence.

Then it has been said that the manners and tone of good society are ultimately based upon this principle of honor,

* Knightly honor is the child of pride and folly, and it is need, not pride, which is the heritage of the human race. It is a very remarkable fact that this extreme form of pride should be found exclusively among the adherents of the religion which teaches the deepest humility. Still, this pride must not be put down to religion, but, rather, to the feudal system, which made every nobleman a petty sovereign who recognized no human judge, and learned to regard his person as sacred and inviolable, and any attack upon it, or any blow or insulting word, as an offense punishable by death. The principle of knightly honor and of the duel was at first confined to the nobles, and, later on, also to officers in the army, who, enjoying a kind of off-and-on relationship with the upper classes, though they were never incorporated with them, were anxious not to be behind them. It is true that duels were the product of the old ordeals; but the latter are not the foundation, but rather the consequence and application of the principle of honor: the man who recognized no human judge appealed to the divine. Ordeals, however, are not peculiar to Christendom: they may be found in great force among the Hindoos, especially of ancient times; and there are traces of them even now.

which, with its system of duels, is made out to be a bulwark against the assaults of savagery and rudeness. But Athens, Corinth and Rome could assuredly boast of good, nay, excellent society, and manners and tone of a high order, without any support from the bogey of knightly honor. It is true that women did not occupy that prominent place in ancient society which they hold now, when conversation has taken on a frivolous and trifling character, to the exclusion of that weighty discourse which distinguished the ancients. This change has certainly contributed a great deal to bring about the tendency, which is observable in good society nowadays, to prefer personal courage to the possession of any other quality. The fact is that personal courage is really a very subordinate virtue—merely the distinguishing mark of a subaltern—a virtue, indeed, in which we are surpassed by the lower animals ; or else you would not hear people say, "as brave as a lion." Far from being the pillar of society knightly honor affords a sure asylum, in general for dishonesty and wickedness, and also for small incivilities, want of consideration and unmannerliness. Rude behavior is often passed over in silence because no one cares to risk his neck in correcting it.

After what I have said, it will not appear strange that the dueling system is carried to the highest pitch of sanguinary zeal precisely in that nation whose political and financial records show that they are not too honorable. What that nation is like in its private and domestic life, is a question which may be best put to those who are experienced in the matter. Their urbanity and social culture have long been conspicuous by their absence.

There is no truth, then, in such pretexts. It can be urged with more justice that as, when you snarl at a dog, he snarls in return, and when you pet him, he fawns ; so it lies in the nature of men to return hostility by hostility, and to be embittered and irritated at any signs of depreciatory treatment or hatred : and, as Cicero says, "there is something so penetrating in the shaft of envy that even men of wisdom and worth find its wound a painful one ;" and nowhere in the world, except, perhaps, in a few religious sects, is an insult or a blow taken with equanimity. And yet a natural view of either would in no case demand anything more than a requital proportionate to the offense, and would never go the length of assigning death as the proper penalty for any one who accuses another of lying or stupidy or cowardice. The old German theory of blood for a blow is a revolting superstition of the age of chivalry. And in any case the return or requital of an insult is dictated by anger, and not by any such obligation of honor and duty as the advocates of chivalry seek to attach to it. The fact is that, the greater the truth, the greater the slander; and it is clear that the slightest hint of some real delinquency will give much greater offense than a most terrible accusation which is perfectly baseless: so that a man who is quite sure that he has done nothing to deserve a reproach may treat it with contempt, and will be safe in doing so. The theory of honor demands that he shall show a susceptibility which he does not possess, and take bloody vengeance for insults which he cannot feel. A man must himself have but a poor opinion of his own worth who hastens to prevent the utterance of an unfavorable opinion by giving his enemy a black eye.

True appreciation of his own value will make a man really indifferent to insult; but if he cannot help resenting it, a little shrewdness and culture will enable him to save appearances and dissemble his anger. If we could only get rid of this superstition about honor—the idea, I mean, that it disappears when you are insulted, and can be restored by returning the insult; if we could only stop people from thinking that wrong, brutality and insolence can be legalized by expressing readiness to give satisfaction, that is, to fight in defense of it, we should all soon come to the general opinion that insult and depreciation are like a battle in which the loser wins; and that, as Vincenzo Monti says, abuse resembles a church procession, because it always returns to the point from which it sets out. If we could only get people to look upon insult in this light, we should no longer have to say something rude in order to prove that we are in the right. Now, unfortunately, if we want to take a serious view of any question, we have first of all to consider whether it will not give offense in some way or other to the dullard, who generally shows alarm and resentment at the merest sign of intelligence: and it may easily happen that the head which contains the intelligent view has to be pitted against the noddle which is empty of everything but narrowness and stupidity. If all this were done away with, intellectual superiority could take the leading place in society which is its due—a place now occupied, though people do not like to confess it, by excellence of physique, mere fighting pluck, in fact : and the natural effect of such a change would be that the best kind of people would have one reason the less for withdrawing from society. This would pave the way for the introduction of real courtesy and genuinely good society, such as undoubtedly existed in Athens, Corinth and Rome. If any one wants to see a good example of what I mean I should like him to read Xenophon's "Banquet."

The last argument in defense of knightly honor no doubt is, that, but for its existence, the world—awful thought! —would be a regular bear-garden. To which I may briefly reply that nine hundred and ninety-nine people out of a thousand who do not recognize the code, have often given and received a blow without any fatal consequences: whereas among the adherents of the code, a blow usually means death to one of the parties. But let me examine this argument more closely.

I have often tried to find some tenable, or at any rate, plausible basis—other than a merely conventional one—some positive reasons, that is to say, for the rooted conviction which a portion of mankind entertains, that a blow is a very dreadful thing; but I have looked for it in vain, either in the animal or in the rational side of human nature. A blow is, and always will be, a trivial physical injury which one man can do to another: proving, thereby, nothing more than his superiority in strength or skill, or that his enemy was off his guard. Analysis will carry us no further. The same knight who regards a blow from the human hand as the greatest of evils, if he gets a ten times harder blow from his horse, will give you the assurance, as he limps away in suppressed pain, that it is a matter of no consequence whatever. So I have come to think that it is the human hand which is at the bottom of the mischief. And yet in a battle the knight may get cuts and thrusts from the same hand, and still assure you that his wounds are not worth mentioning. Now, I hear that a blow from the flat of a sword is not by any means so bad as a blow with a stick; and that, a short time ago, cadets were liable to be punished by the one but not the other, and that the very greatest honor of all is the *accolade*. This is all the psychological or moral basis that I can find; and so there is nothing left me but to pronounce the whole thing an antiquated superstition that has taken deep root, and one more of the many examples which show the force of tradition. My view is confirmed by the well-known fact that in China a beating with a bamboo is a very frequent punishment for the common people, and even for officials of every class; which shows that human nature, even in a highly civilized state, does not run in the same groove here and in China.

On the contrary, an unprejudiced view of human nature shows that it is just as natural for man to beat as it is for savage animals to bite and rend in pieces, or for horned beasts to butt or push. Man may be said to be the animal that beats. Hence it is revolting to our sense of the fitness of things to hear, as we sometimes do, that one man has bitten another; on the other hand, it is a natural and everyday occurrence for him to get blows or give them. It is intelligible enough that, as we become educated, we are glad to dispense with blows by a system of mutual restraint. But it is a cruel thing to compel a nation or a single class to regard a blow as an awful misfortune which must have death and murder for its consequences. There are too many genuine evils in the world to allow of our increasing them by imaginary misfortunes, which bring real ones in their train; and yet this is the precise effect of the superstition, which thus proves itself at once stupid and malign.

It does not seem to me wise of governments and legislative bodies to promote any such folly by attempting to do away with flogging as a punishment in civil or military life. Their idea is that they are acting in the interests of humanity; but, in point of fact, they are doing just the opposite; for the abolition of flogging will serve only to strengthen this inhuman and abominable superstition, to which so many sacrifices have already been made. For all offenses, except the worst, a beating is the obvious, and therefore the natural penalty; and a man who will not listen to reason will yield to blows. It seems to me right and proper to administer corporal punishment to the man who possesses nothing and therefore cannot be fined, or cannot be put in prison because his master's interests would suffer by the loss of his services. There are really no arguments against it: only mere talk about "the dignity of man"—talk which proceeds, not from any clear notions on the subject, but from the pernicious superstition I have been describing. That it is a superstition which lies at the bottom of the whole business is proved by an almost laughable example. Not long ago in the military discipline of many countries, the cat was replaced by the stick. In either case the object was to produce physical pain; but the latter method involved no disgrace, and was not derogatory to honor.

By promoting this superstition, the state is playing into the hands of the principle of knightly honor, and therefore of the duel; while at the same time it is trying, or at any rate it pretends that it is trying to abolish the duel by legislative enactment. As a natural consequence we find that this fragment of the theory that "might is right," which has come down to us from the most savage days of the Middle Age, has still in this nineteenth century a good deal of life left in it—more shame to us! It is high time for the principle to be driven out bag and baggage. Nowadays, no one is allowed to set dogs or cocks to fight each other—at any rate in England it is a penal offense—but men are plunged into deadly strife, against their will, by the operation of this ridiculous, superstitious and absurd principle which imposes upon us the obligation as its narrow-minded supporters and advocates declare of fighting with one another like gladiators, for any little trifle. Let me recommend our purists to adopt the expression baiting,* instead of duel, which probably comes to us, not from the Latin *duellum* but from the Spanish *duelo*—meaning suffering, nuisance, annoyance.

In any case, we may well laugh at the pedantic excess to which this foolish system has been carried. It is really revolting that this principle, with its absurd code, can form a power within the state—*imperium in imperio*—a power too easily put in motion, which, recognizing no right but might, tyrannizes over the classes which come within its range, by keeping up a sort of inquisition, before which any one may be haled on the most flimsy pretext, and there and then be tried on an issue of life and death between himself and his opponent. This is the lurking place from which every rascal, if he only belongs to the classes in question, may menace and even exterminate the noblest and best of men, who, as such, must of course be an object of

---

* Ritterhetze.

hatred to him. Our system of justice and police-protection has made it impossible in these days for any scoundrel in the street to attack us with—"Your money or your life!" and common sense ought now to be able to prevent rogues disturbing the peaceable intercourse of society by coming at us with—"Your honor or your life!" An end should be put to the burden, which weighs upon the higher classes— the burden, I mean, of having to be ready every moment to expose life and limb to the mercy of any one who takes it into his rascally head to be coarse, rude, foolish or mali- cious. It is perfectly atrocious that a pair of silly, passion- ate boys should be wounded, maimed or even killed, simply because they have had a few words.

The strength of this tyrannical power within the state, and the force of the superstition, may be measured by the fact that people who are prevented from restoring their knightly honor by the superior or inferior rank of their aggressor, or anything else that puts the persons on a dif- ferent level, often come to a tragic-comic end by committing suicide in sheer despair. You may generally know a thing to be false and ridiculous by finding that, if it is carried to its logical conclusion, it results in a contradiction: and here too, we have a very glaring absurdity. For an officer is forbidden to take part in a duel; but if he is challenged and declines to come out, he is punished by being dismissed the service.

As I am on the matter, let me be more frank still. The important distinction, which is often insisted upon, between killing your enemy in a fair fight with equal weap- ons, and lying in ambush for him, is entirely a corollary of the fact that the power within the state, of which I have spoken, recognizes no other right than might, that is, the right of the stronger, and appeals to a "judgment of God," as the basis of the whole code. For to kill a man in a fair fight, is to prove that you are superior to him in strength or skill; and to justify the deed, you must assume that the right of the stronger is really a right.

But the truth is that, if my opponent is unable to defend himself, it gives me the possibility, but not by any means the right, of killing him. The right, the moral justification, must depend entirely upon the motives which I have for taking his life. Even supposing that I have sufficient motive for taking a man's life, there is no reason why I should make his death depend upon whether I can shoot or fence better than he. In such a case, it is immaterial in what way I kill him, whether I attack him from the front or the rear. From a moral point of view, the right of the stronger is no more convincing than the right of the more skillful; and it is skill which is employed if you murder a man treacherously. Might and skill are in this case equally right: in a duel, for instance, both the one and the other come into play; for a feint is only another name for treachery. If I consider myself morally justified in taking a man's life, it is stupid of me to try first of all whether he can shoot or fence better than I; as, if he can, he will not only have wronged me, but have taken my life into the bargain.

It is Rousseau's opinion that the proper way to avenge an insult is, not to fight a duel with your aggressor, but to assassinate him—an opinion, however, which he is cautious enough only to barely indicate in a mysterious note to one of the books of his "Émile." This shows the philosopher so completely under the influence of the mediæval superstition of knightly honor that he considers it justifiable to murder a man who accuses you of lying: while he must have known that every man, and himself especially, has deserved to have the lie given him times without number.

The prejudice which justifies the killing of your adversary, so long as it is done in an open contest and with equal weapons, obviously looks upon might as really right, and a duel as the interference of God. The Italian who, in a fit of rage, falls upon his aggressor wherever he finds him, and despatches him without any ceremony, acts, at any rate, consistently and naturally: he may be cleverer, but he is not worse, than the duelist. If you say, I am justified in killing my adversary in a duel, because he is at the moment doing his best to kill me; I can reply that it is your challenge which has placed him under the necessity of defending himself: and that by mutually putting it on the ground of self-defense, the combatants are seeking a plausible pretext for committing murder. I should rather justify the deed by the legal maxim *Volenti nonfit injuria*, because the parties mutually agree to set their life upon the issue. This argument may, however, be rebutted by showing that the injured party is not injured *volens;* because it is this tyrannical principle of knightly honor, with its absurd code, which forcibly drags one at least of the combatants before a bloody inquisition.

I have been rather prolix on the subject of knightly honor, but I had good reasons for being so, because the Augean stable of moral and intellectual enormity in this world can be cleaned out only with the besom of philosophy. There are two things which more than all else serve to make the social arrangements of modern life compare unfavorably with those of antiquity, by giving our age a gloomy, dark and sinister aspect, from which antiquity, fresh, natural and, as it were, in the morning of life, is completely free; I mean modern honor and modern disease —*parcnobile fratrum!* which have combined to poison all the relations of life, whether public or private. The second of this noble pair extends its influence much farther than at first appears to be the case, as being not merely a physical, but also a moral disease. From the time that poisoned arrows have been found in Cupid's quiver, an estranging, hostile, nay devilish element has entered into the relations of men and women, like a sinister thread of fear and mistrust in the warp and woof of their intercourse; indirectly shaking the foundations of human fellowship, and so more or less affecting the whole tenor of existence. But it would be beside my present purpose to pursue the subject further.

An influence analogous to this, though working on other lines, is exerted by the principle of knightly honor—that solemn farce, unknown to the ancient world, which makes modern society stiff, gloomy and timid, forcing us to keep the strictest watch on every word that falls. Nor is this all. The principle is a universal Minotaur; and the goodly company of the sons of noble houses which it demands in yearly tribute, comes, not from one country alone as of old, but from every land in Europe. It is high time to make a regular attack upon this foolish system; and that is what I am trying to do now. Would that these two monsters of the modern world might disappear before the end of the century!

Let us hope that medicine may be able to find some means of preventing the one, and that, by clearing our ideas, philosophy may put an end to the other; for it is only by clearing our ideas that the evil can be eradicated. Governments have tried to do so by legislation, and failed.

Still, if they are really concerned to suppress the dueling system; and if the small success that has attended their efforts is really due only to their inability to cope with the evil, I do not mind proposing a law the success of which I am prepared to guarantee. It will involve no sanguinary measures, and can be put into operation without recourse either to the scaffold or the gallows, or to imprisonment for life. It is a small homœpathic pilule, with no serious after effects. If any man send or accept a challenge, let the corporal take him before the guard house, and there give him, in broad daylight twelve strokes with a stick *à la Chinoise;* a non-commissioned officer or a private to receive six. If a duel has actually taken place, the usual criminal proceeding should be instituted.

A person with knightly notions might, perhaps, object that, if such a punishment were carried out, a man of honor would possibly shoot himself; to which I should answer that it is better for a fool like that to shoot himself rather than other people. However, I know very well that governments are not really in earnest about putting down dueling. Civil officials, and much more so, officers in the army (except those in the highest positions), are paid most inadequately for the services they perform; and the deficiency is made up by honor, which is represented by titles and orders, and, in general, by the system of rank and distinction. The duel is, so to speak, a very serviceable extra-horse for people of rank: so they are trained in the knowledge of it at the universities. The accidents which happen to those who use it make up in blood for the deficiency of the pay.

Just to complete the discussion, let me here mention the subject of national honor. It is the honor of a nation as a unit in the aggregate of nations. And as there is no court to appeal to but the court of force; and as every nation must be prepared to defend its own interests, the honor of a nation consists in establishing the opinion, not only that it may be trusted (its credit), but also that it is to be feared. An attack upon its rights must never be allowed to pass unheeded. It is a combination of civic and of knightly honor.

Section 5.—*Fame.*

Under the heading of place in the estimation of the

world we have put *Fame;* and this we must now proceed to consider.

Fame and honor are twins; and twins, too, like Castor and Pollux, of whom the one was mortal and the other was not. Fame is the undying brother of ephemeral honor. I speak, of course, of the highest kind of fame, that is, of fame in the true and genuine sense of the word; for, to be sure, there are many sorts of fame, some of which last but a day. Honor is concerned merely with such qualities as every one may be expected to show under similar circumstances; fame only of those which cannot be required of any man. Honor is of qualities which every one has a right to attribute to himself; fame only of those which should be left to others to attribute. While our honor extends as far as people have knowledge of us; fame runs in advance, and makes us known wherever it finds its way. Every one can make a claim to honor; very few to fame, as being attainable only in virtue of extraordinary achievements.

These achievements may be of two kinds, either actions or work; and so to fame there are two paths open. On the path of actions, a great heart is the chief recommendation; on that of works, a great head. Each of the two paths has its own peculiar advantages and detriments; and the chief difference between them is that actions are fleeting, while works remain. The influence of an action, be it never so noble, can last but a short time; but a work of genius is a living influence, beneficial and ennobling throughout the ages. All that can remain of actions is a memory, and that becomes weak and disfigured by time—a matter of indifference to us, until at last it is extinguished altogether; unless, indeed, history takes it up, and presents it, fossilized, to posterity. Works are immortal in themselves, and once committed to writing, may live forever. Of Alexander the Great we have but the name and the record: but Plato and Aristotle, Homer and Horace are alive, and as directly at work to-day as they were in their own life-time. The "Vedas" and their "Upanishads," are still with us: but of all contemporaneous actions not a trace has come down to us.*

---

* Accordingly it is a poor compliment, though sometimes a fashionable one, to try to pay honor to a work by calling it an action.

Another disadvantage under which actions labor is that they depend upon chance for the possibility of coming into existence; and hence, the fame they win does not flow entirely from their intrinsic value, but also from the circumstances which happened to lend them importance and luster. Again, the fame of actions, if, as in war, they are purely personal, depends upon the testimony of fewer witnesses; and these are not always present, and even if present, are not always just or unbiased observers. This disadvantage, however, is counterbalanced by the fact that actions have the advantage of being of a practical character, and, therefore, within the range of general human intelligence; so that once the facts have been correctly reported, justice is immediately done; unless, indeed, the motive underlying the action is not at first properly understood or appreciated. No action can be really understood apart from the motive which prompted it.

It is just the contrary with works. Their inception does not depend upon chance, but wholly and entirely upon their author; and whatever they are in and for themselves, that they remain as long as they live. Further, there is a difficulty in properly judging them, which become all the harder, the higher their character; often there are no persons competent to understand the work, and often no unbiased or honest critics. Their fame, however, does not depend upon one judge only; they can enter an appeal to another. In the case of actions, as I have said, it is only their memory which comes down to posterity, and then

---

For a work is something essentially higher in its nature. An action is always something based on motive, and, therefore, fragmentary and fleeting—a part, in fact, of that Will which is the universal and original element in the constitution of the world. But a great and beautiful work has a permanent character, as being of universal significance, and sprung from the Intellect, which rises, like a perfume, above the faults and follies of the world of Will.

The fame of a great action has this advantage, that it generally starts with a loud explosion; so loud, indeed, as to be heard all over Europe: whereas the fame of a great work is slow and gradual in its beginnings; the noise it makes is at first slight, but it goes on growing greater, until at last, after a hundred years perhaps, it attains its full force; but then it remains, because the works remain, for thousands of years. But in the other case, when the first explosion is over, the noise it makes grows less and less, and is heard by fewer and fewer persons; until it ends by the actions having only a shadowy existence in the pages of history.

only in the traditional form ; but works are handed down themselves, and, except when parts of them have been lost, in the form in which they first appeared. In this case there is no room for any disfigurement of the facts ; and any circumstances which may have prejudiced them in their origin, fall away with the lapse of time. Nay, it is often only after the lapse of time that the persons really competent to judge them appear—exceptional critics sitting in judgment on exceptional works, and giving their weighty verdicts in succession. These collectively form a perfectly just appreciation ; and though there are cases where it has taken some hundreds of years to form it, no further lapse of time is able to reverse the verdict; so secure and inevitable is the fame of a great work.

Whether authors ever live to see the dawn of their fame depends upon the chance of circumstance; and the higher and more important their works are, the less likelihood there is of their doing so. That was an incomparably fine saying of Seneca's, that fame follows merit as surely as the body casts a shadow; sometimes falling in front, and sometimes behind. And he goes on to remark that "though the envy of contemporaries be shown by universal silence, there will come those who will judge without enmity or favor." From this remark it is manifest that even in Seneca's age there were rascals who understood the art of suppressing merit by maliciously ignoring its existence, and of concealing good work from the public in order to favor the bad: it is an art well understood in our day, too, manifesting itself, both then and now, in "an envious conspiracy of silence."

As a general rule, the longer a man's fame is likely to last, the later it will be in coming; for all excellent products require time for their development. The fame which lasts to posterity is like an oak, of very slow growth: and that which endures but a little while, like plants which spring up in a year and then die; while false fame is like a fungus, shooting up in a night and perishing as soon.

And why? For this reason; the more a man belongs to posterity, in other words, to humanity in general, the more of an alien he is to his contemporaries; since his work is not meant for them as such, but only for them in so far as they form part of mankind at large; there is none of that familiar local color about his productions which would appeal to them: and so what he does, fails of recognition be-

cause it is strange. People are more likely to appreciate
the man who serves the circumstances of his own brief hour,
or the temper of the moment—belonging to it, and living
and dying with it.

The general history of art and literature shows that the
highest achievements of the human mind are, as a rule, not
favorably received at first; but remain in obscurity until
they win notice from intelligence of a higher order, by
whose influence they are brought into a position which they
then maintain, in virtue of the authority thus given
them.

If the reason of this should be asked, it will be found
that ultimately, a man can really understand and appreciate those things only which are of like nature with himself.
The dull person will like what is dull, and the common
person what is common; a man whose ideas are mixed will
be attracted by confusion of thought; and folly will appeal
to him who has no brains at all; but first of all, a man will
like his own works, as being of a character thoroughly at
one with himself. This is a truth as old as Epicharmus of
fabulous memory—

> Θαυμαστὸν οὐδὲν ἐστί με ταῦθ' οὕτω λέγειν
> Καὶ ἀνδάνειν αὐτοῖσιν αὐτους, καὶ δοκεῖν
> Καλῶς πεφυκέναι· καὶ γὰρ ὁ κύων κυνί
> Κάλλιστον εἶμεν φαίνεται, καὶ βοῦς βοΐ
> Ονος δ' ὄνῳ κάλλιστόν [ἐστιν], ὗς δ' ὑΐ.

The sense of this passage—for it should not be lost—is
that we should not be surprised if people are pleased with
themselves, and fancy that they are in good case; for to a
dog the best thing in the world is a dog; to an ox, an ox;
to an ass, an ass; and to a sow, a sow.

The strongest arm is unavailing to give impetus to a
feather-weight; for, instead of speeding on its way and hit-
ting its mark with effect, it will soon fall to the ground,
having expended what little energy was given to it, and
possessing no mass of its own to be the vehicle of momen-
tum. So it is with great and noble thoughts, nay, with
the very masterpieces of genius when there are none but
little, weak, and perverse minds to appreciate them—a
fact which has been deplored by a chorus of the wise in all
ages. Jesus the son of Sirach, for instance, declares that

"He that telleth a tale to a fool speaketh to one in slumber: when he hath told his tale, he will say, 'What is the matter?'" * And Hamlet says, "A knavish speech sleeps in a fool's ear."† And Goethe is of the same opinion, that a dull ear mocks at the wisest word,

> " Das glucklichste Wort es wird verhohnt,
>   Wenn der Horer ein Schiefohr ist; "

and again, that we should not be discouraged if people are stupid, for you can make no rings if you throw your stone into a marsh.

> " Du wirkest nicht, Alles bleibt so stumpf;
>   Sei guter Dinge !
>   Der Stein in Sumpf
>   Macht keine Ringe."

Lichtenberg asks: "When a head and a book come into collision, and one sounds hollow, is it always the book?" And in another place: "Works like this are as a mirror; if an ass looks in, you cannot expect an apostle to look out." We should do well to remember old Gellert's fine and touching lament, that the best gifts of all find the fewest admirers, and that most men mistake the bad for the good —a daily evil that nothing can prevent, like a plague which no remedy can cure. There is but one thing to be done, though how difficult!—the foolish must become wise—and that they can never be. The value of life they never know: they see with the outer eye but never with the mind, and praise the trivial because the good is strange to them:

> " Nie kennen sie den Werth der Dinge,
>   Ihr Auge schliesst, nicht ihr Verstand;
>   Sie loben ewig das Geringe
>   Wiel sie das Gutrinie gekannt."

To the intellectual incapacity which, as Goethe says fails to recognize and appreciate the good which exists, must be added something which comes into play everywhere, the moral baseness of mankind, here taking the form of envy. The new fame that a man wins raises him afresh over the heads of his fellows, who are thus degraded in proportion. All conspicuous merit is obtained at the cost of

---

* Ecclesiasticus, xxii., 8.   † Act., iv., sc. 2.

those who possess none: or, as Goethe has it in the "West östlicher Divan," another's praise is one's own depreciation—

> "Wenn wir Andern Ehre geben
> Mussen wir uns selbst entadeln."

We see, then, how it is that, whatever be the form which excellence takes, mediocrity, the common lot of by far the greatest number, is leagued against it in a conspiracy to resist, and if possible, to suppress it. The pass-word of this league is *a bas le mérite.* Nay more; those who have done something themselves, and enjoy a certain amount of fame, do not care about the appearance of a new reputation, because its success is apt to throw theirs into the shade. Hence, Goethe declares that if we had to depend for our life upon the favor of others, we should never have lived at all; from their desire to appear important themselves, people gladly ignore our very existence;

> "Hatte ich gezaudert zu werden,
> Bis man mir's Leben gegöunt,
> Ich, ware noch nicht auf Erden,
> Wenn ihr seht, wie sie sich geberden,
> Die um etwas zu scheinen,
> Mich gerne möchten verneinen."

Honor, on the contrary, generally meets with fair appreciation, and is not exposed to the onslaught of envy; nay, every man is credited with the possession of it until the contrary is proved. But fame has to be won in despite of envy, and the tribunal which awards the laurel is composed of judges biased against the applicant from the very first. Honor is something which we are able and ready to share with every one; fame suffers encroachment and is rendered more unattainable in proportion as more people come by it. Further, the difficulty of winning fame by any given work stands in inverse ratio to the number of people who are likely to read it; and hence it is so mucn harder to become famous as the author of a learned work than as a writer who aspires only to amuse. It is hardest of all in the case of philosophical works, because the result at which they aim is rather vague and, at the same time, useless from a material point of view; they appeal chiefly to readers who are working on the same lines themselves.

It is clear, then, from what I have said as to the difficulty of winning fame, that those who labor, not out of love for their subject, nor from pleasure in pursuing it, but under the stimulus of ambition, rarely or never leave mankind a legacy of immortal works. The man who seeks to do what is good and genuine, must avoid what is bad, and be ready to defy the opinions of the mob, nay, even to despise it and its misleaders. Hence the truth of the remark (especially insisted upon by Osorius *de Gloria*), that fame shuns those who seek it, and seeks those who shun it; for the one adapt themselves to the taste of their contemporaries, and the others work in defiance of it.

But, difficult though it be to acquire fame, it is an easy thing to keep it when once acquired. Here, again, fame is in direct opposition to honor, with which every one is presumably to be accredited. Honor has not to be won ; it must only not be lost. But there lies the difficulty ! For by a single unworthy action, it is gone irretrievably. But fame, in the proper sense of the word. can never disappear ; for the action or work by which it was acquired can never be undone ; and fame attaches to its author, even though he does nothing to deserve it anew. The fame which vanishes, or is outlived. proves itself thereby to have been spurious, in other words, unmerited, and due to a momentary over-estimate of a man's work ; not to speak of the kind of fame which Hegel enjoyed, and which Lichtenberg describes as "trumpeted forth by a clique of admiring under-graduates—the resounding echo of empty heads; such a fame as will make posterity smile when it lights upon a grotesque architecture of words, a fine nest with the birds long ago flown ; it will knock at the door of this decayed structure of conventionalities and find it utterly empty ! not even a trace of thought there to invite the passer-by."

The truth is that fame means nothing but what a man is in comparison with others. It is essentially relative in character, and therefore only indirectly valuable ; for it vanishes the moment other people become what the famous man is. Absolute value can be predicated only of what a man possesses under any and all circumstances—here, what a man is directly and in himself. It is the possession of a great heart or a great head, and not the mere fame of it which is worth having, and conducive to happiness. Not fame, but that which deserves to be famous, is what a man should hold in esteem. This is, as it were, the true underlying substance, and fame is only an accident, affecting its subject chiefly as a kind of external symptom, which serves to confirm his own opinion of himself. Light is not visible unless it meets with something to reflect it; and talent is sure of itself only when its fame is noised abroad. But fame is not a certain symptom of merit; because you can have the one without the other; or, as Lessing nicely puts it, "Some people obtain fame, and others deserve it."

It would be a miserable existence which should make its value or want of value depend upon what other people think; but such would be the life of a hero or a genius if its worth consisted in fame, that is, in the applause of the world. Every man lives and exists on his own account, and, therefore, mainly in and for himself; and what he is and the whole manner of his being concern himself more than any one else; so if he is not worth much in this respect, he cannot be worth much otherwise. The idea which other people form of his existence is something secondary, derivative, exposed to all the chances of fate, and in the end affecting him but very indirectly. Besides, other people's heads are a wretched place to be the home of a man's true happiness—a fanciful happiness perhaps, but not a real one.

And what a mixed company inhabits the Temple of Universal Fame! generals, ministers, charlatans, jugglers, dancers, singers, millionaires and Jews! It is a temple in which more sincere recognition, more genuine esteem, is given to the several excellences of such folk, than to superiority of mind, even of a high order, which obtains from the great majority only a verbal acknowledgment.

From the point of view of human happiness, fame is, surely, nothing but a very rare and delicate morsel for the appetite that feeds on pride and vanity—an appetite which, however carefully concealed, exists to an immoderate degree in every man, and is perhaps, strongest of all in those who set their hearts on becoming famous at any cost. Such people generally have to wait some time in uncertainty as to their own value, before the opportunity comes which will put it to the proof and let other people see what they are made of ; but until then, they feel as if they were suffering secret injustice.*

But, as I explained at the beginning of this chapter, an unreasonable value is set upon other people's opinion, and one quite disproportionate to its real worth. Hobbes has some strong remarks on this subject ; and no doubt he is quite right. "Mental pleasure," he writes, "and ecstasy of any kind, arise when, on comparing ourselves with others, we come to the conclusion that we may think well of ourselves." So we can easily understand the great value which is always attached to fame, as worth any sacrifices if there is the slighest hope of attaining it.

> " Fame is the spur that the clear spirit doth raise
> (That last infirmity of noble mind)
> To scorn delights and live laborious days."†

And again :

> " How hard it is to climb
> The heights where Fame's proud temple shines afar !"

We can thus understand how it is that the vainest people in the world are always talking about *la gloire*, with the most implicit faith in it as a stimulus to great actions and great works. But there can be no doubt that fame is something secondary in its character, a mere echo or reflection —as it were, a shadow or symptom—of merit : and, in any case, what excites admiration must be of more value than the admiration itself. The truth is that a man is made happy, not by fame, but by that which brings him fame, by his merits, or to speak more correctly, by the disposition and capacity from which his merits proceed, whether they be moral or intellectual. The best side of a man's nature must of necessity be more important for him than for any one else : the reflection of it, the opinion which exists in the heads of others, is a matter that can affect him only in

---

* Our greatest pleasure consists in being admired ; but those who admire us, even if they have every reason to do so, are slow to express their sentiments. Hence he is the happiest man who, no matter how, manages sincerely to admire himself—so long as other people leave him alone.

† Milton " Lycidas."

a very subordinate degree. He who deserves fame without getting it possesses by far the more important element of happiness, which should console him for the loss of the other. It is not that a man is thought to be great by masses of incompetent and often infatuated people, but that he really is great, which should move us to envy his position; and his happiness lies, not in the fact that posterity will hear of him, but that he is the creator of thoughts worthy to be treasured up and studied for hundreds of years.

Besides, if a man has done this, he possesses something which cannot be wrested from him, and, unlike fame, it is a possession dependent entirely upon himself. If admiration were his chief aim, there would be nothing in him to admire. This is just what happens in the case of false, that is, unmerited, fame; for its recipient lives upon it without actually possessing the solid substratum of which fame is the outward and visible sign. False fame must often put its possessor out of conceit with himself; for the time may come when, in spite of the illusions born of self-love, he will feel giddy on the heights which he was never meant to climb, or look upon himself as spurious coin; and in the anguish of threatened discovery and well-merited degradation, he will read the sentence of posterity on the foreheads of the wise—like a man who owes his property to a forged will. The truest fame, the fame that comes after death, is never heard of by its recipient: and yet he is called a happy man. His happiness lay both in the possession of those great qualities which won him fame, and in the opportunity that was granted him of developing them—the leisure he had to act as he pleased, to dedicate himself to his favorite pursuits. It is only work done from the heart that ever gains the laurel.

Greatness of soul, or wealth of intellect, is what makes a man happy—intellect, such as, when stamped on its productions, will receive the admiration of centuries to come—thoughts which made him happy at the time, and will in their turn be a source of study and delight to the noblest minds of the most remote posterity. The value of posthumous fame lies in deserving it; and this is its own reward. Whether works destined to fame attain it in the lifetime of their author is a chance affair, of no very great importance. For the average man has no critical power of his own, and is absolutely incapable of appreciating the difficulty of a great work. People are always swayed by authority; and where fame is widespread, it means that ninety-nine out of a hundred take it on faith alone. If a man is famed far and wide in his own lifetime, he will, if he is wise, not set too much value upon it, because it is no more than the echo of a few voices, which the chance of a day has touched in his favor.

Would a musician feel flattered by the loud applause of an audience if he knew that they were nearly all deaf, and that, to conceal their infirmity, they set to work to clap vigorously as soon as ever they saw one or two persons applauding? And what would he say if he got to know that those one or two persons had often taken bribes to secure the loudest applause for the poorest player!

It is easy to see why contemporary praise so seldom develops into posthumous fame. D'Alembert, in an extremely fine description of the temple of literary fame, remarks that the sanctuary of the temple is inhabited by the great dead, who during their life had no place there, and by a very few living persons, who are nearly all ejected on their death. Let me remark, in passing, that to erect a monument to a man in his lifetime is as much as declaring that posterity is not to be trusted in its judgment of him. If a man does happen to see his own true fame, it can very rarely be before he is old, though there have been artists and musicians who have been exceptions to this rule, but very few philosophers. This is confirmed by the portraits of people celebrated by their works; for most of them are taken only after their subjects have attained celebrity, generally depicting them as old and gray; more especially if philosophy has been the work of their lives. From a eudæmonistic standpoint, this is a very proper arrangement; as fame and youth are too much for a mortal at one and the same time. Life is such a poor business that the strictest economy must be exercised in its good things Youth has enough and to spare in itself, and must rest content with what it has. But when the delights and joys of life fall away in old age, as the leaves from a tree in autumn, fame buds forth opportunely, like a plant that is green in winter. Fame is, as it were, the fruit that must grow all the summer before it can be enjoyed at Yule. There is no greater consolation in age than the feeling of having put the whole force of one's youth into works which still remain young.

Finally, let us examine a little more closely the kinds of fame which attach to various intellectual pursuits; for it is with fame of this sort that my remarks are more immediately concerned.

I think it may be said broadly that the intellectual superiority it denotes consists in forming theories, that is, new combinations of certain facts. These facts may be of very different kinds; but the better they are known, and the more they come within every-day experience, the greater and wider will be the fame which is to be won by theorizing about them. For instance, if the facts in question are numbers or lines or special branches of science, such as physics, zoölogy, botany, anatomy, or corrupt passages in ancient authors, or undecipherable inscriptions, written, it may be, in some unknown alaphabet, or obscure points in history; the kind of fame which may be obtained by correctly manipulating such facts will not extend much beyond those who make a study of them—a small number of persons, most of whom live retired lives and are envious of others who become famous in their special branch of knowledge.

But if the facts be such as are known to every one, for example, the fundamental characteristics of the human mind or the human heart, which are shared by all alike; or the great physical agencies which are constantly in operation before our eyes, or the general course of natural laws; the kind of fame which is to be won by spreading the light of a new and manifestly true theory in regard to them, is such as in time will extend almost all over the civilized world; for if the facts be such as every one can grasp, the theory also will be generally intelligible. But the extent of the fame will depend upon the difficulties overcome; and the more generally known the facts are, the harder it will be to form a theory that shall be both new and true; because a great many heads will have been occupied with them and there will be little or no possibility of saying anything that has not been said before. On the other hand, facts which are not accessible to everybody, and can be got at only after much difficulty and labor, nearly always admit of new combinations and theories; so that, if sound understanding and judgment are brought to bear upon them—

qualities which do not involve very high intellectual power —a man may easily be so fortunate as to light upon some new theory in regard to them which shall be also true. But fame won on such paths does not extend much beyond those who possess a knowledge of the facts in question. To solve problems of this sort requires, no doubt, a great deal of study and labor, if only to get at the facts: while on the path where the greatest and most widespread fame is to be won, the facts may be grasped without any labor at all. But just in proportion as less labor is necessary, more talent or genius is required; and between such qualities and the drudgery of research no comparison is possible, in respect either of their intrinsic value, or of the estimation in which they are held.

And so people who feel that they possess solid intellectual capacity and a sound judgment, and yet cannot claim the highest mental powers, should not be afraid of laborious study; for by its aid they may work themselves above the great mob of humanity who have the facts constantly before their eyes, and reach those secluded spots which are accessible to learned toil. For this is a sphere where there are infinitely fewer rivals, and a man of only moderate capacity may soon find an opportunity of proclaiming a theory that shall be both new and true; nay, the merit of his discovery will partly rest upon the difficulty of coming at the facts. But applause from one's fellow-students, who are the only persons with a knowledge of the subject, sounds very faint to the far-off multitude. And if we follow up this sort of fame far enough, we shall at last come to a point where facts very difficult to get at are in themselves sufficient to lay a foundation of fame, without any necessity for forming a theory—travels, for instance, in remote and little-known countries, which make a man famous by what he has seen, not by what he has thought. The great advantage of this kind of fame is that to relate what one has seen, is much easier than to impart one's thoughts and people are apt to understand descriptions better than ideas, reading the one more readily than the other; for, as Asmus says:

> " When one goes forth a-voyaging
> He has a tale to tell."

And yet, for all that, a personal acquaintance with cele-

brated travelers often reminds us of a line from Horace—
new scenes do not always mean new ideas—

"Coelum non animum mutant qui trans mare currunt."*

But if a man finds himself in possession of great mental
faculties, such as alone should venture on the solution of
the hardest of all problems—those which concern nature
as a whole and humanity in its widest range, he will do
well to extend his view equally in all directions, without
ever straying too far amid the intricacies of various by-
paths, or invading regions little known ; in other words,
without occupying himself with special branches of knowledge, to say nothing of their petty details. There is no
necessity for him to seek out subjects difficult of access,
in order to escape a crowd of rivals ; the common objects
of life will give him material for new theories at once
serious and true ; and the service he renders will be appreciated by all those—and they form a great part of mankind
who know the facts of which he treats. What a vast distinction there is between students of physics, chemistry,
anatomy, mineralogy, zoology, philology, history, and the
men who deal with the great facts of human life, the poet
and the philosopher !

---

* Epist. I. II.

COUNSELS AND MAXIMS.

" Le bonheur n'est pas chose aisée: il est trèsdifficile de le trouver en nous,
et impossible de le trouver ailleurs."—CHAMFORT.

COUNSELS AND MAXIMS.*

INTRODUCTION.

IF MY object in these pages were to present a complete scheme of counsels and maxims for the guidance of life, I should have to repeat the numerous rules—some of them excellent—which have been drawn up by thinkers of all ages, from Theognis and Solomon† down to La Rochefoucauld ; and, in so doing, I should inevitably entail upon the reader a vast amount of well-worn commonplace. But the fact is that in this work I make still less claim to exhaust my subject than in any other of my writings.

An author who makes no claims to completeness must also, in a great measure, abandon any attempt at systematic arrangement. For his double loss in this respect, the reader may console himself by reflecting that a complete and systematic treatment of such a subject as the guidance of life could hardly fail to be a very wearisome business. I have simply put down those of my thoughts which appear to be worth communicating—thoughts which, as far as I know, have not been uttered, or, at any rate, not just in the same form, by any one else ; so that my remarks may

---

* For convenience of publication, I have divided this translation of Schopenhauer's "Aphorismen zur Lebensweisheit" into two parts ; and for the sake of appearances, a new series of chapters has been begun in the present volume. But it should be understood that there is no such division in the original, and that "The Wisdom of Life" and "Counsels and Maxims" form a single treatise, devoted to a popular exposition of the author's views on matters of practice. To the former volume I have prefixed some remarks which may help the reader to appreciate the value of Schopenhauer's teaching, and to determine its relation to certain well-known theories of life.

† I refer to the proverbs and maxims ascribed, in the Old Testament, to the king of that name.

be taken as a supplement to what has been already achieved in the immense field.

However, by way of introducing some sort of order into the great variety of matters upon which advice will be given in the following pages, I shall distribute what I have to say under the following heads : (1) general rules ; (2) our relation to ourselves; (3) our relation to others ; and finally, (4) rules which concern our manner of life and our worldly circumstances. I shall conclude with some remarks on the changes which the various periods of life produce in us.

CHAPTER I.

GENERAL RULES.

§ 1. The first and foremost rule for the wise conduct of life seems to me to be contained in a view to which Aristotle parenthetically refers in the "Nichomachean Ethics" * ὁ φρονιμος τὸ ἄλυπον διώκει οὐ τὸ ἡδυ, or, as it may be rendered, " not pleasure, but freedom from pain is what the wise man will aim at."

The truth of this remark turns upon the negative character of happiness—the fact that pleasure is only the negation of pain, and that pain is the positive element in life. Though I have given a detailed proof of this proposition in my chief work,† I may supply one more illustration of it here, drawn from a circumstance of daily occurrence. Suppose that, with the exception of some sore or painful spot, we are physically in a sound and healthy condition; the pain of this one spot will completely absorb our attention, causing us to lose the sense of general well-being, and destroying all our comfort in life. In the same way, when all our affairs but one turn out as we wish, the single instance in which our aims are frustrated is a constant trouble to us, even though it be something quite trivial. We think a great deal about it, and very little about those other and more important matters in which we have been successful. In both these cases what has met with resist-

---

* vii. (11) 12.

† " Welt als Wille und Vorstellung." Vol. I. p. 58.

ance is the will; in the one case as it is objectified in the organism, in the other, as it presents itself in the struggle of life; and in both, it is plain that the satisfaction of the will consists in nothing else than that it meets with no resistance. It is, therefore, a satisfaction which is not directly felt; at most, we can become conscious of it only when we reflect upon our condition. But that which checks or arrests the will is something positive; it proclaims its own presence. All pleasure consists in merely removing this check—in other words, in freeing us from its action; and hence pleasure is a state which can never last very long.

This is the true basis of the above excellent rule quoted from Aristotle, which bids us direct our aim, not toward securing what is pleasurable and agreeable in life, but toward avoiding, as far as possible, its innumerable evils. If this were not the right course to take, that saying of Voltaire's "Happiness is but a dream and sorrow is real," would be as false as it is, in fact, true. A man who desires to make up the book of his life and determine where the balance of happiness lies, must put down in his accounts, not the pleasures which he has enjoyed, but the evils which he has escaped. That is the true method of eudæmonology for all eudæmonology must begin by recognizing that its very name is a euphemism, and that "to live happily" only means "to live less unhappily"—to live a tolerable life. There is no doubt that life is given us, not to be enjoyed, but to be overcome— to be got over. There are numerous expressions illustrating this—such as *degere vitam, vita defungi:* or in Italian *si scampa così;* or in German, *man muss suchen durchzukommen; er wird schon durch die Welt kommen,* and so on. In old age it is indeed a consolation to think that the work of life is over and done with. The happiest lot is not to have experienced the keenest delights or the greatest pleasures, but to have brought life to a close without any very great pain, bodily or mental. To measure the happiness of a life by its delights or pleasures, is to apply a false standard. For pleasures are and remain something negative; that they produce happiness is a delusion; cherished by envy to its own punishment. Pain is felt to be something positive, and hence its absence is the true standard of happiness. And if, over and above freedom from pain, there is also an absence of boredom, the essential conditions of earthly happiness are attained: for all else is chimerical.

It follows from this that a man should never try to purchase pleasure at the cost of pain, or even at the risk of incurring it; to do so is to pay what is positive and real for what is negative and illusory; while there is a net profit in sacrificing pleasure for the sake of avoiding pain. In either case it is a matter of indifference whether the pain follows the pleasure or precedes it. While it is a complete inversion of the natural order to try and turn this scene of misery into a garden of pleasure, to aim at joy and pleasure rather than at the greatest possible freedom from pain—and yet how many do it ! there is some wisdom in taking a gloomy view, in looking upon the world as a kind of hell, and in confining one's efforts to securing a little room that shall not be exposed to the fire. The fool rushes after the pleasures of life and finds himself their dupe; the wise man avoids its evils; and even if, notwithstanding his precautions, he falls into misfortune, that is the fault of fate, not of his own folly. As far as he is successful in his endeavors, he cannot be said to have lived a life of illusion; for the evils which he shuns are very real. Even if he goes too far out of his way to avoid evils, and makes an unnecessary sacrifice of pleasure, he is, in reality, not the worse off for that; for all pleasures are chimerical, and to mourn for having lost any of them is a frivolous, and even ridiculous proceeding.

The failure to recognize this truth—a failure promoted by optimistic ideas—is the source of much unhappiness. In moments free from pain, our restless wishes present, as it were in a mirror, the image of a happiness that has no counterpart in reality, seducing us to follow it; in doing so we bring pain upon ourselves, and that is something undeniably real. Afterward we come to look with regret upon that lost state of painlessness; it is a paradise which we have gambled away; it is no longer with us, and we long in vain to undo what has been done. One might well fancy that these visions of wishes fulfilled were the work of some evil spirit, conjured up in order to entice us away from that painless state which forms our highest happiness.

A careless youth may think that the world is meant to be enjoyed, as though it were the abode of some real or positive happiness, which only those fail to attain who are not clever enough to overcome the difficulties that lie in the way. This false notion takes a stronger hold on him when he comes to read poetry and romance, and to be deceived by outward show—the hypocrisy that characterizes the world from beginning to end ; on which I shall have something to say presently. The result is that his life is the more or less deliberate pursuit of positive happiness; and happiness he takes to be equivalent to a series of definite pleasures. In seeking for these pleasures he encounters danger—a fact which should not be forgotten. He hunts for game that does not exist ; and so he ends by suffering some very real and positive misfortune—pain, distress, sickness, loss, care, poverty, shame, and all the thousand ills of life. Too late he discovers the trick that has been played upon him.

But if the rule I have mentioned is observed, and a plan of life is adopted which proceeds by avoiding pain—in other words, by taking measures of precaution against want, sickness, and distress in all its forms, the aim is a real one, and something may be achieved which will be great in proportion as the plan is not disturbed by striving after the chimera of positive happiness. This agrees with the opinion expressed by Goethe in the " Elective Affinities," and there put into the mouth of Mittler—the man who is always trying to make other people happy : " To desire to get rid of an evil is a definite object, but to desire a better fortune than one has is blind folly." The same truth is contained in that fine French proverb : *le mieux est l'ennemi du bien*—leave well alone. And, as I have remarked in my chief work,* this is the leading thought underlying the philosophical system of the cynics. For what was it led the cynics to repudiate pleasure in every form, if it was not the fact that pain is, in a greater or less degree, always bound up with pleasure ? To go out of the way of pain seemed to them so much easier than to secure pleasure. Deeply impressed as they were by the negative nature of pleasure and the positive nature of pain, they consistently devoted all their efforts to the avoidance of pain. The first step to that end was, in their opinion, a complete and deliberate repudiation of

---

* " Welt als Wille und Vorstellung," vol. ii., ch. 16.

pleasure, as something which served only to entrap the victim in order that he might be delivered over to pain.

We are all born, as Schiller says, in Arcadia. In other words, we come into the world full claims to happiness and pleasure, and we cherish the fond hope of making them good. But, as a rule, Fate soon teaches us, in a rough and ready way, that we really possess nothing at all, but that everything in the world is at its command, in virtue of an unassailable right, not only to all we have or acquire, to wife or child, but even to our very limbs, our arms, legs, eyes and ears, nay, even to the nose in the middle of our face. And in any case, after some little time, we learn by experience that happiness and pleasure are a *fata morgana*, which, visible from afar, vanish as we approach ; that, on the other hand, suffering and pain are a reality, which makes its presence felt without any intermediary; and for its effect, stands in no need of illusion or the play of false hope.

If the teaching of experience bears fruit in us, we soon give up the pursuit of pleasure and happiness, and think much more about making ourselves secure against the attacks of pain and suffering. We see that the best the world has to offer is an existence free from pain—a quiet tolerable life; and we confine our claims to this, as to something we can more surely hope to achieve. For the safest way of not being very miserable is not to expect to be very happy. Merck, the friend of Goethe's youth, was conscious of this truth when he wrote: "It is the wretched way people have of setting up a claim to happiness—and that, too, in a measure corresponding with their desires—that ruins everything in this world. A man will make progress if he can get rid of this claim, and desire nothing but what he sees before him."* Accordingly it is advisable to put very moderate limits upon our expectations of pleasure, possessions, rank, honor and so on; because it is just this striving and struggling to be happy, to dazzle the world, to lead a life full of pleasure, which entail great misfortune. It is prudent, and wise, I say, to reduce one's claims, if only for the reason that it is extremely easy to be very unhappy; while to be very happy is not indeed dif-

---

* Letters to and from Merck.

ficult, but quite impossible. With justice sings the poet
of life's wisdom:

> " Auream quisquis mediocritatem
> Diligit, tutus caret obsoleti
> Sordibus tecti, caret invidenda
> Sobrius aula.

> " Sævius ventis agitatur ingens
> Pinus: et celsæ graviori casu
> Decidunt turres; feriuntque summos
> Fulgura montes " *

—the golden mean is best—to live free from the squalor of
a mean abode, and yet not be a mark for envy. It is the
tall pine which is cruelly shaken by the wind, and the lofty
towers that fall so heavily; the highest summits that are
struck in the storm.

He who has taken to heart the teaching of my philosophy
—who knows, therefore, that our whole existence is something which had better not have been, and that to disown
and disclaim it is the highest wisdom—he will have no
great expectations from anything or any condition in life;
he will spend passion upon nothing in the world, nor lament over-much if he fails in any of his undertakings. He
will feel the deep truth of what Plato† says: οὔτε τι τῶν
ἀνθρωπίνων ἄξιον ὂν μεγάλης σπουδῆς—nothing in human
affairs is worth any great anxiety; or, as the Persian poet
has it:

> " Though from thy grasp all worldly things should flee,
> Grieve not for them, for they are nothing worth:
> And though a world in thy possession be,
> Joy not, for worthless are the things of earth.
> Since to that better world 'tis given to thee
> To pass, speed on, for this is nothing worth." ‡

The chief obstacle to our arriving at these salutary
views is that hypocrisy of the world to which I have already alluded—an hypocrisy which should be early revealed to the young. Most of the glories of the world are

---

* Horace. Odes II. x.

* "Republic," x, 604.

* *Translator's Note.*—From the "Anvár-i Suhailí"—"The Lights of
Canopus"—being the Persian version of the Tables of Bidpai." Trans-
alted by E. B. Eastwick, ch iii. Story iv., p. 289.

mere outward show, like the scenes on a stage : there is
nothing real about them. Ships festooned and hung with
pennants, firing of cannon, illuminations, beating of drums
and blowing of trumpets, shouting and applauding—these
are all the outward sign, the pretense and suggestion—as
it were the hieroglyphic—of joy : but just there, joy is as
a rule, not to be found ; it is the only guest who has de-
clined to be present at the festival. Where this guest may
really be found, he comes generally without invitation ;
he is not formally announced, but slips in quietly by himself *sans façon ;* often making his appearance under the
most unimportant and trivial circumstances, and in the
commonest company—anywhere, in short, but where the
society is brilliant and distinguished. Joy is like the gold
in the Australian mines—found only now and then, as it
were, by the caprice of chance, and according to no rule
or law ; oftenest in very little grains, and very seldom in
heaps. All that outward show which I have described, is
only an attempt to make people believe that it is really joy
which has come to the festival ; and to produce this impression upon the spectators is, in fact, the whole object
of it.

With mourning it is just the same. That long funeral
procession, moving up so slowly ; how melancholy it looks !
what an endless row of carriages ! But look into them—
they are all empty ; the coachmen of the whole town are the
sole escort the dead man has to his grave. Eloquent
picture of the friendship and esteem of the world ! This
is the falsehood, the hallowness, the hypocrisy of human
affairs !

Take another example—a roomful of guests in full dress,
being received with great ceremony. You could almost
believe that this is a noble and distinguished company ;
but, as a matter of fact, it is compulsion, pain and boredom who are the real guests. For where many are invited,
it is a rabble—even if they all wear stars. Really good
society is everywhere of necessity very small. In brilliant
festivals and noisy entertainments, there is always, at
bottom, a sense of emptiness prevalent. A false tone is
there : such gatherings are in strange contrast with the
misery and barrenness of our existence. The contrast
brings the true condition into greater relief. Still, these
gatherings are effective from the outside ; and that is just

their purpose.   Chamfort* makes the excellent remark that society—*les cercles, les salons, ce qu'on appelle le monde* —is like a miserable play, or a bad opera, without any interest in itself, but supported for a time by mechanical aid, costumes and scenery.

And so, too, with academies and chairs of philosophy. You have a kind of a sign-board hung out to show the apparent abode of wisdom : but wisdom is another guest who declines the invitation ; she is to be found elsewhere. The chiming of bells, ecclesiastical millinery, attitudes of devotion, insane antics—these are the pretense, the false show of piety.   And so on.   Everything in the world is like a hollow nut ; there is little kernel anywhere, and when it does exist, it is still more rare to find it in the shell.   You may look for it elsewhere, and find it, as a rule, only by chance.

§ 2.   To estimate a man's condition in regard to happiness, it is necessary to ask, not what things please him, but what things trouble him: and the more trivial these things are in themselves, the happier the man will be.   To be irritated by trifles, a man must be well off: for in misfortune trifles are unfelt.

§ 3.   Care should be taken not to build the happiness of life upon a "broad foundation"—not to require a great many things in order to be happy.   For happiness on such a foundation is the most easily undermined; it offers many more opportunities for accidents; and accidents are always happening.   The architecture of happiness follows a plan in this respect just the opposite of that adopted in every other case, where the broadest foundation offers the greatest security.   Accordingly, to reduce your claims to the lowest possible degree, in comparison with your means—of whatever kind these may be—is the surest way of avoiding extreme misfortune.

To make extensive preparations for life—no matter what form they may take—is one of the greatest and commonest of follies.   Such preparations presuppose, in the first place,

---

* *Translator's Note.*—Nicholas " Chamfort " (1741-94), a French miscellaneous writer, whose brilliant conversation, power of sarcasm, and epigrammatic force, coupled with an extraordinary career, render him one of the most interesting and remarkable men of his time.   Schopenhauer undoubtedly owed much to this writer, to whom he constantly refers.

a long life, the full and complete term of years appointed to man—and how few reach it! and even if it be reached; it is still too short for all the plans that have been made, for to carry them out requires more time than was thought necessary at the beginning. And then how many mischances and obstacles stand in the way! how seldom the goal is ever reached in human affairs! And lastly even though the goal be reached, the changes which time works in us have been left out of the reckoning; we forget that the capacity whether for achievement or for enjoyment does not last a whole lifetime. So we often toil for things which are no longer suited to us when we attain them; and again, the years we spend in preparing for some work, unconsciously rob us of the power for carrying it out. How often it happens that a man is unable to enjoy the wealth which he acquired at so much trouble and risk, and that the fruits of his labor are reserved for others; or that he is incapable of filling the position which he has won after so many years of toil and struggle. Fortune has come too late for him; or, contrarily, he has come too late for fortune —when, for instance, he wants to achieve great things, say in art or literature; the popular taste has changed, it may be; a new generation has grown up, which takes no interest in his work; others have gone a shorter way and got the start of him. These are the facts of life which Horace must have had in view, when he lamented the uselessness of all advice:

" quid eternis minorem
Consiliis animum fatigas?" *

The cause of this commonest of all follies is that optical illusion of the mind from which every one suffers, making life, at its beginning, seem of long duration, and at its end, when one looks back over the course of it, how short a time it seems! There is some advantage in the illusion; but for it, no great work would ever be done.

Our life is like a journey on which, as we advance, the landscape takes a different view from that which it presented at first, and changes again, as we come nearer. This is just what happens—especially with our wishes. We often find something else, nay, something better than what

* Odes II. xi.

we were looking for: and what we look for, we often find on a very different path from that on which we began a vain search. Instead of finding, as we expected, pleasure, happiness, joy, we get experience, insight, knowledge—a real and permanent blessing, instead of a fleeting and illusory one.

This is the thought that runs through "Wilhelm Meister," like the bass in a piece of music. In this work of Goethe's, we have a novel of the "intellectual" kind, and, therefore, superior to all others, even to Sir Walter Scott's, which are, one and all, "ethical;" in other words, they treat of human nature only from the side of the will. So, too, in the Zauberflöte—that grotesque, but still significant, and even ambiguous hieroglyphic—the same thought is symbolized, but in great, coarse lines, much in the way in which scenery is painted. Here the symbol would be complete if Tamino were in the end to be cured of his desire to possess Tamina, and received, in her stead initiation into, the mysteries of the Temple of Wisdom. It is quite right for Papageno, his necessary contrast, to succeed in getting his Papagena.

Men of any worth or value soon come to see that they are in the hands of Fate, and gratefully submit to be molded by its teachings. They recognize that the fruit of life is experience, and not happiness; they become accustomed and content to exchange hope for insight: and, in the end, they can say, with Petrarch, that all they care for is to learn:

" Altro diletto che 'mparar, non provo."

It may even be that they to some extent still follow their old wishes and aims, trifling with them, as it were, for the sake of appearances; all the while really and seriously looking for nothing but instruction; a process which lends them an air of genius, a trait of something contemplative and sublime.

In their search for gold, the alchemists discovered other things—gunpowder, china, medicines, the laws of nature. There is a sense in which we are all alchemists.

CHAPTER II.

OUR RELATION TO OURSELVES.

§ 4. The mason employed on the building of a house may be quite ignorant of its general design: or, at any rate, he may not keep it constantly in mind. So it is with man in working through the days and hours of his life, he takes little thought of its character as a whole.

If there is any merit or importance attaching to a man's career, if he lays himself out carefully for some special work, it is all the more necessary and advisable for him to turn his attention now and then to its plan, that is to say, the miniature sketch of its general outlines. Of course, to do that, he must have applied the maxim Γνῶθι σεαυτόν; he must have made some little progress in the art of understanding himself. He must know what is his real, chief, and foremost object in life—what it is that he most wants in order to be happy; and then, after that, what occupies the second and third place in his thoughts; he must find out what, on the whole, his vocation really is—the part he has to play, his general relation to the world. If he maps out important work for himself on great lines, a glance at this miniature plan of his life will more than anything else stimulate, rouse and ennoble him, urge him on to action and keep him from false paths.

Again, just as the traveler, on reaching a height gets a connected view over the road he has taken, with its many turns and windings; so it is only when we have completed a period in our life, or approach the end of it altogether, that we recognize the true connection between all our actions—what it is we have achieved, what work we have done. It is only then that we see the precise chain of cause and effect, and the exact value of all our efforts. For as long as we are actually engaged in the work of life, we always act in accordance with the nature of our character, under the influence of motive, and within the limits of our capacity—in a word, from beginning to end, under a law of necessity; at every moment we do just what appears to us right and proper. It is only afterward, when we come to look back at the whole course of our life and its general result, that we see the why and wherefore of it all.

When we are actually doing some great deed, or creating some immortal work, we are not conscious of it as such; we think only of satisfying present aims, of fulfilling the intentions we happen to have at the time, of doing the right thing at the moment. It is only when we come to view our life as a connected whole that our character and capacities show themselves in their true light; that we see how in particular instances, some happy inspiration, as it were, led us to choose the only true path out of a thousand which might have brought us to ruin. It was our genius that guided us, a force felt in the affairs of the intellect as in those of the world; and working by its defect just in the same way in regard to evil and disaster.

§ 5. Another important element in the wise conduct of life is to preserve a proper proportion between our thought for the present and our thought for the future ; in order not to spoil the one by paying over-great attention to the other. Many live too much in the present—frivolous people, I mean ; others, too much in the future, ever anxious and full of care. It is seldom that a man holds the right balance between the two extremes. Those who strive and hope and live only in the future, always looking ahead and impatiently anticipating what is coming, as something which will make them happy when they get it, are, in spite of their very clever airs, exactly like those donkeys one sees in Italy, whose pace may be hurried by fixing a stick on their heads with a wisp of hay at the end of it ; this is always just in front of them, and they keep on trying to get it. Such people are in a constant state of illusion as to their whole existence ; they go on living *ad interim*, until at last they die.

Instead, therefore, of always thinking about our plans and anxiously looking to the future, or of giving ourselves up to regret for the past, we should never forget that the present is the only reality, the only certainty ; that the future almost always turns out contrary to our expectations ; that the past, too, was very different from what we suppose it to have been. Both the past and the future are, on the whole, of less consequence than we think. Distance, which makes objects look small to the outward eye, makes them look big to the eye of thought. The present alone is true and actual ; it is the only time which possesses full reality, and our existence lies in it exclusively.

Therefore we should always be glad of it, and give it the welcome it deserves, and enjoy every hour that is bearable by its freedom from pain and annoyance with a full consciousness of its value. We shall hardly be able to do this if we make a wry face over the failure of our hopes in the past or over our anxiety for the future. It is the height of folly to refuse the present hour of happiness, or wantonly to spoil it by vexation at by-gones or uneasiness about what is to come. There is a time, of course, for forethought, nay, even for repentance ; but when it is over let us think of what is past as of something to which we have said farewell, of necessity subduing our hearts—

ἀλλὰ τὰ μὲν προτετύχθαι ἐάσομεν ἀχνύμενόι περ
θυμὸν ἐνὶ στήθεσσι φίλον δαμάσαντες ἀνάγκῃ,*

and of the future as of that which lies beyond our power, in the lap of the gods—

ἀλλ' ἤτοι μὲν ταῦτα θεῶν ἐν γούνασι κεῖται.†

But in regard to the present let us remember Seneca's advice, and live each day as if it were our whole life — *singulas dies singulas vitas puta:* let us make it as agreeable as possible, it is the only real time we have.

Only those evils which are sure to come at a definite date have any right to disturb us ; and how few there are which fulfill this description. For evils are of two kinds ; either they are possible only, at most probable ; or they are inevitable. Even in the case of evils which are sure to happen, the time at which they will happen is uncertain. A man who is always preparing for either class of evil will not have a moment of peace left him. So, if we are not to lose all comfort in life through the fear of evils some of which are uncertain in themselves, and others, in the time at which they will occur, we should look upon the one kind as never likely to happen, and the other as not likely to happen very soon.

Now, the less our peace of mind is disturbed by fear, the more likely it is to be agitated by desire and expectation. This is the true meaning of that song of Goethe's which is such a favorite with every one : *Ich hab' mein'*

* "Iliad," xix. 65   † Ibid, xvii. 514.

Sach' auf nichts gestellt. It is only after a man has got
rid of all pretension, and taken refuge in mere unembel-
lished existence, that he is able to attain that peace of
mind which is the foundation of human happiness.
Peace of mind! that is something essential to any enjoyment of the present moment; and unless its separate
moments are enjoyed, there is an end of life's happiness as
a whole. We should always recollect that to-day comes
only once, and never returns. We fancy that it will come
again to-morrow; but to-morrow is another day, which,
in its turn, comes once only. We are apt to forget that
every day is an integral, and therefore irreplaceable portion
of life, and to look upon life as though it were a collective
idea or name which does not suffer if one of the individuals it covers is destroyed.

We should be more likely to appreciate and enjoy the
present, if, in those good days when we are well and strong,
we did not fail to reflect how, in sickness and sorrow, every
past hour that was free from pain and privation seemed in
our memory so infinitely to be envied—as it were, a lost
paradise, or some one who was only then seen to have acted
as a friend. But we live through our days of happiness
without noticing them; it is only when evil comes upon
us that we wish them back. A thousand gay and pleasant
hours are wasted in ill-humor; we let them slip by unenjoyed, and sigh for them in vain when the sky is overcast.
Those present moments that are bearable, be they never so
trite and common—passed by in indifference, or, it may be,
impatiently pushed away—those are the moments we
should honor; never failing to remember that the ebbing
tide is even now hurrying them into the past, where memory will store them transfigured and shining with an imperishable light—in some after-time, and above all, when
our days are evil, to raise the veil and present them as the
object of our fondest regret.

§ 6. "Limitation always makes for happiness." We
are happy in proportion as our range of vision, our sphere
of work, our points of contact with the world, are restricted
and circumscribed. We are more likely to feel worried and
anxious if these limits are wide; for it means that our
cares, desires and terrors are increased and intensified.
That is why the blind are not so unhappy as we might be
inclined to suppose, otherwise there would not be that

gentle and almost serene expression of peace in their faces.

Another reason why limitation makes for happiness is that the second half of life proves even more dreary than the first. As the years wear on, the horizon of our aims and our points of contact with the world become more extended. In childhood our horizon is limited to the narrowest sphere about us; in youth there is already a very considerable widening of our view; in manhood it comprises the whole range of our activity, often stretching out over a very distant sphere—the care, for instance, of a state or a nation in old age it embraces posterity.

But even in the affairs of the intellect limitation is necessary, if we are to be happy. For the less the will is excited the less we suffer. We have seen that suffering is something positive, and that happiness is only a negative condition. To limit the sphere of outward activity is to relieve the will of external stimulus: to limit the sphere of our intellectual efforts is to relieve the will of internal sources of excitement. This latter kind of limitation is attended by the disadvantage that it opens the door to boredom, which is a direct source of countless sufferings: for to banish boredom, a man will have recourse to any means that may be handy—dissipation, society, extravagance, gaming, and drinking, and the like, which in their turn bring mischief, ruin and misery in their train. *Difficiles in otio quies*—it is difficult to keep quiet if you have nothing to do. That limitation in the sphere of outward activity is conducive, nay, even necessary to human happiness such as it is, may be seen in the fact that the only kind of poetry which depicts men in a happy state of life—idyllic poetry, I mean—always aims, as an intrinsic part of its treatment, at representing them in very simple and restricted circumstances. It is this feeling too, which is at the bottom of the pleasure we take in what are called *genre* pictures.

"Simplicity," therefore, as far as it can be attained, and even monotony, in our manner of life, if it does not mean that we are bored, will contribute to happiness; just because under such circumstances, life, and consequently the burden which is the essential concomitant of life, will be least felt. Our existence will glide on peacefully like a stream which no waves or whirlpools disturb.

§ 7. Whether we are in a pleasant or a painful state depends, ultimately, upon the kind of matter that pervades and engrosses our consciousness. In this respect purely intellectual occupation, for the mind that is capable of it, will, as a rule, do much more in the way of happiness than any form of practical life, with its constant alternations of success and failure, and all the shocks and torments it produces. But it must be confessed that for such occupation a pre-eminent amount of intellectual capacity is necessary. And in this connection it may be noted that, just as a life devoted to outward activity will distract and divert a man from study and also deprive him of that quiet concentration of mind which is necessary for such work; so, on the other hand, a long course of thought will make him more or less unfit for the noisy pursuits of real life. It is advisable, therefore, to suspend mental work for awhile, if circumstances happen which demand any degree of energy in affairs of a practical nature.

§ 8. To live a life that shall be entirely prudent and discreet, and to draw from experience all the instruction it contains, it is requisite to be constantly thinking back— to make a kind of recapitulation of what we have done, of our impressions and sensations, to compare our former with our present judgments—what we set before us and struggled to achieve, with the actual result and satisfaction we have obtained. To do this is to get a repetition of the private lessons of experience—lessons which are given to every one.

Experience of the world may be looked upon as a kind of text, to which reflection and knowledge form the commentary. Where there is a great deal of reflection and intellectual knowledge, and very little experience, the result is like those books which have on each page two lines of text to forty lines of commentary. A great deal of experience with little reflection and scanty knowledge, gives us books like those of the "editio Bipontina,"* where there are no notes and much that is unintelligible.

The advice here given is on a par with a rule recommended

---

* "*Translator's Note*—A series of Greek, Latin and French classics published at Zweibrücken in the Palatinate, from and after the year 1779. Cf. Butter, *Ueber die Bipontiner: und die editiones Bipontinae.*

by Pythagoras—to review, every night before going to sleep what we have done during the day. To live at random, in the hurly-burly of business or pleasure, without ever reflecting upon the past—to go on, as it were, pulling cotton off the reel of life—is to have no clear idea of what we are about: and a man who lives in this state will have chaos in his emotions and certain confusion in his thoughts; as is soon manifest by the abrupt and fragmentary character of his conversation, which becomes a kind of mincemeat. A man will be all the more exposed to this fate in proportion as he lives a restless life in the world, amid a crowd of various impressions and with a correspondingly small amount of activity on the part of his own mind.

And in this connection it will be in place to observe that, when events and circumstances which have influenced us pass away in the course of time, we are unable to bring back and renew the particlar mood or state of feeling which they aroused in us: but we can remember what we were led to say and do in regard to them; and this forms, as it were, the result, expression and measure of those events. We should, therefore, be careful to preserve the memory of our thoughts at important points in our life: and herein lies the great advantage of keeping a journal.

§ 9.   To be self-sufficient, to be all in all to one's self, to want for nothing, to be able to say *omnia mea mecum porto*—that is assuredly the chief qualification for happiness. Hence Aristotle's remark, ἡ εὐδαιμονία τῶν αὐτάρχων ἔστι *—to be happy means to be self-sufficient—cannot be too often repeated. It is, at bottom, the same thought as is present in that very well-turned sentence from Chamfort, which I have prefixed as a motto to this volume. For while a man cannot reckon with certainty upon any one but himself, the burdens and disadvantages, the dangers and annoyances which arise from having to do with others, are not only countless but unavoidable.

There is no more mistaken path to happiness than worldliness, revelry, high life : for the whole object of it is to transform our miserable existence into a succession of joys, delights and pleasures—a process which cannot fail

---

* "Eudem. Eth." VII. ii. 37.

to result in disappointment and delusion ; on a par, in this respect with its *obbligato* accompaniment the interchange of lies.*

All society necessarily involves, as the first condition of its existence, mutual accommodation and restraint upon the part of its members. This means that the larger it is, the more insipid will be its tone. A man can be himself only so long as he is alone ; and if he does not love solitude, he will not love freedom ; for it is only when he is alone that he is really free. Constraint is always present in society, like a companion of whom there is no riddance ; and in proportion to the greatness of a man's individuality, it will be hard for him to bear the sacrifices which all intercourse with others demands. Solitude will be welcomed or endured or avoided, according as a man's personal value is large or small—the wretch feeling, when he is alone, the whole burden of his misery; the great intellect delighting in its greatness ; and every one, in short, being just what he is.

Further, if a man stands high in Nature's list, it is natural and inevitable that he should feel solitary. It will be an advantage to him if his surroundings do not interfere with this feeling ; for if he has to see a great deal of other people who are not of like character with himself, they will exercise a disturbing influence upon him, adverse to his peace of mind ; they will rob him, in fact, of himself, and give him nothing to compensate for the loss.

But while Nature sets very wide differences between man and man in respect both of morality and of intellect, society disregards and effaces them ; or, rather, it sets up artificial differences in their stead—gradations of rank and position, which are very often diametrically opposed to those which Nature establishes. The result of this arrangement is to elevate those whom Nature has placed low, and to depress the few who stand high. These latter, then, usually withdraw from society, where, as soon as it is at all numerous, vulgarity reigns supreme.

---

* As our body is concealed by the clothes we wear, so our mind is veiled in lies. The veil is always there, and it is only through it that we can sometimes guess at what a man really thinks ; just as from his clothes we arrive at the general shape of his body.

What offends a great intellect in society is the equality of rights, leading to equality of pretensions, which every one enjoys ; while at the same time, inequality of capacity means a corresponding disparity of social power. So-called good society recognizes every kind of claim but that of intellect, which is a contraband article : and people are expected to exhibit an unlimited amount of patience toward every form of folly and stupidity, perversity and dullness while personal merit has to beg pardon, as it were, for being present, or else conceal itself altogether. Intellectual superiority offends by its very existence, without any desire to do so.

The worst of what is called good society is not only that it offers us the companionship of people who are unable to win either our praise or our affection, but that it does not allow of our being that which we naturally are; it compels us, for the sake of harmony, to shrivel up, or even alter our shape altogether. Intellectual conversation whether grave or humorous, is only fit for intellectual society; it is downright abhorrent to ordinary people, to please whom it is absolutely necessary to be commonplace and dull. This demands an act of severe self-denial; we have to forfeit three-fourths of ourselves in order to become like other people. No doubt their company may be set down against our loss in this respect; but the more a man is worth, the more he will find that what he gains does not cover what he loses, and that the balance is on the debit side of the account; for the people with whom he deals are generally bankrupt—that is to say, there is nothing to be got from their society which can compensate either for its boredom, annoyance and disagreeableness, or for the self-denial which it renders necessary. Accordingly, most society is so constituted as to offer a good profit to any one who will exchange it for solitude.

Nor is this all. By way of providing a substitute for real—I mean intellectual—superiority, which is seldom to be met with, and intolerable when it is found, society has capriciously adopted a false kind of superiority, conventional in its character, and resting upon abitrary principles —a tradition, as it were, handed down in the higher circles and. like a password, subject to alterations; I refer to *bon ton* fashion. Whenever this kind of superiority comes into collision with the real kind, its weakness is manifest.

Moreover, the presence of "good tone" means the absence of good sense.

No man can be in perfect accord with any one but himself—not even with a friend or the partner of his life; differences of individuality and temperament are always bringing in some degree of discord, though it may be a very slight one. That genuine, profound peace of mind, that perfect tranquillity of soul, which, next to health, is the highest blessing the earth can give, is to be attained only in solitude, and, as a permanent mood, only in complete retirement: and then, if there is anything great and rich in the man's own self, his way of life is the happiest that may be found in this wretched world.

Let me speak plainly. However close the bond of friendship, love, marriage, a man, ultimately, looks to himself, to his own welfare alone: at most, to his child's too. The less necessity there is for you to come into contact with mankind in general, in the relations whether of business or of personal intimacy, the better off you are. Loneliness and solitude have their evils, it is true; but if you cannot feel them all at once, you can at least see where they lie; on the other hand, society is insidious in this respect; as in offering you what appears to be the pastime of pleasing social intercourse, it works great and often irreparable mischief. The young should early be trained to bear being left alone; for it is a source of happiness and peace of mind.

It follows from this that a man is best off if he be thrown upon his own resources and can be all in all to himself: and Cicero goes so far as to say that a man who is in this condition cannot fail to be very happy—*nemo potest non beatissimus esse qui est totus aptus ex sese, quique in se uno ponit omnia.** The more a man has himself, the less others can be to him. The feeling of self-sufficiency! it is that which restrains those whose personal value is in itself great riches, from such considerable sacrifices as are demanded by intercourse with the world, let alone, then, from actually practicing self-denial by going out of their way to seek it. Ordinary people are sociable and complaisant just from the very opposite feeling; to bear others' company is easier for them than to bear their own. Moreover, respect is not paid in this world to that which has real

* "Paradoxa Stoicorum," II.

merit; it is reserved for that which has none. So retirement is at once a proof and a result of being distinguished by the possession of meritorious qualities. It will therefore show real wisdom on the part of any one who is worth anything in himself, to limit his requirements as may be necessary, in order to preserve or extend his freedom, and, —since a man must come into some relations with his fellow-men—to admit them to his intimacy as little as possible.

I have said that people are rendered sociable by their inability to endure solitude, that is to say, their own society. They become sick of themselves. It is this vacuity of soul which drives them to intercourse with others—to travels in foreign countries. Their mind is wanting in elasticity; it has no movement of its own, and so they try to give it some—by drink, for instance. How much drunkenness is due to this cause alone! They are always looking for some form of excitement, of the strongest kind they can bear—the excitement of being with people of like nature with themselves; and if they fail in this, their mind sinks by its own weight, and they fall into a grievous lethargy.* Such people, it may be said, possess only a small fraction of humanity in themselves; and it requires a great many of them put together to make up a fair amount of it—to attain any degree of consciousness as men. A man, in the full sense of the word—a man *par excel*

---

* It is a well-known fact, that we can more easily bear up under evils which fall upon a great many people besides ourselves. As boredom seems to be an evil of this kind, people band together to offer it a common resistance. The love of life is at bottom only the fear of death; and, in the same way, the social impulse does not rest directly upon the love of society, but upon the fear of solitude; it is not alone the charm of being in others' company that people seek, it is the dreary oppression of being alone—the monotony of their own consciousness—that they would avoid. They will do anything to escape it—even tolerate bad companions, and put up with the feeling of constraint which all society involves, in this case a very burdensome one. But if aversion to such society conquer the aversion to being alone, they become accustomed to solitude and hardened to its immediate effects. They no longer find solitude to be such a very bad thing, and settle down comfortably to it without any hankering after society; and this, partly because it is only indirectly that they need others' company and partly because they have become accustomed to the benefits of being alone.

lence—does not represent a fraction, but a whole number; he is complete in himself.

Ordinary society is, in this respect, very like the kind of music to be obtained from an orchestra composed solely of Russian horns. Each horn has only one note; and the music is produced by each note coming in just at the right moment. In the monotonous sound of a single horn, you have a precise illustration of the effect of most people's minds. How often there seems to be only one thought there! and no room for any other. It is easy to see why people are so bored; and also why they are so sociable, why they like to go about in crowds—why mankind is so *gregarious*. It is the monotony of his own nature that makes a man find solitude intolerable. *Omnis stultitia laborat fastidio sui:* folly is truly its own burden. Put a great many men together, and you may get some result—some music from your horns!

A man of intellect is like an artist who gives a concert without any help from any one else, playing on a single instrument—a piano, say, which is a little orchestra in itself. Such a man is a little world in himself; and the effect produced by various instruments together he produces single-handed, in the unity of his own consciousness. Like the piano, he has no place in a symphony: he is a soloist and performs by himself—in solitude, it may be; or, if in company with other instruments, only as principal; or for setting the tone, as in singing. However, those who are fond of society from time to time may profit by this simile, and lay it down as a general rule that deficiency of quality in those we meet may be to some extent compensated by an increase in quantity. One man's company may be quiet enough, if he is clever; but where you have only ordinary people to deal with, it is advisable to have a great many of them, so that some advantage may accrue by letting them all work together—on the analogy of the horns; and may Heaven grant you patience for your task!

That mental vacuity and barrenness of soul to which I have alluded, is responsible for another misfortune. When men of the better class form a society for promoting some noble or ideal aim, the result almost always is that the innumerable mob of humanity comes crowding in too, as it always does everywhere, like vermin—their object being to try and get rid of boredom, or some other defect of their nature; and anything that will effect that, they seize upon at once, without the slightest discrimination. Some of them will slip into that society, or push themselves in, and then either soon destroy it altogether, or alter it so much that in the end it comes to have a purpose the exact opposite of that which it had at first.

This is not the only point of view from which the social impulse may be regarded. On cold days people manage to get some warmth by crowding together; and you can warm your mind in the same way—by bringing it into contact with others. But a man who has a great deal of intellectual warmth in himself will stand in no need of such resources. I have written a little fable illustrating this: it may be found elsewhere.* As a general rule, it may be said that a man's sociability stands very nearly in inverse ratio to his intellectual value: to say that "so and so" is very unsociable, is almost tantamount to saying that he is a man of great capacity.

Solitude is doubly advantageous to such a man. Firstly it allows him to be with himself, and, secondly, it prevents him being with others—an advantage of great moment; for how much constraint, annoyance, and even danger there is in all intercourse with the world. *Tout notre mal*, says La Bruyère, *vient de ne pouvoir être seul*. It is really a very risky, nay, a fatal thing, to be sociable; because it means contact with natures, the great majority of which are bad

---

* *Translator's Note.*—The passage to which Schopenhauer refers is "Parrega;" vol. ii. § 413. (4th. edition). The fable is of certain porcupines, who huddled together for warmth on a cold day; but as they began to prick one another with their quills, they were obliged to disperse. However the cold drove them together again, when just the same thing happened. At last, after many turns of huddling and dispersing, they discovered that they would be best off by remaining at a little distance from one another. In the same way, the need of society drives the human porcupines together—only to be mutually repelled by the many prickly and disagreeable qualities of their nature. The moderate distance which they at last discover to be the only tolerable condition of intercourse, is the code of politeness and fine manners; and those who transgress it are roughly told—in the English phrase—"to keep their distance." By this arrangement the mutual need of warmth is only very moderately satisfied—but then people do not get pricked. A man who has some heat in himself prefers to remain outside, where he will neither prick other people nor get pricked himself.

morally, and dull or perverse, intellectually. To be un-sociable is not to care about such people; and to have enough in one's self to dispense with the necessity of their company is a great piece of good fortune; because almost all our sufferings spring from having to do with other people and that destroys the peace of mind, which, as I have said comes next after health in the elements of happiness. Peace of mind is impossible without a considerable amount of solitude. The cynics renounced all private property in order to attain the bliss of having nothing to trouble them; and to renounce society with the same object is the wisest thing a man can do. Bernardin de Saint Pierre has the very excellent and pertinent remark that to be sparing in regard to food is a means of health; in regard to society, a means of tranquillity—*la diète des alimens nous rend la santé du corps, et celledes hommes la tranquillité de l'âme.* To be soon on friendly, or even affectionate, terms with solitude is like winning a gold mine: but this is not some-thing which everybody can do. The prime reason for social intercourse is mutual need; and as soon as that is satisfied, boredom drives people together once more. If it were not for these two reasons, a man would probably elect to remain alone; if only because solitude is the sole condition of life which gives full play to that feeling of exclusive importance which every man has in his own eyes—as if he were the only person in the world! a feeling which, in the throng and press of real life, soon shrivels up to nothing, getting, at every step, a painful *démenti.* From this point of view it may be said that solitude is the original and natural state of man, where, like another Adam, he is as happy as his nature will allow.

But still, had Adam no father or mother? There is an-other sense in which solitude is not the natural state; for, at his entrance into the world, a man finds himself with parents, brothers, sisters, that is to say, in society, and not alone. Accordingly it cannot be said that the love of soli-tude is an original characteristic of human nature; it is rather the result of experience and reflection, and these in their turn depend upon the development of intellectual power, and increase with the years.

Speaking generally, sociability stands in inverse ratio with age. A little child raises a piteous cry of fright if it is left alone for only a few minutes; and later on, to be shut up by itself is a great punishment. Young people soon get on very friendly terms with one another; it is only the few among them of any nobility of mind who are glad now and then to be alone—but to spend the whole day thus would be disagreeable. A grown-up man can easily do it;.it is little trouble to him to be much alone, and it becomes less and less trouble as he advances in years. An old man who has outlived all his friends, and is either indifferent or dead to the pleasures of life, is in his proper element in solitude and in individual cases the special tendency to retirement and seclusion will always be in direct proportion to intellectual capacity.

For this tendency is not, as I have said, a purely natural one; it does not come into existence as a direct need of human nature; it is rather the effect of the experience we go through, the product of reflection upon what our needs really are; proceeding, more especially, from the insight we attain into the wretched stuff of which most people are made, whether you look at their morals or their intellects. The worst of it all is that, in the individual, moral and intellectual shortcomings are closely connected and play into each other's hands, so that all manner of disagreeable results are obtained, which make intercourse with most people not only unpleasant but intolerable. Hence, though the world contains many things which are thoroughly bad, the worst thing in it is society. Even Voltaire, that sociable Frenchman, was obliged to admit that there are everywhere crowds of people not worth talking to; *la terre est couverte de gens qui ne méritent pas qu'on leur parle.* And Petrarch gives a similar reason for wishing to be alone—that tender spirit! so strong and constant in his love of seclusion. The streams, the plains and woods know well, he says, how he has tried to escape the perverse and stupid people who have missed the way to heaven:

> " Cercato ho sempre solitaria vita
> (Le rive il sanno, e le campagne e i boschi)
> Per fuggir quest' ingegni storti e loschi
> Che la strada del ciel' hanno smarrita."

He pursues the same strain in that delightful book of his "De Vita Solitaria," which seems to have given Zimmerman the idea of his celebrated work on "Solitude." It is the secondary and indirect character of the love of seclusion to which Chamfort alludes in the following passage, couched in his sarcastic vein: *"On dit quelquefois d'un homme qui vit seul, il n'aime pas la société. C'est souvent comme si on disait d'un homme qu'il n'aime pas la prome-nade, sous le prétexte qu'il ne se promène pas volontiers le soir dans la forêt de Bondy.*

You will find a similar sentiment expressed by the Persian poet Sadi, in his "Garden of Roses." "Since that time," he says, "we have taken leave of society, preferring the path of seclusion; for there is safety in solitude. Angelus Silesius,* a very gentle and Christian writer, confesses to the same feeling, in his own mythical language. Herod, he says, is the common enemy; and when, as with Joseph, God warns us of danger, we fly from the world to solitude, from Bethlehem to Egypt; or else suffering and death await us!

> "Herodes ist ein Feind; der Joseph der Verstand,
> Dem machte Gott die Gefahr im Traum (in Geist) bekannt;
> Die Welt ist Bethlehem, Aegypten Einsamkeit,
> Fleuch, meine Seele! fleuch, sonst stirbest du vor Leid."

Giordano Bruno also declares himself a friend of seclusion. *Tanti uomini,* he says, *che in terra hanne voluto gustare vita celeste, dissero con una voce, "ecce elongavi fugiens et mansi in solitudine"*—those who in this world have desired a foretaste of the divine life, have always proclaimed with one voice:

> "Lo ! then would I wander far off:
> I would lodge in the wilderness." †

And in the work from which I have already quoted Sadi says of himself: "In disgust with my friends at Damascus I withdraw into the desert about Jerusalem, to seek the society of the beasts of the field." In short, the same thing has been said by all whom Prometheus has formed out of better clay. What pleasure could they find in the company of people with whom their only common ground is just what is lowest and least noble in their own nature—the

---

* *Translator's Note*—Angelus Silesius, pseudonym for Johannes Scheffler, a physician and mystic poet of the seventeenth century (1624-77).

† Psalms, lv. 7.

part of them that is commonplace, trivial and vulgar? What do they want with people who cannot rise to a higher level, and for whom nothing remains but to drag others down to theirs? for this is what they aim at. It is an aristocratic feeling that is at the bottom of this propensity to seclusion and solitude.

Rascals are always sociable—more's the pity! and the chief sign that a man has any nobility in his character is the little pleasure he takes in others' company. He prefers solitude more and more, and, in course of time, comes to see that with few exceptions, the world offers no choice beyond solitude on one side and vulgarity on the other. This may sound a hard thing to say; but even Angelus Silesius, with all his Christian feelings of gentleness and love, was obliged to admit the truth of it. However painful solitude may be, he says, be careful not to be vulgar; for then you may find a desert everywhere:

"Die Einsamkeit ist noth: doch sei nur nicht gemein,
  So kannst du uberall in einer Wüste sein."

It is natural for great minds—the true teachers of humanity—to care little about the constant company of others just as little as the schoolmaster cares for joining in the gambols of the noisy crowd of boys which surrounds him. The mission of these great minds is to guide mankind over the sea of error to the haven of truth—to draw it forth from the dark abysses of a barbarous vulgarity up into the light of culture and refinement. Men of great intellect live in the world without really belonging to it; and so, from their earliest years, they feel that there is a perceptible difference between them and other people. But it is only gradually, with the lapse of years, that they come to a clear understanding of their position. Their intellectual isolation is then reinforced by actual seclusion in their manner of life; they let no one approach who is not in some degree emancipated from the prevailing vulgarity.

From what has been said it is obvious that the love of solitude is not a direct, original impulse in human nature, but rather something secondary and of gradual growth. It is the more distinguishing feature of nobler minds, developed not without some conquest of natural desires, and now and then in actual opposition to the promptings of Mephistopheles—bidding you exchange a morose and soul-destroying solitude for life among men, for society ; even the worst, he says, will give a sense of human fellowship :

> "Hor' auf mit deinem Gram zu spielen,
>   Der, wie ein Geier, dir am Leben frisst :
>   Die schlechteste Gesellschaft lässt dich fühlen
>   Dass du ein Mensch mit Menschen bist." *

To be alone is the fate of all great minds—a fate deplored at times, but still always chosen as the less grievous of two evils. As the years increase, it always becomes easier to say, Dare to be wise—*sapere aude*. And after sixty, the inclination to be alone grows into a kind of real, natural instinct ; for at that age everything combines in favor of it. The strongest impulse—the love of women's society—has little or no effect ; it is the sexless condition of old age which lays the foundation of a certain self-sufficiency, and that gradually absorbs all desire for others' company. A thousand illusions and follies are overcome ; the active years of life are in most cases gone ; a man has no more expectations or plans or intentions. The generation to which he belonged has passed away, and a new race has sprung up which looks upon him as essentially outside its sphere of activity. And then the years pass more quickly as we become older, and we want to devote our remaining time to the intellectual rather than to the practical side of life. For, provided that the mind retains its faculties, the amount of knowledge and experience we have acquired, together with the facility we have gained in the use of our powers, makes it then more than ever easy and interesting to us to pursue the study of any subject. A thousand things become clear which were formerly enveloped in obscurity, and results are obtained which give a feeling of difficulties overcome. From long experience of men, we cease to expect much from them ; we find that, on the whole, people do not gain by a nearer acquaintance ; and that—apart from a few rare and fortunate exceptions —we have come across none but defective specimens of human nature which it is advisable to leave in peace. We are no more subject to the ordinary illusions of life ; and

---

* "Goethe's "Faust," Part I., 1281-5.

as, in individual instances, we soon see what a man is made of, we seldom feel any inclination to come into closer relations with him. Finally, isolation—our own society—has become a habit, as it were a second nature, with us, more especially if we have been on friendly terms with it from our youth up. The love of solitude which was formerly indulged only at the expense of our desire for society, has now come to be the simple quality of our natural disposition—the element proper to our life, as water to a fish. This is why any one who possesses a unique individuality—unlike others and therefore necessarily isolated—feels that, as he becomes older, his position is no longer so burdensome as when he was young.

For as a matter of fact, this very genuine privilege of old age is one which can be enjoyed only if a man is possessed of a certain amount of intellect; it will be appreciated most of all where there is real mental power: but in some degree by every one. It is only people of very barren and vulgar nature who will be just as sociable in their old age as they were in their youth. But then they become troublesome to a society to which they are no longer suited, and, at most, manage to be tolerated; whereas they were formerly in great request.

There is another aspect of this inverse proportion between age and sociability—the way in which it conduces to education. The younger people are, the more in every respect they have to learn; and it is just in youth that Nature provides a system of mutual education, so that mere intercourse with others, at that time of life, carries instruction with it. Human society, from this point of view, resembles a huge academy of learning, on the Bell and Lancaster system, opposed to the system of education by means of books and schools, as something artificial and contrary to the institutions of Nature. It is therefore a very suitable arrangement that, in his young days, a man should be a very diligent student at the place of learning provided by Nature herself.

But there is nothing in life which has not some drawback—*nihil est ab omni parte beatum*, as Horace says; or, in the words of an Indian proverb, "no lotus without a stalk." Seclusion, which has so many advantages, has also its little annoyances and drawbacks, which are small, however, in comparison with those of society; hence any one who is worth much in himself will get on better without other people than with them. But among the disadvantages of seclusion there is one which is not so easy to see as the rest. It is this: when people remain indoors all day, they become physically very sensitive to atmospheric changes, so that every little draught is enough to make them ill; so with our temper; a long course of seclusion makes it so sensitive that the most trivial incidents, words, or even looks, are sufficient to disturb or to vex and offend us—little things which are unnoticed by those who live in the turmoil of life.

When you find human society disagreeable and feel yourself justified in flying to solitude, you may be so constituted as to be unable to bear the depression of it for any length of time, which will probably be the case if you are young. Let me advise you, then, to form the habit of taking some of your solitude with you into society, to learn to be to some extent alone even though you are in company: not to say at once what you think, and, on the other hand, not to attach too precise a meaning to what others say; rather not to expect much of them, either morally or intellectually and to strengthen yourself in the feeling of indifference to their opinion, which is the surest way of always practicing a praiseworthy toleration. If you do that, you will not live so much with other people, though you may appear to move among them; your relation to them will be of purely objective character. This precaution will keep you from too close contact with society, and therefore secure you against being contaminated or even outraged by it. * Society is in this respect like a fire—the wise man warming himself at a proper distance from it; not coming too close like the fool, who, on getting scorched, runs away and shivers in solitude, loud in his complaint that the fire burns.

§ 10.   Envy is natural to man: and still, it is at once a vice and a source of misery.† We should treat it as the

---

* This restricted, or, as it were, entrenched kind of sociability has been dramatically illustrated in a play—well worth reading—of Moratin's, entitled "El Café o sea la Comedia Nuova" (The Cafe or the New Comedy), chiefly by one of the characters, Don Pedro, and especially in the second and third scenes of the first act.

† Envy shows how unhappy people are: and in their constant attention to what others do and leave undone, how much they are bored.

enemy of our happiness, and stifle it like an evil thought. This is the advice given by Seneca; as he well puts it, we shall be pleased with what we have, if we avoid the self-torture of comparing our own lot with some other and happier one—*nostra nos sine comparatione delectent; nunquam erit felix quem torquebit felicior.** And again: *quum adspexeris quot te antecedant, cogita quot sequantur*†—if a great many people appear to be better off than yourself, think how many there are in a worse position. It is a fact that if real calamity comes upon us, the most effective consolation—though it springs from the same source as envy—is just the thought of greater misfortunes than ours; and the next best is the society of those who are in the same ill luck as we—the partners of our sorrows.

So much for the envy which we may feel toward others. As regards the envy which we may excite in them, it should always be remembered that no form of hatred is so implacable as the hatred that comes from envy; and therefore we should always carefully refrain from doing anything to rouse it; nay, as with many another form of vice, it is better altogether to renounce any pleasure there may be in it because of the serious nature of its consequences.

Aristocracies are of three kinds: (1) of birth and rank; (2) of wealth; and (3) of intellect. The last is really the most distinguished of the three, and its claim to occupy the first position comes to be recognized, if it is only allowed time to work. So eminent a king as Frederick the Great admitted it—*les âmes privilegiées rangent à l'ègal des souverains*, as he said to his chamberlain, when the latter expressed his surprise that Voltaire should have a seat at the table reserved for kings and princes, while ministers and generals were relegated to the chamberlain's.

Every one of these aristocracies is surrounded by a host of envious persons. If you belong to one of them, they will be secretly embittered against you; and unless they are restrained by fear, they will always be anxious to let you understand that you are no better than they. It is by their anxiety to let you know this, that they betray how greatly they are conscious that the opposite is the truth.

The line of conduct to be pursued if you are exposed to envy is to keep the envious persons at a distance, and,

---

* "De Ira:" iii., 30.   † "Epist.," xv.

as far as possible, avoid all contact with them, so that there may be a wide gulf fixed between you and them ; if this cannot be done, to bear their attacks with the greatest composure. In the latter case, the very thing that provokes the attack will also neutralize it. This is what appears to be generally done.

The members of one of these aristocracies usually get on very well with those of another, and there is no call for envy between them, because their several privileges effect an equipoise.

§ 11. Give mature and repeated consideration to any plan before you proceed to carry it out ; and even after you have thoroughly turned it over in your mind, make some concession to the incompetency of human judgment ; for it may always happen that circumstances which cannot be investigated or foreseen, will come in and upset the whole of your calculation. This is a reflection that will always influence the negative side of the balance—a kind of warning to refrain from unnecessary action in matters of importance—*quieta non movere.* But having once made up your mind and begun your work, you must let it run its course and abide the result—not worry yourself by fresh reflections on what is already accomplished, or by a renewal of your scruples on the score of possible danger : free your mind from the subject altogether, and refuse to go into it again, secure in the thought that you gave it mature attention at the proper time. This is the same advice as is given by an Italian proverb—*legala bene e poi lascia la andare*—which Goethe has translated thus : see well to your girths, and then ride on boldly.*

And if, notwithstanding that, you fail, it is because all human affairs are the sport of chance and error. Socrates, the wisest of men, needed the warning voice of his good genius, or δαιμόνιον to enable him to do what was right in regard to his own personal affairs, or, at any rate, to avoid mistakes ; which argues that the human intellect is incompetent for the purpose. There is a saying—which is reported to have originated with one the popes—that when

---

* It may be observed, in passing, that a great many of the maxims which Goethe puts under the head of *Proverbial*, are translations from the Italian.

misfortune happens to us, the blame of it, at least in some
degree, attaches to ourselves. If this is not true absolutely
and in every instance, it is certainly true in the great
majority of cases. It even looks as if this truth had a
great deal to do with the effort people make as far as possible to conceal their misfortunes, and to put the best face
they can upon them, for fear lest their misfortunes may
show how much they are to blame.

§ 12. In the case of a misfortune which has already
happened and therefore cannot be altered, you should not
allow yourself to think that it might have been otherwise ;
still less, that it might have been avoided by such and
such means ; for reflections of this kind will only add
to your distress and make it intolerable, so that you will
become a tormentor of yourself—ἑαυτοντιμωρούμενος. It is
better to follow the example of King David ; who, as long
as his son lay on the bed of sickness, assailed Jehovah with
unceasing supplications and entreaties for his recovery ;
but when he was dead, snapped his fingers and thought no
more of it. If you are not light-hearted enough for that, you
can take refuge in fatalism, and have the great truth
revealed to you that everything which happens is the result
of necessity, and therefore inevitable.

However good this advice may be, it is one sided and
partial. In relieving and quieting us for the moment, it
is no doubt effective enough ; but when our misfortunes
have resulted—as is usually the case—from our own care-
lessness or folly, or, at any rate, partly by our own fault,
it is a good thing to consider how they might have been
avoided, and to consider it often in spite of its being a
tender subject—a salutary form of self-discipline, which
will make us wiser and better men for the future. If we
have made obvious mistakes, we should not try, as we
generally do, to gloss them over, or to find something to
excuse or extenuate them ; we should admit to ourselves
that we have committed faults, and open our eyes wide to
all their enormity, in order that we may firmly resolve to
avoid them in time to come. To be sure, that means a
great deal of self-inflicted pain, in the shape of discontent,
but it should be remembered that to spare the rod is to
spoil the child—ὁ μὴ δαρεὶς ἄνθρωπος οὐ παιδεύεται.*

---

* Menander. Monost : 422.

§ 13. In all matters affecting our weal or woe, we should be careful not to let our imagination run away with us, and build no castles in the air. In the first place, they are expensive to build, because we have to pull them down again immediately, and that is a source of grief. We should be still more on our guard against distressing our hearts by depicting possible misfortunes. If these were misfortunes of a purely imaginary kind, or very remote and unlikely, we should at once see, on awaking from our dream, that the whole thing was mere illusion; we should rejoice all the more in a reality better than our dreams, or, at most, be warned against misfortunes which, though very remote, were still possible. These, however, are not the sort of playthings in which imagination delights; it is only in idle hours that we build castles in the air, and they are always of a pleasing description. The matter which goes to form gloomy dreams are mischances which to some extent really threaten us, though it be from some distance; imagination makes them look larger and nearer and more terrible than they are in reality. This is a kind of dream which cannot be so readily shaken off on awaking as a pleasant one; for a pleasant dream is soon dispelled by reality, leaving, at most, a feeble hope lying in the lap of possibility. When we have abandoned ourselves to a fit of the blues, visions are conjured up which do not so easily vanish again; for it is always just possible that the visions may be realized. But we are not always able to estimate the exact degree of possibility: possibility may easily pass into probability; and thus we deliver ourselves up to torture. Therefore we should be careful not to be over-anxious on any matter affecting our weal or our woe, not to carry our anxiety to unreasonable or injudicious limits; but coolly and dispassionately to deliberate upon the matter, as though it were an abstract question which did not touch us in particular. We should give no play to imagination here; for imagination is not judgment—it only conjures up visions, inducing an unprofitable and often very painful mood.

The rule on which I am here insisting should be most carefully observed toward evening. For as darkness makes us timid and apt to see terrifying shapes everywhere, there is something similar in the effect of indistinct thought; and uncertainty always brings with it a sense of

danger. Hence, toward evening, when our powers of
thought and judgment are relaxed—at the hour, as it were,
of subjective darkness—the intellect becomes tired, easily
confused, and unable to get at the bottom of things ; and
if, in that state, we meditate on matters of personal interest
to ourselves, they soon assume a dangerous and terrifying
aspect.   This is mostly the case at night, when we are in
bed ; for then the mind is fully relaxed, and the power of
judgment quite unequal to its duties ; but imagination is
still awake.   Night gives a black look to everything, whatever it may be.   This is why our thoughts, just before we
go to sleep, or as we lie awake through the hours of the
night, are usually such confusions and perversions of facts
as dreams themselves ; and when our thoughts at that
time are concentrated upon our own concerns, they are
generally as black and monstrous as possible.   In the
morning all such nightmares vanish like dreams ; as the
Spanish proverb has it, *noche tinta, blanco el dia*—the
night is colored, the day is white.

But even toward nightfall, as soon as the candles are lit,
the mind, like the eye, no longer sees things so clearly as
by day ; it is a time unsuited to serious meditation, especially on unpleasant subjects.   The morning is the proper
time for that—as indeed for all efforts without exception,
whether mental or bodily.   For the morning is the youth
of the day, when everything is bright, fresh and easy of
attainment ; we feel strong then, and all our faculties are
completely at our disposal.   Do not shorten the morning
by getting up late, or waste it in unworthy occupations
or in talk ; look upon it as the quintessence of life, as to a
certain extent sacred.   Evening is like old age : we are
languid, talkative, silly.   Each day is a little life ; every
waking and rising a little birth, every fresh morning a
little youth, every going to rest and sleep a little death.

But condition of health, sleep, nourishment, temperature
weather, surroundings, and much else that is purely external, have, in general, an important influence upon our
mood and therefore upon our thoughts.   Hence both our
view of any matter and our capacity for any work are very
much subject to time and place.   So it is best to profit by
a good mood—for how seldom it comes—

> "Nehmt die gute Stimmung wahr,
>   Denn sie kommt so selten." *

We are not always able to form new ideas about our surroundings, or to command original thoughts; they come if
they will, and when they will. And so, too, we cannot always succeed in completely considering some personal matter at the precise time at which we have determined beforehand to consider it, and just when we set ourselves to do
so. For the peculiar train of thought which is favorable to
it may suddenly become active without any special call being made upon it, and we may then follow it up with keen
interest. In this way reflection, too, chooses its own
time.

This reining-in of the imagination which I am recommending, will also forbid us to summon up the memory of
past misfortune, to paint a dark picture of the injustice or
harm that has been done us, the losses we have sustained,
the insults, slights and annoyances to which we have been
exposed; for to do that is to rouse into fresh life all those
hateful passions long laid asleep—the anger and resentment
which disturb and pollute our nature. In an excellent parable, Proclus, the Neoplatonist, points out how in every
town the mob dwell side by side with those who are rich and
distinguished: so, too, in every man, be he never so noble
and dignified, there is, in the depths of his nature, a mob
of low and vulgar desires which constitute him an animal.
It will not do to let this mob revolt or even so much as peep
forth from its hiding-place; it is hideous of mien, and its
rebel leaders are those flights of imagination which I have
been describing. The smallest annoyance whether it comes
from our fellow-men or from the things around us, may
swell up into a monster of dreadful aspect, putting us at
our wits' end—and all because we go on brooding over our
troubles and painting them in the most glaring colors and
on the largest scale. It is much better to take a very calm
and prosaic view of what is disagreeable; for that is the
easiest way of bearing it.

If you hold small objects close to your eyes, you limit
your field of vision and shut out the world. And, in the
same way, the people or the things which stand nearest,
even though they are of the very smallest consequence, are

* Goethe.

apt to claim an amount of attention much beyond their due, occupying us disagreeably, and leaving no room for serious thoughts and affairs of importance. We ought to work against this tendency.

§ 14. The sight of things which do not belong to us is very apt to raise the thought: "Ah, if that were only mine!" making us sensible of our privation. Instead of that we should do better by more frequently putting to ourselves the opposite case: "Ah, if that were not mine!" What I mean is that we should sometimes try to look upon our possessions in the light in which they would appear if we had lost them; whatever they may be, property, health, friends, a wife or child or some one else we love, our horse or our dog—it is usually only when we have lost them that we begin to find out their value. But if we come to look at things in the way I recommend, we shall be doubly the gainers; we shall at once get more pleasure out of them than we did before, and we shall do everything in our power to prevent the loss of them; for instance, by not risking our property, or angering our friends, or exposing our wives to temptation, or being careless about our children's health, and so on.

We often try to banish the gloom and despondency of the present by speculating upon our chances of success in the future; a process which leads us to invent a great many chimerical hopes. Every one of them contains the germ of illusion, and disappointment is inevitable when our hopes are shattered by the hard facts of life.

It is less hurtful to take the chances of misfortune as a theme for speculation: because in doing so, we provide ourselves at once with measures of precaution against it, and a pleasant surprise when it fails to make its appearance. Is it not a fact that we always feel a marked improvement in our spirits when we begin to get over a period of anxiety? I may go further and say that there is some use in occasionally looking upon terrible misfortunes—such as might happen to us—as though they had actually happened, for then the trivial reverses which subsequently come in reality, are much easier to bear. It is a source of consolation to look back upon those great misfortunes which never happened. But in following out this rule, care must be taken not to neglect what I have said in the preceding section.

§ 15.   The things which engage our attention—whether they are matters of business or ordinary events—are of such diverse kinds, that, if taken quite separately and in no fixed order or relation, they present a medley of the most glaring contrasts, with nothing in common, except that they one and all affect us in particular.   There must be a corresponding abruptness in the thoughts and anxieties which these various matters arouse in us, if our thoughts are to be in keeping with their various subjects.   Therefore, in setting about anything, the first step is to withdraw our attention from everything else; this will enable us to attend to each matter at its own time, and to enjoy or put up with it, quite apart from any thought of our remaining interests. Our thoughts must be arranged, as it were, in little drawers so that we may open one without disturbing any of the others.

In this way we can keep the heavy burden of anxiety from weighing upon us so much as to spoil the little pleasures of the present, or from robbing us of our rest; otherwise the consideration of one matter will interfere with every other, and attention to some important business may lead us to neglect many affairs which happen to be of less moment. It is most important for any one who is capable of higher and nobler thoughts to keep his mind from being so completely engrossed with private affairs and vulgar troubles as to let them take up all his attention and crowd out worthier matter; for that is, in a very real sense, to lose sight of the true end of life—*propter vitam vivendi perdere causas.*

Of course for this—as for so much else—self-control is necessary; without it, we cannot manage ourselves in the way I have described.   And self-control may not appear so very difficult, if we consider that every man has to submit to a great deal of very severe control on the part of his surroundings, and that without it no form of existence is possible.   Further, a little self-control at the right moment may prevent much subsequent compulsion at the hands of others; just as a very small section of a circle close to the center may correspond to a part near the circumference a hundred times as large.   Nothing will protect us from external compulsion so much as the control of ourselves; and as Seneca says, to submit yourself to reason is the way to make everything else submit to you—*si tibi vis omnia subjicere, te subjice rationi.*   Self-control, too, is something

which we have in our own power; and if the worst comes
to the worst, and it touches us in a very sensitive part, we
can always relax its severity.   But other people will pay no
regard to our feelings, if they have to use compulsion, and
we shall be treated without pity or mercy.   Therefore it
will be prudent to anticipate compulsion by self-control.

§ 16.   We must set limits to our wishes, curb our desires,
moderate our anger, always remembering that an individual
can attain only an infinitesimal share in anything that is
worth having: and that, on the other hand, every one must
incur many of the ills of life; in a word, we must bear and
forbear—*abstinere et sustinere;* and if we fail to observe
this rule, no position of wealth or power will prevent us
from feeling wretched.   This is what Horace means when
he recommends us to study carefully and inquire diligently
what will best promote a tranquil life—not to be always
agitated by fruitless desires and fears and hopes for things,
which, after all, are not worth very much:

> " Inter cuncta leges et percontabere doctos
>   Qua ratione queas traducere leniter aevum:
>   Ne te semper inops agitet vexetque cupido,
>   Ne pavor. et rerum mediocriter utilium spes." *

§ 17.   Life consists in movement, says Aristotle; and he is
obviously right.   We exist, physically, because our organism
is the seat of constant motion; and if we are to exist intellectually, it can only be by means of continual occupation
—no matter with what so long as it is some form of practical
or mental activity.   You may see that this is so by the way
in which people who have no work or nothing to think
about immediately begin to beat the devil's tattoo with their
knuckles or a stick or anything that comes handy.   The
truth is, that our nature is essentially restless in its character; we very soon get tired of having nothing to do; it is
intolerable boredom.   This impulse to activity should be
regulated, and some sort of method introduced into it,
which of itself will enhance the satisfaction we obtain.
Activity—doing something, if possible creating something,
at any rate learning something—how fortunate it is that
men cannot exist without that!   A man wants to use his

---

* Epist. I. xviii 97.

strength, to see, if he can, what effect it will produce; and
he will get the most complete satisfaction of this desire if
he can make or construct something—be it a book or a
basket. There is a direct pleasure in seeing work grow under one's hands day by day, until at last it is finished. This
is the pleasure attaching to a work of art or a manuscript,
or even mere manual labor; and, of course, the higher the
work, the greater pleasure it will give.

From this point of view, those are happiest of all who
are conscious of the power to produce great works animated by some significant purpose : it gives a higher kind
of interest—a sort of rare flavor—to the whole of their
life, which, by its absence from the life of the ordinary
man, makes it, in comparison, something very insipid.
For richly endowed natures, life and the world have a
special interest beyond the mere everyday personal interest
which so many others share ; and something higher than
that—a formal interest. It is from life and the world
that they get the material for their works; and as soon as
they are freed from the pressure of personal needs, it is to
the diligent collection of material that they devote their
whole existence. So with their intellect : it is to some extent of a twofold character, and devoted partly to the
ordinary affairs of every day—those matters of will which
are common to them and the rest of mankind, and partly
to their peculiar work—the pure and objective contemplation of existence. And while, on the stage of the world,
most men play their little part and then pass away, the genius lives a double life, at once an actor and a spectator.

Let every one, then, do something, according to the
measure of his capacities. To have no regular work, no
set sphere of activity—what a miserable thing it is ! How
often long travels undertaken for pleasure make a man
downright unhappy ; because the absence of anything that
can be called occupation forces him, as it were, out of his
right element. Effort, struggles with difficulties ! that is
as natural to a man as grubbing in the ground is to a mole.
To have all his wants satisfied is something intolerable—the
feeling of stagnation which comes from pleasures that last
too long. To overcome difficulties is to experience the full
delight of existence, no matter where the obstacles are en-
countered ; whether in the affairs of life, in commerce or
business; or in mental effort—the spirit of inquiry that

tries to master its subject. There is always something pleasurable in the struggle and the victory. And if a man has no opportunity to excite himself, he will do what he can to create one, and according to his individual bent, he will hunt or play cup and ball ; or led on by this unsuspected element in his nature, he will pick a quarrel with some one, or hatch a plot or intrigue, or take to swindling and rascally courses generally—all to put an end to a state of repose which is intolerable. As I have remarked, *difficilis in otio quies*—it is difficult to keep quiet if you have nothing to do.

§ 18. A man should avoid being led on by the phantoms of his imagination. This is not the same thing as to submit to the guidance of ideas clearly thought out : and yet these are rules of life which most people pervert. If you examine closely into the circumstances which, in any deliberation, ultimately turn the scale in favor of some particular course, you will generally find that the decision is influenced, not by any clear arrangement of ideas leading to a formal judgment, but by some fanciful picture which seems to stand for one of the alternatives in question.

In one of Voltaire's or Diderot's romances—I forget the precise reference—the hero, standing like a young Hercules at the parting of ways, can see no other representation of Virtue than his old tutor holding a snuff-box in his left hand, from which he takes a pinch and moralizes ; while Vice appears in the shape of his mother's chambermaid. It is in youth, more especially, that the goal of our efforts comes to be a fanciful picture of happiness, which continues to hover before our eyes sometimes for half and even for the whole of our life—a sort of mocking spirit ; for when we think our dream is to be realized, the picture fades away, leaving us the knowledge that nothing of what it promised is actually accomplished. How often this is so with the visions of domesticity—the detailed picture of what our home will be like ; or of life among our fellow-citizens and in society ; or, again, of living in the country —the kind of house we shall have, its surroundings, the marks of honor and respect that will be paid to us, and so on—whatever our hobby may be ; *chaqu fou a samarotte.* It is often the same, too, with our dreams about one we love. And this is all quite natural; for the visions we conjure up affect us directly, as though they were real objects; and so they exercise a more immediate influence upon our will than an abstract idea, which gives merely a vague, general outline, devoid of details; and the details are just the real part of it. We can be only indirectly affected by an abstract idea, and yet it is the abstract idea alone which will do as much as it promises; and it is the function of education to teach us to put our trust in it. Of course the abstract idea must be occasionally explained —paraphrased, as it were—by the aid of pictures; but discreetly, *cum grano salis.*

§ 19. The preceding rule may be taken as a special case of the more general maxim, that a man should never let himself be mastered by the impressions of the moment, or indeed by outward appearances at all, which are incomparably more powerful in their effects than the mere play of thought or a train of ideas; not because these momentary impressions are rich in virtue of the data they supply—it is often just the contrary—but because they are something palpable to the senses and direct in their working; they forcibly invade our mind, disturbing our repose and shattering our resolutions.

It is easy to understand that the thing which lies before our very eyes will produce the whole of its effect at once, but that time and leisure are necessary for the working of thought and the appreciation of argument, as it is impossible to think of everything at one and the same moment. This is why we are so allured by pleasure, in spite of all our determination to resist it; or so much annoyed by a criticism, even though we know that its author is totally incompetent to judge; or so irritated by an insult, though it comes from some very contemptible quarter. In the same way, to mention no other instances, ten reasons for thinking that there is no danger may be outweighed by one mistaken notion that it is actually at hand. All this shows the radical unreason of human nature. Women frequently succumb altogether to this predominating influence of present impressions, and there are few men so overweighted with reason as to escape suffering from a similar cause.

If it is impossible to resist the effects of some external influence by the mere play of thought, the best thing to do is to neutralize it by some contrary influence; for example, the effect of an insult may be overcome by seeking the society of those who have a good opinion of us; and the unpleasant sensation of imminent danger may be avoided by fixing our attention on the means of warding it off.   Leibnitz * tells of an Italian who managed to bear up under the tortures of the rack by never for a moment ceasing to think of the gallows which would have awaited him, had he revealed his secret; he kept on crying out: "I see it! I see it!" —afterward explaining that this was part of his plan.

It is from such reason as this, that we find it so difficult to stand alone in a matter of opinion—not to be made irresolute by the fact that every one else disagrees with us and acts accordingly, even though we are quite sure that they are in the wrong.   Take the case of a fugitive king who is trying to avoid capture; how much consolation he must find in the ceremonious and submissive attitude of a faithful follower, exhibited secretly so as not to betray his master's strict incognito; it must be almost necessary to prevent him doubting his own existence.

§ 20.   In the first part of this work I have insisted upon the great value of health as the chief and most important element in happiness.   Let me emphasize and confirm what I have there said by giving a few general rules as to its preservation.

The way to harden the body is to impose a great deal of labor and effort upon it in the days of good health—to exercise it, both as a whole and in its several parts, and to habituate it to withstand all kinds of noxious influences.   But on the appearance of any illness or disorder, either in the body as a whole or in any of its parts, a contrary course should be taken, and every means used to nurse the body, or the part of it which is affected, and to spare it any effort; for what is ailing and debilitated cannot be hardened.

The muscles may be strengthened by a vigorous use of them ; but not so the nerves ; they are weakened by it. Therefore, while exercising the muscles in every way that is suitable, care should be take to spare the nerves as much as possible.   The eyes, for instance, should be protected from too strong a light—especially when it is is reflected

---

* "Nouveaux Essais."   Liv. I. ch. 2 Sec. 11.

light—from any straining of them in the dark, or from the long-continued examination of minute objects; and the ears from too loud sounds. Above all, the brain should never be forced, or used too much, or at the wrong time; let it have a rest during digestion; for then the same vital energy which forms thoughts in the brain has a great deal of work to do elsewhere—I mean in the digestive organs, where it prepares chyme and chyle. For similar reasons, the brain should never be used during, or immediately after, violent muscular exercise. For the motor nerves are in this respect on a par with the sensory nerves; the pain felt when a limb is wounded has its seat in the brain; and, in the same way, it is not really our legs and arms which work and move—it is the brain, or, more strictly, that part of it which, through the medium of the spine, excites the nerves in the limbs and sets them in motion. Accordingly, when our arms and legs feel tired, the true seat of this feeling is in the brain. This is why it is only in connection with those muscles which are set in motion consciously and voluntarily—in other words, depend for their action upon the brain—that any feeling of fatigue can arise; this is not the case with those muscles which work involuntarily, like the heart. It is obvious, then, that injury is done to the brain if violent muscular exercise and intellectual exertion are forced upon it at the same moment, or at very short intervals.

What I say stands in no contradiction with the fact that at the beginning of a walk, or at any period of a short stroll, there often comes a feeling of enhanced intellectual vigor. The parts of the brain that come into play have had no time to become tired: and besides, slight muscular exercise conduces to activity of the respiratory organs, and causes a purer and more oxydated supply of arterial blood to mount to the brain.

It is most important to allow the brain the full measure of sleep which is necessary to restore it; for sleep is to a man's whole nature what winding up is to a clock.* This measure will vary directly with the development and activity of the brain; to overstep the measure is mere

* Cf. "Welt als Wille und Vorstellung," 4th Edition. Bk. II. pp. 236-40.

waste of time because if that is done, sleep gains only so much in length as it loses in depth.*

It should be clearly understood that thought is nothing but the organic function of the brain ; and it has to obey the same laws in regard to exertion and repose as any other organic function. The brain can be ruined by overstrain, just like the eyes. As the function of the stomach is to digest, so it is that of the brain to think. The notion of a soul—as something elementary and immaterial, merely lodging in the brain and needing nothing at all for the performance of its essential function, which consists in always and unweariedly thinking—has undoubtedly driven many people to foolish practices, leading to a deadening of the intellectual powers ; Frederick the Great, even, once tried to form the habit of doing without sleep altogether. It would be well if professors of philosophy refrained from giving currency to a notion which is attended by practical results of a pernicious character ; but then this is just what professorial philosophy does, in its old-womanish endeavor to keep on good terms with the catechism. A man should accustom himself to view his intellectual capacities in no other light than that of physiological functions, and to manage them accordingly—nursing or exercising them as the case may be ; remembering that every kind of physical suffering, malady or disorder, in whatever part of the body it occurs, has its effect upon the mind. The best advice that I know on this subject is given by Cabanis in his *Rapports du physique et du moral de l'homme.*†

Through neglect of this rule, many men of genius and and great scholars have become weak-minded and childish, or even gone quite mad, as they grew old. To take no

---

* Cf. loc : cit : p. 275. Sleep is a morsel of death borrowed to keep up and renew the part of life which is exhausted by the day —*le sommeil est un emprunt fait a la mort.* Or it might be said that sleep is the interest we have to pay on the capital which is called in at death ; and the higher the rate of interest and the more regularly it is paid, the further the date of redemption is postponed.

† *Translator's Note.*—The work to which Schopenhauer here refers is a series of essays by Cabanis, a French philosopher (1757-1808), treating of mental and moral phenomena on a physiological basis. In his later days, Cabanis completely abandoned his materialistic standpoint.

other instances, there can be no doubt that the celebrated English poets of the early part of this century, Scott, Wordsworth, Southey, became intellectually dull and incapable toward the end of their days, nay, soon after passing their sixtieth year ; and that their imbecility can be traced to the fact that, at that period of life, they were all led on, by the promise of high pay, to treat literature as a trade and to write for money. This seduced them into an unnatural abuse of their intellectual powers ; and a man who puts his Pegasus into harness, and urges on his Muse with the whip, will have to pay a penalty similar to that which is exacted by the abuse of other kinds of power.

And even in the case of Kant, I suspect that the second childhood of his last four years was due to overwork in later life, and after he had succeeded in becoming a famous man.

Every month of the year has its own peculiar and direct influence upon health and bodily condition generally ; nay, even upon the state of the mind. It is an influence dependent upon the weather.

CHAPTER III.

OUR RELATION TO OTHERS.

§ 21. IN MAKING his way through life, a man will find it useful to be ready and able to do two things ; to look ahead and to overlook : the one will protect him from loss and injury, the other from disputes and squabbles.

No one who has to live among men should absolutely discard any person who has his due place in the order of nature, even though he is very wicked or contemptible or ridiculous. He must accept him as an unalterable fact— unalterable, because the necessary outcome of an eternal, fundamental principle ; and in bad cases he should remember the words of Mephistopheles : *es muss auch solche Käuze geben**—there must be fools and rogues in the world. If he acts otherwise, he will be committing an injustice, and giving a challenge of life and death to the man he discards. No one can alter his own peculiar individuality,

---

* Goethe's " Faust," Part I.

his moral character, his intellectual capacity, his temperament or physique ; and if we go so far as to condemn a
man from every point of view, there will be nothing left
him but to engage us in deadly conflict; for we are practically allowing him the right to exist only on condition
that he becomes another man—which is impossible ; his
nature forbids it.

So if you have to live among men, you must allow every
one the right to exist in accordance with the character he
has, whatever it turns out to be : and all you should strive
to do is to make use of this character in such a way as its
kind and nature permit, rather than to hope for any alter-
ation in it, or to condemn it offhand for what it is.   This
is the true sense of the maxim—"Live and let live."
That, however, is a task which is difficult in proportion
as it is right; and he is a happy man who can once
for all avoid having to do with a great many of his fellow
creatures.

The art of putting up with people may be learned by
practicing patience on inanimate objects, which, in virtue
of some mechanical or general physical necessity, oppose a
stubborn resistance to our freedom of action—a form of
patience which is required every day.   The patience thus
gained may be applied to our dealings with men, by accus-
toming ourselves to regard their opposition, wherever we
encounter it, as the inevitable outcome of their nature,
which sets itself up against us in virtue of the same rigid law
of necessity as governs the resistance of inanimate objects.
To become indignant at their conduct is as foolish as to be
angry with a stone because it rolls into your path.   And
with many people the wisest thing you can do is to resolve
to make use of those whom you cannot alter.

§ 22. It is astonishing how easily and how quickly
similarity, or difference of mind and disposition, makes
itself felt between one man and another as soon as they
begin to talk ; every little trifle shows it.   When two
people of totally different natures are conversing, almost
everything said by the one will, in a greater or less degree,
displease the other, and in many cases produce positive
annoyance ; even though the conversation turn upon
the most out-of-the way subject, or one in which neither
of the parties has any real interest.   People of similar

nature, on the other hand, immediately come to feel a kind of general agreement ; and if they are cast very much in the of same mold, complete harmony or even unison will flow from their intercourse.

This explains two circumstances. First of all, it shows why it is that common, ordinary people are so sociable and find good company wherever they go. Ah ! those good, dear, brave people. It is just the contrary with those who are not of the common run ; and the less they are so, the more unsociable they become ; so that if, in their isolation, they chance to come across some one in whose nature they can find even a single sympathetic chord, be it never so minute, they show extraordinary pleasure in his society. For one man can be to another only so much as the other is to him. Great minds are like eagles, and build their nest in some lofty solitude.

Secondly, we are enabled to understand how it is that people of like disposition so quickly get on with one another, as though they were drawn together by magnetic force—kindred souls greeting each other from afar. Of course the most frequent opportunity of observing this is afforded by people of vulgar tastes and inferior intellect, but only because their name is legion ; while those who are better off in this respect and of a rarer nature, are not often to be met with : they are called rare because you can seldom find them.

Take the case of a large number of people who have formed themselves into a league for the purpose of carrying out some practical object ; if there be two rascals among them, they will recognize each other as readily as if they bore a similar badge, and will at once conspire for some misfeasance or treachery. In the same way, if you can imagine—*per impossibile*—a large company of very intelligent and clever people, among whom there are only two blockheads, these two will be sure to be drawn together by a feeling of sympathy, and each of them will very soon secretly rejoice at having found at least one intelligent person in the whole company. It is really quite curious to see how two such men, especially if they are morally and intellectually of an inferior type, will recognize each other at first sight ; with what zeal they will strive to become intimate ; how affably and cheerily they will run to greet each other, just as though they were old friends—it

is all so striking that one is tempted to embrace the Buddhist doctrine of metempsychosis and presume that they
were on familiar terms in some former state of existence.

Still, in spite of all this general agreement, men are
kept apart who might come together; or, in some cases
a passing discord springs up between them. This is due
to diversity of mood. You will hardly ever see two people exactly in the same frame of mind; for that is something which varies with their condition of life, occupation,
surroundings, health, the train of thought they are in at
the moment, and so on. These differences give rise to
discord between persons of the most harmonious disposition. To correct the balance properly, so as to remove the
disturbance—to introduce, as it were, a uniform temperature—is a work demanding a very high degree of culture.
The extent to which uniformity of mood is productive of
good fellowship may be measured by its effects upon a
large company. When, for instance, a great many people
are gathered together and presented with some objective
interest which works upon all alike and influences them in
a similar way, no matter what it be—a common danger or
hope, some great news, a spectacle, a play, a piece of
music, or anything of that kind—you will find them
roused to a mutual expression of thought, and a display of
sincere interest. There will be a general feeling of pleasure among them; for that which attracts their attention
produces a unity of mood by overpowering all private and
personal interests.

And in default of some objective interest of the kind I
have mentioned, recourse is usually had to something subjective. A bottle of wine is not an uncommon means of
introducing a mutual feeling of fellowship; and even tea
and coffee are used for a like end.

The discord which so easily finds its way into all society
as an effect of the different moods in which people happen
to be for the moment, also in part explains why it is that
memory always idealizes, and sometimes almost transfig-
ures, the attitude we have taken up at any period of the
past—a change due to our inability to remember all the
fleeting influences which disturbed us on any given occasion. Memory is in this respect like the lens of a *camera
obscura*: it contracts everything within its range, and so
produces a much finer picture than the actual landscape

affords. And, in the case of a man, absence always goes
some way toward securing this advantageous light; for
though the idealizing tendency of the memory requires
time to complete its work, it begins it at once. Hence
it is a prudent thing to see your friends and acquaintances
only at considerable intervals of time; and on meeting
them again, you will observe that memory has been at
work.

§ 23. No man can see "over his own height." Let me
explain what I mean.

You cannot see in another man any more than you have
in yourself; and your own intelligence strictly determines the
extent to which he comes within its grasp. If your intelligence is of a very low order, mental qualities in another,
even though they be of the highest kind, will have no
effect at all upon you; you will see nothing in their possessor except the meanest side of his individuality—in
other words, just those parts of his character and disposition which are weak and defective. Your whole estimate
of the man will be confined to his defects, and his higher
mental qualities will no more exist for you than colors
exist for those who cannot see.

Intellect is invisible to the man who has none. In any
attempt to criticise another's work, the range of knowledge possessed by the critic is as essential a part of his
verdict as the claims of the work itself.

Hence intercourse with others involves a process of level-
ling down. The qualities which are present in one man,
and absent in another, cannot come into play when they
meet; and the self-sacrifice which this entails upon one of
the parties, calls forth no recognition from the other.

Consider how sordid, how stupid, in a word, how vulgar
most men are, and you will see that it is impossible to talk
to them without becoming vulgar yourself for the time being. Vulgarity is in this respect like electricity; it is easily
distributed. You will then fully appreciate the truth and
propriety of the expression, "to make yourself cheap;" and
you will be glad to avoid the society of people whose only
possible point of contact with you is just that part of your
nature of which you have least reason to be proud. So you
will see that, in dealing with fools and blockheads, there is
only one way of showing your intelligence—by having noth-

ting to do with them. That means, of course, that when you go into society, you may now and then feel like a good dancer who gets an invitation to a ball, and on arriving, finds that every one is lame—with whom is he to dance?

§ 24. I feel respect for the man—and he is one in a hundred—who, when he is waiting or sitting unoccupied, refrains from rattling or beating time with anything that happens to be handy—his stick, or knife and fork, or whatever else it may be. The probability is that he is thinking of something.

With a large number of people, it is quite evident that their power of sight completely dominates over their power of thought; they seem to be conscious of existence only when they are making a noise; unless indeed they happen to be smoking, for this serves a similar end. It is for the same reason that they never fail to be all eyes and ears for what is going on around them.

§ 25. La Rochefoucauld makes the striking remark that it is difficult to feel deep veneration and great affection for one and the same person. If this is so, we shall have to choose whether it is veneration or love that we want from our fellow-men.

Their love is always selfish, though in very different ways; and the means used to gain it are not always of a kind to make us proud. A man is loved by others mainly in the degree in which he moderates his claim on their good feeling and intelligence: but he must act genuinely in the matter and without dissimulation—not merely out of forbearance, which is at bottom a kind of contempt. This calls to mind a very true observation of Helvetius:* "the amount of intellect necessary to please us, is a most accurate measure of the amount of intellect we have ourselves." With these remarks as premises, it is easy to draw the conclusion.

Now with veneration the case is just the opposite; it is wrung from men reluctantly, and for that very reason

---

* Translator's Note.—Helvetius, Claude-Adrien (1715-71), a French philosophical writer much esteemed by Schopenhauer. His chief work "De l'Esprit," excited great interest and opposition at the time of its publication, on account of the author's pronounced materialism.

mostly concealed. Hence, as compared with love, veneration gives more real satisfaction; for it is connected with
personal value, and the same is not directly true of love,
which is subjective in its nature, while veneration is objective. To be sure, it is more useful to be loved than to
be venerated.

§ 26. Most men are so thoroughly subjective that nothing really interests them but themselves. They always think
of their own case as soon as ever any remark is made, and
their whole attention is engrossed and absorbed by the
merest chance reference to anything which affects them
personally, be it never so remote; with the result that they
have no power left for forming an objective view of things
should the conversation take that turn; neither can they
admit any validity in arguments which tell against their
interest or their vanity. Hence their attention is easily distracted. They are so readily offended, insulted or annoyed,
that in discussing any impersonal matter with them, no care
is too great to avoid letting your remarks bear the slightest
possible reference to the very worthy and sensitive individuals
whom you have before you for anything you may say will perhaps hurt their feelings. People really care about nothing
that does not affect them personally. True and striking observations, fine, subtle and witty things are lost upon them;
they cannot understand or feel them. But anything that
disturbs their petty vanity in the most remote and indirect
way, or reflects prejudicially upon their exceedingly precious
selves—to that, they are most tenderly sensitive. In this
respect they are like the little dog whose toes you are so apt
to tread upon inadvertently—you know it by the shrill
bark it sets up: or, again, they resemble a sick man covered
with sores and boils, with whom the greatest care must be
taken to avoid unnecessary handling. And in some people
this feeling reaches such a pass that, if they are talking
with any one, and he exhibits, or does not sufficiently conceal, his intelligence and discernment, they look upon it as
a downright insult; although, for the moment they hide
their ill will, and the unsuspecting author of it afterward
ruminates in vain upon their conduct, and racks his brains
to discover what in the world he could have done to excite
their malice and hatred.

But it is just as easy to flatter and win them over; and

this is why their judgment is usually corrupt, and why their opinions are swayed, not by what is really true and right but by the favor of the party or class to which they belong. And the ultimate reason of it all is, that in such people force of will greatly predominates over knowledge; and hence their meager intellect is wholly given up to the service of the will, and can never free itself from that service for a moment.

Astrology furnishes a magnificent proof of this miserable subjective tendency in men, which leads them to see everything only as bearing upon themselves, and to think of nothing that is not straightway made into a personal matter. The aim of astrology is to bring the motions of the celestial bodies into relation with the wretched *Ego* and to establish a connection between a comet in the sky and squabbles and rascalities on earth. *

§ 27. When any wrong statement is made, whether in public, or in society, or in books, and well received—or, at any rate, not refuted—that is no reason why you should despair or think that there the matter will rest. You should comfort yourself with the reflection that the question will be afterward gradually subjected to examination; light will be thrown upon it; it will be thought over, considered, discussed, and generally in the end the correct view will be reached; so that, after a time—the length of which will depend upon the difficulty of the subject—every one will come to understand that which a clear head saw at once.

In the meantime, of course, you must have patience. He who can see truly in the midst of general infatuation is like a man whose watch keeps good time, when all clocks in the town in which he lives are wrong. He alone knows the right time; but what use is that to him? for every one goes by the clocks which speak false, not even excepting those who know that his watch is the only one that is right.

§ 28. Men are like children, in that, if you spoil them, they become naughty.

Therefore it is well not to be too indulgent or charitable

---

* See for instance, Stobæus, "Eclog." I. xii, 9.

with any one. You may take it as a general rule that you will not lose a friend by refusing him a loan, but that you are very likely to do so by granting it; and, for similar reasons, you will not readily alienate people by being somewhat proud and careless in your behavior; but if you are very kind and complaisant toward them, you will often make them arrogant and intolerable, and so a breach will ensue.

There is one thing that, more than any other, throws people absolutely off their balance—the thought that you are dependent upon them. This is sure to produce an insolent and domineering manner toward you. There are some people, indeed, who become rude if you enter into any kind of relation with them; for instance, if you have occasion to converse with them frequently upon confidential matters, they soon come to fancy that they can take liberties with you, and so they try to transgress the laws of politeness. This is why there are so few with whom you care to become more intimate, and why you should avoid familiarity with vulgar people. If a man comes to think that I am more dependent upon him than he is upon me, he at once feels as though I had stolen something from him; and his endeavor will be to have his vengeance and get it back. The only way to attain superiority in dealing with men, is to let it be seen that you are independent of them.

And in this view it is advisable to let every one of your acquaintance— whether man or woman—feel now and then that you could very well dispense with their company. This will consolidate friendship. Nay, with most people there will be no harm in occasionally mixing a grain of disdain with your treatment of them; that will make them value your friendship all the more. *Chi non istima vien stimato,* as a subtle Italian proverb has it—to disregard is to win regard. But if we really think very highly of a person, we should conceal it from him like a crime. This is not a very gratifying thing to do, but it is right. Why, a dog will not bear being treated too kindly, let alone a man!

§ 29. It is often the case that people of noble character and great mental gifts betray a strange lack of worldly wisdom and a deficiency in the knowledge of men, more especially when they are young; with the result that it is easy to deceive or mislead them; and that, on the other hand, natures of the commoner sort are more ready and successful in making their way in the world.

The reason of this is that, when a man has little or no experience, he must judge by his own antecedent notions; and in matters demanding judgment an antecedent notion is never on the same level as experience. For, with the commoner sort of people, an antecedent notion means just their own selfish point of view. This is not the case with those whose mind and character are above the ordinary; for it is precisely in this respect—their unselfishness—that they differ from the rest of mankind; and as they judge other people's thoughts and actions by their own high standard, the result does not always tally with their calculation.

But if, in the end, a man of noble character comes to see, as the effect of his own experience, or by the lessons he learns from others, what it is that may be expected of men in general—namely, that five-sixths of them are morally and intellectually so constituted that, if circumstances do not place you in relation with them, you had better get out of their way and keep as far as possible from having anything to do with them—still, he will scarcely ever attain an adequate notion of their wretchedly mean and shabby nature: all his life long he will have to be extending and adding to the inferior estimate he forms of them; and in the meantime he will commit a great many mistakes and do himself harm.

Then again, after he has really taken to heart the lessons that have been taught him, it will occasionally happen that, when he is in the society of people whom he does not know, he will be surprised to find how thoroughly reasonable they all appear to be, both in their conversation and in their demeanor—in fact, quite honest, sincere, virtuous and trustworthy people, and at the same time shrewd and clever.

But that ought not to perplex him. Nature is not like those bad poets, who, in setting a fool or a knave before us, do their work so clumsily, and with such evident design, that you might almost fancy you saw the poet standing behind each of his characters, and continually disavowing their sentiments, and telling you in a tone of warning:

"This is a knave; that is a fool; do not mind what he says." But nature goes to work like Shakespeare and Gœthe, poets who make every one of their characters—even if it is the devil himself!—appear to be quite in the right for the moment that they come before us in their several parts; the characters are described so objectively that they excite our interest and compel us to sympathize with their point of view; for, like the works of nature, everyone of these characters is evolved as the result of some hidden law or principle, which makes all they say and do appear natural and therefore necessary. And you will always be the prey or the plaything of the devils and fools in this world, if you expect to see them going about with horns or jangling their bells.

And it should be borne in mind that, in their intercourse with others, people are like the moon or like hunchbacks; they show you only one of their sides. Every man has an innate talent for mimicry—for making a mask out of his physiognomy, so that he can always look as if he really were what he pretends to be; and since he makes his calculations always within the lines of his individual nature, the appearance he puts on suits him to a nicety, and its effect is extremely deceptive. He dons his mask whenever his object is to flatter himself into some one's good opinion; and you may pay just as much attention to it as if it were made of wax or cardboard, never forgetting that excellent Italian proverb: *non è si tristo cane che non meni la coda*—there is no dog so bad but that he will wag his tail.

In any case it is well to take care not to form a highly favorable opinion of a person whose acquaintance you have only recently made, for otherwise you are very likely to be disappointed; and then you will be ashamed of yourself and perhaps even suffer some injury. And while I am on the subject, there is another fact that deserves mention. It is this. A man shows his character just in the way in which he deals with trifles—for then he is off his guard. This will often afford a good opportunity of observing the boundless egoism of a man's nature, and his total lack of consideration for others; and if these defects show themselves in small things, or merely in his general demeanor, you will find that they also underlie his action in matters of importance, although he may disguise the fact. This is an opportunity which should not be missed. If in the little affairs of every day—the trifles of life, those matters to which the rule *de minimis non* applies—a man is inconsiderate and seeks only what is advantageous or convenient to himself, to the prejudice of others' rights; if he appropriates to himself that which belongs to all alike, you may be sure there is no justice in his heart, and that he would be a scoundrel on a wholesale scale, only that law and compulsion bind his hands. Do not trust him beyond your door. He who is not afraid to break the laws of his own private circle, will break those of the state when he can do so with impunity.

If the average man were so constituted that the good in him outweighed the bad, it would be more advisable to rely upon his sense of justice, fairness, gratitude, fidelity, love or compassion, than to work upon his fears; but as the contrary is the case, and it is the bad that outweighs the good, the opposite course is the more prudent one.

If any person with whom we are associated or have to do, exhibits unpleasant or annoying qualities, we have only to ask ourselves whether or not this person is of so much value to us that we can put up with frequent and repeated exhibitions of the same qualities in a somewhat aggravated form.* In case of an affirmative answer to this question, there will not be much to be said, because talking is very little use. We must let the matter pass, with or without some notice; but we should nevertheless remember that we are thereby exposing ourselves to a repetition of the offense. If the answer is in the negative, we must break with our worthy friend at once and forever; or in the case of a servant, dismiss him. For he will inevitably repeat the offense, or do something tantamount to it, should the occasion return, even though for the moment he is deep and sincere in his assurances of the contrary. There is nothing, absolutely nothing, that a man cannot forget—but not himself, his own character. For character is incorrigible; because all a man's actions emanate from an inward principle, in virtue of which he must always do the same thing under like circumstances; and he cannot do otherwise. Let me refer to my prize essay on the so-called

---

* "To forgive and forget" means to throw away dearly bought experience.

" Freedom of the Will," the perusal of which will dissipate any delusions the reader may have on this subject.

To become reconciled to a friend with whom you have broken, is a form of weakness; and you pay the penalty of it when he takes the first opportunity of doing precisely the very thing which brought about the breach; nay, he does it the more boldly, because he is secretly conscious that you cannot get on without him. This is also applicable to servants whom you have dismissed, and then taken into your service again.

For the same reason, you should just as little expect people to continue to act in a similar way under altered circumstances. The truth is that men alter their demeanor and sentiments just as fast as their interest changes; and their design in this respect is a bill drawn for such short payment that the man must be still more short-sighted who accepts the bill without protesting it. Accordingly, suppose you want to know how a man will behave in an office into which you think of putting him; you should not build upon expectations, on his promises or assurances. For, even allowing that he is quite sincere, he is speaking about a matter of which he has no knowledge. The only way to calculate how he will behave, is to consider the circumstances in which he will be placed, and the extent to which they will conflict with his character.

If you wish to get a clear and profound insight—and it is very needful—into the true but melancholy elements of which most men are made, you will find it a very instructive thing to take the way they behave in the pages of literature as a commentary to their doings in practical life, and *vice versâ.* The experience thus gained will be very useful in avoiding wrong ideas, whether about yourself or about others. But if you come across any special trait of meanness or stupidity—in life or in literature—you must be careful not to let it annoy or distress you, but to look upon it merely as an addition to your knowledge—a new fact to be considered in studying the character of humanity. Your attitude toward it will be that of the mineralogist who stumbles upon a very characteristic specimen of a mineral.

Of course there are some facts which are very exceptional, and it is difficult to understand how they arise, and how it is that there come to be such enormous differences between man and man ; but, in general, what was said long ago is quite true, and the world is in a very bad way. In savage countries they eat one another, in civilized countries they deceive one another ; and that is what people call the way of the world! What are states and all the elaborate systems of political machinery, and the rule of force, whether in home or in foreign affairs—what are they but barriers against the boundless iniquity of mankind? Does not all history show that whenever a king is firmly planted on the throne, and his people reach some degree of prosperity, he uses it to lead his army, like a band of robbers, against adjoining countries? Are not almost all wars ultimately undertaken for purposes of plunder? In the most remote antiquity, and to some extent also in the Middle Age, the conquered became slaves—in other words, they had to work for those who conquered them ; and where is the difference between that and paying war-taxes, which represent the product of previous work?

All war, says Voltaire, is a matter of robbery ; and the Germans should take that as a warning.

§ 30. No man is so formed that he can be left entirely to himself, to go his own ways; every one needs to be guided by a preconceived plan, and to follow certain general rules. But if this is carried too far, and a man tries to take on a character which is not natural or innate in him, but is artificially acquired and evolved merely by a process of reasoning, he will very soon discover that Nature cannot be forced, and that if you drive it out, it will return despite your efforts :

"Naturam expellas furca, tamen usque recurret."

To understand a rule governing conduct toward others, even to discover it for one's self and to express it neatly, is easy enough ; and still, very soon afterward, the rule may be broken in practice. But that is no reason for despair ; and you need not fancy that as it is impossible to regulate your life in accordance with abstract ideas and maxims, it is better to live just as you please. Here, as in all theoretical instruction that aims at a practical result, the first thing to do is to understand the rule ; the second thing is to learn the practice of it. The theory may be understood at once by an effort of reason, and yet the practice of it acquired only in course of time.

A pupil may learn the various notes on an instrument of music, or the different positions in fencing ; and when he makes a mistake, as he is sure to do, however hard he tries, he is apt to think it will be impossible to observe the rules, when he is set to read music at sight or challenged to a furious duel. But for all that, gradual practice makes him perfect, through a long series of slips, blunders and fresh efforts. It is just the same in other things ; in learning to write and speak Latin, a man will forget the grammatical rules; it is only by long practice that a blockhead turns into a courtier, that a passionate man becomes shrewd and worldly-wise, or a frank person reserved, or a noble person ironical. But though self-discipline of this kind is the result of long habit, it always works by a sort of external compulsion, which Nature never ceases to resist and sometimes unexpectedly overcomes. The difference between action in accordance with abstract principles, and action as the result of original innate tendency, is the same as that between a work of art, say a watch—where form and movement are impressed upon shapeless and inert matter—and a living organism, where form and matter are one, and each is inseparable from the other.

There is a maxim attributed to the Emperor Napoleon, which expresses this relation between acquired and innate character, and confirms what I have said: "everything that is unnatural is imperfect "—a rule of universal application, whether in the physical or in the moral sphere. The only exception I can think of to this rule is aventurine,* a substance known to mineralogists, which in its natural state cannot compare with the artificial preparation of it.

And in this connection let me utter a word of protest against any and every form of affectation. It always arouses contempt ; in the first place, because it argues deception, and the deception is cowardly, for it is based on fear; and, secondly, it argues self-condemnation, because it means that a man is trying to appear what he is not, and therefore something which he thinks better than he actually is.

---

* *Translator's Note*—Aventurine is a rare kind of quartz ; and the same name is given to a brownish-colored glass much resembling it, which is manufactured at Murano. It is so called from the fact that the glass was discovered by chance (*avventura*).

To affect a quality, and to plume yourself upon it, is just
to confess that you have not got it.   Whether it is courage,
or learning, or intellect, or wit, or success with women, or
riches, or social position, or whatever else it may be that
a man boasts of, you may conclude by his boasting about
it that that is precisely the direction in which he is rather
weak ; for if a man possesses any faculty to the full, it will
not occur to him to make a great show of affecting it ;
he is quite content to know that he has it.   That is the
application of the Spanish proverb: *herradura que chacolo-
tea clavo le falta*—a clattering hoof means a nail gone.
To be sure, as I said at first, no man ought to let the reins
go quite loose, and show himself just as he is; for there are
many evil and bestial sides to our nature which require to
be hidden away out of sight ; and this justifies the negative
attitude of dissimulation, but it does not justify a positive
feigning of qualities which are not there.   It should also
be remembered that affectation is recognized at once, even
before it is clear what it is that is being affected.   And,
finally, affectation cannot last very long and one day the
mask will fall off.   *Nemo potest personam diu ferre fictam*,
says Seneca;* *ficta cito in naturam suam recidunt*—no one
can persevere long in a fictitious character ; for nature will
soon re-assert itself.

§ 31. A man bears the weight of his own body without
knowing it, but he soon feels the weight of any other, if
he tries to move it: in the same way, a man can see other
people's shortcomings and vices, but he is blind to his own.
This arrangement has one advantage: it turns other people
into a kind of mirror, in which a man can see clearly everything that is vicious, faulty, ill-bred and loathsome in his
own nature; only, it is generally the old story of the dog
barking at its own image; it is himself that he sees and not
another dog, as he fancies.

He who criticises others, works at the reformation of
himself.   Those who form the secret habit of scrutinizing
other people's general behavior, and passing severe judgment upon what they do and leave undone, thereby improve
themselves, and work out their own perfection : for they
will have sufficient sense of justice, or at any rate enough

* " De Clementia," I. 1.

pride and vanity, to avoid in their own case that which they condemn so harshly elsewhere. But tolerant people are just the opposite, and claim for themselves the same indulgence that they extend to others—*hanc veniam damus petimusque vicissim.* It is all very well for the Bible to talk about the mote in another's eye and the beam in one's own. The nature of the eye is to look not at itself but at other things; and therefore to observe and blame faults in another is a very suitable way of becoming conscious of one's own. We require a looking-glass for the due dressing of our morals.

The same rule applies in the case of style and fine writing. If, instead of condemning, you applaud some new folly in these matters, you will imitate it. That is just why literary follies have such vogue in Germany. The Germans are a very tolerant people—everybody can see that! Their maxim is—*Hanc veniam damus petimusque vicissim.*

§ 32. When he is young, a man of noble character fancies that the relations prevailing among mankind, and the alliances to which these relations lead, are, at bottom and essentially, ideal in their nature ; that is to say, that they rest upon similarity of disposition or sentiment, or taste, or intellectual power, and so on.

But, later on, he finds out that it is a real foundation which underlies these alliances ; that they are based upon some material interest. This is the true foundation of almost all alliances: nay, most men have no notion of an alliance resting upon any other basis. Accordingly, we find that a man is always measured by the office he holds, or by his occupation, nationality, or family relations—in a word, by the position and character which have been assigned him in the conventional arrangements of life, where he is ticketed and treated as so much goods. Reference to what he is in himself, as a man—to the measure of his own personal qualities–is never made unless for convenience sake: and so that view of a man is something exceptional, to be set aside and ignored, the moment that any one finds it disagreeable; and this is what usually happens. But the more of personal worth a man has, the less pleasure he will take in these conventional arrangements ; and he will try to withdraw from the sphere in which they apply. The

reason why these arrangements exist at all, is simply that
in this world of ours misery and need are the chief ·fea-
tures: therefore it is everywhere the essential and paramount business of life to devise the means of alleviating
them.

§ 33. As paper-money circulates in the world instead of
real coin, so, in the place of true esteem and genuine
friendship, you have the outward appearance of it—a
mimic show made to look as much like the real thing as
possible.

On the other hand, it may be asked whether there are
any people who really deserve the true coin. For my own
part, I should certainly pay more respect to an honest dog
wagging his tail than to a hundred such demonstrations of
human regard.

True and genuine friendship presupposes a strong sympathy with the weal and woe of another—purely objective
in its character and quite disinterested; and this in its turn
means an absolute identification of self with the object of
friendship. The egoism of human nature is so strongly
antagonistic to any such sympathy, that true friendship
belongs to that class of things—the sea-serpent, for instance
—with regard to which no one knows whether they are fabulous or really exist somewhere or other.

Still, in many cases, there is a grain of true and genuine
friendship in the relations of man to man, though generally, of course, some secret personal interest is at the
bottom of them—some one among the many forms that
selfishness can take. But in a world where all is imperfect,
this grain of true feeling is such an ennobling influence
that it gives some warrant for calling those relations by the
name of friendship, for they stand far above the ordinary
friendships that prevail among mankind. The latter are
so constituted that, were you to hear how your dear friends
speak of you behind your back, you would never say
another word to them.

Apart from the case where it would be a real help to you
if your friend were to make some considerable sacrifice to
serve you, there is no better means of testing the genuine-
ness of his feeling than the way in which he receives the
news of a misfortune that has just happened to you. At
that moment the expression of his features will either show

that his one thought is that of true and sincere sympathy for you; or else the absolute composure of his countenance, or the passing trace of something other than sympathy, will confirm the well-known maxim of La Rochefoucauld: *Dans l'adversité de nos meilleurs amis, nous trouvons toujours quelque chose qui ne nous déplait pas.* Indeed, at such a moment, the ordinary so-called friend will find it hard to suppress the signs of a slight smile of pleasure. There are few ways by which you can make more certain of putting people into a good humor than by telling them of some trouble that has recently befallen you, or by unreservedly disclosing some personal weakness of yours. How characteristic this is of humanity!

Distance and long absence are always prejudicial to friendship, however, disinclined a man may be to admit it. Our regard for people whom we do not see—even though they be our dearest friends—gradually dries up in the course of years, and they become abstract notions; so that our interest in them grows to be more and more intellectual—nay, it is kept up only as a kind of tradition; while we retain a lively and deep interest in those who are constantly before our eyes, even if they be only pet animals. This shows how much men are limited by their senses, and how true is the remark that Goethe makes in "Tasso" about the dominant influence of the present moment:

"Die Gegenwart ist eine mächtige Göttin." *

"Friends of the house" are very rightly so called; because they are friends of the house rather than of its master; in other words, they are more like cats than dogs.

Your friends will tell you that they are sincere; your enemies are really so. Let your enemies' censure be like a bitter medicine, to be used as a means of self-knowledge.

A friend in need, as the saying goes, is rare. Nay, it is just the contrary; no sooner have you made a friend than he is in need, and asks you for a loan.

§ 34. A man must be still a greenhorn in the ways of the world, if he imagines that he can make himself popular in

---

* Act iv., sc. 4.

society by exhibiting intelligence and discernment. With
the immense majority of people, such qualities excite hatred
and resentment, which are rendered all the harder to bear
by the fact that people are obliged to suppress—even from
themselves—the real reason of their anger.

What actually takes place is this. A man feels and perceives that the person with whom he is conversing is intellectually very much his superior. He thereupon secretly
and half-unconsciously concludes that his interlocutor must
form a proportionately low and limited estimate of his
abilities. That is a method of reasoning—an enthymeme—
which rouses the bitterest feelings of sullen and rancorous
hatred.* And so Gracian is quite right in saying that the
only way to win affection from people is to show the most
animal-like simplicity of demeanor—*para ser bien quisto,
el unico medio vestirse la piel del mas simple de los brutos.†*

To show your intelligence and discernment is only an
indirect way of reproaching other people for being dull and
incapable. And besides, it is natural for a vulgar man to
be violently agitated by the sight of opposition in any form
and in this case envy comes in as the secret cause of his
hostility. For it is a matter of daily observation that
people take the greatest pleasure in that which satisfies
their vanity; and vanity cannot be satisfied without comparison with others. Now, there is nothing of which a
man is prouder than of intellectual ability, for it is this
that gives him his commanding place in the animal world.
It is an exceedingly rash thing to let any one see that you
are decidedly superior to him in this respect, and to let

---

* Cf. "Welt als Wille und Vorstellung," Bk. II. p. 256 (4th
Edit.), where I quote from Dr. Johnson, and from Merck, the friend
of Goethe's youth. The former says: "There is nothing by which a
man exasperates most people more, than by displaying a superior
ability of brilliancy in conversation. They seem pleased at the time,
but their envy makes them curse him at their hearts." (Boswell's
" Life of Johnson," aetat: 74.)

† *Translator's Note.*—Balthazar Gracian " Oraculo manuel,y arte
de prudencia," 240. Gracian (1584–1658) was a Spanish prose writer
and Jesuit, whose works deal chiefly with the observation of character in the various phenomena of life. Schopenhauer, among others,
had a great admiration for his worldly philosophy, and translated his
" Oraculo manuel "—a system of rules for the conduct of life—into
German. The same book was translated into English toward the
close of the seventeeth century.

other people see it too; because he will then thirst for vengeance, and generally look about for an opportunity of
taking it by means of insult, because this is to pass from
the sphere of intellect to that of will—and there all are on
an equal footing as regards the feeling of hostility. Hence,
while rank and riches may always reckon upon deferential
treatment in society, that is something which intellectual
ability can never expect; to be ignored is the greatest favor
shown to it; and if people notice it at all, it is because they
regard it as a piece of impertinence, or else as something
to which its possessor has no legitimate right, and upon
which he dares to pride himself; and in retaliation and
revenge for his conduct, people secretly try and humiliate
him in some other way; and if they wait to do this, it is
only for a fitting opportunity. A man may be as humble
as possible in his demeanor, and yet hardly ever get people
to overlook his crime in standing intellectually above
them. In the "Garden of Roses," Sadi makes the remark :
"You should know that foolish people are a hundredfold
more averse to meeting the wise than the wise are indis-
posed for the company of the foolish."

On the other hand, it is a real recommendation to be
stupid. For just as warmth is agreeable to the body, so it
does the mind good to feel its superiority ; and a man will
seek company likely to give him this feeling, as instinctively as he will approach the fireplace or walk in the sun
if he wants to get warm. But this means that he will be
disliked on account of his superiority ; and if a man is to
be liked, he must really be inferior in point of intellect ;
and the same thing holds good of a woman in point of
beauty. To give proof of real and unfeigned inferiority to
some of the people you meet—that is a very difficult business indeed !

Consider how kindly and heartily a girl who is passably
pretty will welcome one who is downright ugly. Physical
advantages are not thought so much of in the case of man,
though I suppose you would rather a little man sat next to
you than one who was bigger than yourself. This is why,
among men, it is the dull and ignorant, and among women
the ugly, who are always popular and in request. It is
likely to be said of such people that they are extremely
good-natured, because every one wants to find a pretext for
caring about them—a pretext which will blind both himself

and other people to the real reason why he likes them.
This is also why mental superiority of any sort always tends
to isolate its possessor : people run away from him out of
pure hatred, and say all manner of bad things about him
by way of justifying their action.* Beauty, in the case of
women, has a similar effect : very pretty girls have no
friends of their own sex, and they even find it hard to get
another girl to keep them company. A handsome woman
should always avoid applying for a position as companion,
because the moment she enters the room, her prospective
mistress will scowl at her beauty, as a piece of folly with
which, both for her own and for her daughters' sake, she
can very well dispense. But if the girl has advantages of
rank, the case is very different ; because rank, unlike personal qualities which work by the force of mere contrast,
produces its effect by a process of reflection ; much in the
same way as the particular hue of a person's complexion
depends upon the prevailing tone of his immediate surroundings.

§ 35. Our trust in other people often consists in great
measure of pure laziness, selfishness and vanity on our own
part : I say laziness, because, instead of making inquiries
ourselves, and exercising an active care we prefer to trust
others ; selfishness, because we are led to confide in people
by the pressure of our own affairs ; and vanity, when we
ask confidence for a matter on which we rather pride ourselves. And yet, for all that, we expect people to be true
to the trust we repose in them.

But we ought not to become angry if people put no

---

* If you desire to get on in the world, friends and acquaintances are
by far the best passport to fortune. The possession of a great deal
of ability makes a man proud, and therefore not apt to flatter those
who have very little, and from whom, on that account, the possession
of great ability should be carefully concealed. The consciousness of
small intellectual power has just the opposite effect, and is very compatible with a humble, affable and companionable nature, and with
respect for what is mean and wretched. This is why an inferior sort
of man has so many people to befriend and encourage him.

These remarks are applicable not only to advancement in political
life, but to all competition for places of honor and dignity, nay, even
for reputation in the world of science, literature and art. In learned
societies, for example, mediocrity—that very acceptable quality—is
always to the fore, while merit meets with tardy recognition, or
with none at all. So it is in everything.

trust in us : because that really means that they pay honesty the sincere compliment of regarding it as a very rare thing, so rare, indeed, as to leave us in doubt whether its existence is not merely fabulous.

§ 36. Politeness, which the Chinese hold to be a cardinal virtue, is based upon two considerations of policy. I have explained one of these considerations in my "Ethics" * ; the other is as follows : Politeness is a tacit agreement that people's miserable defects, whether moral or intellectual, shall on either side be ignored and not made the subject of reproach ; and since these defects are thus rendered somewhat less obtrusive, the result is mutually advantageous.

It is a wise thing to be polite ; consequently, it is a stupid thing to be rude. To make enemies by unnecessary and willful incivility, is just as insane a proceeding as to set your house on fire. For politeness is like a counter—an avowedly false coin, with which it is foolish to be stingy. A sensible man will be generous in the use of it. It is customary in every country to end a letter with the words : " your most obedient servant "—*votre tres-humble serviteur—suo devotissimo servo.* (The Germans are the only people who suppress the word servant—*diener*—because, of course, it is not true !) However, to carry politeness to such an extent as to damage your prospects, is like giving money where only counters are expected.

Wax, a substance naturally hard and brittle, can be made soft by the application of a little warmth, so that it will take any shape you please. In the same way, by being polite and friendly, you can make people pliable and obliging, even though they are apt to be crabbed and malevolent. Hence politeness is to human nature what warmth is to wax.

Of course, it is no easy matter to be polite ; in so far, I mean, as it requires us to show great respect for everybody,

* *Translator's Note.*—In the passage referred to ("Grundlage der Moral," collected works, Vol. IV. pp. 187 and 198), Schopenhauer explains politeness as a conventional and systematic attempt to mask the egoism of human nature in the small affairs of life—an egoism so repulsive that some such device is necessary for the purpose of concealing its ugliness. The relation which politeness bears to the true love of one's neighbor is analogous to that existing between justice as an affair of legality, and justice as the real integrity of the heart.

whereas most people deserve none at all ; and again in so far as it demands that we should feign the most lively interest in people, when we must be very glad that we have nothing to do with them. To combine politeness with pride is a masterpiece of wisdom.

We should be much less ready to lose our temper over an insult—which, in the strict sense of the word, means that we have not been treated with respect—if, on the one hand, we had not such an exaggerated estimate of our value and dignity—that is to say, if we were not so immensely proud of ourselves ; and, on the other hand, if we had arrived at any clear notion of the judgment which, in his heart, one man generally passes upon another. If most people resent the slightest hint that any blame attaches to them, you may imagine their feelings if they were to overhear what their acquaintances say about them. You should never lose sight of the fact that ordinary politeness is only a grinning mask : if it shifts its place a little, or is removed for a moment, there is no use raising a hue and cry. When a man is downright rude, it is as though he had taken off all his clothes, and stood before you *in puris naturalibus*. Like most men in this condition, he does not present a very attractive appearance.

§ 37. You ought never to take any man as a model for what you should do or leave undone ; because position and circumstances are in no two cases alike, and difference of character gives a peculiar, individual tone to what a man does. Hence *duo cum faciunt idem, non est idem*—two persons may do the same thing with a different result. A man should act in accordance with his own character, as soon as he has carefully deliberated on what he is about to do.

The outcome of this is that originality cannot be dispensed with in practical matters : otherwise, what a man does will not accord with what he is.

§ 38. Never combat any man's opinion ; for though you reached the age of Methuselah, you would never have done setting him right upon all the absurd things that he believes.

It is also well to avoid correcting people's mistakes in conversation, however good your intentions may be ; for it is easy to offend people, and difficult, if not impossible, to mend them.

If you feel irritated by the absurd remarks of two people whose conversation you happen to overhear, you should imagine that you are listening to the dialogue of two fools in a comedy. *Probatum est.*

The man who comes into the world with the notion that he is really going to instruct it in matters of the highest importance, may thank his stars if he escapes with a whole skin.

§ 39. If you want your judgment to be accepted, express it coolly and without passion. All violence has its seat in the will; and so, if your judgment is expressed with vehemence, people will consider it an effort of will, and not the outcome of knowledge, which is in its nature cold and unimpassioned. Since the will is the primary and radical element in human nature, and intellect merely supervenes as something secondary, people are more likely to believe that the opinion you express with so much vehemence is due to the excited state of your will, rather than that the excitement of the will comes only from the ardent nature of your opinion.

§ 40. Even when you are fully justified in praising yourself, you should never be seduced into doing so. For vanity is so very common, and merit so very uncommon, that even if a man appears to be praising himself, though very indirectly, people will be ready to lay a hundred to one that he is talking out of pure vanity, and that he has not sense enough to see what a fool he is making of himself.

Still, for all that, there may be some truth in Bacon's remark that, as in the case of calumny, if you throw enough dirt, some of it will stick, so it is also in regard to self-praise; with the conclusion that self-praise, in small doses, is to be recommended.*

---

* *Translator's Note.*—Schopenhauer alludes to the following passage in Bacon's "De Augmentis Scientiarum," Bk. viii., ch. 2: *Sicut enim dici solet de calumnia,* audacter calumniare, semper aliquid haeret : *sic dici potest de jacantia* (*nisi plane deformis fuerit et ridicula*), audacter te vendita, semper aliquid haeret. *Haerebeit certe apud populum licet prudentiores subrideant. Itaque existimatio parta apud plurimos paucorum fastidium abunde compensabit.*

§ 41. If you have reason to suspect that a person is telling you a lie, look as though you believed every word he said. This will give him courage to go on; he will become more vehement in his assertions, and in the end betray himself.

Again, if you perceive that a person is trying to conceal something from you, but with only partial success, look as though you did not believe him. This opposition on your part will provoke him into leading out his reserve of truth and bringing the whole force of it to bear upon your incredulity.

§ 42. You should regard all your private affairs as secrets, and, in respect of them, treat your acquaintances, even though you are on good terms with them, as perfect strangers, letting them know nothing more than they can see for themselves. For in course of time, and under altered circumstances, you may find it a disadvantage that they know even the most harmless things about you.

And, as a general rule, it is more advisable to show your intelligence by saying nothing than by speaking out; for silence is a matter of prudence, while speech has something in it of vanity. The opportunities for displaying the one or the other quality occur equally often; but the fleeting satisfaction afforded by speech is often preferred to the permanent advantage secured by silence.

The feeling of relief which lively people experience in speaking aloud when no one is listening, should not be indulged, lest it grow into a habit; for in this way thought establishes such very friendly terms with speech, that conversation is apt to become a process of thinking aloud. Prudence exacts that a wide gulf should be fixed between what we think and what we say.

At times we fancy that people are utterly unable to believe in the truth of some statement affecting us personally, whereas it never occurs to them to doubt it, but if we give them the slightest opportunity of doubting it, they find it absolutely impossible to believe it any more. We often betray ourselves into revealing something, simply because we suppose that people cannot help noticing it—just as a man will throw himself down from a great height because he loses his head, in other words, because he fancies that he cannot retain a firm footing any longer; the torment of his position is so great, that he thinks it better to put an end to it at once. This is the kind of insanity which is called *acrophobia*.

But it should not be forgotten how clever people are in regard to affairs which do not concern them, even though they show no particular sign of acuteness in other matters. This is a kind of algebra in which people are very proficient: give them a single fact to go upon, and they will solve the most complicated problems. So, if you wish to relate some event that happened long ago, without mentioning any names, or otherwise indicating the persons to whom you refer, you should be very careful not to introduce into your narrative anything that might point, however distantly, to some definite fact, whether it is a particular locality or a date, or the name of some one who was only to a small extent implicated, or anything else that was even remotely connected with the event; for that at once gives people something positive to go upon, and by the aid of their talent for this sort of algebra, they will discover all the rest. Their curiosity in these matters becomes a kind of enthusiasm; their will spurs on their intellect, and drives it forward to the attainment of the most remote results. For however unsusceptible and indifferent people may be to general and universal truths, they are very ardent in the matter of particular details.

In keeping with what I have said, it will be found that all those who profess to give instruction in the wisdom of life are specially urgent in commending the practice of silence, and assign manifold reasons why it should be observed; so it is not necessary for me to enlarge upon the subject any further. However, I may just add one or two little known Arabian proverbs, which occur to me as peculiarly appropriate:

"Do not tell a friend anything that you would conceal from an enemy."

"A secret is in my custody, if I keep it; but should it escape me, it is I who am the prisoner."

" The tree of silence bears the fruit of peace."

§ 43. Money is never spent to so much advantage as when you have been cheated out of it; for at one stroke you have purchased prudence.

§ 44. If possible, no animosity should be felt for any one. But carefully observe and remember the manner in which a man conducts himself, so that you may take the measure of his value—at any rate in regard to yourself— and regulate your bearing toward him accordingly; never losing sight of the fact that character is unalterable, and that to forget the bad features in a man's disposition is like throwing away hard-won money. Thus you will protect yourself against the results of unwise intimacy and foolish friendship.

" Give way neither to love nor to hate," is one half of worldly wisdom: " say nothing and believe nothing," the other half. Truly, a world where there is need of such rules as this and the following, is one upon which a man may well turn his back.

§ 45. To speak angrily to a person, to show your hatred by what you say or by the way you look, is an unnecessary proceeding—dangerous, foolish, ridiculous, and vulgar.

Anger or hatred should never be shown otherwise than in what you do; and feelings will be all the more effective in action, in so far as you avoid the exhibition of them in any other way. It is only cold blooded animals whose bite is poisonous.

§ 46. To speak without emphasizing your words—*parler sans accent*—is an old rule with those who are wise in the world's ways. It means that you should leave other people to discover what it is that you have said; and as their minds are slow, you can make your escape in time. On the other hand, to emphasize your meaning—*parler avec accent*—is to address their feelings; and the result is always the opposite of what you expect. If you are only polite enough in your manner and courteous in your tone there are many people whom you may abuse outright, and yet run no immediate risk of offending them.

CHAPTER IV.

WORLDLY FORTUNE.

§ 47. However varied the forms that human destiny may take, the same elements are always present; and so life is everywhere much of a piece, whether it is passed in the cottage or in the palace, in the barrack or in the cloister. Alter the circumstances as much as you please! point to strange adventures, successes, failures! life is like a sweet-shop, where there is a great variety of things, odd in shape and diverse in color—one and all made from the same paste. And when men speak of some one's success, the lot of the man who has failed is not so very different as it seems. The inequalities in the world are like the combinations in a kaleidoscope; at every turn a fresh picture strikes the eye; and yet, in reality, you see only the same bits of glass as you saw before.

§ 48. An ancient writer says, very truly, that there are three great powers in the world: Sagacity, Strength, and Luck—σύνεσις, κράτος, τύχη. I think the last is the most efficacious.

A man's life is like the voyage of a ship, where luck—*secunda aut adversa fortuna*—acts the part of the wind, and speeds the vessel on its way or drives it far out of its course. All that the man can do for himself is of little avail; like the rudder, which, if worked hard and continu-ously, may help in the navigation of the ship; and yet all may be lost again by a sudden squall. But if the wind is only in the right quarter, the ship will sail on so as not to need any steering. The power of luck is nowhere better ex-pressed than in a certain Spanish proverb: *Daventura a tu hijo, y echa lo en el mar*—give your son luck and throw him into the sea.

Still, chance, it may be said, is a malignant power, and as little as possible should be left to its agency. And yet where is there any giver who, in dispensing gifts, tells us quite clearly that we have no right to them, and that we owe them not to any merit on our part but wholly to the goodness and grace of the giver—at the same time allow-ing us to cherish the joyful hope of receiving in all humility. further undeserved gifts from the same hands—where is there any giver like that, unless it be Chance? who understands the kingly art of showing the recipient that all merit is powerless and unavailing against the royal grace and favor.

On looking back over the course of his life—that laby-rinthine way of error—a man must see many points where

luck failed him and misfortune came; and then it is easy to
carry self-reproach to an unjust excess.   For the course of
a man's life is in no wise entirely of his own making: it is
the product of two factors—the series of things that happened and his own resolves in regard to them. and these
two are constantly interacting upon and modifying each
other.   And besides these, another influence is at work in
the very limited extent of a man's horizon, whether it is
that he cannot see very far ahead in respect of the plans he
will adopt, or that he is still less able to predict the course
of future events: his knowledge is strictly confined to present plans and present events.   Hence, as long as a man's
goal is far off, he cannot steer straight for it; he must be
content to make a course that is approximately right;
and in following the direction in which he thinks he ought
to go, he will often have occasion to tack.

All that a man can do is to form such resolves as from
time to time accord with the circumstances in which he is
placed, in the hope of thus managing to advance a step
nearer toward the final goal.   It is usually the case that
the position in which we stand, and the object at which we
aim, resemble two tendencies working with dissimilar
strength in different directions ; and the course of our life
is represented by their diagonal, or resultant force.

Terence makes the remark that life is like a game at
dice, where if the number that turns up is not precisely the
one you want, you can still contrive to use it equally well :
—*in vita est hominum quasi cum ludas tesseris ; si illud
quod maxime opus est jactu non cadit, illud quod cecidit
forte, id arte ut corrigas.** Or, to put the matter
more shortly, life is like a game of cards, when the cards
are shuffled and dealt by fate.   But for my present purpose, the most suitable simile would be that of a game
of chess, where the plan we determined to follow is
conditioned by the play of our rival—in life, by the
caprice of fate.   We are compelled to modify our tactics,
often to such an extent that, as we carry them out, hardly
a single feature of the original plan can be recognized.

But above and beyond all this, there is another influence
that makes itself felt in our lives.   It is a trite saying

---

* He seems to have been referring to a game something like
backgammon.

—only too frequently true—that we are often more foolish than we think. On the other hand, we are often wiser than we fancy ourselves to be. This, however, is a discovery which only those can make, of whom it is really true ; and it takes them a long time to make it. Our brains are not the wisest part of us. In the great moments of life, when a man decides upon an important step, his action is directed not so much by any clear knowledge of the right thing to do, as by an inner impulse—you may almost call it an instinct—proceeding from the deepest foundations of his being. If, later on he attempts to criticise his action by the light of hard and fast ideas of what is right in the abstract—those unprofitable ideas which are learned by rote, or, it may be, borrowed from other people ; if he begins to apply general rules, the principles which have guided others, to his own case, without sufficiently weighing the maxim that one man's meat is another's poison, then he will run great risk of doing himself an injustice. The result will show where the right course lay. It is only when a man has reached the happy age of wisdom that he is capable of just judgment in regard either to his own actions or to those of others.

It may be that this impulse or instinct is the unconscious effect of a kind of prophetic dream which is forgotten when we awake—lending our life a uniformity of tone, a dramatic unity, such as could never result from the unstable moments of consciousness, when we are so easily led into error, so liable to strike a false note. It is in virtue of some such prophetic dream that a man feels himself called to great achievements in a special sphere, and works in that direction from his youth up out of an inner and secret feeling that that is his true path, just as by a similar instinct the bee is led to build up its cells in the comb. This is the impulse which Balthazar Gracian calls *la gran sindéresis*,*—the great power of moral discernment : it is

---

* *Translator's Note.*—This obscure word appears to be derived from the Greek συντηρέω (N.T. and Polyb.) meaning "to observe strictly." It occurs in " The Doctor and Student " a series of dialogues between a doctor of divinity and a student on the laws of England, first published in 1518; and is there (Dialog. I. ch. 13) explained as " a natural power of the soule, set in the highest part thereof, moving and stirring it to good, and abhorring evil." This passage is copied into Milton's Commonplace Book, edit. Horwood, § 79. The word is also found in the Dictionary of the Spanish Academy (vol. vi. of the year

something that a man instinctively feels to be his salvation,
without which he were lost.

To act in accordance with abstract principles is a difficult
matter, and a great deal of practice will be required before
you can be even occasionally successful ; it often happens
that the principles do not fit in with your particular case.
But every man has certain innate concrete principles—a
part, as it were, of the very blood that flows in his veins,
the sum or result, in fact, of all his thoughts, feelings and
volitions. Usually he has no knowledge of them in any
abstract form ; it is only when he looks back upon the
course his life has taken, that he becomes aware of having
been always led on by them—as though they formed an
invisible clue which he had followed unawares.

§ 49. That Time works great changes, and that all
things are in their nature fleeting—these are truths that
should never be forgotten. Hence, in whatever case you
may be, it is well to picture to yourself the opposite : in
prosperity to be mindful of misfortune ; in friendship, of
enmity ; in good weather, of days when the sky is overcast;
in love, of hatred ; in moments of trust, to imagine the be-
trayal that will make you regret your confidence ; and so,
too, when you are in evil plight, to have a lively sense of
happier times—what a lasting source of true worldly wisdom
were there ! We should then always reflect, and not be so
very easily deceived ; because, in general, we should anticipate the very changes that the years will bring.

Perhaps in no form of knowledge is personal experience
so indispensable as in learning to see that all things are unstable and transitory in this world. There is nothing that,
in its own place and for the time it lasts, is not a product
of necessity, and therefore capable of being fully justified ;
and it is this fact that makes the circumstances of every
year, every month, even of every day, seem as though they
might maintain their right to last to all eternity. But we

1739) in the sense of an innate discernment of moral principles, where
a quotation is given from Madre Maria de Jesus, abbess of the convent
of the Conception at Agreda, a mystical writer of the seventeenth
century, frequently consulted by Philip IV.—and again in the Bologn-
ese Dictionary of 1824, with a similar meaning, illustrated from the
writings of Salvini (1653-1729). For these references I am indebted
to the kindness of Mr. Norman Maccoll.

know that this can never be the case, and that in a world where all is fleeting, change alone endures. He is a prudent man who is not only undeceived by apparent stability, but is able to forecast the lines upon which movement will take place.*

But people generally think that present circumstances will last, and that matters will go on in the future much as they have done in the past. Their mistake arises from the fact that they do not understand the causes of the things they see—causes which, unlike the effects they produce, contain in themselves the germ of future change. The effects are all that people know, and they hold fast to them on the supposition that those unknown causes, which were sufficient to bring them about, will also be able to maintain them as they are. This is a very common error; and the fact that it is common is not without its advantage, for it means that people always err in unison; and hence the calamity which results from the error affects all alike, and is therefore easy to bear; whereas, if a philosopher makes a mistake, he is alone in his error, and so at a double disadvantage.†

But in saying that we should anticipate the effects of time, I mean that we should mentally forecast what they are likely to be; I do not mean that we should practically forestall them, by demanding the immediate performance of promises which time alone can fulfill. The man who makes this demand will find out that there is no worse or more exacting usurer than Time; and that, if you compel Time to give money in advance, you will have to pay a rate

---

* Chance plays so great a part in all human affairs that when a man tries to ward off a remote danger by present sacrifice, the danger often vanishes under some new and unforeseen development of events; and then the sacrifice, in addition to being a complete loss, brings about such an altered state of things as to be in itself a source of positive danger in the face of this new development. In taking measures of precaution, then, it is well not to look too far ahead, but to reckon with chance; and often to oppose a courageous front to a danger, in the hope that, like many a dark thunder-cloud, it may pass away without breaking.

† I may remark, parenthically, that all this is a confirmation of the principle laid down in " Die Welt als Wille und Vorstellung," (Bk. I. p. 94: 4th edit.), that error always consists in making a wrong inference, that is, in ascribing a given effect to something that does not cause it.

of interest more ruinous than any Jew would require. It is possible, for instance, to make a tree burst forth into leaf, blossom, or even bear fruit within a few days, by the application of unslaked lime and artificial heat; but after that the tree will wither away. So a young man may abuse his strength—it may be only for a few weeks—by trying to do at nineteen what he could easily manage at thirty, and Time may give him the loan for which he asks; but the interest he will have to pay comes out of the strength of his later years; nay, it is part of his very life itself.

There are some kinds of illness in which entire restoration to health is possible only by letting the complaint run its natural course; after which it disappears without leaving any trace of its existence. But if the sufferer is very impatient, and while he is still affected, insists that he is completely well, in this case, too, Time will grant the loan, and the complaint may be shaken off; but life-long weakness and chronic mischief will be the interest paid upon it.

Again, in time of war or general disturbance, a man may require ready money at once, and have to sell out his investments in land or consols for a third or even a still smaller fraction of the sum he would have received for them, if he could have waited for the market to right itself, which would have happened in due course; but he compels Time to grant him a loan, and his loss is the interest he has to pay. Or perhaps he wants to go on a long journey and requires the money: in one or two years he could lay by a sufficient sum out of his income, but he cannot afford to wait; and so he either borrows it or deducts it from his capital; in other words, he gets Time to lend him the money in advance. The interest he pays is a disordered state of his accounts, and permanent and increasing deficits, which he can never make good.

Such is Time's usury; and all who cannot wait are its victims. There is no more thriftless proceeding than to try and mend the measured pace of Time. Be careful, then, not to become its debtor.

§ 50. In the daily affairs of life, you will have very many opportunities of recognizing a characteristic difference between ordinary people and people of prudence and discretion. In estimating the possibility of danger in connection with any undertaking, an ordinary man will confine his inquiries to the kind of risk that has already attended such undertakings in the past ; whereas a prudent person will look ahead, and consider everything that might possibly happen in the future, having regard to a certain Spanish maxim : *lo que no acaece en un año, acaece en un rato*—a thing may not happen in a year, and yet may happen within two minutes.

The difference in question is, of course, quite natural ; for it requires some amount of discernment to calculate possibilities ; but a man need only have his senses about him to see what has already happened.

Do not omit to sacrifice to evil spirits. What I mean is, that a man should not hesitate about spending time, trouble, and money, or giving up his comfort, or restricting his aims and denying himself, if he can thereby shut the door on the possibility of misfortune. The most terrible misfortunes are also the most improbable and remote—the least likely to occur. The rule I am giving is best exemplified in the practice of insurance—a public sacrifice made on the altar of anxiety. Therefore take out your policy of insurance !

§ 51. Whatever fate befalls you, do not give way to great rejoicings or great lamentation ; partly because all things are full of change, and your fortune may turn at any moment ; partly because men are so apt to be deceived in their judgment as to what is good or bad for them.

Almost every one in his time has lamented over something which afterwards turned out to be the very best thing for him that could have happened—or rejoiced at an event which became the source of his greatest sufferings. The right state of mind has been finely portrayed by Shakespeare :

> " I have felt so many quirks of joy and grief
> That the first face of neither, on the start,
> Can Woman me unto't.*

And, in general, it may be said that, if a man takes misfortunes quietly, it is because he knows that very many

---

* " All's Well that Ends Well," *Act iii. Sc.* 2.

dreadful things may happen in the course of life ; and so
he looks upon the trouble of the moment as only a very
small part of that which might come.   This is the Stoic
temper—never to be unmindful of the sad fate of humanity—*condicionis humanæ oblitus ;* but always to remember
that our existence is full of woe and misery, and that the
ills to which we are exposed are innumerable.   Wherever
he be, a man need only cast a look around, to revive the
sense of human misery : there before his eyes he can see
mankind struggling and floundering in torment—all for
the sake of a wretched existence, barren and unprofitable !
If he remembers this, a man will not expect very much
from life, but learn to accommodate himself to a world
where all is relative and no perfect state exists ; always
looking misfortune in the face, and if he cannot avoid it,
meeting it with courage.

It should never be forgotten that misfortune, be it great
or small, is the element in which we live.   But that is no
reason why a man should indulge in fretful complaints,
and, like Beresford,* pull a long face over the " Miseries
of Human Life "—and not a single hour is free from them ;
or still less, call upon the Deity at every flea-bite—*in
pulicis morsu Deum invocare.*   Our aim should be to look
well about us, to ward off misfortune by going to meet it,
to attain such perfection and refinement in averting the
disagreeble things of life—whether they come from our
fellow-men or from the physical world—that, like a clever
fox, we may slip out of the way of every mishap, great or
small ; remembering that a mishap is generally only our
own awkwardness in disguise.

The main reason why misfortune falls less heavily upon us,
if we have looked upon its occurrence as not impossible, and,
as the saying is, prepared ourselves for it, may be this : if,
before the misfortune comes, we have quietly thought over
it as something which may or may not happen, the whole
of its extent and range is known to us, and we can, at least,
determine how far it will affect us ; so that, if it really
arrives, it does not depress us unduly—its weight is not
felt to be greater than it actually is.   But if no preparation

---

* *Translator's Note.*—Rev. James Beresford (1764-1840), miscel-
laneous writer.   The full title of this, his chief work, is " The
Miseries of Human Life ; or the last groans of Timothy Testy and
Samuel Sensitive, with a few supplementary sighs from Mrs. Testy."

has been made to meet it, and it comes unexpectedly, the mind is in a state of terror for the moment and unable to measure the full extent of the calamity ; it seems so far-reaching in its effects that the victim might well think there was no limit to them in any case, its range is exaggerated. In the same way, darkness and uncertainty always increase the sense of danger. And, of course, if we have thought over the possibility of misfortune, we have also at the same time considered the sources to which we shall look for help and consolation ; or, at any rate, we have accustomed ourselves to the idea of it.

There is nothing that better fits us to endure the misfortunes of life with composure, than to know for certain that everything that happens—from the smallest up to the greatest facts of existence—happens of necessity.* A man soon accommodates himself to the inevitable—to something that must be ; and if he knows that nothing can happen except of necessity, he will see that things cannot be other than they are, and that even the strangest chances in the world are just as much a product of necessity as phenomena which obey well-known rules and turn out exactly in accordance with expectation. Let me here refer to what I have said elsewhere on the soothing effect of the knowledge that all things are inevitable and a product of necessity.†

If a man is steeped in the knowledge of this truth, he will, first of all, do what he can, and then readily endure what he must.

We may regard the petty vexations of life that are constantly happening, as designed to keep us in practice for bearing great misfortunes, so that we may not become completely enervated by a career of prosperity. A man should be a Siegfried, armed *cap-à-pie*, toward the small troubles of every day—those little differences we have with our fellow-men, insignificant disputes, unbecoming conduct in other people, petty gossip, and many other similar annoyances of life ; he should not feel them at all, much less take them to heart and brood over them, but hold them at

---

* This is a truth which I have firmly established in my prize-essay on the "Freedom of the Will," where the reader will find a detailed explanation of the grounds on which it rests. Cf. especially p. 60. [Schopenhauer's Works, 4th Edit., vol. iv.—*Tr.*]

† Cf. "Welt als Wille und Vorstellung," Bk. I. p. 361 (4th edit.).

arm's length and push them out of his way, like stones
that lie in the road, and upon no account think about them
and give them a place in his reflections.

§ 52.   What people commonly call "Fate" is, as a general rule, nothing but their own stupid and foolish conduct
There is a fine passage in Homer,* illustrating the truth ol
this remark, where the poet praises μῆτις—shrewd counsel;
and his advice is worthy of all attention.   For if wickedness is atoned for only in another world, stupidity gets its
reward here—although, now and then, mercy may be
shown to the offender.

It is not ferocity but cunning that strikes fear into the
heart and forebodes danger; so true it is that the human
brain is a more terrible weapon than the lion's paw.

The most finished man of the world would be one who
was never irresolute and never in a hurry.

§ 53.   Courage comes next to prudence as a quality of
mind very essential to happiness.   It is quite true that no one
can endow himself with either, since a man inherits prudence from his mother and courage from his father ; still,
if he has these qualities, he can do much to develop them
by means of resolute exercise.

In this world, "where the game is played with loaded
dice," a man must have a temper of iron, with armor proof
to the blows of fate, and weapons to make his way against
men.   Life is one long battle ; we have to fight at every
step : and Voltaire very rightly says that if we succeed, it
is at the point of the sword, and that we die with the
weapon in our hand—on ne réussit dans ce monde qu'à la
pointe de l'épé, et on meurt les armes à la main.   It is a
cowardly soul that shrinks or grows faint and despondent
as soon as the storm begins to gather, or even when the
first cloud appears on the horizon.   Our motto should be
"No surrender ;" and far from yielding to the ills of life,
let us take fresh courage from misfortune;

"Tu ne cede malis sed contra audentior ito." *

As long as the issue of any matter fraught with peril is

---

* "Iliad," xxiii. 313, sqq.   * Virgil, " Æneid," vi., 95.

still in doubt, and there is yet some possibility left that all may come right, no one should ever tremble or think of anything but resistance—just as a man should not despair of the weather if he can see a bit of blue sky anywhere. Let our attitude be such that we should not quake even if the world fell in ruins about us :

> "Si fractus illabatur orbis
> Impavidum ferient ruinæ." *

Our whole life itself—let alone its blessings—would not be worth such a cowardly trembling and shrinking of the heart. Therefore, let us face life courageously and show a firm front to every ill :

> " Quocirca vivite fortes
> Fortiaque adversis opponite pectora rebus."

Still, it is possible for courage to be carried to an excess and to degenerate into rashness. It may even be said that some amount of fear is necessary, if we are to exist at all in the world, and cowardice is only the exaggerated form of it. This truth has been very well expressed by Bacon, in his account of " Terror Panicus ; " and the etymological account which he gives of its meaning, is very superior to the ancient explanation preserved for us by Plutarch.† He connects the expression with *Pan*, the personification of Nature ;‡ and observes that fear is innate in every living thing ; and, in fact, tends to its preservation, but that it is apt to come into play without due cause, and that man especially exposed to it. The chief feature of this " Panic Terror " is that there is no clear notion of any definite danger bound up with it ; that it presumes rather than knows that danger exists ; and that, in case of need, it pleads fright itself as the reason for being afraid.

---

* Horace, Odes iii. 3.   † " De Iside et Osiride," ch. 14.

‡ " De Sapientia Veterum," c. 6. " Natura enim rerum omnibus viventibus indidit metum ac formidinem, vitæ atque essentiæ suæ conservatricem, ac mala ingruentia vitantem et depellentem. Verumtamen eadem natura modum tenere nescia est : sed timoribus salutaribus semper vanos et innanes admiscet ; adeo ut omnia (si intus conspici darentur) Panicis terroribus plenissima sint, praesertim humana."

CHAPTER V.

THE AGES OF LIFE.

THERE is a very fine saying of Voltaire's to the effect that every age of life has its own peculiar mental character, and that a man will feel completely unhappy if his mind is not in accordance with his years:

> "Qui n'a pas l'esprit de son âge,
>   De son âge a tout le malheur."

It will, therefore, be a fitting close to our speculations upon the nature of happiness, if we glance at the changes which the various periods of life produce in us.

Our whole life long it is the present, and the present alone, that we actually possess; the only difference is that at the beginning of life we look forward to a long future, and that toward the end we look back upon a long past; also that our temperament, but not our character, undergoes certain well-known changes, which make the present wear a different color at each period of life.

I have elsewhere stated that in childhood we are more given to using our intellect than our will; and I have explained why this is so.* It is just for this reason that the first quarter of life is so happy; as we look back upon it in after years, it seem a sort of lost paradise. In childhood our relations with others are limited, our wants are few—in a word, there is little stimulus for the will; and so our chief concern is the extension of our knowledge. The intellect—like the brain, which attains its full size in the seventh year,† is developed early, though it takes time to

---

Translator's Note.—Schopenhauer refers to "Die Welt als Wille und Vorstellung," Bk. II. c. 31, p. 451 (4th. edit.), where he explains that this is due to the fact that at that period of life the brain and nervous system are much more developed than any other part of the organism.

†*Translator's Note.*—This statement is not quite correct. The weight of the brain increases rapidly up to the seventh year, more slowly between the sixteenth and the twentieth year, still more slowly till between thirty and forty years of age, when it attains its maximum. At each decennial period after this, it is supposed to decrease in weight on the average an ounce for every ten years.

mature and it explores the whole world of its surroundings in its constant search for nutriment: it is then that existence is in itself an ever fresh delight, and all things sparkle with the charm of novelty.

This is why the years of childhood are like a long poem. For the function of poetry, as of all art, is to grasp the idea —in the Platonic sense; in other words, to apprehend a particular object in such a way as to perceive its essential nature, the characteristics it has in common with all other objects of the same kind: so that a single object appears as the representative of a class, and the results of one experience hold good for a thousand.

It may be thought that my remarks are opposed to fact, and that the child is never occupied with anything beyond the individual objects or events which are presented to it from time to time, and then only in so far as they interest and excite its will for the moment; but this is not really the case. In those early years, life—in the full meaning of the word, is something so new and fresh, and its sensations are so keen and unblunted by repetition, that, in the midst of all its pursuits and without any clear consciousness of what it is doing, the child is always silently occupied in grasping the nature of life itself—in arriving at its fundamental character and general outline by means of separate scenes and experiences; or, to use Spinoza's phraseology, the child is learning to see the things and persons about it *sub specie æternitatis*—as particular manifestations of universal law.

The younger we are, then, the more does every individual object represent for us the whole class to which it belongs; but as the years increase, this becomes less and less the case. That is the reason why youthful impressions are so different from those of old age. And that is also why the slight knowledge and experience gained in childhood and youth afterward come to stand as the permanent rubric, or heading, for all the knowledge acquired in later life— those early forms of knowledge passing into categories, as it were, under which the results of subsequent experience are classified; though a clear consciousness of what is being done, does not always attend upon the process.

In this way the earliest years of a man's life lay the foundation of his view of the world, whether it be shallow or deep, and although this view may be extended and perfected later on, it is not materially altered. It is an effect of this purely objective and therefore poetical view of the world—essential to the period of childhood and promoted by the as yet undeveloped state of the volitional energy—that, as children, we are concerned much more with the acquisition of pure knowledge than with exercising the power of will. Hence that grave, fixed look observable in so many children, of which Raphael makes such a happy use in his depiction of cherubs, especially in the picture of the "Sistine Madonna." The years of childhood are thus rendered so full of bliss that the memory of them is always coupled with longing and regret.

While we thus eagerly apply ourselves to learning the outward aspect of things, as the primitive method of understanding the objects about us, education aims at instilling into us ideas. But ideas furnish no information as to the real and essential nature of objects, which, as the foundation and true content of all knowledge, can be reached only by the process called intuition. This is a kind of knowledge which can in no wise be instilled into us from without; we must arrive at it by and for ourselves.

Hence a man's intellectual as well as his moral qualities proceed from the depths of his own nature, and are not the result of external influences ; and no educational scheme—of Pestalozzi, or of any one else—can turn a born simpleton into a man of sense. The thing is impossible ! He was born a simpleton, and a simpleton he will die.

It is the depth and intensity of this early intuitive knowledge of the external world that explain why the experiences of childhood take such a firm hold on the memory. When we were young, we were completely absorbed in our immediate surroundings ; there was nothing to distract our attention from them ; we looked upon the objects about us as though they were the only ones of their kind, as though, indeed, nothing else existed at all. Later on, when we come to find out how many things there are in the world, this primitive state of mind vanishes, and with it our patience.

I have said elsewhere* that the world, considered as

---

* "Die Welt als Wille und Vorstellung," Bk. II.c 31, p 426-7 (4th Edit.), to which the reader is referred for a detail explanation of my meaning.

object—in other words, as it is presented to us objectively—wears in general a pleasing aspect; but that in the world, considered as the subject—that is, in regard to its inner nature, which is will—pain and trouble predominates I may be allowed to express the matter, briefly, thus : the world is glorious to look at, but dreadful in reality.

Accordingly, we find that, in the years of childhood, the world is much better known to us on its outer or objective side, namely as the presentation of will, than on the side of its inner nature, namely, as the will itself. Since the objective side wears a pleasing aspect, and the inner or subjective side, with its tale of horror, remains as yet unknown, the youth, as his intelligence develops, takes all the forms of beauty that he sees, in nature and in art, for so many objects of blissful existence : they are so beautiful to the outward eye that, on their inner side, they must, he thinks, be much more beautiful still. So the world lies before him like another Eden ; and this is the Arcadia in which we are all born.

A little later, this state of mind gives birth to a thirst for real life—the impulse to do and suffer—which drives a man forth into the hurly-burly of the world. There he learns the other side of existence—the inner side, the will, which is thwarted at every step. Then comes the great period of disillusion, a period of very gradual growth, but once it has fairly begun, a man will tell you that he has got over all his false notions—*l'âge des illusions est passé;* and yet the process is only beginning, and it goes on extending its sway and applying more and more to the whole of life. So it may be said that in childhood life looks like the scenery in a theater, as you view it from a distance; and that in old age it is like the same scenery when you come up quite close to it.

And lastly, there is another circumstance that contributes to the happiness of childhood. As spring commences, the young leaves on the trees are similar in color and much the same in shape: and in the first years of life we all resemble one another and harmonize very well. But with puberty divergence begins; and, like the radii of a circle, we go further and further apart.

The period of youth, which forms the remainder of this earlier half of our existence—and how many advantages it has over the later half—is troubled and made miserable by the pursuit of happiness, as though there were no doubt that it can be met with somewhere in life—a hope that always ends in failure and leads to discontent. An illusory image of some vague future bliss—born of a dream and shaped by fancy—floats before our eyes: and we search for the reality in vain. So it is that the young man is generally dissatisfied with the position in which he finds himself, whatever it may be; he ascribes his disappointment solely to the state of things that meets him on his first introduction to life, when he had expected something very different; whereas it is only the vanity and wretchedness of human life everywhere that he is now for the first time experiencing.

It would be a great advantage to a young man if his early training could eradicate the idea that the world has a great deal to offer him. But the usual result of education is to strengthen this delusion; and our first ideas of life are generally taken from fiction rather than from fact.

In the bright dawn of our youthful days, the poetry of life spreads out a gorgeous vision before us, and we torture ourselves by longing to see it realized. We might as well wish to grasp the rainbow! The youth expects his career to be like an interesting romance; and there lies the germ of that disappointment which I have been describing.* What lends a charm to all these visions is just the fact that they are visionary and not real, and that in contemplating them we are in the sphere of pure knowledge, which is sufficient in itself and free from the noise and struggle of life. To try and realize those visions is to make them an object of will—a process which always involves pain.†

If the chief feature of the earlier half of life is a never-satisfied longing after happiness, the later half is characterized by the dread of misfortune. For, as we advance in years, it becomes in a greater or less degree clear that all happiness is chimaerical in its nature, and that pain alone is real. Accordingly, in later years, we, or at least, the more prudent among us, are more intent upon eliminating what is painful from our lives and making our

---

* Cf. loc. cit. p. 428.

† Let me refer the reader, if he is interested in the subject, to the volume already cited, chapter 37.

position secure, than on the pursuit of positive pleasure. I may observe, by the way, that in old age we are better able to prevent misfortunes from coming, and in youth better able to bear them when they come.

In my young days, I was always pleased to hear a ring at my door: ah! thought I, now for something pleasant. But in later life my feelings on such occasions were rather akin to dismay than to pleasure; heaven help me! thought I, what am I to do? A similar revulsion of feeling in regard to the world of men takes place in all persons of any talent or distinction. For that very reason they cannot be said properly to belong to the world; in a greater or less degree, according to the extent of their superiority, they stand alone. In their youth they have a sense of being abandoned by the world; but later on, they feel as though they had escaped it. The earlier feeling is an unpleasant one, and rests upon ignorance, the second is pleasurable—for in the meantime they have come to know what the world is.

The consequence of this is that, as compared with the earlier, the later half of life, like the second part of a musical period, has less of passionate longing and more restfulness about it. And why is this the case? Simply because, in youth, a man fancies that there is a prodigious amount of happiness and pleasure to be had in the world, only that it is difficult to come by it; whereas, when he becomes old, he knows that there is nothing of the kind; he makes his mind completely at ease on the matter, enjoys the present hour as well as he can, and even takes a pleasure in trifles.

The chief result gained by experience of life is clearness of view. This is what distinguishes the man of mature age, and makes the world wear such a different aspect from that which it presented in his youth or boyhood. It is only then that he sees things quite plain, and takes them for that which they really are; while in earlier years he saw a phantom-world put together out of the whims and crotchets of his own mind, inherited prejudice and strange delusion; the real world was hidden from him, or the vision of it distorted. The first thing that experience finds to do is to free us from the phantoms of the brain—those false notions that have been put into us in youth.

To prevent their entrance at all would, of course, be the best form of education, even though it were only negative in aim; but it would be a task full of difficulty. At first the child's horizon would have to be limited as much as possible, and yet within that limited sphere none but clear and correct notions would have to be given; only after the child had properly appreciated everything within it, might the sphere be gradually enlarged; care being always taken that nothing was left obscure, or half or wrongly understood. The consequence of this training would be that the child's notions of men and things would always be limited and simple in their character; but on the other hand, they would be clear and correct, and only need to be extended, not to be rectified. The same line might be pursued on into the period of youth. This method of education would lay special stress upon the prohibition of novel reading; and the place of novels would be taken by suitable biographical literature—the life of Franklin, for instance, or Moritz's "Anton Reiser." *

In our early days we fancy that the leading events in our life, and the persons who are going to play an important part in it, will make their entrance to the sound of drums and trumpets; but when, in old age, we look back, we find that they all came in quite quietly, slipped in, as it were, by the side-door, almost unnoticed.

From the point of view we have been taking up until now, life may be compared to a piece of embroidery, of which, during the first half of his time, a man gets a sight of the right side, and during the second half, of the wrong. The wrong side is not so pretty as the right, but it is more instructive; it shows the way in which the threads have been worked together.

Intellectual superiority, even if it is of the highest kind, will not secure for a man a preponderating place in conversation until after he is forty years old. For age and experience, though they can never be a substitute for intellectual talent, may far outweigh it; and even in a person of the meanest capacity, they give a certain counterpoise to the power of an extremely intellectual man so long as the latter is young. Of course I allude here to personal superiority, not to the place a man may gain by his works.

And on passing his fortieth year any man of the slightest

Translator's Note.—Moritz was a miscellaneous writer of the last century (1757-93). His "Anton Reiser," composed in the form of a novel, is practically an autobiography.

power of mind—any man, that is, who has more than the
sorry share of intellect with which Nature has endowed
five-sixths of mankind—will hardly fail to show some trace
of misanthropy. For, as is natural, he has by that time
inferred other people's character from an examination of
his own; with the result that he has been gradually disappointed to find that in the qualities of the head or in those
of the heart—and usually in both—he reaches a level to
which they do not attain; so he gladly avoids having anything more to do with them. For it may be said, in general, that every man will love or hate solitude—in other
words, his own society—just in proportion as he is worth
anything in himself. Kant has some remarks upon this
kind of misanthropy in his "Critique of the Faculty of
Judgment." *

In a young man, it is a bad sign, as well from an intellectual as from a moral point of view, if he is precocious in
understanding the ways of the world, and in adapting himself to its pursuits; if he at once knows how to deal with
men, and enters upon life, as it were, fully prepared. It
argues a vulgar nature. On the other hand, to be surprised and astonished at the way people act, and to be
clumsy and cross-grained in having to do with them, indicates a character of the nobler sort.

The cheerfulness and vivacity of youth are partly due
to the fact that, when we are ascending the hill of life,
death is not visible : it lies down at the bottom of the
other side. But once we have crossed the top of the hill,
death comes in view—death, which, until then, was known
to us only by hearsay. This makes our spirits droop, for
at the same time we begin to feel that our vital powers
are on the ebb. A grave seriousness now takes the place
of that early extravagance of spirit ; and the change is
noticeable even in the expression of a man's face. As long
as we are young, people may tell us what they please ! we
look upon life as endless and use our time recklessly ; but
the older we become, the more we practice economy. For
toward the close of life, every day we live gives us the
same kind of sensation as the criminal experiences at every
step on his way to be tried.

From the standpoint of youth, life seems to stretch

---

* "Kritik der Urtheilskraft," Part I., § 29, Note ad fin.

away into an endless future; from the standpoint of old age, to go back but a little way into the past; so that, at the beginning, life presents us with a picture in which the objects appear a great way off, as though we had reversed our telescope; while in the end everything seems to close. To see how short life is, a man must have grown old, that is to say, he must have lived long.

On the other hand, as the years increase, things look smaller, one and all; and life, which had so firm and stable a base in the days of our youth, now seems nothing but a rapid flight of moments, every one of them illusory; we have come to see that the whole world is vanity!

Time itself seems to go at a much slower pace when we are young; so that not only is the first quarter of life the happiest, it is also the longest of all; it leaves more memories behind it. If a man were put to it, he could tell you more out of the first quarter of his life than out of two of the remaining periods. Nay, in the spring of life, as in the spring of the year, the days reach a length that is positively tiresome; but in the autumn, whether of the year or of life, though they are short, they are more genial and uniform.

But why is it that to an old man his past life appears so short? For this reason: his memory is short; and so he fancies that his life has been short too. He no longer remembers the insignificant parts of it, and much that was unpleasant is now forgotten; how little, then, there is left! For, in general, a man's memory is as imperfect as his intellect; and he must make a practice of reflecting upon the lessons he has learned and the events he has experienced, if he does not want them both to sink gradually into the gulf of oblivion. Now, we are unaccustomed to reflect upon matters of no importance, or, as a rule, upon things that we have found disagreeable, and yet that is necessary if the memory of them is to be preserved. But the class of things that may be called insignificant is continually receiving fresh additions: much that wears an air of importance at first, gradually becomes of no consequence at all from the fact of its frequent repetition; so that in the end we actually lose count of the number of times it happens. Hence we are better able to remember the events of our early than of our later years. The longer we live, the fewer are the things that we can call important or significant enough to deserve further consideration, and by this alone can they be fixed in the memory ; in other words, they are forgotten as soon as they are past. Thus it is that time runs on, leaving always fewer traces of its passage.

Further, if disagreeable things have happened to us we do not care to ruminate upon them, least of all when they touch our vanity, as is usually the case ; for few misfortunes fall upon us for which we can be held entirely blameless: So people are very ready to forget many things that are disagreeable, as well as many that are unimportant.

It is from this double cause that our memory is so short ; and a man's recollection of what has happened always becomes proportionately shorter, the more things that have occupied him in life. The things we did in years gone by, the events that happened long ago, are like those objects on the coast which, to the seafarer on his outward voyage, become smaller every minute, more unrecognizable and harder to distinguish.

Again, it sometimes happens that memory and imagination will call up some long past scene as vividly as if it had occurred only yesterday; so that the event in question seems to stand very near to the present time. The reason of this is that it is impossible to call up all the intervening period in the same vivid way, as there is no one figure pervading it which can be taken in at a glance; and besides most of the things that happened in that period are forgotten, and all that remains of it is the general knowledge that we have lived through it—a mere notion of abstract existence, not a direct vision of some particular experience. It is this that causes some single event of long ago to appear as though it took place but yesterday: the intervening time vanishes, and the whole of life looks incredibly short. Nay, there are occasional moments in old age when we can scarcely believe that we are so advanced in years, or that the long past lying behind us has had any real existence— a feeling which is mainly due to the circumstance that the present always seems fixed and immovable as we look at it. These and similar mental phenomena are ultimately to be traced to the fact that it is not our nature in itself, but only the outward presentation of it, that lies in time, and that the present is the point of contact between the world as subject and the world as object. *

Again, why is it that in youth we can see no end to the years that seem to lie before us? Because we are obliged to find room for all the things we hope to attain in life. We cram the years so full of projects that if we were to try and carry them all out, death would come prematurely though we reached the age of Methuselah.

Another reason why life looks so long when we are young is that we are apt to measure its length by the few years we have already lived. In those early years things are new to us and so they appear important; we dwell upon them after they have happened and often call them to mind: and thus in youth life seems replete with incident, and therefore of long duration.

Sometimes we credit ourselves with a longing to be in some distant spot, whereas, in truth, we are only longing to have the time back again which we spent there—days when we were younger and fresher than we are now. In those moments Time mocks us by wearing the mask of space, and if we travel to the spot, we can see how much we have been deceived.

There are two ways of reaching a great age, both of which presuppose a sound constitution as a *conditio sine quâ non.* They may be illustrated by two lamps, one of which burns a long time with very little oil, because it has a very thin wick: and the other just as long, though it has a very thick one, because there is plenty of oil to feed it. Here, the oil is the vital energy, and the difference in the wick is the manifold way in which the vital energy is used.

Up to our thirty-sixth year, we may be compared, in respect of the way in which we use our vital energy, to people who live on the interest of their money; what they spend to-day, they have again to-morrow. But from the age of thirty-six onward, our position is like that of the investor

---

Translator's Note.—By this remark Schopenhauer means that will, which, as he argues, forms the inner reality underlying all the phenomena of life and nature, is not in itself affected by time; but that on the other hand, time is necessary for the objectification of the will for the will as presented in the passing phenomena of the world. Time is thus definable as the condition of change, and the present time as the only point of contact between reality and appearance.

who begins to entrench upon his capital. At first he hardly notices any difference at all, as the greater part of his expenses is covered by the interest of his securities; and if the deficit is but slight, he pays no attention to it. But the deficit goes on increasing, until he awakes to the fact that it is becoming more serious every day; his position becomes less and less secure, and he feels himself growing poorer and poorer, while he has no expectation of this drain upon his resources coming to an end. His fall from wealth to poverty becomes faster every moment—like the fall of a solid body in space, until at last he has absolutely nothing left. A man is truly in a woeful plight if both the terms of this comparison—his vital energy and his wealth—really begin to melt away at one and the same time. It is the dread of this calamity that makes love of possession increase with age.

On the other hand, at the beginning of life—in the years before we attain majority, and for some little time afterward—the state of our vital energy puts us on a level with those who each year lay by a part of their interest and add it to their capital: in other words, not only does their interest come in regularly, but the capital is constantly receiving additions. This happy condition of affairs is sometimes brought about—with health as with money—under the watchful care of some honest guardian. Oh happy youth, and sad old age!

Nevertheless, a man should economize his strength even when he is young. Aristotle * observes that among those who were victors at Olympia only two or three gained a prize at two different periods, once in boyhood and then when they came to be men; and the reason of this was that the premature efforts which the training involved, so completely exhausted their powers that they failed to last on into manhood. As this is true of muscular, so it is still more true of nervous energy, of which all intellectual achievements are the manifestation. Hence, those infant prodigies—*ingenia praecocia*—the fruit of a hot-house education, who surprise us by their cleverness as children, afterward turn out very ordinary folk. Nay, the manner in which boys are forced into an early acquaintance with the ancient tongues may, perhaps be to blame for the dull-

---

* "Politics."

ness and lack of judgment which distinguish so many learned persons.

I have said that almost every man's character seems to be specially suited to some one period of life, so that on reaching it the man is at his best. Some people are charming so long as they are young, and afterward there is nothing attractive about them; others are vigorous and active in manhood, and then lose all the value they possess as they advance in years; many appear to best advantage in old age, when their character assumes a gentler tone, as becomes men who have seen the world and take life easily. This is often the case with the French.

This peculiarity must be due to the fact that the man's character has something in it akin to the qualities of youth or manhood or old age—something which accords with one or another of these periods of life, or perhaps acts as a corrective to its special failings.

The mariner observes the progress he makes only by the way in which objects on the coast fade away into the distance and apparently decrease in size. In the same way a man becomes conscious that he is advancing in years when he finds that people older than himself begin to seem young to him.

It has been already remarked that the older a man becomes, the fewer are the traces left in his mind by all that he sees, does or experiences, and the cause of this has been explained. There is thus a sense in which it may be said that it is only in youth that a man lives with a full degree of consciousness and that he is only half alive when he is old. As the years advance, his consciousness of what goes on about him dwindles, and the things of life hurry by without making any impression upon him, just as none is made by a work of art seen for the thousandth time. A man does what his hand finds to do, and afterward he does not know whether he has done it or not.

As life becomes more and more unconscious the nearer it approaches the point at which all consciousness ceases, the course of time itself seems to increase in rapidity. In childhood all the things and circumstances of life are novel and that is sufficient to awake us to the full consciousness of existence: hence, at that age, the day seems of such immense length. The same thing happens when we are traveling; one month seems longer then than four spent at home. Still, though time seems to last longer when we are young or on a journey, the sense of novelty does not prevent it from now and then in reality hanging heavily upon our hands under both these circumstances, at any rate more than is the case when we are old or staying at home. But the intellect gradually becomes so rubbed down and blunted by long habituation to such sensations that things have a constant tendency to produce less and less impression upon us as they pass by; and this makes time seem increasingly less important, and therefore shorter in duration: the hours of the boy are longer than the days of the old man. Accordingly, time goes faster and faster the longer we live, like a ball rolling down hill. Or, to take another example; as in a revolving disc the further a point lies from the center the more rapid is its rate of progression, so it is in the wheel of life; the further you stand from the beginning, the faster time moves for you. Hence it may be said that as far as concerns the immediate sensation that time makes upon our minds, the length of any given year is in direct proportion to the number of times it will divide our whole life: for instance, at the age of fifty the year appears to us only one-tenth as long as it did at the age of five.

This variation in the rate at which time appears to move, exercises a most decided influence upon the whole nature of our existence at every period of it. First of all, it causes childhood—even though it embrace only a span of fifteen years—to seem the longest period of life, and therefore the richest in reminiscences. Next, it brings it about that a man is apt to be bored just in proportion as he is young. Consider, for instance, that constant need of occupation—whether it is work or play—that is shown by children : if they come to an end of both work and play, a terrible feeling of boredom ensues. Even in youth people are by no means free from this tendency, and dread the hours when they have nothing to do. As manhood approaches, boredom disappears ; and old men find the time too short when their days fly past them like arrows from a bow. Of course, I must be understood to speak of men, not of decrepit brutes. With this increased rapidity of time, boredom mostly passes away as we advance in life ;

and as the passions with all their attendant pain are then
laid asleep, the burden of life is, on the whole, appreciably
lighter in later years than in youth, provided, of course,
that health remains. So it is that the period immediately
preceding the weakness and troubles of old age receives
the name of a man's best years.

That may be a true appellation, in view of the comfortable feeling which those years bring ; but for all that the
years of youth, when our consciousness is lively and open
to every sort of impression, have this privilege—that then
the seeds are sown and the buds come forth ; it is the
springtime of the mind. Deep truths may be perceived,
but can never be excogitated—that is to say, the first
knowledge of them is immediate, called forth by some
momentary impression. This knowledge is of such a kind
as to be attainable only when the impressions are strong,
lively and deep ; and if we are to be acquainted with deep
truth, everything depends upon a proper use of our early
years. In later life, we may be better able to work upon
other people—upon the world, because our natures are
then finished and rounded off, and no more a prey to fresh
views ; but then the world is less able to work upon us.
These are the years of action and achievement ; while youth
is the time for forming fundamental conceptions and laying down the groundwork of thought.

In youth it is the outward aspect of things that most
engages us ; while in age, thought or reflection is the
predominating quality of the mind. Hence, youth is the
time for poetry, and age is more inclined to philosophy.
In practical affairs it is the same : a man shapes his
resolutions in youth more by the impression that the outward world makes upon him ; whereas, when he is old, it
is thought that determines his actions. This is partly to
be explained by the fact that it is only when a man is old
that the results of outward observation are present in
sufficient numbers to allow of their being classified according to the ideas they represent—a process which in
its turn causes those ideas to be more fully understood in
all their bearings, and the exact value and amount of trust
to be placed in them, fixed and determined, while at the
same time he has grown accustomed to the impressions
produced by the various phenomena of life, and their
effects on him are no longer what they were.

Contrarily, in youth, the impressions that things make, that is to say, the outward aspects of life, are so overpoweringly strong, especially in the case of people of lively and imaginative disposition, that they view the world like a picture ; and their chief concern is the figure they cut in it, the appearance they present ; nay, they are unaware of the extent to which this is the case. It is a quality of mind that shows itself—if in no other way—in that personal vanity, and that love of fine clothes, which distinguish young people.

There can be no doubt that the intellectual powers are most capable of enduring great and sustained efforts in youth, up to the age of thirty-five at latest ; from which period their strength begins to decline, though very gradually. Still, the later years of life, and even old age itself, are not without their intellectual compensation. It is only then that a man can be said to be really rich in experience or in learning ; he has then had time and opportunity enough to enable him to see and think over life from all its sides ; he has been able to compare one thing with another, and to discover points of contact and connecting links, so that only then are the true relations of things rightly understood. Further, in old age there comes an increased depth in the knowledge that was acquired in youth ; a man has now many more illustrations of any ideas he may have attained ; things which he thought he knew when he was young, he now knows in reality. And besides, his range of knowledge is wider ; and in whatever direction it extends, it is thorough, and therefore formed into a consistent and connected whole ; whereas in youth knowledge is always defective and fragmentary.

A complete and adequate motion of life can never be attained by any one who does not reach old age ; for it is only the old man who sees life whole and knows its natural course ; it is only he who is acquainted—and this is most important—not only with its entrance, like the rest of mankind, but with its exit too ; so that he alone has a full sense of its utter vanity ; while the others never cease to labor under the false notion that everything will come right in the end.

On the other hand, there is more conceptive power in

youth, and at that time of life a man can make more out of
the little that he knows.   In age, judgment, penetration
and thoroughness predominate.   Youth is the time for
amassing the material for a knowledge of the world that
shall be distinctive and peculiar—for an original view of life,
in other words, the legacy that a man of genius leaves to
his fellow-men; it is, however, only in later years that he
becomes master of his material.   Accordingly it will be
found that, as a rule, a great writer gives his best work to
the world when he is about fifty years of age.   But though
the tree of knowledge must reach its full height before it can
bear fruit, the roots of it lie in youth.

Every generation, no matter how paltry its character,
thinks itself much wiser than the one immediately preceding it, let alone those that are more remote.   It is just
the same with the different periods in a man's life; and yet
often, in the one case no less than in the other, it is a mistaken opinion.   In the years of physical growth, when our
powers of mind and our stores of knowledge are receiving
daily additions, it becomes a habit for to-day to look down
with contempt upon yesterday.   The habit strikes root, and
remains even after the intellectual powers have begun to decline—when to-day should rather look up with respect to
yesterday.   So it is that we often unduly depreciate the
achievements as well as the judgments of our youth.

This seems the place for making the general observation
that, although in its main qualities a man's intellect or
head as well as his character or heart, is innate, yet the
former is by no means so unalterable in its nature as the
latter.   The fact is that the intellect is subject to very many
transformations, which, as a rule do not fail to make their
actual appearance; and this is so, partly because the intellect has a deep foundation in the physique, and partly
because the material with which it deals is given in
experience.   And so, from a physical point of view, we
find that if a man has any peculiar power, it first gradually increases in strength until it reaches its acme after
which it enters upon a path of slow decadence, until
it ends in imbecility.   But, on the other hand, we must not
lose sight of the fact that the material which gives employment to a man's powers and keeps them in activity—the
subject matter of thought and knowledge, experience, intellectual attainments, the practice of seeing to the bottom

of things, and so a perfect mental vision, form in themselves a mass which continues to increase in size, until the time comes when weakness shows itself, and the man's powers suddenly fail. The way in which these two distinguishable elements combine in the same nature—the one absolutely unalterable, and the other subject to change in two directions opposed to each other—explains the variety of mental attitude and the dissimilarity of value which attach to a man at different periods of life.

The same truth may be more broadly expressed by saying that the first forty years of life furnish the text, while the remaining thirty supply the commentary; and that without the commentary we are unable to understand aright the true sense and coherence of the text, together with the moral it contains and all the subtle application of which it admits.

Toward the close of life, much the same thing happens as at the end of a *bal masqué*—the masks are taken off. Then you can see who the people really are, with whom you have come into contact in your passage through the world. For by the end of life characters have come out in their true light, actions have borne fruit, achievements have been rightly appreciated, and all shams have fallen to pieces. For this, Time was in every case requisite.

But the most curious fact is that it is also only toward the close of life that a man really recognizes and understands his own true self—the aims and objects he has followed in life, more especially the kind of relation in which he has stood to other people and to the world. It will often happen that as a result of this knowledge, a man will have to assign himself a lower place than he formerly thought was his due. But there are exceptions to this rule; and it will occasionally be the case that he will take a higher position than he had before. This will be owing to the fact that he had no adequate notion of the baseness of the world and that he set up a higher aim for himself than was followed by the rest of mankind.

The progress of life shows a man the stuff of which he is made.

It is customary to call youth the happy, and age the sad part of life. This would be true if it were the passions that made a man happy. Youth is swayed to and fro by them; and they give a great deal of pain and little pleasure. In age the passions cool and leave a man at rest, and then forthwith his mind takes a contemplative tone; the intellect is set free and attains the upper hand. And since, in itself, intellect is beyond the range of pain, a man feels happy just in so far as his intellect is the predominating part of him.

It need only be remembered that all pleasure is negative, and that pain is positive in its nature, in order to see that the passions can never be a source of happiness, and that age is not the less to be envied on the ground that many pleasures are denied it. For every sort of pleasure is never anything more than the quietive of some need or longing; and that pleasure should come to an end as soon as the need ceases, is no more a subject of complaint than that a man cannot go on eating after he has had his dinner, or fall asleep again after a good night's rest.

So far from youth being the happiest period of life, there is much more truth in the remark made by Plato, at the beginning of the "Republic," that the prize should rather be given to old age, because then at last a man is freed from the animal passion which has hitherto never ceased to disquiet him. Nay, it may even be said that the countless and manifold humors which have their source in this passion, and the emotions that spring from it, produce a mild state of madness: and this lasts as long as the man is subject to the spell of the impulse—this evil spirit, as it were, of which there is no riddance—so that he never really becomes a reasonable being until the passion is extinguished.

There is no doubt that, in general, and apart from individual circumstances and particular dispositions, youth is marked by a certain melancholy and sadness, while genial sentiments attach to old age; and the reason of this is nothing but the fact that the young man is still under the service, nay, the forced labor, imposed by that evil spirit, which scarcely ever leaves him a moment to himself. To this source may be traced, directly or indirectly, almost all and every ill that befalls or menaces mankind. The old man is genial and cheerful because, after long lying in the bonds of passion, he can now move about in freedom.

Still, it should not be forgotten that, when this passion is extinguished, the true kernel of life is gone, and nothing remains but the hollow shell; or, from another point of view, life then becomes like a comedy, which, begun by real actors, is continued and brought to an end by automata dressed in their clothes.

However that may be, youth is the period of unrest, and age of repose; and from that very circumstance, the relative degree of pleasure belonging to each may be inferred. The child stretches out its little hand in the eager desire to seize all the pretty things that meet its sight, charmed by the world because all its senses are still so young and fresh. Much the same thing happens with the youth, and he displays greater energy in his quest. He, too, is charmed by all the pretty things and the many pleasing shapes that surround him; and forthwith his imagination conjures up pleasures which the world can never realize. So he is filled with an ardent desire for he knows not what delights—robbing him of all rest and making happiness impossible. But when old age is reached, all this is over and done with, partly because the blood runs cooler and the senses are no longer so easily allured; partly because experience has shown the true value of things and the futility of pleasure, whereby illusion has been gradually dispelled, and the strange fancies and prejudices which previously concealed or distorted a free and true view of the world, have been dissipated and put to flight; with the result that a man can now get a juster and clearer view, and see things as they are, and also in a measure attain more or less insight into the nullity of all things on this earth.

It is this that gives almost every old man, no matter how ordinary his faculties may be, a certain tincture of wisdom, which distinguishes him from the young. But the chief result of all this change is the peace of mind that ensues —a great element in happiness, and, in fact, the condition and essence of it. While the young man fancies that there is a vast amount of good things in the world, if he could only come at them, the old man is steeped in the truth of the Preacher's words, that "all things are vanity" —knowing that, however gilded the shell, the nut is hollow.

In these later years, and not before, a man comes to a true appreciation of Horace's maxim: *Nil admirari.*

He is directly and sincerely convinced of the vanity of everything and that all the glories of the world are as nothing, his illusions are gone.   He is no more beset with the idea that there is any particular amount of happiness anywhere, in the palace or in the cottage, any more than he himself enjoys when he is free from bodily or mental pain.   The worldly distinctions of great and small, high and low, exist for him no longer; and in this blissful state of mind the old man may look down with a smile upon all false notions.   He is completely undeceived, and knows that, whatever may be done to adorn human life and deck it out in finery, its paltry character will soon show through the glitter of its surroundings; and that, paint and bejewel it as one may, it remains everywhere much the same—an existence which has no true value except in freedom from pain, and is never to be estimated by the presence of pleasure, let alone, then, of display.*

Disillusion is the chief characteristic of old age; for by that time the fictions are gone which gave life its charm and spurred on the mind to activity; the splendors of the world have been proved null and vain ; its pomp, grandeur and magnificence are faded.   A man has then found out that behind most of the things he wants, and most of the pleasures he longs for, there is very little after all ; and so he comes by degrees to see that our existence is all empty and void.   It is only when he is seventy years old that he quite understands the first words of the Preacher; and this again explains why it is that old men are sometimes fretful and morose.

It is often said that the common lot of old age is disease and weariness of life.   Disease is by no means essential to old age ; especially where a really long span of years is to be attained; for as life goes on, the conditions of health and disorder tend to increase—*crescent vita, crescit sanitas et morbus.*   And as far as weariness or boredom is concerned, I have stated above why old age is even less exposed to that form of evil than youth.   Nor is boredom by any means to be taken as a necessary accompaniment of that solitude, which, for reasons that do not require to be explained, old age certainly cannot escape; it is rather the fate that awaits those who have never known any other

---

* Cf. Horace, "Epist." I. 12., 1-4.

pleasures but the gratification of the senses and the delights of society—who have left their minds unenlightened and their faculties unused. It is quite true that the intellectual faculties decline with the approach of old age; but where they were originally strong, there will always be enough left to combat the onslaught of boredom. And then again, as I have said, experience, knowledge, reflection, and skill in dealing with men, combine to give an old man an increasingly accurate insight into the ways of the world; his judgment becomes keen and he attains a coherent view of life; his mental vision embraces a wider range. Constantly finding new uses for his stores of knowledge and adding to them at every opportunity, he maintains uninterrupted that inward process of self-education which gives employment and satisfaction to the mind, and thus forms the due reward of all its efforts.

All this serves in some measure as a compensation for decreased intellectual power. And besides, Time, as I have remarked, seems to go much more quickly when we are advanced in years; and this is in itself a preventive of boredom. There is no great harm in the fact that a man's bodily strength decreases in old age, unless, indeed, he requires it to make a living. To be poor when one is old, is a great misfortune. If a man is secure from that, and retains his health, old age may be a very passable time of life. Its chief necessity is to be comfortable and well off; and, in consequence, money is then prized more than ever, because it is a substitute for failing strength. Deserted by Venus, the old man likes to turn to Bacchus to make him merry. In the place of wanting to see things, to travel and learn, comes the desire to speak and teach. It is a piece of good fortune if the old man retains some of his love of study or of music or of the theater—if, in general, he is still somewhat susceptible to the things about him; as is, indeed, the case with some people to a very late age. At that time of life, what a man has in himself, is of greater advantage to him than ever it was before.

There can be no doubt that most people who have never been anything but dull and stupid, become more and more of automata as they grow old. They have always thought, said and done the same things as their neighbors; and nothing that happens now can change their disposition, or make them act otherwise. To talk to old people of this kind is like writing on the sand; if you produce any impression at all it is gone almost immediately; old age is here nothing but the *caput mortuum* of life—all that is essential to manhood is gone. There are cases in which nature supplies a third set of teeth in old age, thereby apparently demonstrating the fact that that period of life is a second childhood.

It is certainly a very melancholy thing that all a man's faculties tend to waste away as he grows old, and at a rate that increases in rapidity: but still this is a necessary nay a beneficial arrangement, as otherwise death, for which it is a preparation, would be too hard to bear. So the greatest boon that follows the attainment of extreme old age is *euthanasia*—an easy death, not ushered in by disease, and free from all pain and struggle.* For let a man live as long as he may, he is never conscious of any moment but the present, one and indivisible; and in those late years the mind loses more every day by sheer forgetfulness than ever it gains anew.

The main difference between youth and age will always be that youth looks forward to life, and old age to death; and that while the one has a short past and a long future before it, the case is just the opposite with the other. It is quite true that when a man is old, to die is the only thing that awaits him; while if he is young, he may expect to live; and the question arises, Which of the two fates is the more hazardous, and if life is not a matter which, on the whole, it is better to have behind one than before? Does not the Preacher say: "the day of death [is better] than the day of one's birth?" † It is certainly a rash thing to wish for long life; ‡ for, as the Spanish proverb has it, it means to see much evil—*Quien larga vida vive mucho mal vide.*

---

* See "Die Welt als Wille und Vorstellung," Bk. II. ch. 41, for a further description of this happy end to life.

† Ecclesiastes vii. 1.

‡ The life of man cannot, strictly speaking be called either long or short, since it is the ultimate standard by which duration of time in regard to all other things is measured.

In one of the Vedic "Upanishads" (*Oupnekhat,* II.) the "natural length" of human life is put down at one hundred years. And I believe this to be right. I have observed, as a matter of fact, that it is only people who exceed the age of ninety who attain *euthanasia*—who die, that is to say, of no disease, apoplexy or convulsion, and pass

A man's individual career is not as astrology wishes to make out, to be predicted from observation of the planets; but the course of human life in general, as far as the various periods of it are concerned, may be likened to the succession of the planets; so that we may be said to pass under the influence of each one of them in turn.

At ten, Mercury is in the ascendant; and at that age, a man, like this planet, is characterized by extreme mobility within a narrow sphere, where trifles have a great effect upon him; but under the guidance of so crafty and eloquent a god, he easily makes great progress. Venus begins her sway during his twentieth year, and then a man is wholly given up to the love of women. At thirty, Mars comes to the front, and he is now all energy and strength—daring, pugnacious and arrogant.

When a man reaches the age of forty, he is under the rule of the four Asteroids: that is to say, his life has gained something in extension. He is frugal; in other words, by the help of Ceres, he favors what is useful; he has his own hearth, by the influence of Vesta; Pallas has taught him that which is necessary for him to know; and his wife—his Juno—rules as the mistress of his house. *

---

away without agony of any sort; nay, who sometimes even show no pallor, but expire generally in a sitting attitude, and often after a meal—or I may say, simply cease to live rather than die. To come to one's end before the age of ninety, means to die of disease, in other words, prematurely.

Now the Old Testament (Psalms xc. 10) puts the limit of human life at seventy, and if it is very long, at eighty years, and what is more noticeable still, Herodotus (i. 32 and iii. 22) says the same thing. But this is wrong; and the error is due simply to a rough and superficial estimate of the results of daily experience. For if the natural length of life were from seventy to eighty years, people, would die about that time of mere old age. Now this is certainly not the case. If they die then, they die, like younger people, of disease; and disease is something abnormal. Therefore it is not natural to die at that age. It is only when they are between ninety and a hundred that people die of old age. die I mean, without suffering from any disease, or showing any special signs of their condition, such as a struggle, death rattle, convulsion, pallor—the absence of all which constitutes *euthanasia.* The natural length of human life is a hundred years and in assigning that limit the Upanishads are right once more.

* The other asteroids which have been discovered since, are an innovation, and I shall have nothing to do with them. My relation to them is that of the professors of philosophy to me—I ignore them, because they do not suit my book.

But at the age of fifty, Jupiter is the dominant influence. At that period a man has outlived most of his contemporaries, and he can feel himself superior to the generation about him. He is still in the full enjoyment of his strength, and rich in experience and knowledge; and if he has any power and position of his own, he is endowed with authority over all who stand in his immediate surroundings. He is no more inclined to receive orders from others; he wants to take command himself. The work most suitable to him now is to guide and rule within his own sphere. This is the point where Jupiter culminates, and where the man of fifty years is at his best.

Then comes Saturn, at about the age of sixty, a weight as of lead, dull and slow:

> " But old folks, many feign as they were dead,
> Unwieldy, slow, heavy and pale as lead." *

Last of all, *Uranus;* or, as the saying is, a man goes to heaven.

I cannot find a place for Neptune, as this planet has been very thoughtlessly named; because I may not call it as it should be called—Eros. Otherwise I should point out how Beginning and End meet together, and how closely and intimately Eros is connected with Death ; how Orcus, or Amenthes, as the Egyptians called him,† is not only the receiver but the giver of all things—λαμβάνων καὶ διδούς. Death is the great reservoir of Life. Everything comes from Orcus ; everything that is alive now was once there. Could we but understand the great trick by which that is done, all would be clear!

---

* " Romeo and Juliet," ii. 5.

† Plutarch, " De Iside et Osiride," c. 29.

RELIGION AND OTHER ESSAYS.

RELIGION.

A DIALOGUE.

DEMOPHELES.—Between ourselves, my dear fellow, I don't care about the way you sometimes have of exhibiting your talent for philosophy; you make religion a subject for sarcastic remarks, and even for open ridicule. Every one thinks his religion sacred, and therefore you ought to respect it.

PHILALETHES.—That doesn't follow! I don't see why, because other people are simpletons, I should have any regard for a pack of lies. I respect truth everywhere, and so I can't respect what is opposed to it. My maxim is *Vigeat veritas et pereat mundus*, like the lawyers' *Fiat justitia et pereat mundus*. Every profession ought to have an analogous device.

DEMOPHELES.—Then I suppose doctors should say *Fiant pilulæ et pereat mundus*—there wouldn't be much difficulty about that!

PHILALETHES.—Heaven forbid! You must take everything *cum grano salis*.

DEMOPHELES.—Exactly; that's why I want you to take religion *cum grano salis*. I want you to see that you must meet the requirements of the people according to the measure of their comprehension. Where you have masses of people, of crude susceptibilities and clumsy intelligence, sordid in their pursuits and sunk in drudgery, religion provides the only means of proclaiming and making them feel the high import of life. For the average man takes an interest, primarily, in nothing but what will satisfy his physical needs and hankerings, and beyond this, give him a little amusement and pastime. Founders of religion and philosophers come into the world to rouse him from his stupor and point to the lofty meaning of existence; philosophers for the few, the emancipated, founders of religion for the many, for humanity at large. For, as your friend Plato has said, the multitude can't be philosophers, and you shouldn't forget that. Religion is the metaphysics of the masses; by all means let them keep it: let it therefore command external respect, for to discredit it is to take it away. Just as they have popular poetry, and the popular wisdom of proverbs, so they must have popular metaphysics too: for mankind absolutely needs an interpretation of life; and this, again, must be suited to popular comprehension. Consequently, this interpretation is always an allegorical investiture of the truth: and in practical life and in its effects on the feelings, that is to say, as a rule of action and as a comfort and consolation in suffering and death, it accomplishes perhaps just as much as the truth itself could achieve if we possessed it. Don't take offense at its unkempt, grotesque and apparently absurd form: for with your education and learning, you have no idea of the round-about ways by which people in their crude state have to receive their knowledge of deep truths. The various religions are only various forms in which the truth, which taken by itself is above their comprehension, is grasped and realized by the masses; and truth becomes inseparable from these forms. Therefore, my dear sir, don't take it amiss if I say that to make a mockery of these forms is both shallow and unjust.

PHILALETHES.—But isn't it every bit as shallow and unjust to demand that there shall be no other system of metaphysics but this one, cut out as it is to suit the requirements and comprehension of the masses? that its doctrines shall be the limit of human speculation, the standard of all thought, so that the metaphysics of the few, the emancipated, as you call them, must be devoted only to confirming, strengthening, and explaining the metaphysics of the masses? that the highest powers of human intelligence shall remain unused and undeveloped, even be nipped in the bud in order that their activity may not thwart the popular metaphysics? And isn't this just the very claim which religion sets up? Isn't it a little too much to have tolerance and delicate forbearance preached by what is intolerance and cruelty itself? Think of the heretical tribunals, inquisitions, religious wars, crusades, Socrates' cup of poison,

Bruno's and Vanini's death in the flames! Is all this to-day quite a thing of the past? How can genuine philosophical effort, sincere search after truth, the noblest calling of the noblest men, be let and hindered more completely than by a conventional system of metaphysics enjoying a state monopoly, the principles of which are impressed into every head in earliest youth so earnestly, so deeply, and so firmly, that, unless the mind is miraculously elastic, they remain indelible. In this way the groundwork of all healthy reason is once for all deranged; that is to say, the capacity for original thought and unbiased judgment, which is weak enough in itself, is, in regard to those subjects to which it might be applied, forever paralyzed and ruined.

DEMOPHELES.—Which means, I suppose, that people have arrived at a conviction which they won't give up in order to embrace yours instead.

PHILALETHES.—Ah! if it were only a conviction based on insight. Then one could bring arguments to bear, and the battle would be fought with equal weapons. But religions admittedly appeal, not to conviction as the result of argument, but to belief as demanded by revelation. And as the capacity for believing is strongest in childhood, special care is taken to make sure of this tender age. This has much more to do with the doctrines of belief taking root than threats and reports of miracles. If, in early childhood, certain fundamental views and doctrines are paraded with unusual solemnity, and an air of the greatest earnestness never before visible in anything else; if, at the same time, the possibility of a doubt about them be completely passed over, or touched upon only to indicate that doubt is the first step to eternal perdition, the resulting impression will be so deep that, as a rule, that is, in almost every case, doubt about them will be almost as impossible as doubt about one's own existence. Hardly one in ten thousand will have the strength of mind to ask himself seriously and earnestly is that true? To call such as can do it strong minds, *esprits forts*, is a description apter than is generally supposed. But for the ordinary mind there is nothing so absurd or revolting but what, if inculcated in that way, the strongest belief in it will strike root. If, for example, the killing of a heretic or infidel were essential to the future salvation of his soul, almost every one would make it the chief event of his life, and in dying would draw consolation and strength from the remembrance that he had succeeded. As a matter of fact, almost every Spaniard in days gone by used to look upon an *auto da fe* as the most pious of all acts and one most agreeable to God. A parallel to this may be found in the way in which the Thugs (a religious sect in India, suppressed a short time ago by the English, who executed numbers of them) express their sense of religion and their veneration for the goddess Kali; they take every opportunity of murdering their friends and traveling companions, with the object of getting possession of their goods, and in the serious conviction that they are thereby doing a praiseworthy action, conducive to their eternal welfare.* The power of religious dogma, when inculcated early, is such as to stifle conscience, compassion and finally every feeling of humanity. But if you want to see with your own eyes and close at hand what timely inoculation of belief will accomplish, look at the English. Here is a nation favored before all others by nature; endowed, more than all others, with discernment, intelligence, power of judgment, strength of character; look at them, abased and made ridiculous, beyond all others, by their stupid ecclesiastical superstition, which appears among their other abilities like a fixed idea or monomania; For this they have to thank the circumstance that education is in the hands of the clergy, whose endeavor it is to impress all the articles of belief, at the earliest age, in a way that amounts to a kind of paralysis of the brain; this in its turn expresses itself all their life in an idiotic bigotry, which makes otherwise most sensible and intelligent people among them degrade themselves so that one can't make head or tail of them. If you consider how essential to such a masterpiece is inoculation in the tender age of childhood, the missionary system appears no longer only as the acme of human importunity, arrogance and impertinence, but also as an absurdity, if it doesn't confine itself to nations, which are still in their infancy, like Kaffirs, Hottentots, South Sea Islanders, etc. Among these races it is successful; but in India the Brahmans treat the discourses of the missionaries with contemptuous smiles of approbation, or

---

* Cf. Illustrations of the history and practice of the Thugs, London, 1837; also the *Edinburgh Review*, Oct.-Jan., 1836-7.

simply shrug their shoulders. And one may say generally that the proselytizing efforts of the missionaries in India, in spite of the most advantageous facilities, are, as a rule, a failure. An authentic report in Vol. XXI. of the Asiatic Journal (1826) states that after so many years of missionary activity not more than three hundred living converts were to be found in the whole of India, where the population of the English possessions alone comes to one hundred and fifteen millions; and at the same time it is admitted that the Christian converts are distinguished for their extreme immorality. Three hundred venal and bribed souls out of so many millions! There is no evidence that things have gone better with Christianity in India since then, in spite of the fact that the missionaries are now trying, contrary to stipulation and in schools exclusively designed for secular English instruction, to work upon the children's minds as they please. in order to smuggle in Christianity; against which the Hindoos are most jealously on their guard. As I have said, childhood is the time to sow the seeds of belief, and not manhood; more especially where an earlier faith has taken root. An acquired conviction such as is feigned by adults is, as a rule, only the mask for some kind of personal interest. And it is the feeling that this is almost bound to be the case which makes a man who has changed his religion in mature years an object of contempt to most people everywhere; who thus show that they look upon religion, not as a matter of reasoned conviction, but merely as a belief inoculated in childhood, before any test can be applied. And that they are right in their view of religion is also obvious from the way in which not only the masses, who are blindly credulous, but also the clergy of every religion, who, as such, have faithfully and zealously studied its sources, foundations, dogmas and disputed points, cleave as a body to the religion of their particular country; consequently for a minister of one religion or confession to go over to another is the rarest thing in the world. The Catholic clergy, for example, are fully convinced of the truth of all the tenets of their church, and so are the Protestant clergy of theirs, and both defend the principles of their creeds with like zeal. And yet the conviction is governed merely by the country native to each; to the South German ecclesiastic the truth of the Catholic dogma is quite obvious, to the

North German, the Protestant. If, then, these convictions are based on objective reasons, the reasons must be climatic, and thrive, like plants, some only here, some only there. The convictions of those who are thus locally convinced are taken on trust and believed by the masses everywhere.

DEMOPHELES.—Well, no harm is done, and it doesn't make any real difference. As a fact, Protestantism is more suited to the north, Catholicism to the south.

PHILALETHES.—So it seems. Still I take a higher standpoint, and keep in view a more important object, the progress, namely, of the knowledge of truth among mankind. And from this point of view, it is a terrible thing that, wherever a man is born, certain propositions are inculcated in him in earliest youth, and he is assured that he may never have any doubts about them, under penalty of thereby forfeiting eternal salvation; propositions, I mean, which affect the foundation of all our other knowledge and accordingly determine forever, and, if they are false, distort forever, the point of view from which our knowledge starts; and as, further, the corollaries of these propositions touch the entire system of our intellectual attainments at every point, the whole of human knowledge is thoroughly adulterated by them. Evidence of this is afforded by every literature; the most striking by that of the Middle Age, but in a too considerable degree by that of the fifteenth and sixteenth centuries. Look at even the first minds of all those epochs; how paralyzed they are by false fundamental positions like these; how, more especially, all insight into the true constitution and working of Nature is, as it were, blocked up. During the whole of the Christian period Theism presents a solid barrier to all intellectual effort, and chiefly to philosophy, arresting or stunting all progress. For the scientific men of these ages God, devil, angels, demons hid the whole of nature; no inquiry was followed to the end, nothing ever thoroughly examined; everything which went beyond the most obvious causal nexus was immediately set down to those personalities. "It was at once explained by a reference to God, angels or demons," as Pomponatius expressed himself when the matter was being discussed, "and philosophers at any rate have nothing analogous." There is, to be sure, a suspicion of irony in this statement of Pomponatius, as his perfidy in other matters is known; still, he is only giving expression to the general way of thinking of his age. And if, on the other hand, any one possessed the rare quality of an elastic mind, which alone could burst the bonds, his writings and he himself with them were burned; as happened to Bruno and Vanini. How completely an ordinary mind is paralyzed by that early preparation in metaphysics is seen in the most vivid way and on its most ridiculous side whenever it undertakes to criticise the doctrines of an alien creed. The efforts of the ordinary man are generally found to be directed to a careful exhibition of the incongruity of its dogmas with those of his own belief: he is at great pains to show that not only do they not say, but certainly do not mean, the same thing; and with that he thinks, in his simplicity, that he has demonstrated the falsehood of the alien creed. He really never dreams of putting the question which of the two may be right; his own articles of belief he looks upon as *à priori* true and certain principles.

DEMOPHELES.—So that's your higher point of view! I assure you there is a higher still. "First live, then philosophize" is a maxim of more comprehensive import than appears at first sight. The first thing to do is to control the raw and evil dispositions of the masses, so as to keep them from pushing injustice to extremes, and from committing cruel, violent and disgraceful acts. If you were to wait until they had recognized and grasped the truth, you would undoubtedly come too late; and truth, supposing that it had been found, would surpass their powers of comprehension. In any case an allegorical investiture of it, a parable or myth, is all that would be of any service to them. As Kant said, there must be a public standard of Right and Virtue; it must always flutter high overhead. It is a matter of indifference what heraldic figures are inscribed on it, so long as they signify what is meant. Such an allegorical representation of truth is always and everywhere, for humanity at large, a serviceable substitute for a truth to which it can never attain, for a philosophy which it can never grasp; let alone the fact that it is daily changing its shape, and has in no form as yet met with general acceptance. Practical aims, then, my good Philalethes, are in every respect superior to theoretical.

PHILALETHES.—What you say is very like the ancient advice of Timæus of Locrus, the Pythagorean, "stop the mind with falsehood if you can't speed it with truth." I almost suspect that your plan is the one which is so much in vogue just now, that you want to impress upon us that

> " The hour is nigh
> When we may feast in quiet."

You recommend us, in fact, to take timely precautions so that the waves of the discontented raging masses mayn't disturb us at table. But the whole point of view is as false as it is nowadays popular and commended; and so I make haste to enter a protest against it. It is false that state, justice, law cannot be upheld without the assistance of religion and its dogmas; and that justice and public order need religion as a necessary complement, if legislative enactments are to be carried out. It is false, were it repeated a hundred times! An effective and striking argument to the contrary is afforded by the ancients, especially the Greeks. They had nothing at all of what we understand by religion. They had no sacred documents, no dogma to be learned and its acceptance furthered by every one, its principles to be inculcated early on the young. Just as little was moral doctrine preached by the ministers of religion, nor did the priests trouble themselves about morality or about what the people did or left undone. Not at all. The duty of the priests was confined to temple-ceremonial, prayers, hymns, sacrifices, processions, lustrations and the like, the object of which was anything but the moral improvement of the individual. What was called religion consisted, more especially in the cities, in giving temples here and there to some of the gods of the greater tribes, in which the worship described was carried on as a state matter, and was consequently, in fact, an affair of police. No one, except the functionaries performing, was in any way compelled to attend, or even to believe in it. In the whole of antiquity there is no trace of any obligation to believe in any particular dogma. Merely in the case of an open denial of the existence of the gods, or any other reviling of them, a penalty was imposed, and that on account of the insult offered to the state, which served those gods: beyond this it was free to every one to think of them what he pleased. If any one wanted to gain the favor of those gods privately, by prayer or sacrifice, it was open to him to do so at his own expense and at his own risk; if he didn't do it, no one made any objection, least of all the state. In the case of the Romans every one had his own Lares and Penates at home: these were, however, in reality, only the venerated busts of ancestors. Of the immortality of the soul and a life beyond the grave, the ancients had no firm, clear or, least of all, dogmatically fixed idea, but very loose, fluctuating, indefinite and problematical notions, every one in his own way: and the ideas about the gods were just as varying, individual and vague. There was therefore really no religion, in our sense of the word, among the ancients. But did anarchy and lawlessness prevail among them on that account? Is not law and civil order, rather, so much their work, that it still forms the foundation of our own? Was there not complete protection for property, even though it consisted for the most part of slaves? And did not this state of things last for more than a thousand years? So that I can't recognize, I must even protest against the practical aims and the necessity of religion in the sense indicated by you, and so popular nowadays, that is, as an indispensable foundation of all legislative arrangements. For, if you take that point of view, the pure and sacred endeavor after truth will, to say the least, appear quixotic, and even criminal, if it ventures, in its feeling of justice, to denounce the authoritative creed as a usurper who has taken possession of the throne of truth and maintained his position by keeping up the deception.

DEMOPHELES.—But religion is not opposed to truth; it itself teaches truth. And as the range of its activity is not a narrow lecture room, but the world and humanity at large, religion must conform to the requirements and comprehension of an audience so numerous and so mixed. Religion must not let truth appear in its naked form; or, to use a medical simile, it must not exhibit it pure, but must employ a mythical vehicle, a medium, as it were. You can also compare truth in this respect to certain chemical stuffs which in themselves are gaseous, but which for medicinal uses, as also for preservation or transmission, must be bound to a stable, solid base, because they would otherwise volatilize. Chlorine gas, for example, is for all purposes applied only in the form of chlorides. But if truth, pure, abstract and free from all mythical alloy, is always to remain unattainable, even by philosophers, it might be compared to fluorine, which cannot even be isolated, but must always appear in combination with other elements. Or, to take a less scientific simile, truth, which is inexpressible except by means of myth and allegory, is like water, which can be carried about only in vessels: a philosopher who insists on obtaining it pure is like a man who breaks the jug in order to get the water by itself. This is, perhaps, an exact analogy. At any rate, religion is truth allegorically and mythically expressed, and so rendered attainable and digestible by mankind in general. Mankind couldn't possibly take it pure and unmixed, just as we can't breathe pure oxygen; we require an addition of four times its bulk in nitrogen. In plain language, the profound meaning, the high aim of life, can only be unfolded and presented to the masses symbolically, because they are incapable of grasping it in its true signification. Philosophy, on the other hand, should be like the Eleusinian mysteries, for the few, the *élite*.

PHILALETHES.—I understand. It comes, in short, to truth wearing the garment of falsehood. But in doing so it enters on a fatal alliance. What a dangerous weapon is put into the hands of those who are authorized to employ falsehood as the vehicle of truth! If it is as you say, I fear the damage caused by the falsehood will be greater than any advantage the truth could ever produce. Of course, if the allegory were admitted to be such, I should raise no objection; but with the admission it would rob itself of all respect, and consequently, of all utility. The allegory must, therefore, put in a claim to be true in the proper sense of the word, and maintain the claim; while, at the most, it is true only in an allegorical sense. Here lies the irreparable mischief, the permanent evil; and this is why religion has always been and will always be in conflict with the noble endeavor after pure truth.

DEMOPHELES.—Oh no! that danger is guarded against. If religion mayn't exactly confess its allegorical nature, it gives sufficient indication of it.

PHILALETHES.—How so?

DEMOPHELES.—In its mysteries. "Mystery," is in reality only a technical theological term for religious allegory. All religions have their mysteries. Properly speaking, a mystery is a dogma which is plainly absurd, but which, nevertheless, conceals in itself a lofty truth, and one which by itself would be completely incomprehensible to the ordinary understanding of the raw multitude. The multitude accepts it in this disguise on trust, and believes it, without being led astray by the absurdity of it, which even to its intelligence is obvious; and in this way it participates in the kernel of the matter so far as it is possible for it to do so. To explain what I mean, I may add that even in philosophy an attempt has been made to make use of a mystery. Pascal, for example, who was at once a pietist, a mathematician, and a philosopher, says in this threefold capacity: "God is everywhere center and nowhere periphery." Malebranche has also the just remark: "Liberty is a mystery." One could go a step further and maintain that in religions everything is mystery. For to impart truth, in the proper sense of the word, to the multitude in its raw state is absolutely impossible; all that can fall to its lot is to be enlightened by a mythological reflection of it. Naked truth is out of place before the eyes of the profane vulgar; it can only make its appearance thickly veiled. Hence, it is unreasonable to require of a religion that it shall be true in the proper sense of the word; and this, I may observe in passing, is nowadays the absurd contention of Rationalists and Supernaturalists alike. Both start from the position that religion must be the real truth; and while the former demonstrate that it is not the truth, the latter obstinately maintain that it is; or rather, the former dress up and arrange the allegorical element in such a way, that, in the proper sense of the word, it could be true, but would be, in that case, a platitude; while the latter wish to maintain that it is true in the proper sense of the word, without any further dressing; a belief, which, as we ought to know, is only to be enforced by inquisitions and the stake. As a fact, however, myth and allegory really form the proper element of religion; and under this indispensable condition, which is imposed by the intellectual limitation of the multitude, religion provides a sufficient satisfaction for those metaphysical requirements of mankind which are indestructible. It takes the place of that pure philosophical truth which is infinitely difficult and perhaps never attainable.

PHILALETHES.—Ah! just as a wooden leg takes the place of a natural one; it supplies what is lacking, barely does duty for it, claims to be regarded as a natural leg, and is more or less artfully put together. The only difference is that, while a natural leg as a rule preceded the wooden one, religion has everywhere got the start of philosophy.

DEMOPHELES.—That may be, but still for a man who hasn't a natural leg, a wooden one is of great service. You must bear in mind that the metaphysical needs of mankind absolutely require satisfaction, because the horizon of man's thoughts must have a back-ground and not remain unbounded. Man has, as a rule, no faculty for weighing reasons and discriminating between what is false and what is true; and besides, the labor which nature and the needs of nature impose upon him, leaves him no time for such inquiries, or for the education which they presuppose. In his case, therefore, it is no use talking of a reasoned conviction; he has to fall back on belief and authority. If a really true philosophy were to take the place of religion, nine-tenths at least of mankind would have to receive it on authority; that is to say, it too would be a matter of faith, for Plato's dictum, that the multitude can't be philosophers, will always remain true. Authority, however, is an affair of time and circumstance alone, and so it can't be bestowed on that which has only reason in its favor; it must accordingly be allowed to nothing but what has acquired it in the course of history, even if it is only an allegorical representation of truth. Truth in this form, supported by authority, appeals first of all to those elements in the human constitution which are strictly metaphysical, that is to say, to the need man feels of a theory in regard to the riddle of existence which forces itself upon his notice, a need arising from the consciousness that behind the physical in the world there is a metaphysical, something permanent as the foundation of constant change. Then it appeals to the will, to the fears and hopes of mortal beings living in constant struggle; for whom, accordingly, religion creates gods and demons whom they can cry to, appease and win over. Finally, it appeals to that moral consciousness which is undeniably present in man, lends to it that corroboration and support without which it would not easily maintain itself in the struggle against so many temptations. It is just from this side that religion affords an inexhaustible source of con solation and comfort in the innumerable trials of life, a comfort which does not leave men in death, but rather then only unfolds its full efficacy. So religion may be compared to one who takes a blind man by the hand and leads him, because he is unable to see for himself, whose concern it is to reach his destination, not to look at every-thing by the way.

PHILALETHES.--That is certainly the strong point of religion. If it is a fraud, it is a pious fraud; that is un-deniable. But this makes priests something between de-ceivers and teachers of morality: they daren't teach the real truth, as you have quite rightly explained, even if they knew it, which is not the case. A true philosophy, then, can always exist, but not a true religion; true, I mean, in the proper understanding of the word, not merely in that flowery or allegorical sense which you have de-scribed; a sense in which all religions would be true, only in various degrees. It is quite in keeping with the in-extricable mixture of weal and woe, honesty and deceit, good and evil, nobility and baseness, which is the average characteristic of the world everywhere, that the most im-portant, the most lofty the most sacred truths can make their appearance only in combination with a lie, can even borrow strength from a lie as from something that works more powerfully on mankind: and, as revelation, must be ushered in by a lie. This might indeed be regarded as the *cachet* of the moral world. However, we won't give up the hope that mankind will eventually reach a point of maturity and education at which it can on the one side produce, and on the other receive, the true philosophy. *Simplex sigillum veri:* the naked truth must be so simple and intelligible that it can be imparted to all in its true form, without any admixture of myth and fable, without disguising it in the form of religion.

DEMOPHELES.--You've no notion how stupid most people are.

PHILALETHES.--I am only expressing a hope which I can't give up. If it were fulfilled, truth in its simple and intelligible form would of course drive religion from the place it has so long occupied as its representative, and by that very means kept open for it The time would have come when religion would have carried out her object and completed her course: the race she had brought to years of discretion she could dismiss, and herself depart in peace: that would be the *euthanasia* of religion. But as long as she lives, she has two faces, one of truth, one of fraud. According as you look at one or the other, you will bear her favor or ill-will. Religion must be regarded as a necessary evil, its necessity resting on the pitiful imbecility of the great majority of mankind, incapable of grasping the truth, and therefore requiring, in its pressing need, something to take its place.

DEMOPHELES.—Really, one would think that you philosophers had truth in a cupboard, and that all you had to do was to go and get it!

PHILALETHES.—Well, if we haven't got it, it is chiefly owing to the pressure put upon philosophy by religion at all times and in all places. People have tried to make the expression and communication of truth, even the contemplation and discovery of it, impossible, by putting children, in their earliest years, into the hands of priests to be manipulated; to have the lines in which their fundamental thoughts are henceforth to run, laid down with such firmness as, in essential matters, to be fixed and determined for this whole life. When I take up the writings even of the best intellects of the sixteenth and seventeenth centuries (more especially if I have been engaged in oriental studies), I am sometimes shocked to see how they are paralyzed and hemmed in on all sides by Jewish ideas. How can any one think out the true philosophy when he is prepared like this?

DEMOPHELES.—Even if the true philosophy were to be discovered, religion wouldn't disappear from the world, as you seem to think. There can't be one system of metaphysics for everybody; that's rendered impossible by the natural differences of intellectual power between man and man, and the differences, too, which education makes. It is a necessity for the great majority of mankind to engage in that severe bodily labor which cannot be dispensed with if the ceaseless requirements of the whole race are to be satisfied. Not only does this leave the majority no time for education, for learning, for contemplation; but by virtue of the hard and fast antagonism between muscles and mind, the intelligence is blunted by so much exhausting bodily labor, and becomes heavy, clumsy, awkward and consequently incapable of grasping any other than quite simple situations. At least nine-tenths of the human race falls under this category. But still people require a system of metaphysics, that is, an account of the world and our existence, because such an account belongs to the most natural needs of mankind, they require a popular system; and to be popular it must combine many rare qualities. It must be easily understood, and at the same time possess, on the proper points, a certain amount of obscurity, even of impenetrability; then a correct and satisfactory system of morality must be bound up with its dogmas; above all, it must afford inexhaustible consolation in suffering and death; the consequence of all this is, that it can only be true in an allegorical and not in a real sense. Further, it must have the support of an authority which is impressive by its great age, by being universally recognized, by its documents, their tone and utterances; qualities which are so extremely difficult to combine that many a man wouldn't be so ready, if he considered the matter, to help to undermine a religion, but would reflect that what he is attacking is a people's most sacred treasure. If you want to form an opinion on religion, you should always bear in mind the character of the great multitude for which it is destined, and form a picture to yourself of its complete inferiority, moral and intellectual. It is incredible how far this inferiority goes, and how perseveringly a spark of truth will glimmer on even under the crudest covering of monstrous fable or grotesque ceremony, clinging indestructibly, like the odor of musk, to everything that has once come into contact with it. In illustration of this, consider the profound wisdom of the Upanishads, and then look at the mad idolatry in the India of to-day, with its pilgrimages, processions and festivities, or at the insane and ridiculous goings-on of the Saniassi. Still one can't deny that in all this insanity and nonsense there lies some obscure purpose which accords with, or is a reflection of the profound wisdom I mentioned. But for the brute multitude, it has to be dressed up in this form. In such a contrast as this we have the two poles of humanity, the wisdom of the individual and the bestiality of the many, both of which find their point of contact in the moral sphere. That saying from the

Kurral must occur to everybody, "Base people look like men, but I have never seen their exact counterpart." The man of education may, all the same, interpret religion to himself *cum grano salis;* the man of learning, the contemplative spirit may secretly exchange it for a philosophy. But here again one philosophy wouldn't suit everybody; by the laws of affinity every system would draw to itself that public to whose education and capacities it was most suited. So there is always an inferior metaphysical system of the schools for the educated multitude, and a higher one for the *élite.* Kant's lofty doctrine, for instance, had to be degraded to the level of the schools and ruined by such men as Fries, Krug and Salat. In short, here, if anywhere, Goethe's maxim is true, "One does not suit all." Pure faith in revelation and pure metaphysics are for the two extremes, and for the intermediate steps mutual modifications of both in innumerable combinations and gradations. And this is rendered necessary by the immeasurable differences which nature and education have placed between man and man.

PHILALETHES.—The view you take reminds me seriously of the mysteries of the ancients, which you mentioned just now. Their fundamental purpose seems to have been to remedy the evil arising from the differences of intellectual capacity and education. The plan was out of the great multitude utterly impervious to unveiled truth, to select certain persons who might have it revealed to them up to a given point; out of these, again to choose others to whom more would be revealed, as being able to grasp more; and so on up to the Epopts. These grades corresponded to the little, greater and greatest mysteries. The arrangement was founded on a correct estimate of the intellectual inequality of mankind.

DEMOPHELES.—To some extent the education in our lower, middle and high schools corresponds to the varying grades of initiation into the mysteries.

PHILALETHES.—In a very approximate way: and then only in so far as subjects of higher knowledge are written about exclusively in Latin. But since that has ceased to be the case, all the mysteries are profaned.

DEMOPHELES.—However that may be, I wanted to remind you that you should look at religion more from the practical than from the theoretical side. Personified metaphysics may be the enemy of religion, but all the same personified morality will be its friend. Perhaps the metaphysical element in all religions is false; but the moral element in all is true. This might perhaps be presumed from the fact that they all disagree in their metaphysics, but are in accord as regards morality.

PHILALETHES.—Which is an illustration of the rule of logic that false premises may give a true conclusion.

DEMOPHELES.—Let me hold you to your conclusion let me remind you that religion has two sides. If it can't stand when looked at from its theoretical, that is, its intellectual side; on the other hand, from the moral side, it proves itself the only means of guiding, controlling and mollifying those races of animals endowed with reason, whose kinship with the ape does not exclude a kinship with the tiger. But at the same time religion is, as a rule, a sufficient satisfaction for their dull metaphysical necessities. You don't seem to me to possess a proper idea of the difference, wide as the heavens asunder, the deep gulf between your man of learning and enlightenment, accustomed to the process of thinking, and the heavy, clumsy, dull and sluggish consciousness of humanity's beasts of burden, whose thoughts have once and for all taken the direction of anxiety about their livelihood, and cannot be put in motion in any other; whose muscular strength is so exclusively brought into play that the nervous power, which makes intelligence, sinks to a very low ebb. People like that must have something tangible which they can lay hold of on the slippery and thorny pathway of their life, some sort of beautiful fable, by means of which things can be imparted to them which their crude intelligence can entertain only in picture and parable. Profound explanations and fine distinctions are thrown away upon them. If you conceive religion in this light, and recollect that its aims are above all practical, and only in a subordinate degree theoretical, it will appear to you as something worthy of the highest respect.

PHILALETHES.—A respect which will finally rest upon the principle that the end sanctifies the means. I don't feel in favor of a compromise on a basis like that. Religion may be an excellent means of taming and training the perverse, obtuse and ill-disposed members of the biped race: in the eyes of the friend of truth every fraud, even though it be a pious one, is to be condemned. A system of deception, a pack of lies, would be a strange means of inculcating virtue. The flag to which I have taken the oath is truth: I shall remain faithful to it everywhere, and whether I succeed or not, I shall fight for light and truth! If I see religion on the wrong side——

DEMOPHELES.—But you won't. Religion isn't a deception: it is true and the most important of all truths. Because its doctrines are, as I have said, of such a lofty kind that the multitude can't grasp them without an intermediary; because, I say, its light would blind the ordinary eye, it comes forward wrapped in the veil of allegory and teaches, not indeed what is exactly true in itself, but what is true in respect of the lofty meaning contained in it; and, understood in this way, religion is the truth.

PHILALETHES.—It would be all right if religion were only at liberty to be true in a merely allegorical sense. But its contention is that it is downright true in the proper sense of the word. Herein lies the deception, and it is here that the friend of truth must take up a hostile position.

DEMOPHELES.—This deception is a *sine qua non.* If religion were to admit that it was only the allegorical meaning in its doctrines which was true, it would rob itself of all efficacy. Such rigorous treatment as this would destroy its invaluable influence on the hearts and morals of mankind. Instead of insisting on that with pedantic obstinacy, look at its great achievements in the practical sphere, its furtherance of good and kindly feelings, its guidance in conduct, the support and consolation it gives to suffering humanity in life and death. How much you ought to guard against letting theoretical cavils discredit in the eyes of the multitude, and finally wrest from it, something which is an inexhaustible source of consolation and tranquillity, something which, in its hard lot, it needs so much, even more than we do. On that score alone, religion should be free from attack.

PHILALETHES.—With that kind of argument you could have driven Luther from the field, when he attacked the sale of indulgences. How many a man got consolation from the letters of indulgence, a consolation which nothing else could give, a complete tranquillity: so that he joyfully departed with the fullest confidence in the packet of them which he held in his hand at the hour of death, convinced that they were so many cards of admission to all the nine heavens. What is the use of grounds of consolation and tranquillity which are constantly overshadowed by the Damocles-sword of illusion? The truth, my dear sir, is the only safe thing; the truth alone remains steadfast and trusty; it is the only solid consolation; it is the indestructible diamond.

DEMOPHELES.—Yes, if you had truth in your pocket, ready to favor us with it on demand. All you've got are metaphysical systems, in which nothing is certain but the headaches they cost. Before you take anything away, you must have something better to put in its place.

PHILALETHES.—That's what you keep on saying. To free a man from error is to give, not to take away. Knowledge that a thing is false is a truth. Error always does harm: sooner or later it will bring mischief to the man who harbors it. Then give up deceiving people; confess ignorance of what you don't know, and leave every one to form his own articles of faith for himself. Perhaps they won't turn out so bad, especially as they'll rub one another's corners down, and mutually rectify mistakes. The existence of many views will at any rate lay a foundation of tolerance. Those who possess knowledge and capacity may betake themselves to the study of philosophy, or even in their own persons carry the history of philosophy a step further.

DEMOPHELES.—That'll be a pretty business! A whole nation of raw metaphysicians, wrangling and eventually coming to blows with one another!

PHILALETHES.—Well, well, a few blows here and there are the sauce of life; or at any rate a very inconsiderable evil, compared with such things as priestly dominion, plundering of the laity, persecution of heretics, courts of inquisition, crusades, religious wars, massacres of St. Bartholomew. These have been the results of popular metaphysics imposed from without; so I stick to the old saying that you can't get grapes from thistles, nor expect good to come from a pack of lies.

DEMOPHELES.—How often must I repeat that religion is anything but a pack of lies? It is the truth itself, only in a mythical, allegorical vesture. But when you spoke of your plan of every one being his own founder of religion.

I wanted to say that a particularism like this is totally opposed to human nature, and would consequently destroy all social order. Man is a metaphysical animal—that is to say, he has paramount metaphysical necessities; accordingly, he conceives life above all in its metaphysical significance and wishes to bring everything into line with that. Consequently, however strange it may sound in view of the uncertainty of all dogmas, agreement in the fundamentals of metaphysics is the chief thing; because a genuine and lasting bond of union is only possible among those who are of one opinion on these points. As a result of this, the main point of likeness and of contrast between nations is rather religion than government, or even language; and so the fabric of society, the state, will stand firm only when founded on a system of metaphysics which is acknowledged by all. This, of course, can only be a popular system—that is, a religion: it becomes part and parcel of the constitution of the state, of all the public manifestations of the national life, and also of all solemn acts of individuals. This was the case in ancient India, among the Persians, Egyptians, Jews, Greeks and Romans: it is still the case in the Brahman, Buddhist and Mohammedan nations. In China there are three faiths, it is true, of which the most prevalent—Buddhism—is precisely the one which is not protected by the state: still, there is a saying in China, universally acknowledged, and of daily application, that "the three faiths are only one," —that is to say, they agree in essentials. The emperor confesses all three together at the same time. And Europe is the union of Christian states: Christianity is the basis of every one of the members, and the common bond of all. Hence Turkey, though geographically in Europe, is not properly to be reckoned as belonging to it. In the same way, the European princes hold their place " by the grace of God:" and the pope is the vicegerent of God. Accordingly, as his throne was the highest, he used to wish all thrones to be regarded as held in fee from him. In the same way, too, archbishops and bishops, as such, possessed temporal power; and in England they still have seats and votes in the Upper House. Protestant princes, as such, are heads of their churches: in England, a few years ago, this was a girl eighteen years old. By the revolt from the pope, the Reformation shattered the European fabric, and in a special degree dissolved the true unity of Germany by destroying its common religious faith. This union, which had practically come to an end, had, accordingly, to be restored later on by artificial and purely political means. You see, then, how closely connected a common faith is with the social order and the constitution of every state. Faith is everywhere the support of the laws and the constitution, the foundation, therefore, of the social fabric, which could hardly hold together at all if religion did not lend weight to the authority of government and the dignity of the ruler.

PHILALETHES.—Oh, yes, princes use God as a kind of bogey to frighten grown-up children to bed with, if nothing else avails: that's why they attach so much importance to the Deity. Very well. Let me, in passing, recommend our rulers to give their serious attention, regularly twice every year, to the fifteenth chapter of the First Book of Samuel, that they may be constantly reminded of what it means to prop the throne on the altar. Besides, since the stake, that *ultima ratio theologorum*, has gone out of fashion, this method of government has lost its efficacy. For, as you know, religions are like glow-worms; they shine only when it's dark. A certain amount of general ignorance is the condition of all religions, the element in which alone they can exist. And as soon as astronomy, natural science, geology, history, the knowledge of countries and peoples have spread their light broadcast, and philosophy finally is permitted to say a word, every faith founded on miracles and revelation must disappear; and philosophy takes its place. In Europe the day of knowledge and science dawned toward the end of the fifteenth century with the appearance of the Renaissance Platonists: its sun rose higher in the sixteenth and seventeenth centuries so rich in results, and scattered the mists of the Middle Age. Church and Faith were compelled to disappear in the same proportion; and so in the eighteenth century English and French philosophers were able to take up an attitude of direct hostility; until, finally, under Frederick the Great, Kant appeared, and took away from religious belief the support it had previously enjoyed from philosophy: he emancipated the handmaid of theology, and in attacking the question with German thoroughness and patience, gave it an earnest, instead of a frivolous tone. The consequence of this is that we see Christianity undermined in the nineteenth century, a serious faith in it almost completely gone; we see it fighting even for bare existence, while anxious princes try to set it up a little by artificial means, as a doctor uses a drug on a dying patient. In this connection there is passage in Condorcet's "*Des Progrès de l'esprit humain*," which looks as if written as a warning to our age: " the religious zeal shown by philosophers and great men was only a political devotion; and every religion which allows itself to be defended as a belief that may usefully be left to the people, can only hope for an agony more or less prolonged." In the whole course of the events which I have indicated, you may always observe that faith and knowledge are related as the two scales of a balance; when the one goes up, the other goes down. So sensitive is the balance that it indicates momentary influences. When, for instance, at the beginning of this century, those inroads of French robbers under the leadership of Buonaparte, and the enormous efforts necessary for driving them out and punishing them, had brought about a temporary neglect of science, and consequently a certain decline in the general increase of knowledge, the Church immediately began to raise her head again and Faith began to show fresh signs of life: which, to be sure, in keeping with the times, was partly poetical in its nature. On the other hand, in the more than thirty years of peace which followed, leisure and prosperity furthered the building up of science and the spread of knowledge in an extraordinary degree· the consequence of which is what I have indicated, the dissolution and threatened fall of religion. Perhaps the time is approaching which has so often been prophesied, when religion will take her departure from European humanity, like a nurse which the child has out-grown: the child will now be given over to the instructions of a tutor. For there is no doubt that religious doctrines which are founded merely on authority, miracles and revelations, are only suited to the childhood of humanity. Every one will admit that a race, the past duration of which on the earth all accounts, physical and historical, agree in placing at not more than some hundred times the life of a man of sixty, is as yet only in its first childhood.

DEMOPHELES.—Instead of taking an undisguised pleas-are in prophesying the downfall of Christianity, how I wish you would consider what a measureless debt of gratitude European humanity owes to it, how greatly it has benefitted by the religion which, after a long interval, followed it from its old home in the East. Europe received from Christianity ideas which were quite new to it, the knowledge, I mean, of the fundamental truth that life cannot be an end in itself, that the true end of our existence lies beyond it. The Greeks and Romans had placed this end altogether in our present life, so that in this sense they may certainly be called blind heathens. And, in keeping with this view of life, all their virtues can be reduced to what is serviceable to the community, to what is useful, in fact. Aristotle says quite naïvely, "Those virtues must necessarily be the greatest which are the most useful to others." So the ancients thought patriotism the highest virtue, although it is really a very doubtful one, since narrowness, prejudice, vanity and an enlightened self-interest are main elements in it. Just before the passage I quoted, Aristotle enumerates all the virtues, in order to discuss them singly. They are Justice, Courage, Temperance, Magnificence, Magnanimity, Liberality, Gentleness, Good Sense and Wisdom. How different from the Christian virtues! Plato himself, incomparably the most transcendent philosopher of pre-Christian antiquity, knows no higher virtue than justice; and he alone recommends it unconditionally and for its own sake, whereas the rest make a happy life, *vita beata,* the aim of all virtue, and moral conduct the way to attain it. Christianity freed European humanity from this shallow, crude identification of itself with the hollow uncertain existence of every day,

" cœlumque tueri
Jussit, et erectos ad sidera tollere vultus."

Christianity, accordingly, does not preach mere Justice, but the Love of Mankind, Compassion, Good Works, Forgiveness, Love of your Enemies, Patience, Humility, Resignation, Faith and Hope. It even went a step further, and taught that the world is of evil, and that we need deliverance. It preached despisal of the world, self-denial, chastity, giving up of one's own will, that is, turning away from life and its illusory pleasures. It taught the healing power of pain: an instrument of torture is the symbol of Christianity. I am quite ready to admit that this earnest, this only correct view of life was thousands of years previously spread all over Asia in other forms, as it is still, independently of Christianity; but for European humanity it was a new and great revelation. For it is well known that the population of Europe consists of Asiatic races driven out as wanderers from their own homes, and gradually settling down in Europe; on their wanderings these races lost the original religion of their homes, and with it the right view of life: so, under a new sky, they formed religions for themselves, which were rather crude; the worship of Odin, for instance, the Druidic or the Greek religion, the metaphysical content of which was little and shallow. In the meantime the Greeks developed a special, one might almost say, an instinctive sense of beauty, belonging to them alone of all the nations who have ever existed on the earth, peculiar, fine and exact: so that their mythology took, in the mouth of their poets, and in the hands of their artists, an exceedingly beautiful and pleasing shape. On the other hand, the true and deep significance of life was lost to the Greeks and Romans. They lived on like grown-up children, till Christianity came and recalled them to the serious side of existence.

PHILALETHES.—And to see the effects you need only compare antiquity with the Middle Age; the time of Pericles, say, with the fourteenth century. You could scarcely, believe you were dealing with the same kind of beings. There, the finest development of humanity, excellent institutions, wise laws, shrewdly apportioned offices, rationally ordered freedom, all the arts, including poetry and philosophy, at their best; the production of works which, after thousands of years, are unparalleled, the creations, as it were, of a higher order of beings, which we can never imitate; life embellished by the noblest fellowship, as portrayed in Xenophon's "Banquet." Look on the other picture, if you can; a time at which the Church had enslaved the minds, and violence the bodies of men, that knights and priests might lay the whole weight of life upon the common beast of burden, the third estate. There, you have might as right, Feudalism and Fanati-

cism in close alliance, and in their train abominable
ignorance and darkness of mind, a corresponding intolerance, discord of creeds, religious wars, crusades, inquisitions and persecutions; as the form of fellowship, chivalry,
compounded of savagery and folly, with its pedantic
system of ridiculous false pretenses carried to an extreme,
its degrading superstition and apish veneration for
women. Gallantry is the residue of this veneration, de-
servedly requited as it is by feminine arrogance: it affords
continual food for laughter to all Asiatics, and the Greeks
would have joined in it. In the golden Middle Age the
practice developed into a regular and methodical service of
women; it imposed deeds of heroism, *cours d'amour*,
bombastic troubadour songs etc.; although it is to be
observed that these last buffooneries, which had an intellectual side, were chiefly at home in France; whereas
among the material sluggish Germans, the knights distinguished themselves rather by drinking and stealing;
they were good at boozing and filling their castles with
plunder; though in the courts to be sure, there was no
lack of insipid love-songs. What caused this utter transformation? Migration and Christianity.

DEMOPHELES.—I am glad you reminded me of it.
Migration was the source of the evil; Christianity the dam
on which it broke. It was chiefly by Christianity that the
raw, wild hordes which came flooding in were controlled
and tamed. The savage man must first of all learn to
kneel, to venerate, to obey; after that, he can be civilized.
This was done in Ireland by St. Patrick, in Germany by
Winifried the Saxon, who was a genuine Boniface. It
was migration of peoples, the last advance of Asiatic races
toward Europe, followed only by the fruitless attempts of
those under Attila, Genghis Khan, and Timur, and as a
comic afterpiece, by the gypsies—it was this movement
which swept away the humanity of the ancients. Christianity was precisely the principle which set itself to work
against this savagery; just as later, through the whole of
the Middle Age, the Church and its hierarchy were most
necessary to set limits to the savage barbarism of those
masters of violence, the princes and knights; it was what
broke up the ice-floes in that mighty deluge. Still, the
chief aim of Christianity is not so much to make this life
pleasant as to render us worthy of a better. It looks away

over this span of time, over this fleeting dream, and seeks
to lead us to eternal welfare. Its tendency is ethical in
the highest sense of the word, a sense unknown in Europe
till its advent; as I have shown you, by putting the
morality and religion of the ancients side by side with
those of Christendom.

PHILALETHES.—You are quite right as regards theory;
but look at the practice! In comparison with the ages of
Christianity the ancient world was unquestionably less
cruel than the Middle Age, with its deaths by exquisite
torture, its innumerable burnings at the stake. The ancients, further, were very enduring, laid great stress o
justice, frequently sacrificed themselves for their country,
showed such traces of every kind of magnanimity, and
such genuine manliness, that to this day an acquaintance
with their thoughts and actions is called the study of
Humanity. The fruits of Christianity were religious wars,
butcheries, crusades, inquisitions, extermination of the
natives in America, and the introduction of African slaves
in their place; and among the ancients there is nothing
analogous to this, nothing that can be compared with it;
for the slaves of the ancients, the *familia*, the *vernœ*,
were a contented race, and faithfully devoted to their
masters' service, and as different from the miserable
negroes of the sugar plantations, which are a disgrace to
humanity, as their two colors are distinct. Those special
moral delinquencies for which we reproach the ancients,
and which are perhaps less uncommon nowadays than
appears on the surface to be the case, are trifles compared
with the Christian enormities I have mentioned. Can
you then, all considered, maintain that mankind has been
really made morally better by Christianity?

DEMOPHELES.—If the results haven't everywhere been
in keeping with the purity and truth of the doctrine, it
may be because the doctrine has been too noble
too elevated for mankind, that its aim has been
placed too high. It was so much easier to come up to the
heathen system, or to the Mohammedan. It is precisely
what is noble and dignified that is most liable everywhere
to misuse and fraud: *abusus optimi pessimus.* Those
high doctrines have accordingly now and then served as a
pretext for the most abominable proceedings, and for acts
of unmitigated wickedness. The downfall of the in-

stitutions of the old world, as well as of its arts and
sciences, is, as I have said, to be attributed to the inroad
of foreign barbarians. The inevitable result of this inroad
was that ignorance and savagery got the upper hand;
consequently violence and knavery established their
dominion, and knights and priests became a burden to
mankind. It is partly, however, to be explained by the fact
that the new religion made eternal and not temporal welfare the object of desire, taught that simplicity of heart
was to be preferred to knowledge, and looked askance at
all worldly pleasure. Now the arts and sciences subserve
worldly pleasure; but in so far as they could be made
serviceable to religion they were promoted, and attained
a certain degree of perfection.

PHILALETHES.—In a very narrow sphere. The sciences
were suspicious companions, and as such, were placed
under restrictions: on the other hand darling ignorance,
that element so necessary to a system of faith, was carefully nourished.

DEMOPHELES.—And yet mankind's possessions in the
way of knowledge up to that period, which were preserved
in the writings of the ancients, were saved from destruction by the clergy, especially by those in the monasteries.
How would it have fared if Christianity hadn't come in
just before the migration of peoples?

PHILALETHES.—It would really be a most useful inquiry
to try and make, with the coldest impartiality, an unprejudiced, careful and accurate comparison of the advantages
and disadvantages which may be put down to religion.
For that, of course, a much larger knowledge of historical
and psychological data than either of us command, would
be necessary. Academies might make it a subject for a
prize essay.

DEMOPHELES.—They'll take good care not to do so.

PHILALETHES.—I'm surprised to hear you say that: it's
a bad lookout for religion. However, there are academies which, in proposing a subject for competition,
make it a secret condition that the prize is to go to the
man who best interprets their own view. If we could only
begin by getting a statistician to tell us how many crimes
are prevented every year by religious, and how many by
other motives, there would be very few of the former.
If a man feels tempted to commit a crime, you may rely

upon it that the first consideration which enters his head is the penalty appointed for it, and the chances that it will fall upon him: then comes, as a second consideration, the risk to his reputation. If I am not mistaken, he will ruminate by the hour on these two impediments, before he ever takes a thought of religious considerations. If he gets safely over those two first bulwarks against crime, I think religion alone will very rarely hold him back from it.

DEMOPHELES.—I think that it will very often do so, especially when its influence works through the medium of custom. An atrocious act is at once felt to be repulsive. What is this but the effect of early impressions? Think, for instance, how often a man, especially if of noble birth, will make tremendous sacrifices to perform what he has promised, motived entirely by the fact that his father has often earnestly impressed upon him in his childhood that " a man of honor " or " a gentleman " or " a cavalier " always keeps his word inviolate.

PHILALETHES.—That's no use unless there is a certain inborn honorableness. You mustn't ascribe to religion what results from innate goodness of character, by which compassion for the man who would suffer by the crime keeps a man from committing it. This is the genuine moral motive, and as such it is independent of all religions.

DEMOPHELES.—But this is a motive which rarely affects the multitude unless it assumes a religious aspect. The religious aspect at any rate strengthens its power for good. Yet without any such natural foundation, religious motives alone are powerful to prevent crime. We need not be surprised at this in the case of the multitude when we see that even people of education pass now and then under the influence, not indeed of religious motives, which are founded on something which is at least allegorically true, but of the most absurd superstition, and allow themselves to be guided by it all their life long; as, for instance, undertaking nothing on a Friday, refusing to sit down thirteen at table, obeying chance omens, and the like. How much more likely is the multitude to be guided by such things. You can't form any adequate idea of the narrow limits of the mind in its raw state; it is a place of absolute darkness, especially when, as often happens, a bad, unjust, and malicious heart is at the bottom of it. People in this condition—and they form the great bulk of humanity—must be led and controlled as well as may be, even if it be by really superstitious motives; until such time as they become susceptible to truer and better ones. As an instance of the direct working of religion, may be cited the fact, common enough, in Italy especially, of a thief restoring stolen goods, through the influence of his confessor, who says he won't absolve him if he doesn't. Think again of the case of an oath, where religion shows a most decided influence: whether it be that a man places himself expressly in the position of a purely moral being, and as such looks upon himself as solemnly appealed to, as seems to be the case in France, where the formula is simply *je le jure,* and also among the Quakers, whose solemn yea or nay is regarded as a substitute for the oath; or whether it be that a man really believes he is pronouncing something which may affect his eternal happiness—a belief which is presumably only the investiture of the former feeling. At any rate, religious considerations are a means of awaking and calling out a man's moral nature. How often it happens that a man agrees to take a false oath, and then, when it comes to the point, suddenly refuses, and truth and right win the day.

PHILALETHES.—Oftener still false oaths are really taken, and truth and right trampled under foot, though all witnesses of the oath know it well. Still you are quite right to quote the oath as an undeniable example of the practical efficacy of religion. But, in spite of all you've said, I doubt whether the efficacy of religion goes much beyond this. Just think; if a public proclamation were suddenly made, announcing the repeal of all the criminal laws; I fancy neither you nor I would have the courage to go home from here under the protection of religious motives. If, in the same way, all religions were declared untrue, we could, under the protection of the laws alone, go on living as before, without any special addition to our apprehensions or our measures of precaution. I will go beyond this, and say that religions have very frequently exercised a decidedly demoralizing influence. One may say generally that duties toward God and duties toward humanity are in inverse ratio. It is easy to let adulation of the Deity make amends for lack of proper behavior toward man. And so we see that in all times and in all countries the great majority of mankind find it much easier to beg their way to heaven by prayers than to deserve to go there by their actions. In every religion it soon comes to be the case that faith, ceremonies, rites and the like are proclaimed to be more agreeable to the Divine will than moral actions; the former, especially if they are bound up with the emoluments of the clergy, gradually come to be looked upon as a substitute for the latter. Sacrifices in temples, the saying of masses, the founding of chapels, the planting of crosses by the roadside, soon come to be the most meritorious works, so that even great crimes are expiated by them, as also by penance, subjection to priestly authority, confessions, pilgrimages, donations to the temples and the clergy, the building of monasteries and the like. The consequence of all this is that the priests finally appear as middlemen in the corruption of the gods. And if matters don't go quite so far as that, where is the religion whose adherents don't consider prayers, praise and manifold acts of devotion, a substitute, at least in part, for moral conduct? Look at England, where by an audacious piece of priestcraft, the Christian Sunday, introduced by Constantine the Great as a substitute for the Jewish Sabbath, is in a mendacious way identified with it, and takes its name—and this in order that the commands of Jehovah for the Sabbath (that is, the day on which the Almighty had to rest from his six days' labor, so that it is essentially the last day of the week), might be applied to the Christian Sunday, the *dies solis,* the first day of the week which the sun opens in glory, the day of devotion and joy. The consequence of this fraud is that "Sabbath-breaking," or "the desecration of the Sabbath," that is, the slightest occupation, whether of business or pleasure, all games, music, sewing, worldly books, are on Sundays looked upon as great sins. Surely the ordinary man must believe that if, as his spiritual guides impress upon him, he is only constant in "a strict observance of the holy Sabbath," and "a regular attendance on Divine Service," that is, if he only invariably idles away his time on Sundays and doesn't fail to sit two hours in church to hear the same litany for the thousandth time and mutter it in tune with the others, he may reckon on indulgence in regard to those little peccadilloes which he occasionally allows himself. Those devils in human form—the slave owners and traders in the free states of North America (they should be called the slave states)—are, as a rule, orthodox, pious Anglicans who would consider it a grave sin to work on Sundays: and in confidence in this, and their regular attendance at church, they hope for eternal happiness. The demoralizing tendency of religion is less problematical than its moral influence. How great and how certain that moral influence must be to make amends for the enormities which religions, especially the Christian and Mohammedan religions, have produced and spread over the earth! Think of the fanaticism, the endless persecutions, the religious wars, that sanguinary frenzy of which the ancients had no conception! think of the crusades, a butchery lasting two hundred years and inexcusable, its war-cry " It is the will of God," its object to gain possession of the grave of one who preached love and sufferance! think of the cruel expulsion and extermination of the Moors and Jews from Spain! think of the orgies of blood, the inquisitions, the heretical tribunals, the bloody and terrible conquests of the Mohammedans in three continents, or those of Christianity in America, whose inhabitants were for the most part, and in Cuba entirely, exterminated. According to Las Casas, Christianity murdered twelve millions in forty years, of course, *all in majorem Dei gloriam*, and for the propagation of the Gospel, and because what wasn't Christian wasn't even looked upon as human! I have, it is true, touched upon these matters before; but when in our day, we hear of " Latest News from the Kingdom of God,"* we shall not be weary of bringing old news to mind. And, above all, don't let us forget India, the cradle of the human race, or at least of that part of it to which we belong, where first Mohammedans, and then Christians, were most cruelly infuriated against the adherents of the original faith of mankind. The destruction or disfigurement of the ancient temples and idols, a lamentable, mischievous and barbarous act, still bears witness to the monotheistic fury of the Mohammedans, carried on from Marmud the Ghaznevid of cursed memory down to Aureng Zeb, the

---

* A missionary periodical, the fortieth annual number of which appeared in 1856.

fratricide, whom the Portuguese Christians have zealously imitated by destruction of temples and the *auto da fè* of the inquisition at Goa. Don't let us forget the chosen people of God, who after they had, by Jehovah's express command, stolen from their old and trusty friends in Egypt the gold and silver vessels which had been lent to them, made a murderous and plundering inroad into " the Promised Land," with the murderer Moses at their head, to tear it from the rightful owners, again by the same Jehovah's express and repeated commands, showing no mercy, exterminating the inhabitants, women, children and all (Joshua, ch. 9 and 10). And all this, simply because they weren't circumcised and didn't know Jehovah, which was reason enough to justify every enormity against them; just as for the same reason, in earlier times, the infamous knavery of the Patriarch Jacob and his chosen people against Hamor, king of Shalem, and his people, is reported to his glory because the people were unbelievers! (Genesis xxxiii. 18.) Truly, it is the worst side of religions that the believers of one religion have allowed themselves every sin against those of another, and with the utmost ruffianism and cuelty persecuted them; the Mohammedans against the Christians and Hindoos; the Christians against the Hindoos, Mohammedans, American natives, negroes, Jews, heretics, and others.

Perhaps I go too far in saying all religions. For the sake of truth, I must add that the fanatical enormities perpetrated in the name of religion are only to be put down to the adherents of monotheistic creeds, that is, the Jewish faith and its two branches, Christianity and Islamism. We hear of nothing of the kind in the case of Hindoos and Buddhists. Although it is a matter of common knowledge that about the fifth century of our era Buddhism was driven out by the Brahmans from its ancient home in the southernmost part of the Indian peninsula, and afterward spread over the whole of the rest of Asia; as far as I know, we have no definite account of any crimes of violence, or wars, or cruelties, perpetrated in the course of it. That may, of course, be attributable to the obscurity which veils the history of those countries; but the exceedingly mild character of their religion, together with their unceasing inculcation of forbearance toward all living things, and the fact that Brahmanism by its caste system properly admits no proselytes, allows one to hope that their adherents may be acquitted of shedding of blood on a large scale, and of cruelty in any form. Spence Hardy, in his excellent book on "Eastern Monachism," praises the extraordinary tolerance of the Buddhists, and adds his assurance that the annals of Buddhism will furnish fewer instances of religious persecution than those of any other religion. As a matter of fact, it is only to monotheism that intolerance is essential: an only god is by his nature a jealous god, who can allow no other god to exist. Polytheistic gods, on the other hand, are naturally tolerant; they live and let live; their own colleagues are the chief objects of their sufferance, as being gods of the same religion. This toleration is afterward extended to foreign gods, who are, accordingly, hospitably received, and later on admitted, in some cases, to an equality of rights; the chief example of which is shown by the fact that the Romans willingly admitted and venerated Phrygian, Egyptian and other gods. Hence, it is that monotheistic religions alone furnish the spectacle of religious wars, religious persecutions, heretical tribunals, that breaking of idols and destruction of images of the gods, that razing of Indian temples, and Egyptian colossi, which had looked on the sun three thousand years; just because a jealous god had said, "Thou shalt make no graven image."

But to return to the chief point. You are certainly right in insisting on the strong metaphysical needs of mankind; but religion appears to me to be not so much a satisfaction as an abuse of those needs. At any rate, we have seen that in regard to the furtherance of morality, its utility is, for the most part, problematical, its disadvantages, and especially the atrocities which have followed in its train, patent to the light of day. Of course it is quite a different matter if we consider the utility of religion as a prop of thrones; for where these are held "by the grace of God," throne and altar are intimately associated; and every wise prince who loves his throne and his family will appear at the head of his people as an exemplar of true religion. Even Machiavelli, in the eighteenth chapter of his book, most earnestly recommended religion to princes. Beyond this, one may say that revealed religions stand to philosophy exactly in the relation of "sovereigns by the grace of God," to "the sovereignty of the people;" so that the two former terms of the parallel are in natural alliance.

DEMOPHELES.—Oh, don't take that tone! You're going hand in hand with ochlocracy and anarchy, the arch-enemy of all legislative order, all civilization and all humanity.

PHILALETHES.—You are right. It was only a sophism of mine, what the fencing-master calls a feint. I retract it. But see how disputing sometimes makes an honest man unjust and malicious. Let us stop.

DEMOPHELES.—I can't help regretting that, after all the trouble I've taken, I haven't altered your disposition in regard to religion. On the other hand, I can assure you that everything you have said hasn't shaken my conviction of its high value and necessity.

PHILALETHES.—I believe you; for as we read in Hudibras:

> "He that complies against his will
> Is of his own opinion still."

My consolation is that, alike in controversies and in taking mineral waters, the after effects are the true ones.

DEMOPHELES.—Well, I hope it'll be beneficial in your case.

PHILALETHES.—It might be so, if I could digest a certain Spanish proverb.

DEMOPHELES.—Which is?

PHILALETHES.—" Behind the cross stands the devil."

DEMOPHELES.—Come, don't let us part with sarcasms. Let us rather admit that religion, like Janus, or better still, like the Brahman god of death, Yama, has two faces, and like him, one friendly, the other sullen. Each of us has kept his eyes fixed on one alone.

PHILALETHES.—You are right, old fellow!

A FEW WORDS ON PANTHEISM.

THE controversy between Theism and Pantheism might be presented in an allegorical or dramatic form by supposing a dialogue between two persons in the pit of a theater at Milan during the performance of a piece. One of them, convinced that he is in Girolamo's renowned marionette-theater, admires the art by which the director gets up the dolls and guides their movements. " Oh, you are quite mistaken," says the other, " we're in the Teatro della Scala; it is the manager and his troop who are on the stage; they are the persons you see before you; the poet too is taking a part."

The chief objection I have to Pantheism is that it says nothing. To call the world "God" is not to explain it; it is only to enrich our language with a superfluous synonym for the word " world." It comes to the same thing whether you say " the world is God," or " God is the world." But if you start from "God" as something that is given in experience, and has to be explained, and then say, "God is the world," you are affording what is, to some extent, an explanation, in so far as you are reducing what is unknown to what is partly known (*ignotum per notius*); but it is only a verbal explanation. If however, you start from what is really given, that is to say, from the world, and say, " the world is God," it is clear that you say nothing, or at least you are explaining what is unknown by what is more unknown.

Hence Pantheism presupposes Theism; only in so far as you start from a god, that is, in so far as you possess him as something with which you are already familiar, can you end by identifying him with the world; and your purpose in doing so is to put him out of the way in a decent fashion. In other words, you do not start clear from the world as something that requires explanation; you start from God as something that is given, and not knowing what to do with him, you make the world take over his ·ôle. This is the origin of Pantheism. Taking an unprejudiced view of the world as it is, no one would dream of regarding it as a god. It must be a very ill-advised god who knows no better way of diverting himself than by turning into such a world as ours, such a mean, shabby world, there to take the form of innumerable millions who live indeed, but are fretted and tormented, and who manage to exist awhile together only by preying on one another; to bear misery, need and death, without measure and without object, in the form, for instance, of millions of negro slaves, or of the three million weavers in Europe who, in hunger and care, lead a miserable existence in damp rooms or the cheerless halls of a factory. What a pastime this for a god, who must, as such, be used to another mode of existence!

We find accordingly that what is described as the great advance from Theism to Pantheism, if looked at seriously, and not simply as a masked negation of the sort indicated above, is a transition from what is unproved and hardly conceivable to what is absolutely absurd. For, however obscure, however loose or confused may be the idea which we connect with the word "God," there are two predicates which are inseparable from it, the highest power and the highest wisdom. It is absolutely absurd to think that a being endowed with these qualities should have put himself into the position described above. Theism, on the other hand, is something which is merely unproved; and if it is difficult to look upon the infinite world as the work of a personal, and therefore individual, Being, the like of which we know only from our experience of the animal world, it is nevertheless not an absolutely absurd idea. That a Being, at once almighty and all-good, should create a world of torment is always conceivable; even though we do not know why he does so; and accordingly we find that when people ascribe the height of goodness to this Being, they set up the inscrutable nature of his wisdom as the refuge by which the doctrine escapes the charge of absurdity. Pantheism, however, assumes that the creative God is himself the world of infinite torment, and, in this little world alone, dies every second, and that entirely of his own will; which is absurd. It would be much more correct to identify the world with the devil, as the venerable author of the *"Deutsche Theologie"* has, in fact, done in a passage of his immortal work, where he says, "Wherefore the evil spirit and nature are one, and where nature is not overcome, neither is the evil adversary overcome."

It is manifest that the Pantheists give the Sansara the name of God. The same name is given by the mystics to the Nirvana. The latter, however, state more about the Nirvana than they know, which is not done by the Buddhists, whose Nirvana is accordingly a relative nothing. It is only Jews, Christians, and Mohammedans who give its proper and correct meaning to the word "God."

The expression, often heard nowadays, "the world is an end-in-itself," leaves it uncertain whether Pantheism or a simple Fatalism is to be taken as the explanation of it. But, whichever it be, the expression looks upon the world from a physical point of view only, and leaves out of sight its moral significance, because you cannot assume a moral significance without presenting the world as means to a higher end. The notion that the world has a physical but not a moral meaning is the most mischievous error sprung from the greatest mental perversity.

ON BOOKS AND READING.

IGNORANCE is degrading only when found in company with riches. The poor man is restrained by poverty and need: labor occupies his thoughts, and takes the place of knowledge. But rich men who are ignorant live for their lusts only, and are like the beasts of the field; as may be seen every day; and they can also be reproached for not having used wealth and leisure for that which gives them their greatest value.

When we read, another person thinks for us: we merely repeat his mental process. In learning to write, the pupil goes over with his pen what the teacher has outlined in pencil: so in reading; the greater part of the work of thought is already done for us. This is why it relieves us to take up a book after being occupied with our own thoughts. And in reading, the mind is, in fact, only the playground of another's thoughts. So it comes about that if any one spends almost the whole day in reading, and by way of relaxation devotes the intervals to some thoughtless pastime, he gradually loses the capacity for thinking; just as the man who always rides, at last forgets how to walk. This is the case with many learned persons; they have read themselves stupid. For to occupy every spare moment in reading, and to do nothing but read, is even more paralyzing to the mind than constant manual labor, which at least allows those engaged in it to follow their own thoughts. A spring never free from the pressure of some foreign body at last loses its elasticity: and so does the mind if other people's thoughts

are constantly forced upon it. Just as you can ruin the
stomach and impair the whole body by taking too much
nourishment, so you can overfill and choke the mind by
feeding it too much. The more you read, the fewer are
the traces left by what you have read; the mind becomes
like a tablet crossed over and over with writing. There
is no time for ruminating, and in no other way can you
assimilate what you have read. If you read on and on
without setting your own thoughts to work, what you have
read cannot strike root, and is generally lost. It is, in
fact, just the same with mental as with bodily food;
hardly the fifth part of what one takes is assimilated.
The rest passes off in evaporation, respiration, and the like.

The result of all this is that thoughts put on paper are
nothing more than footsteps in the sand; you see the way
the man has gone, but to know what he saw on his walk,
you want his eyes.

There is no quality of style that can be gained by reading
writers who possess it; whether it be persuasiveness, imagination, the gift of drawing comparisons, boldness,
bitterness, brevity, grace, ease of expression or wit, unexpected contrasts, a laconic or naïve manner, and the like.
But if these qualities are already in us, exist, that is to
say, potentially, we can call them forth and bring them to
consciousness; we can learn the purposes to which they
can be put; we can be strengthened in our inclination to
use them, or get courage to do so; we can judge by examples the effect of applying them, and so acquire the
correct use of them; and of course it is only when we have
arrived at that point that we actually possess these
qualities. The only way in which reading can form style
is by teaching us the use to which we can put our own
natural gifts. We must have these gifts before we begin
to learn the use of them. Without them, reading teaches
us nothing but cold, dead mannerisms and makes us
shallow imitators.

The strata of the earth preserve in rows the creatures
which lived in former ages; and the array of books on the
shelves of a library stores up in like manner the errors of
the past and the way in which they have been exposed.
Like those creatures, they too were full of life in their

time, and made a great deal of noise; but now they are stiff and fossilized, and an object of curiosity to the literary palæontologist alone.

Herodotus relates that Xerxes wept at the sight of his army, which stretched further than the eye could reach, in the thought that of all these, after a hundred years, not one would be alive. And in looking over a huge catalogue of new books, one might weep at thinking that, when ten years have passed, not one of them will be heard of.

It is in literature as in life: wherever you turn, you stumble at once upon the incorrigible mob of humanity, swarming in all directions, crowding and soiling everything, like flies in summer. Hence the number, which no man can count, of bad books, those rank weeds of literature, which draw nourishment from the corn and choke it. The time, money and attention of the public, which rightfully belong to good books and their noble aims, they take for themselves: they are written for the mere purpose of making money or procuring places. So they are not only useless, they do positive mischief. Nine-tenths of the whole of our present literature has no other aim than to get a few shillings out of the pockets of the public; and to this end author, publisher and reviewer are in league.

Let me mention a crafty and wicked trick, albeit a profitable and successful one, practiced by *littérateurs*, hack writers and voluminous authors. In complete disregard of good taste and the true culture of the period, they have succeeded in getting the whole of the world of fashion into leading strings, so that they are all trained to read in time, and all the same thing, viz,. the newest books; and that for the purpose of getting food for conversation in the circles in which they move. This is the aim served by bad novels, produced by writers who were once celebrated, as Spindler, Bulwer-Lytton, Eugene Sue. What can be more miserable than the lot of a reading public like this, always bound to peruse the latest works of extremely commonplace persons who write for money only, and who are therefore never few in number? and for this advantage they are content to know by name only the works of the few superior minds of all ages and all countries. Literary newspapers, too, are a singularly cunning device for robbing the reading public of the time which, if culture is to be attained, should be devoted to the genuine productions of literature, instead of being occupied by the daily bungling of commonplace persons.

Hence, in regard to reading, it is a very important thing to be able to refrain. Skill in doing so consists in not taking into one's hands any book merely because at the time it happens to be extensively read; such as political or religious pamphlets, novels, poetry, and the like, which make a noise, and may even attain to several editions in the first and last year of their existence. Consider, rather, that the man who writes for fools is always sure of a large audience; be careful to limit your time for reading, and devote it exclusively to the works of those great minds of all times and countries, who o'ertop the rest of humanity, those whom the voice of fame points to as such. These alone really educate and instruct. You can never read bad literature too little, nor good literature too much. Bad books are intellectual poison; they destroy the mind. Because people always read what is new instead of the best of all ages, writers remain in the narrow circle of the ideas which happen to prevail in their time; and so the period sinks deeper and deeper into its own mire.

There are at all times two literatures in progress, running side by side, but little known to each other: the one real, the other only apparent. The former grows into permanent literature; it is pursued by those who live *for* science or poetry; its course is sober and quiet, but extremely slow; and it produces in Europe scarcely a dozen works in a century; these, however, are permanent. The other kind is pursued by persons who live *on* science or poetry; it goes at a gallop, with much noise and shouting of partisans; and every twelvemonth puts a thousand works on the market. But after a few years one asks, "Where are they? where is the glory which came so soon and made so much clamor?" This kind may be called fleeting, and the other, permanent literature.

In the history of politics, half a century is always a

considerable time; the matter which goes to form them is ever on the move; there is always something going on. But in the history of literature there is often a complete standstill for the same period; nothing has happened, for clumsy attempts don't count. You are just where you were fifty years previously.

To explain what I mean, let me compare the advance of knowledge among mankind to the course taken by a planet. The false paths on which humanity usually enters after every important advance are like the epicycles in the Ptolemaic system, and after passing through one of them, the world is just where it was before it entered it. But the great minds, who really bring the race further on its course, do not accompany it on the epicycles it makes from time to time. This explains why posthumous fame is often bought at the expense of contemporary praise, and *vice versâ*. An instance of such an epicycle is the philosophy started by Fichte and Schelling, and crowned by Hegel's caricature of it. This epicycle was a deviation from the limit to which philosophy had been ultimately bought by Kant; and at that point I took it up again afterward, to carry it further. In the intervening period the sham philosophers I have mentioned and some others went through their epicycle, which has just came to an end; so that those who went with them on their course are conscious of the fact that they are exactly at the point from which they started.

This circumstance explains why it is that, every thirty years or so, science, literature, and art, as expressed in the spirit of the age are declared bankrupt. The errors which appear from time to time mount to such a height in that period that the mere weight of their absurdity makes the fabric fall; while the opposition to them has been gathering force at the same time. So an upset takes place, often followed by an error in the opposite direction. To exhibit these movements in their periodical return would be the true practical aim of the history of literature: little attention, however, is paid to it. And besides, the comparatively short duration of these periods makes it difficult to collect the data of epochs long gone by, so that it is most convenient to observe how the matter stands in one's own generation. An instance of this tendency, drawn from physical science, is supplied in the Neptunian

geology of Werter. But let me keep to the example cited
above, the nearest we can take. In German philosophy,
the brilliant epoch of Kant was immediately followed by a
period which aimed rather at being imposing than at convincing. Instead of being thorough and clear, it tried to
be dazzling, hyperbolical, and, in a special degree, unintelligible: instead of seeking truth, it intrigued. Philosophy could make no progress in this fashion; and at last
the whole school and its method became bankrupt.
For the effrontery of Hegel and his fellows came to such a
pass—whether because they talked such sophisticated
nonsense, or were so unscrupulously puffed, or because the
entire aim of this pretty piece of work was quite obvious—
that in the end there was nothing to prevent the char-
latanry of the whole business from becoming manifest to
everybody: and when, in consequence of certain dis-
closures, the favor it had enjoyed in high quarters was
withdrawn, the system was openly ridiculed. This most
miserable of all the meager philosophies that have ever
existed came to grief, and dragged down with it into the
abysm of discredit the systems of Fichte and Schelling
which had preceded it. And so, as far as Germany is
concerned, the total philosophical incompetence of the
first half of the century following upon Kant is quite
plain: and still the Germans boast of their talent for
philosophy in comparison with foreigners, especially since
an English writer has been so maliciously ironical as to
call them "a nation of thinkers."

For an example of the general system of epicycles drawn
from the history of art, look at the school of sculpture
which flourished in the last century and took its name
from Bernini, more especially at the development of it
which prevailed in France. The ideal of this school was
not antique beauty, but commonplace nature: instead of
the simplicity and grace of ancient art, it represented the
manners of a French minuet. This tendency became
bankrupt when, under Winckelmann's direction, a return
was made to the antique school. The history of painting
furnishes an illustration in the first quarter of the century,
when art was looked upon merely as a means and instrument of mediæval religious sentiment and its themes consequently drawn from ecclesiastical subjects alone: these,
however, were treated by painters who had none of the

true earnestness of faith, and in their delusion they followed Francesco Francia, Pietro Perugino, Angelico da Fiesole and others like them, rating them higher even than the really great masters who followed. It was in view of this error, and because in poetry an analogous aim had at the same time found favor, that Goethe wrote his "Pfaffenspiel." This school, too, got the reputation of being whimsical, became bankrupt, and was followed by a return to nature, which proclaimed itself in *genre* pictures and scenes of life of every kind, even though it now and then strayed into what was vulgar.

The progress of the human mind in literature is similar. The history of literature is for the most part like the catalogue of a museum of deformities; the spirit in which they keep best is pigskin. The few creatures that have been born in goodly shape need not be looked for there. They are still alive, and are everywhere to be met with in the world, immortal, and with their years ever green. They alone form what I have called real literature; the history of which, poor as it is in persons, we learn from our youth up out of the mouths of all educated people, before compilations recount it for us.

As an antidote to the prevailing monomania for reading literary histories, in order to be able to chatter about everything, without having any real knowledge at all, let me refer to a passage in Lichtenberg's works, (vol. II. p. 302), which is well worth perusal.

I believe that the over-minute acquaintance with the history of science and learning, which is such a prevalent feature of our day, is very prejudicial to the advance of knowledge itself. There is pleasure in following up this history; but, as a matter of fact, it leaves the mind, not empty indeed, but without any power of its own, just because it makes it so full. Whoever has felt the desire, not to fill up his mind, but to strengthen it, to devolop his faculties and aptitudes, and generally, to enlarge his powers, will have found that there is nothing so weakening as intercourse with a so-called littérateur, on a matter of knowledge on which he has not thought at all, though he knows a thousand little facts appertaining to its history and literature. It is like reading a cookery-book when you are hungry. I believe that so-called literary history will never thrive among thoughtful people, who are conscious of their own worth and the worth of real knowledge. These people are more given to employing their own reason than to troubling themselves to know how others have employed theirs. The worst of it is that, as you will find, the more knowledge takes the direction of literary research, the less the power of promoting knowledge becomes; the only thing that increases is pride in the possession of it. Such persons believe that they possess knowledge in a greater degree than those who really possess it. It is surely a well-founded remark, that knowledge never makes its possessor proud. Those alone let themselves be blown out with pride, who, incapable of extending knowledge in their own persons, occupy themselves with clearing up dark points in its history, or are able to recount what others have done. They are proud, because they consider this occupation, which is mostly of a mechanical nature, the practice of knowledge. I could illustrate what I mean by examples, but it would be an odious task.

Still, I wish some one would attempt a tragical history of literature, giving the way in which the writers and artists, who form the proudest possession of the various nations which have given them birth, have been treated by them during their lives. Such a history would exhibit the ceaseless warfare, which what was good and genuine in all times and countries has had to wage with what was bad and perverse. It would tell of the martyrdom of almost all those who truly enlightened humanity, of almost all the great masters of every kind of art: it would show us how, with few exceptions, they were tormented to death, without recognition, without sympathy, without followers; how they lived in poverty and misery, while fame, honor, and riches, were the lot of the unworthy; how their fate was that of Esau, who, while he was hunting and getting venison for his father, was robbed of the blessing by Jacob, disguised in his brother's clothes; how, in spite of all, they were kept up by the love of their work, until at last the bitter fight of the teacher of humanity is over, until the immortal laurel is held out to him, and the hour strikes when it can be said:

> "Der schwere Panzer wird zum Flügelkleide
> Kurz ist der Schmerz, unendlich ist die Freude."

PHYSIOGNOMY.

THAT the outer man is a picture of the inner, and the face an expression and revelation of the whole character, is a presumption likely enough in itself, and therefore a safe one to go by; evidenced as it is by the fact that people are always anxious to see any one who has made

himself famous by good or evil, or as the author of some
extraordinary work; or if they cannot get a sight of him,
to hear at any rate from others what he looks like. So
people go to places where they may expect to see the
person who interests them; the press, especially in
England, endeavors to give a minute and striking description of his appearance; painters and engravers lose
no time in putting him visibly before us; and finally
photography, on that very account of such high value,
affords the most complete satisfaction of our curiosity.
It is also a fact that in private life every one criticises the
physiognomy of those he comes across, first of all secretly
trying to discern their intellectual and moral character
from their features. This would be a useless proceeding
if, as some foolish people fancy, the exterior of a man is a
matter of no account; if, as they think, the soul is one
thing and the body another, and the body related to the
soul merely as the coat to the man himself.

On the contrary, every human face is a hieroglyphic,
and a hieroglyphic, too, which admits of being deciphered,
the alphabet of which we carry about with us already perfected. As a matter of fact, the face of a man gives us
fuller and more interesting information than his tongue;
for his face is the compendium of all he will ever say, as it
is the one record of all his thoughts and endeavors.
And, moreover, the tongue tells the thought of one man only,
whereas the face expresses a thought of nature itself: so
that every one is worth attentive observation, even though
every one may not be worth talking to. And if every
individual is worth observation as a single thought of
nature, how much more so is beauty, since it is a higher
and more general conception of nature, is, in fact, her
thought of a species. This is why beauty is so captivating.
it is a fundamental thought of nature: whereas the individual is only a by-thought, a corollary.

In private, people always proceed upon the principle
that a man is what he looks; and the principle is a right
one, only the difficulty lies in its application. For though
the art of applying the principle is partly innate and may
be partly gained by experience, no one is a master of it,
and even the most experienced is not infallible. But for
all that, whatever Figaro may say, it is not the face which
deceives; it is we who deceive ourselves in reading in it
what is not there.

The deciphering of a face is certainly a great and difficult art, and the principles of it can never be learned in the abstract. The first condition of success is to maintain a purely objective point of view, which is no easy matter. For, as soon as the faintest trace of anything subjective is present, whether dislike or favor, or fear or hope, or even the thought of the impression we ourselves are making upon the object of our attention, the characters we are trying to decipher become confused and corrupt. The sound of a language is really appreciated only by one who does not understand it, and that because, in thinking of the signification of a word, we pay no regard to the sign itself. So, in the same way, a physiognomy is correctly gauged only by one to whom it is still strange, who has not grown accustomed to the face by constantly meeting and conversing with the man himself. It is, therefore, strictly speaking, only the first sight of a man which affords that purely objective view which is necessary for deciphering his features. An odor affects us only when we first come in contact with it, and the first glass of a wine is the one which gives us its true taste: in the same way, it is only at the first encounter that a face makes its full impression upon us. Consequently the first impression should be carefully attended to and noted, even written down if the subject of it is of personal importance, provided of course, that one can trust one's own sense of physiognomy. Subsequent acquaintance and intercourse will obliterate the impression, but time will one day prove whether it is true.

Let us, however, not conceal from ourselves the fact that this first impression is for the most part extremely unedifying. How poor most faces are! With the exception of those that are beautiful, good-natured or intellectual, that is to say, the very few and far between, I believe a person of any fine feeling scarcely ever sees a new face without a sensation akin to a shock, for the reason that it presents a new and surprising combination of unedifying elements. To tell the truth, it is, as a rule, a sorry sight. There are some people whose faces bear the stamp of such artless vulgarity and baseness of character, such an animal limitation of intelligence, that one wonders how they can appear in public with such a countenance, instead of wearing a mask. There are faces, indeed, the very sight of which produces a feeling of pollution. One cannot therefore take it amiss of people, whose privileged position admits of it, if they manage to live in retirement and completely free from the painful sensation of "seeing new faces." The metaphysical explanation of this circumstance rests upon the consideration that the individuality of a man is precisely that by the very existence of which he should be reclaimed and corrected. If, on the other hand, a psychological explanation is satisfactory, let any one ask himself what kind of physiognomy he may expect in those who have all their life long, except on the rarest occasions, harbored nothing but petty, base and miserable thoughts, and vulgar, selfish, envious, wicked and malicious desires. Every one of these thoughts and desires has set its mark upon the face during the time it lasted, and by constant repetition, all these marks have in course of time become furrows and blotches, so to speak. Consequently, most people's appearance is such as to produce a shock at first sight: and it is only gradually that one gets accustomed to it, that is to say, becomes so deadened to the impression that it has no more effect on one.

And that the prevailing facial expression is the result of a long process of innumerable, fleeting and characteristic contractions of the features is just the reason why intellectual countenances are of gradual formation. It is indeed only in old age that intellectual men attain their sublime expression, while portraits of them in their youth show only the first traces of it. But, on the other hand, what I have just said about the shock which the first sight of a face generally produces is in keeping with the remark that it is only at that first sight that it makes its true and full impression. For to get a purely objective and uncorrupted impression of it, we must stand in no kind of relation to the person; if possible, we must not yet have spoken with him. For every conversation places us to some extent upon a friendly footing, establishes a certain *rapport*, a mutual subjective relation, which is at once unfavorable to an objective point of view. And as every one's endeavor is to win esteem or friendship for himself, the man who is under observation will at once employ all those arts of dissimulation in which he is already versed, and corrupt us with his airs, hypocrisies and flatteries; so that what the first look clearly showed will soon be seen by us no more.

This fact is at the bottom of the saying that "most people gain by further acquaintance;" it ought, however, to run, "delude us by it." It is only when, later on, the bad qualities manifest themselves that our first judgment, as a rule receives its justification and makes good its scornful verdict. It may be that "a further acquaintance" is an unfriendly one, and if that is so, we do not find in this case either that people gain by it. Another reason why people apparently gain on a nearer acquaintance is that the man whose first aspect warns us from him, as soon as we converse with him, no longer shows his own being and character, but also his education; that is, not only what he really is by nature, but also what he has appropriated to himself out of the common wealth of mankind. Three-fourths of what he says belongs not to him, but to the sources from which he obtained it; so that we are often surprised to hear a minotaur speak so humanly. If we make a still closer acquaintance, the animal nature, of which his face gave promise, will manifest itself "in all its splendor." If one is gifted with an acute sense for physiognomy, one should take special note of those verdicts which preceded a closer acquaintance and were therefore genuine. For the face of a man is the exact expression of what he is; and if he deceives us, that is our fault, not his. What a man says, on the other hand, is what he thinks, more often what he has learned, or it may be even, what he pretends to think. And besides. this, when we talk to him, or even hear him talking to others, we pay no attention to his physiognomy proper. It is the underlying substance, the fundamental *datum*, and we disregard it; what interests us is its pathognomy, its play of feature during conversation. This, however, is so arranged as to turn the good side upward.

When Socrates said to a young man who was introduced to him to have his capabilities tested, "Talk in order that I may see you," if indeed by "seeing" he did not simply mean "hearing" he was right, so far as it is only in conversation that the features and especially the eyes become animated, and the intellectual resources and capacities set their mark upon the countenance. This puts us in a position to form a provisional notion of the degree and capacity of intelligence; which was in that case Socrates' aim. But in this connection it is to be observed, firstly, that the rule does not apply to moral qualities, which lie deeper; and in the second place, that what from an objective point of view we gain by the clearer development of the countenance in conversation, we lose from a subjective standpoint on account of the personal relation into which the speaker at once enters in regard to us, and which produces a slight fascination, so that, as explained above, we are not left impartial observers. Consequently from the last point of view we might say with greater accuracy, "Do not speak in order that I may see you."

For to get a pure and fundamental conception of a man's physiognomy, we must observe him when he is alone and left to himself. Society of any kind and conversation throw a reflection upon him which is not his own, generally to his advantage; as he is thereby placed in a state of action and re-action which sets him off. But alone and left to himself, plunged in the depths of his own thoughts and sensations, he is wholly himself, and a penetrating eye for physiognomy can at one glance take a general view of his entire character. For his face, looked at by and in itself, expresses the keynote of all his thoughts and endeavors, the *arrêt irrevocable*, the irrevocable decree of his destiny, the consciousness of which only comes to him when he is alone.

The study of physiognomy is one of the chief means of a knowledge of mankind, because the cast of a man's face is the only sphere in which his arts of dissimulation are of no avail, since these arts extend only to that play of feature which is akin to mimicry. And that is why I recommend such a study to be undertaken when the subject of it is alone and given up to his own thoughts, and before he is spoken to: and this partly for the reason that it is only in such a condition that inspection of the physiognomy pure and simple is possible, because conversation at once lets in a pathognomical element, in which a man can apply the arts of dissimulation which he has learned: partly again because personal contact, even of the very slightest kind, gives a certain bias and so corrupts the judgment of the observer.

And in regard to the study of physiognomy in general,

it is further to be observed that intellectual capacity is much easier of discernment than moral character. The former naturally takes a much more outward direction, and expresses itself not only in the face and the play of feature, but also in the gait, down even to the very slightest movement. One could perhaps discriminate from behind between a blockhead, a fool and a man of genius. The blockhead would be discerned by the torpidity and sluggishness of all his movements: folly sets its mark upon every gesture, and so does intellect and a studious nature. Hence that remark of La Bruyère that there is nothing so slight, so simple or imperceptible but that our way of doing it enters in and betrays us: a fool neither comes nor goes, nor sits down, nor gets up, nor holds his tongue, nor moves about in the same way as an intelligent man. (And this is, be it observed by way of parenthesis, the explanation of that sure and certain instinct which, according to Helvetius, ordinary folk possess of discerning people of genius, and of getting out of their way.)

The chief reason for this is that, the larger and more developed the brain, and the thinner, in relation to it the spine and nerves, the greater is the intellect; and not the intellect alone, but at the same time the mobility and pliancy of all the limbs: because the brain controls them more immediately and resolutely; so that everything hangs more upon a single thread, every movement of which gives a precise expression to its purpose. This is analogous to, nay, is immediately connected with the fact that the higher an animal stands in the scale of development, the easier it becomes to kill it by wounding a single spot. Take, for example, batrachia: they are slow, cumbrous and sluggish in their movements; they are unintelligent, and at the same time, extremely tenacious of life; the reason of which is that with a very small brain, their spine and nerves are very thick. Now gait and movement of the arms are mainly functions of the brain; our limbs receive their motion and every little modification of it from the brain through the medium of the spine. This is why conscious movements fatigue us; the sensation of fatigue, like that of pain, has its seat in the brain, not, as people commonly suppose, in the limbs themselves; hence motion induces sleep. On the other hand those motions which are not excited by the brain, that is, the unconscious movements of organic life, of the heart, of the lungs, etc., go on in their course without producing fatigue. And as thought equally with motion is a function of the brain, the character of the brain's activity is expressed equally in both, according to the constitution of the individual; stupid people move like lay-figures, while every joint of an intelligent man is eloquent. But gesture and movement are not nearly so good an index of intellectual qualities as the face, the shape and size of the brain, the contraction and movement of the features, and above all the eye—from the small, dull, dead-looking eye of a pig up through all gradations to the irradiating, flashing eyes of a genius. The look of good sense and prudence, even of the best kind, differs from that of genius, in that the former bears the stamp of subjection to the will, while the latter is free from it. And therefore one can well believe the anecdote told by Squarzafichi in his life of Petrarch, and taken from Joseph Brivius, a contemporary of the poet, how once at the court of the Visconti, when Petrarch and other noblemen and gentlemen were present, Galeazzo Visconti told his son, who was then a mere boy (he was afterward first duke of Milan), to pick out the wisest of the company; how the boy looked at them all for a little, and then took Petrarch by the hand and led him up to his father, to the great admiration of all present. For so clearly does nature set the mark of her dignity on the privileged among mankind that even a child can discern it. Therefore I should advise my sagacious countrymen, if ever again they wish to trumpet about for thirty years a very commonplace person as a great genius, not to choose for the purpose such a beerhouse-keeper physiognomy as was possessed by that philosopher, upon whose face nature had written, in her clearest characters, the familiar inscription, "commonplace person."

But what applies to intellectual capacity will not apply to moral qualities, to character. It is more difficult to discern its physiognomy, because, being of a metaphysical nature, it lies incomparably deeper. It is true that moral character is also connected with the constitution, with the organism, but not so immediately or in such direct connection with definite parts of its system as is intellectual capacity. Hence while every one makes a show of his intelligence and endeavors to exhibit it at every opportunity, as something with which he is in general quite contented, few expose their moral qualities freely, and most people intentionally cover them up; and long practice makes the concealment perfect. In the meantime, as I explained above, wicked thoughts and worth'ess efforts gradually set their mark upon the face, especially the eyes. So that, judging by physiognomy, it is easy to warrant that a given man will never produce an immortal work; but not that he will never commit a great crime.

PSYCHOLOGICAL OBSERVATIONS.

For every animal, and more especially for man, a certain conformity and proportion between the will and the intellect is necessary for existing or making any progress in the world. The more precise and correct the proportion which nature establishes, the more easy, safe and agreeable will be the passage through the world. Still, if the right point is only approximately reached, it will be enough to ward off destruction. There are, then, certain limits within which the said proportion may vary, and yet preserve a correct standard of conformity. The normal standard is as follows. The object of the intellect is to light and lead the will on its path, and therefore, the greater the force, impetus and passion, which spurs on the will from within, the more complete and luminous must be the intellect which is attached to it, that the vehement strife of the will, the glow of passion, and the intensity of the emotions, may not lead man astray, or urge him on to ill considered, false or ruinous action; this will, inevitably, be the result, if the will is very violent and the intellect very weak. On the other hand, a phlegmatic character, a weak and languid will, can get on and hold its own with a small amount of intellect; what is naturally moderate needs only moderate support. The general tendency of a want of proportion between the will and the intellect, in other words, of any variation from the normal proportion I have mentioned, is to produce unhappiness, whether it be that the will is greater than the intellect, or the intellect greater than the will, Especially is this the case when the intellect is developed to an abnormal degree of strength and superiority, so as to be out of all proportion to the will, a condition which is the essence of real genius; the intellect is then not only more than enough for the needs and aims of life, it is absolutely prejudicial to them. The result is that, in youth, excessive energy in grasping the objective world, accompanied by a vivid imagination and a total lack of experience, makes the mind susceptible, and an easy prey to extravagant ideas, nay, even to chimeras; and this issues in an eccentric and fantastic character. And when, in later years, this state of mind yields and passes away under the teaching of experience, still the genius never feels himself at home in the common world of every day and the ordinary business of life; he will never take his place in it, and accommodate himself to it as accurately as the person of normal intellect; he will be more likely to make curious mistakes. For the ordinary mind feels itself so completely at home in the narrow circle of its ideas and views of the world that no one can get the better of it in that sphere; its faculties remain true to their original purpose, viz., to promote the service of the will; it devotes itself steadfastly to this end, and abjures extravagant aims. The genius, on the other hand, is at bottom a *monstrum per excessum* just as, conversely, the passionate, violent and unintelligent man, the brainless barbarian, is a *monstrum per defectum.*

———————

The will to live, which forms the inmost core of every living being, exhibits itself most conspicuously in the higher order of animals, that is, the cleverer ones; and so in them the nature of the will may be seen and examined most clearly. For in the lower orders its activity is not so evident; it has a lower degree of objectivation; whereas, in the class which stands above the higher order of animals, that is, in men, reason enters in; and with reason comes discretion, and with discretion, the capacity for dissimulation, which throws a veil over the operations of the will. And in mankind, consequently, the will appears without its mask only in the affections and the passions. And this is the reason why passion, when it speaks, always wins credence, no matter what the passion may be; and rightly so. For the same reason the passions are the main theme of poets and the stalking horse of actors. The conspicuousness of the will in the lower order of animals explains the delight we take in dogs, apes, cats, etc,; it is the entirely naïve way in which they express themselves that gives us so much pleasure.

The sight of any free animal going about its business undisturbed, seeking its food, or looking after its young, or mixing in the company of its kind, all the time being exactly what it ought to be and can be—what a strange pleasure it gives us! Even if it is only a bird, I can watch it for a long time with delight; or a water rat or a hedgehog; or better still, a weasel, a deer or a stag. The main reason why we take so much pleasure in looking at animals is that we like to see our own nature in such a simplified form. There is only one mendacious being in the world, and that is man. Every other is true and sincere, and makes no attempt to conceal what it is, expressing its feelings just as they are.

Many things are put down to the force of habit which are rather to be attributed to the constancy and immutability of orginal, innate character, according to which under like circumstances we always do the same thing: whether it happens for the first or the hundredth time, it is in virtue of the same necessity. Real force of habit, as a matter of fact, rests upon that indolent, passive disposition which seeks to relieve the intellect and the will of a fresh choice, and so makes us do what we did yesterday and have done a hundred times before, and of which we know that it will attain its object.

But the truth of the matter lies deeper, and a more precise explanation of it can be given than appears at first sight. Bodies which may be moved by mechanical means only are subject to the power of inertia; and applied to bodies which may be acted on by motives, this power becomes the force of habit. The actions which we perform by mere habit come about, in fact, without any individual separate motive brought into play for the particular case: hence in performing them, we really do not think about them. A motive was present only on the first few occasions on which the action happened, which has since become a habit: the secondary after-effect of this motive is the present habit, and it is sufficient to enable the action to continue: just as when a body has been set in motion by a push, it requires no more pushing in order to continue its motion; it will go on to all eternity, if it meets with no friction. It is the same in the case of animals: training is a habit which is forced upon them. The horse goes on drawing his cart quite contentedly, without having to be urged on: the motion is the continued effect of those strokes of the whip which urged him on at first: by the law of inertia they have become perpetuated as habit. All this is really more than a mere parable: it is the underlying identity of the will at very different degrees of its objectivation, in virtue of which the same law of motion takes such different forms.

Vive muchos años is the ordinary greeting in Spain, and all over the earth it is quite customary to wish people a long life. It is presumably not a knowledge of life which directs such a wish; it is rather knowledge of what man is in his inmost nature, the will to live.

The wish which every one has that he may be remembered after his death—a wish which rises to the longing for posthumous glory in the case of those whose aims are high—seems to me to spring from this clinging to life. When the time comes which cuts a man off from every possibility of real existence, he strives after a life which is still attainable, even though it be a shadowy and ideal one.

The deep grief we feel at the loss of a friend arises from the feeling that in every individual there is something which no words can express, something which is peculiarly his own and therefore irreparable. *Omne individuum ineffabile.*

We may come to look upon the death of our enemies and adversaries, even long after it has occurred, with just as much regret as we feel for that of our friends, viz., when we miss them as witnesses of our brilliant success.

That the sudden announcement of a very happy event may easily prove fatal rests upon the fact that happiness and misery depend merely on the proportion which our claims bear to what we get. Accordingly, the good things we possess, or are certain of getting, are not felt to be such: because all pleasure is in fact of a negative nature and effects the relief of pain, while pain or evil is what is really positive; it is the object of immediate sensation. With the possession or certain expectation of good things our demand rises, and increases our capacity for further possessions and larger expectations. But if we are depressed by continual misfortune, and our claims reduced to a minimum, the sudden advent of happiness finds no capacity for enjoying it. Neutralized by an absence of pre-existing claims, its effects are apparently positive, and so its whole force is brought into play; hence it may possibly break our feelings, *i. e.* be fatal to them. And so, as is well known, one must be careful in announcing great happiness. First, one must get the person to hope for it, then open up the prospect of it, then communicate part of it, and at last make it fully known. Every portion of the good news loses its efficacy, because it is anticipated by a demand, and room is left for an increase in it. In view of all this, it may be said that our stomach for good fortune is bottomless, but the entrance to it is narrow. These remarks are not applicable to great misfortunes in the same way. They are more seldom fatal, because hope always sets itself against them. That an analogous part is not played by fear in the case of happiness results from the fact that we are instinctively more inclined to hope than to fear; just as our eyes turn themselves toward light rather than darkness.

Hope is the result of confusing the desire that something should take place with the probability that it will. Perhaps no man is free from this folly of the heart, which deranges the intellect's correct appreciation of probability to such an extent that, if the chances are a thousand to one against it, yet the event is thought a likely one. Still in spite of this, a sudden misfortune is like a death-stroke, while a hope that is always disappointed and still never dies, is like death by prolonged torture.

He who has lost all hope has also lost all fear; this is the meaning of the expression "desperate." It is natural to a man to believe what he wishes to be true, and to believe it because he wishes it. If this characteristic of our nature, at once beneficial and assuaging, is rooted out by many hard blows of fate, and a man comes, conversely, to a condition in which he believes a thing must happen because he does not wish it, and what he wishes to happen can never be, just because he wishes it, this is in reality the state described as "desperation."

That we are so often deceived in others is not because our judgment is at fault, but because in general, as Bacon says, "*Intellectus luminis sicci non est, sed recipit infusionem a voluntate et affectibus:*" that is to say, trifles unconsciously bias us for or against a person from the very beginning. It may also be explained by our not abiding by the qualities which we really discover; we go on to conclude the presence of others which we think inseparable from them, or the absence of those which we consider incompatible. For instance, when we perceive generosity, we infer justice; from piety, we infer honesty; from lying, deception; from deception, stealing, etc; a procedure which opens the door to many false views, partly because human nature is so strange, partly because our stand-point is so one-sided. It is true, indeed, that character always forms a consistent and connected whole; but the roots of all its qualities lie too deep to allow of our concluding from particular data in a given case whether certain qualities can or cannot exist together.

We often happen to say things that may in some way or other be prejudicial to us; but we keep silent about things that might make us look ridiculous; because in this case effect follows very quickly on cause.

The pain of an unfulfilled wish is small in comparison with that of repentance; for the one stands in the presence of the vast open future, while the other has the irrevocable past closed behind it.

———

Geduld, patientia, patience, especially the Spanish *sufrimiento,* is strongly connected with the notion of suffering. It is therefore a passive state, just as the opposite is an active state of the mind, with which, when great, patience is incompatible. It is the innate virtue of phlegmatic, indolent, and spiritless people, as also of women. But that it is nevertheless so very useful and necessary is a sign that the world is very badly constituted.

———

Money is human happiness in the abstract: he, then, who is no longer capable of enjoying human happiness in the concrete, devotes his heart entirely to money.

———

Obstinacy is the result of the will forcing itself into the place of the intellect.

———

If you want to find out your real opinion of any one, observe the impression made upon you by the first sight of a letter from him.

———

The course of our individual life and the events in it, as far as their true meaning and connection is concerned, may be compared to a piece of rough mosaic. So long as you stand close in front of it, you cannot get a right view of the objects presented, nor perceive their significance or beauty. Both come in sight only when you stand a little way off. And in the same way you often understand the true connection of important events in your life not while they are going on nor soon after they are past, but only a considerable time afterward.

Is this so, because we require the magnifying effect of imagination? or because we can get a general view only from a distance? or because the school of experience makes our judgment ripe? Perhaps all of these together: but it is certain that we often view in the right light the actions of others, and occasionally even our own, only after the lapse of years. And as it is in one's own life, so it is in history.

Happy circumstances in life are like certain groups of trees. Seen from a distance they look very well: but go up to them and among them, and the beauty vanishes; you don't know where it can be; it is only trees you see. And so it is that we often envy the lot of others.

The doctor sees all the weakness of mankind, the lawyer all the wickedness, the theologian all the stupidity.

A person of phlegmatic disposition who is a block head, would with a sanguine nature, be a fool.

Now and then one learns something, but one forgets the whole day long.

Moreover our memory is like a sieve, the holes of which in time get larger and larger; the older we get, the quicker anything intrusted to it slips from the memory, whereas, what was fixed fast in it in early days is there still. The memory of an old man gets clearer and clearer, the further it goes back, and less clear the nearer it approaches the present time; so that his memory, like his eyes, becomes long-sighted.

In the process of learning you may be apprehensive about bewildering and confusing the memory, but not about overloading it, in the strict sense of the word. The faculty for remembering is not diminished in proportion to what one has learned, just as little as the number of molds in which you cast sand, lessens its capacity for being cast in new molds. In this sense the memory is bottomless. And yet the greater and more various any one's knowledge, the longer he takes to find out anything that may suddenly be asked him; because he is like a shopkeeper who has to get the article wanted from a large and multifarious store; or, more strictly speaking, because out of many possible trains of thought he has to recall exactly that one which, as a result of previous training, leads to the matter in question. For the memory is not a repository of things you wish to preserve, but a mere dexterity of the intellectual powers; hence the mind always contains its sum of knowledge only potentially, never actually.

It sometimes happens that my memory will not reproduce some word in a foreign language, or a name, or some artistic expression, although I know it very well. After I have bothered myself in vain about it for a longer or a shorter time, I give up thinking about it altogether. An hour or two afterward, in rare cases even later still, sometimes only after four or five weeks, the word I was trying to recall occurs to me while I am thinking of something else, as suddenly as if some one had whispered it to me. After noticing this phenomenon with wonder for very many years, I have come to think that the probable explanation of it is as follows. After the troublesome and unsuccessful search, my will retains its craving to know the word, and so sets a watch for it in the intellect. Later on, in the course and play of thought, some word by chance occurs having the same initial letters or some other resemblance to the word which is sought; then the sentinel springs forward and supplies what is wanting to make up the word, seizes it, and suddenly brings it up in triumph, without my knowing where and how he got it; so it seems as if some one had whispered it to me. It is the same process as that adopted by a teacher toward a child who cannot repeat a word; the teacher just suggests the first letter of the word, or even the second too; then the child remembers it. In default of this process, you can end by going methodically through all the letters of the alphabet.

In the ordinary man, injustice rouses a passionate desire for vengeance; and it has often been said that vengeance is sweet. How many sacrifices have been made just to enjoy the feeling of vengeance, without any intention of causing an amount of injury equivalent to what one has suffered. The bitter death of the centaur Nessus was sweetened by the certainty that he had used his last moments to work out an extremely clever vengeance. Walter Scott expresses the same human inclination in language as true as it is strong: "Vengeance is the sweetest morsel to the mouth that ever was cooked in hell!" I shall now attempt a psychological explanation of it.

Suffering which falls to our lot in the course of nature, or by chance, or fate, does not, *ceteris paribus*, seem so painful as suffering which is inflicted on us by the arbitrary will of another. This is because we look upon nature and chance as the fundamental masters of the world; we see that the blow we received from them might just as well have fallen on another. In the case of suffering which springs from this source, we bewail the common lot of humanity rather than our own misfortune. But that it is the arbitrary will of another which inflicts the suffering, is a peculiarly bitter addition to the pain or injury it causes, viz., the consciousness that some one else is superior to us, whether by force or cunning, while we lie helpless. If amends are possible, amends heal the injury; but that bitter addition, "and it was you who did that to me," which is often more painful than the injury itself, is only to be neutralized by vengeance. By inflicting injury on the one who has injured us, whether we do it by force or cunning, is to show our superiority to him, and to annul the proof of his superiority to us. That gives our hearts the satisfaction toward which it yearns. So where there is a great deal of pride or vanity, there also will there be a great desire of vengeance. But as the fulfillment of every wish brings with it more or less of a sense of disappointment, so it is with vengeance. The delight we hope to get from it is mostly embittered by compassion. Vengeance taken will often tear the heart and torment the conscience: the motive to it is no longer active, and what remains is the evidence of our malice.

THE CHRISTIAN SYSTEM.

WHEN the Church says that, in the dogmas of religion, reason is totally incompetent and blind, and its use to be reprehended, it is in reality attesting the fact that these dogmas are allegorical in their nature, and are not to be judged by the standard which reason. taking all things *sensu proprio*, can alone apply. Now the absurdities of a dogma are just the mark and sign of what is allegorical and mythical in it. In the case under consideration, however, the absurdities spring from the fact that two such heterogeneous doctrines as those of the Old and New Testaments had to be combined. The great allegory was of gradual growth. Suggested by external and adventitious circumstances, it was developed by the interpretation put upon them, an interpretation in quiet touch with certain deep-lying truths only half realized. The allegory was finally completed by Augustine, who penetrated deepest into its meaning, and so was able to conceive it as a systematic whole and supply its defects. Hence the Augustinian doctrine, confirmed by Luther, is the complete form of Christianity; and the Protestants of to-day, who take Revelation *sensu proprio* and confine it to a single individual, are in error in looking upon the first beginnings of Christianity as its most perfect expression. But the bad thing about all religions is that, instead of being able to confess their allegorical nature, they have to conceal it; accordingly, they parade their doctrines in all seriousness as true *sensu proprio*, and as absurdities from an essential part of these doctrines, you have the great mischief of a continual fraud. And, what is worst, the day arrives when they are no longer true *sensu proprio*, and then there is an end of them; so that, in that respect, it would be better to admit their allegorical nature at once. But the difficulty is to teach the multitude that something can be both true and untrue at the same time. And as all religions are in a greater or less degree of this nature, we must recognize the fact that mankind cannot get on without a certain amount of absurdity, that absurdity is an element in its existence, and illusion indispensable; as indeed other aspects of life testify.

I have said that the combination of the Old Testament with the New gives rise to absurdities. Among the examples which illustrate what I mean, I may cite the Christian doctrine of Predestination and Grace, as formulated by Augustine and adopted from him by Luther; according to which one man is endowed with grace and another is not. Grace, then comes to be a privilege received at birth and brought ready into the world; a privilege, too, in a matter second to none in importance. What is obnoxious and absurd in this doctrine may be traced to the idea contained in the Old Testament, that man is the creation of an external will, which called him into existence out of nothing. It is quite true that genuine moral excellence is really innate; but the meaning of the Christian doctrine is expressed in another and more rational way by the theory of metempsychosis, common to Brahmans and Buddhists. According to this theory, the qualities which distinguish one man from another are received at birth, are brought, that is to say, from another world and a former life; these qualities are not an external gift of grace, but are the fruits of the acts committed in that other world. But Augustine's dogma of Predestination is connected with another dogma, namely, that the mass of humanity is corrupt and doomed to eternal damnation, that very few will be found righteous and attain salvation, and that only in consequence of the gift of grace, and because they are predestined to be saved; while the remainder will be overwhelmed by the perdition they have deserved, viz., eternal torment in hell. Taken in its ordinary meaning, the dogma is revolting, for it comes to this; it condemns a man, who may be, perhaps, scarcely twenty years of age, to expiate his errors, or even his unbelief, in everlasting torment; nay, more, it makes this almost universal damnation the natural effect of original sin, and therefore the necessary consequence of the Fall. This is a result which must have been foreseen by him who made mankind, and who, in the first place, made them not better than they are, and secondly, set a trap for them into which he must have known they would fall; for he made the whole world, and nothing is hidden from him. According to this doctrine, then, God created out of nothing a weak race prone to sin, in order to give them over to endless torment. And, as a last characteristic, we are told that this God, who prescribes forbearance and forgiveness of every fault, exercises none himself, but does the exact opposite; for a punishment which comes at the end of all things, when the world is over and done with, cannot have for its object either to improve or deter, and is therefore pure vengeance. So that, on this view, the whole race is actually destined to eternal torture and damnation, and created expressly for this end, the only exception being those few persons who are rescued by election of grace, from what motive one does not know.

Putting these aside, it looks as if the Blessed Lord had created the world for the benefit of the devil! it would have been so much better not have made it at all. So much, then, for a dogma taken *sensu proprio.* But look at it *sensu allegorico,* and the whole matter becomes capable of a satisfactory interpretation. What is absurd and revolting in this dogma is, in the main, as I said, the simple outcome of Jewish theism, with its "creation out of nothing," and the really foolish and paradoxical denial of the doctrine of metempsychosis which is involved in that idea, a doctrine which is natural, to a certain extent self-evident, and, with the exception of the Jews, accepted by nearly the whole human race at all times. To remove the enormous evil arising from Augustine's dogma, and to modify its revolting nature, Pope Gregory I., in the sixth century, very prudently matured the doctrine of *Purgatory,* the essence of which already existed in Origen (cf. Bayle's article on Origen, note B.). The doctrine was regularly incorporated into the faith of the church, so that the original view was much modified, and a certain substitute provided for the doctrine of metempsychosis; for both the one and the other admit a process of purification. To the same end, the doctrine of "the Restoration of all things" (ἀποκατάστασις) was established, according to which, in the last act of the Human Comedy, the sinners one and all will be reinstated *in integrum.* It is only Protestants, with their obstinate belief in the Bible, who cannot be induced to give up eternal punishment in hell. If one were spiteful, one might say, "much good may it do them," but it is consoling to think that they really do not believe the doctrine; they leave it alone, thinking in their hearts, "It can't be so bad as all that."

The rigid and systematic character of his mind led

Augustine, in his austere dogmatism and his resolute definition of doctrines only just indicated in the Bible and, as a matter of fact, resting on very vague grounds, to give hard outlines to these doctrines and to put a harsh construction on Christianity: the result of which is that his views offend us, and just as in his day Pelagianism arose to combat them, so now in our day Rationalism does the same. Take, for example, the case as he states it generally in the "De Civitate Dei." Bk. xii. ch. 21. It comes to this: God creates a being out of nothing, forbids him some things, and enjoins others upon him; and because these commands are not obeyed, he tortures him to all eternity with every conceivable anguish; and for this purpose, binds soul and body inseparably together, so that, instead of the torment destroying this being by splitting him up into his elements, and so setting him free, he may live to eternal pain. This poor creature, formed out of nothing! At least, he has a claim on his original nothing: he should be assured, as a matter of right, of this last retreat, which, in any case, cannot be a very evil one: it is what he has inherited. I, at any rate, cannot help sympathizing with him. If you add to this Augustine's remaining doctrines, that all this does not depend on the man's own sins and omissions, but was already predestined to happen, one really is at a loss what to think. Our highly educated Rationalists say, to be sure, "It's all false, it's a mere bugbear; we're in a state of constant progress, step by step raising ourselves to ever greater perfection." Ah! what a pity we didn't begin sooner; we should already be there.

In the Christian system the devil is a personage of the greatest importance. God is described as absolutely good, wise and powerful; and unless he were counterbalanced by the devil, it would be impossible to see where the innumerable and measureless evils, which predominate in the world, come from, if there were no devil to account for them. And since the Rationalists have done away with the devil, the damage inflicted on the other side has gone on growing, and is becoming more and more palpable; as might have been foreseen, and was foreseen, by the orthodox. The fact is, you cannot take away one pillar from a building without endangering the rest of it.

And this confirms the view, which has been established on other grounds, that Jehovah is a transformation of Ormuzd, and Satan of the Ahriman who must be taken in connection with him. Ormuzd himself is a transformation of Indra.

Christianity has this peculiar disadvantage, that, unlike other religions, it is not a pure system of doctrine: its chief and essential feature is that it is a history, a series of events, a collection of facts, a statement of the actions and sufferings of individuals: it is this history which constitutes dogma, and belief in it is salvation. Other religions, Buddhism, for instance, have, it is true, historical appendages, the life, namely of their founders: this, however, is not part and parcel of the dogma, but is taken along with it. For example, the Lalitavistara may be compared with the Gospel so far it contains the life of Säkya-muni, the Buddha of the present period of the world's history: but this is something which is quite separate and different from the dogma, from the system itself: and for this reason; the lives of former Buddhas were quite other, and those of the future will be quite other, than the life of the Buddha of to-day. The dogma is by no means one with the career of its founder; it does not rest on individual persons or events; it is something universal and equally valid at all times. The Lalitavistara is not, then, a gospel in the Christian sense of the word; it is not the joyful message of an act of redemption; it is the career of him who has shown how each one may redeem himself. The historical constitution of Christianity makes the Chinese laugh at missionaries as story-tellers.

I may mention here another fundamental error of Christianity, an error which cannot be explained away, and the mischievous consequences of which are obvious every day: I mean the unnatural distinction Christianity makes between man and the animal world to which he really belongs. It sets up man as all-important, and looks upon animals as merely things. Brahmanism, and Buddhism, on the other hand, true to the facts, recognize in a positive way that man is related generally to the whole of nature, and specially and principally to animal nature; and in their systems man is always represented, by the theory of metempsychosis and otherwise, as closely connected with the animal world. The important part played by animals all through Buddhism and Brahmanism, compared with the total disregard of them in Judaism and Christianity, puts an end to any question as to which system is nearer perfection, however much we in Europe may have become accustomed to the absurdity of the claim. Christianity contains, in fact, a great and essential imperfection in limiting its precepts to man, and in refusing rights to the entire animal world. As religion fails to protect animals against the rough, unfeeling and often more than bestial multitude, the duty falls to the police; and as the police are unequal to the task, societies for the protection of animals are now formed all over Europe and America. In the whole of uncircumcised Asia, such a procedure would be the most superfluous thing in the world, because animals are there sufficiently protected by religion, which even makes them objects of charity. How such charitable feelings bear fruit may be seen, to take an example, in the great hospital for animals at Surat, whither Christians, Mohammedans and Jews can send their sick beasts, which, if cured, are very rightly not restored to their owners. In the same way, when a Brahman or Buddhist has a slice of good luck a happy issue in any affair, instead of mumbling a *Te Deum,* he goes to the market place and buys birds and opens their cages at the city gate; a thing which may be frequently seen in Astrachan, where the adherents of every religion meet together: and so on in a hundred similar ways. On the other hand, look at the revolting ruffianism with which our Christian public treats its animals; killing them for no object at all, and laughing over it, or mutilating or torturing them: even its horses, who form its most direct means of livelihood, are strained to the utmost in their old age, and the last strength worked out of their poor bones until they succumb at last under the whip. One might say with truth, Mankind are the devils or the earth, and the animals the souls they torment. But what can you expect from the masses, when there are men of education, zoölogists even, who, instead of admitting what is so familiar to them, the essential identity of man and animal, are bigoted and stupid enough to offer a zealous opposition to their honest and rational colleagues, when they class man under the proper head as an animal, or demonstrate the resemblance between him and the chimpanzee or ourang-outang. It is a revolting thing that a writer who is so pious and Christian in his sentiments as Jung Stilling should use a simile like this, in his "Scenen aus dem Geisterreich." (Bk. II. sc. i., p. 15.) "Suddenly the skeleton shriveled up into an indescribably hideous and dwarf-like form, just as when you bring a large spider into the focus of a burning glass, and watch the purulent blood hiss and bubble in the heat." This man of God then was guilty of such infamy! or looked on quietly when another was committing it! in either case it comes to the same thing here. So little harm did he think of it that he tells us of it in passing, and without a trace of emotion. Such are the effects of the first chapter of Genesis, and, in fact, of the whole of the Jewish conception of nature. The standard recognized by the Hindus and Buddhists is the Mahavakya (the great word) —"tat-twam-asi," (this is thyself), which may always be spoken of every animal, to keep us in mind of the identity of his inmost being with ours. Perfection of morality, indeed! Nonsense.

The fundamental characteristics of the Jewish religion are realism and optimism, views of the world which are closely allied; they form, in fact, the conditions of theism. For theism looks upon the material world as absolutely real, and regards life as a pleasant gift bestowed upon us. On the other hand, the fundamental characteristics of the Brahman and Buddhist religions are idealism and pessimism, which look upon the existence of the world as in the nature of a dream, and life as the result of our sins. In the doctrines of the Zendavesta, from which, as is well known, Judaism sprang, the pessimistic element is represented by Ahriman. In Judaism, Ahriman has as Satan only a subordinate position; but, like Ahriman, he is the lord of snakes, scorpions, and vermin. But the Jewish system forthwith employs Satan to correct its fundamental error of optimism, and in the Fall introduces the element of pessimism, a doctrine demanded by the most obvious facts of the world. There is no truer idea in Judaism than this, although it transfers to the course of existence what must be represented as its foundation and antecedent.

The New Testament, on the other hand, must be in some way traceable to an Indian source: its ethical system, its ascetic view of morality, its pessimism, and its Avatar, are all thoroughly Indian. It is its morality which places it in a position of such emphatic and essential antagonism to the Old Testament, so that the story of the Fall is the only possible point of connection between the two. For when the Indian doctrine was imported into the land of promise, two very different things had to be combined: on the one hand the consciousness of the corruption and misery of the world, its need of deliverance and salvation through an Avatar, together with a morality based on self-denial and repentance; on the other hand the Jewish doctrine of Monotheism, with its corollary that "all things are very good" (παντα καλα λίαν.) And the task succeeded as far as it could, as far, that is, as it was possible to combine two such heterogeneous and antagonistic creeds.

As ivy clings for the support and stay it wants to a rough-hewn post, everywhere conforming to its irregularities and showing their outline, but at the same time covering them with life and grace, and changing the former aspect into one that is pleasing to the eye; so the Christian faith, sprung from the wisdom of India, overspreads the old trunk of rude Judaism, a tree of alien growth; the original form must in part remain, but it suffers a complete change and becomes full of life and truth, so that it appears to be the same tree, but is really another.

Judaism had represented the Creator as separated from the world, which he produced out of nothing. Christianity identifies this Creator with the Saviour, and through him, with humanity: he stands as their representative; they are redeemed in him, just as they fell in Adam, and have lain ever since in the bonds of iniquity, corruption, suffering and death. Such is the view taken by Christianity in common with Buddhism: the world can no longer be looked at in the light of Jewish optimism, which found "all things very good:" nay, in the Christian scheme, the devil is named as its Prince or Ruler, (ὅ ἄρχωνιτ τὸν κόσμου τούτου. John 12, 33). The world is no longer an end, but a means; and the realm of everlasting joy lies beyond it and the grave. Resignation in this world and direction of all our hopes to a better form the spirit of Christianity. The way to this end is opened by the Atonement, that is, the Redemption from this world and its ways. And in the moral system, instead of the law of vengeance, there is the command to love your enemy; instead of the promise of innumerable posterity, the assurance of eternal life; instead of visiting the sins of the fathers upon the children to the third and fourth generations, the Holy Spirit which over-shadows all.

We see, then, that the doctrines of the Old Testament are rectified and their meaning changed by those of the New, so that, in the most important and essential matters, an agreement is brought about between them and the old religions of India. Everything which is true in Christianity may also be found in Brahmanism and Buddhism. But in Hinduism and Buddhism you will look in vain for any parallel to the Jewish doctrines of "a nothing quickened into life," or of "a world made in time," which cannot be humble enough in its thanks and praises to Jehovah for an ephemeral existence full of misery, anguish and need.

Whoever seriously thinks that superhuman beings have ever given our race information as to the aim of its existence and that of the world, is still in his childhood. There is no other revelation than the thoughts of the wise, even though these thoughts, liable to error as is the lot of everything human, are often clothed in strange allegories and myths under the name of religion. So far, then, it is a matter of indifference whether a man lives and dies in reliance on his own or another's thoughts; for it is never more than human thought, human opinion, which he trusts. Still, instead of trusting what their own minds tell them, men have as a rule a weakness for trusting others who pretend to supernatural sources of knowledge. And in view of the enormous intellectual inequality between man and man, it is easy to see that the thoughts of one mind might appear as in some sense a revelation to another.

THE FAILURE OF PHILOSOPHY:

A BRIEF DIALOGUE.

A. PHILOSOPHY has hitherto been a failure. It could not, indeed, have been otherwise; because, instead of confining himself to the better understanding of the world as given in experience, the philosopher has aspired to pass at one bound beyond it, in the hope of discovering the last foundation of all existence and the eternal relations of things. Now these are matters which our intellect is quite incapable of grasping. Its power of comprehension never reaches beyond what philosophers call "finite things," or, as they sometimes say, "phenomena;" in short, just the fleeting shadows of this world, and the interests of the individual, the furtherance of his aims and the maintenance of his person. And since our intellect is thus immanent, our philosophy should be immanent too, and not soar to supramundane things, but be content with gaining a thorough grasp of the world of experience. It surely provides matter enough for such a study.

B. If that is so, intellect is a miserable present for Nature to give us. According to your view, the mind serves only to grasp the relations that constitute our wretched existence as individuals—relations which cease with the brief span of our temporal life; and is utterly unsuited to face those problems which are alone worthy to interest a thinking being—what our existence really is, and what the world means as a whole; in short, how we are to solve the riddle of this dream of life. If all this is so, and our mind could never grasp these things even though they were explained to it, then I cannot see that it is worth my while to educate my mind, or to pay any attention to it at all; it is a thing unworthy of any respect.

A. My dear sir, if we wrangle with Nature, we are usually in the wrong. For Nature does nothing that is useless or in vain—*nihil facit frustra nec supervacaneum.* We are only temporal, finite, fleeting beings creatures of a dream: and our existence passes away like a shadow. What do we want with an intellect to grasp things that are infinite, eternal, absolute? And how should such an intellect ever leave the consideration of these high matters to apply itself again to the small facts of our ephemeral life—the facts that are the only realities for us and our proper concern? How could it ever be of any use for them again? If nature had bestowed this intellect upon us, the gift would not only have been an immense mistake and quite in vain; it would even have conflicted with the very aims that nature has designed for us. For what good do we do, as Shakespeare says,

> " We fools of nature,
> So horridly to shake our disposition
> With thoughts beyond the reaches of our souls." *

If we had this perfect, this all embracing, metaphysical insight, should we be capable of any physical insight at all, or of going about our proper business? Nay, it might plunge us forever into a state of chill horror, like that of one who has seen a ghost.

B. But surely in all this you are making a notorious *petitio principii.* In saying that we are merely temporal, fleeting, finite beings, you beg the whole question. We are also infinite, eternal, and the original principle of nature itself. Is it not then well worth our while to go on trying if we cannot fathom nature after all—*ob nicht Natur zuletzt sich doch ergründe?*

A. Yes; but according to your own philosophy we are infinite and eternal, only in a certain sense. We are infinite and eternal not as phenomena, but as the original principle of nature; not as individuals, but as the inmost essence of the world; not because we are subjects of knowledge, but merely as manifestations of the will to live. The qualities of which you speak are qualities that have to do with intelligence, not will. As intelligent beings we are individual and finite. Our intellect, then, is also of this character. The aim of our life, if I may use a metaphorical expression, is a practical, not a theoretical one; our actions, not our knowledge, appertain to eternity. The use of the intellect is to guide our actions, and at the same time to hold up the mirror to our will; and this is, in effect, what it does. If the intellect

---

* " Hamlet," I., Sc. 4.

had more to do, it would very probably become unfit even for this. Think how a small superfluity of intellect is a bar to the career of the man endowed with it. Take the case of genius: while it may be an inward blessing to its possessor, it may also make him very unhappy in his relations with the world.*

B. Good, that you reminded me of genius. To some extent it upsets the facts you are trying to vindicate. A genius is a man whose theoretical side enormously outweighs his practical. Even though he cannot grasp eternal relations, he can see a little deeper into the things of this world; *attamen est quodam prodire tenus.* It is quite true that this does render the intellect of genius less fit to grasp the finite things of earth; just as a telescope is a good thing, but not in a theater. Here we seem to have reached a point where we agree, and we need not pursue the subject further.

THE METAPHYSICS OF FINE ART.

THE REAL problem in the philosophy of art may be very simply stated thus: How is it possible to take pleasure in something that does not come into any relation with the will?

Let me put this more fully. It is commonly felt that pleasure and enjoyment in a thing can arise only when it comes into some relation with our will, or, as we prefer to say, when it serves some end which we have in view. If this were so, it would seem to be a contradiction to talk of pleasure which did not involve bringing the will into play. And yet it is quite obvious that we derive pleasure and enjoyment from the beautiful as such, quite apart from any connection it may have with our personal aims, or, in other words, with our will.

This problem I have solved in the following way: by the beautiful we mean the essential and original forms of animate and inanimate nature—in Platonic language,

---

* *Translator's Note.*—This is a favorite remark of Schopenhauer's. Some account of his interesting theory of Genius touched upon at the conclusion of this dialogue may be found in the concluding section of this volume emitted: "The Art of Literature."

the Ideas; and they can be apprehended only by their essential correlate, a knowing subject free from will; in other words, a pure intelligence without purpose or ends in view. Hence in the act of æsthetic perception the will has absolutely no place in consciousness. But it is the will alone which is the fount of all our sorrows and sufferings, and if it thus vanishes from consciousness, the whole possibility of suffering is taken away. This it is that explains the feeling of pleasure which accompanies the perception of the beautiful.

If it should be objected that to take away the possibility of suffering is also to take away the possibility of enjoyment, it should be remembered that, as I have often explained, happiness and satisfaction are negative, in their nature; in other words, they are merely freedom from suffering; while pain is the positive element of existence. So that, when will vanishes from consciousness, there yet remains over the state of enjoyment: that is to say, the state in which there is a complete absence, not only of pain, but in this case, even of the very possibility of it.

To be freed from one's self is what is meant by becoming a pure intelligence. It consists in forgetfulness of one's own aims and complete absorption in the object of contemplation; so that all we are conscious of is this one object. And since this is a state of mind unattainable by most men, they are, as a rule, unfitted for an objective attitude toward the world; and it is just this that constitutes the artistic faculty.

To the will as it exists in the individual is superadded an intellectual faculty, which enables the will to become conscious of itself and of the objects about it. This intellectual faculty came into being in order to perform the service of the will. Now, let us suppose that the will sets the intellect at liberty for awhile and grants it a full release from its service, so that the intellect may for the moment dismiss its concern for the will; in other words, abandon the personal service which forms its only natural task, and, therefore, its regular occupation. If, at the same time that it is thus released, the intellect does not cease to be active and energetic, and use every endeavor to arrive at a clear apprehension of the world, it becomes completely objective; that is to say, it becomes a faithful mirror of the things about it.

It is only in this way, with a pure intelligence as subject, that the object, pure and simple, can come into existence. For this postulated relation between subject and object to arise at all, it is necessary that the intellectual faculty should not only be withdrawn from its original service and be left altogether to itself, but also that, when released, it should nevertheless preserve its whole energy of activity; in spite of the fact that the stimulus of this activity, the impulse of the will, is now absent.

Therein lies the difficulty, and this is just why the condition of mind necessary in artistic creation is so rare; because all our thoughts and endeavors, our powers of sight and hearing, are always naturally exerted, directly or indirectly, in the service of our numerous personal aims, great and small. It is the will that drives the intellect to the fulfillment of its function, and the intellect flags at once if the spur is withdrawn. Rendered active in this way, the intellect is perfectly sufficient for the needs of practical life, nay, even for the kind of knowledge required in professional business. For there the aim is to understand only the relations of things, not the inner reality peculiar to them; and this kind of knowledge proceeds by applying such principles of reasoning as govern the relation in which things may stand to one another.

But though in the conception of a work of art the intellect is all in all, in the execution of it, where the aim is to communicate and represent what has been conceived, the will may, nay, must become active again; just because there is an aim to be carried out. Accordingly, in this sphere, the principles of reasoning which govern the relations of things again come into play. It is in conformity with these principles that the means used by art are so contrived as to produce artistic effects. Thus we find the painter concerned with the accuracy of his drawing and the manipulation of his colors, and the poet looking first to the arrangement of his subject and then to a right use of expression and the laws of metre.

In the selection of a theme, both poetry and the plastic arts take some one individual person or thing and endeavor to present it as a separate entity, with all its peculiarities, even down to the minutest, exhibited with the most accurate precision. Science, on the other hand, works by the treatment of abstract ideas, every one of them representing innumerable individuals; and it proceeds to define and mark out the characteristics of these ideas, so as to fix them once for all. A comparison between these two methods might lead one to suppose that art is an insignificant, petty, nay, almost childish pursuit. But the nature of art is such that with it one case holds good for a thousand; for by a careful and detailed preservation of a single individual, person or thing, it aims at revealing the idea of the genus to which that person or thing belongs. Thus some one event or scene in the life of a man, described with complete truth— described, that is to say, so as to exhibit precisely all the individuals which go to make it what it is—gives us a clear and profound insight into the idea of humanity itself, as seen from this particular point of view. But, in spite of this difference of method between science and art, there is some similarity in their treatment of single facts. For just as the botanist picks a single flower from the boundless realm of the vegetable world, and then takes it to pieces in order to demonstrate, from the single specimen, the nature of the plant itself; so the poet chooses out of the endless turmoil of human life as it hurries incessantly on its way, some one scene, nay, often only some one mood, some one sensation, so that he may show us from it what is the life and character of man.

And thus it is that the greatest minds, Shakespeare and Goethe, Raphael and Rembrandt, do not think it unworthy of them to bring some quite ordinary person before us—not even one that is anything beyond the common— to delineate him with the greatest accuracy, in the endeavor to show him to us in the most minute particularity. For it is only when they are put before us in this way that we can apprehend individual and particular facts of life; and that is why I have defined poetry as the art of rousing the imagination by means of words.

If the reader wishes for a direct example of the advantage which intuitive knowledge—the primary and fundamental kind—has over abstract thought, as showing that art reveals to us more than we can gain from all the sciences, let him look at a beautiful human face, full of expressive emotion; and that too whether in nature itself or as presented to us by the mediation of art. How much deeper is the insight gained into the essential character of man, nay, into nature in general, by this sight than by all the words and abstract expressions which may be used to describe it. When a beautiful face beams with laughter, it is as though a fine landscape were suddenly illuminated by a ray of light darting from the clouds. Therefore *ridete, puellæ, ridete!*

Let me here state the general reason why the idea, in the Platonic meaning of the word, may be more easily apprehended from a picture than from reality; in other language, why a picture makes a nearer approach to the idea. A work of art is some objective reality as it appears after it has passed through a subject. From this point of view, it may be said to bear the same relation to the mind as animal food, which is vegetable food already assimilated, bears to the body.

But there is another and deeper reason for the fact in question. The product of plastic and pictorial art does not present us, as reality does, with something that exists once only and then is gone forever—the connection, I mean, between this particular matter and this particular form. It is this connection which is the essence of any concrete individuality, in the strict sense of the word. This kind of art shows us the form alone; and this, if it were given in its whole entirety, would be the idea. The picture, therefore leads us at once from the individual to the mere form; and this separation of the form from the matter brings the form very much nearer the idea. Now every artistic representation, whether painting or statue, is just such a separation; and hence this separation, this disjunction of the form from the matter is part of the character of a work of æsthetic art, because it is just the aim of such art to bring us to the knowledge of the idea.

It is, therefore, essential to a work of art that it should give the form alone without the matter; and, further, that it should do so without any possibility of mistake on the part of the spectator. This is really the reason why wax figures produce no æsthetic impression, and therefore are not, in the æsthetic sense, works of art at all; although if they were well made, they produce an illusion a hundred times greater than the best picture or statue could effect; so that if deceptive imitation of reality were the object of art, they would have to take the first place. For a wax figure of a man appears to give not only the mere form but with it the matter as well, so that it produces the illusion that the man himself is standing before you. The true work of art should lead us from the individual fact, in other words, that which exists once only, and then is gone forever, to the mere form or the idea—in other words, that which always exists an infinite number of times in an infinite number of ways. Instead of doing this, the wax figure appears to present us with the individual himself—in other words, with that which exists once only, and then never again; and yet, at the same time, it fails to represent the life which gives such a fleeting existence its value. This is why a wax figure is repulsive; it is stiff and stark, and reminds us of a corpse.

It might be thought that it is sculpture alone which gives form without matter; and that painting gives matter as well as form, by making color serve to imitate matter and its composition. But this objection would imply that form is to be taken in a purely geometrical sense; and that is not what is here meant. Form must be taken in the philosophical sense of the word, as the opposite of matter; and therefore it includes color, surface, texture; in short, quality, in whatever it may consist. It is quite true that sculpture alone gives form in the purely geometrical sense, exhibiting it on a matter which the eye can see to be foreign to the form, namely, marble; and in this way the form comes to stand by itself so as to strike the eye at once.

But painting does not give matter at all, and it gives only the mere appearance of the form, not in the geometrical, but in the philosophical, sense just described. Painting, I say, does not give even the form itself, but only the mere appearance of it—that is to say, merely its effect on one of our senses, the sense of sight; and that, too, only in so far as a particular act of vision is concerned. This is why a picture in oils does not really produce the illusion that the thing represented is actually before us, both in form and matter. The imitative truth of a picture is always subordinated to certain admitted conditions of this method of representation. Thus, by the unavoidable suppression of the parallax of our two eyes, a picture always makes things appear in the way in which a one eyed person would see them. Therefore painting, equally with sculpture, gives the form alone; for it presents nothing but the effect of the form—an effect confined to one of the senses only, namely, that of sight.

In connection with this subject it is to be observed that copper-plates and monochromes answer to a more noble and elevated taste than chromographs and water-colors; while the latter are preferred by persons of little culture. This is obviously due to the fact that pictures in black and white give the form alone, the form, as it were, in the abstract; and the apprehension of this is, as we know, intellectual, in other words, a matter of the intuitive understanding. Color, on the other hand, is merely an affair of sense, nay more, of a particular arrangement in the organ of sight which depends upon the activity of the retina. In respect of the taste to which they appeal, colored prints may be likened to rhymed, and copper-plates to blank verse.* The union of beauty and grace in the human form is the clearest manifestation of the will on the topmost stage of its objectivation, and for that very reason the highest achievement of the plastic and pictorial arts. But still, everything that is natural is beautiful If there are some animals of which we find a difficulty in believing this to be true, the reason of it is that we are unable to look at them in a purely objective light, so as to apprehend their idea. We are prevented from doing so by some unavoidable association of thought, chiefly the result of some similarity which forces itself upon our notice; as, for instance, the similarity of the ape with man; so that instead of apprehending the idea of an ape, what we see is the caricature of a man. In the same way a toad appears to produce an effect upon us similar to that of dirt and slime, and yet this is not enough to explain the unbounded aversion, nay, the feeling of dread and horror, which comes over some people at the sight of this animal, as over others when they see a spider. The feeling appears to be deeper than any mere association can explain, and to be traceable to some mysterious fact of a metaphysical nature.

The inorganic world, so far as it does not consist of mere water, produces a very sad, nay, an oppressive effect upon the feelings, whenever it is presented to us quite by

---

* Cf. Welt als und Vorstellung, Vol. II., p.488.

itself.   Examples of what I mean are afforded by districts which offer to the eye nothing but a mass of bare crags; that long valley of rocks, for instance, without a trace of vegetation, near Toulon, on the way to Marseilles.   The same effect is produced on a large scale, and in a much more striking degree, by the African desert.   The melancholy impression which this kind of scenery makes is mainly due to the fact that masses of inorganic matter obey one law only, the law of gravity; and consequently everything is disposed in accordance with it.

Contrarily, the sight of vegetation produces a feeling of direct pleasure, and that too in a high degree; and the pleasure is greater in proportion as the vegetation is rich, various, luxuriant, and left to itself.   The more immediate reason of this is that, in the case of vegetation, the law of gravity appears to be overcome, as the vegetable world tends to move in a direction the exact contrary of that taken by gravity.   This is, indeed, the direct way in which the phenomenon of life announces its presence, as a new and higher order of things.   It is an order to which we ourselves belong; it is something akin to us and the element of our being.   And so at the sight of it, our heart is moved.   That straight upward direction is the source of our pleasurable feeling.   This is why a fine group of trees looks so much better if a few tall tapering pines shoot out from the middle of it.   On the other hand, a tree that has been cut down has lost all its effect upon us: and one that grows obliquely has not so much as one that stands straight up.

A tree which bends over the earth with its branches obedient to the law of gravity, makes us melancholy; and and we call it the weeping willow.

Water neutralizes in a great measure the oppressive effect of its inorganic composition by its exceeding mobility, which gives it an appearance of life, and also by its constant interplay of light and shade.   Besides, water is absolutely indispensable for the existence of life.

But above and beyond this, the pleasurable feeling which the sight of vegetable nature gives us, comes from that look of rest, peace and satisfaction which it wears; while the animal world is mostly presented to us in a state of unrest, pain, even of struggle.   This explains why it is so easy for the sight of vegetation to put us into a state where we become a pure intelligence, freed from ourselves.

It is a very astonishing thing that vegetation, even of the commonest and humblest kind, is no sooner withdrawn from the capricious influence of man than it straightway groups itself picturesquely and strikes the eye, as beautiful. This is true of every little spot of earth that has been left wild and uncultivated, even though thistles, thorns and the commonest flowers of the field were all it bore. Where the ground is tilled—in cornfields, for instance, and kitchen-gardens, the æsthetic element in the vegetable world sinks to a minimum.

It has long been observed that everything constructed for the use of man, whether it is a building or only an utensil, must, if it is to be beautiful, preserve a certain similarity with the works of Nature. But a mistake has been made in thinking that the similarity must directly strike the eye and have to do with the shape the thing takes; as, for instance, that pillars should represent trees or human limbs; that receptacles should be shaped like mussels or snail-shells, or the calyx of a flower, and that vegetable or animal forms should be met with everywhere in Art.

The similarity should be indirect; that is to say, it should lie not in the shape itself, but in its character. One shape may differ from another in actual appearance and yet be the same in character. Accordingly, buildings and utensils should not be imitated from Nature, but should be constructed in the spirit of Nature. This will show itself in a perfect adaptation of means to ends, so that the thing itself and every part of it may directly proclaim what its purpose is. This will be effected when that purpose is attained in the shortest way and in the simplest manner. It is just this striking conformity to a certain end that stamps the products of Nature.

In Nature the will works from within outward, after completely dominating its material. But in Art it works from without, by a process of intuition; it may be, by setting up the abstract idea of the purpose which the object of art is to serve; it then attains its end and delivers itself of its meaning by impressing it upon some alien material; that is to say, some material originally devoted to another form of will. Yet for all that, the character I have described as belonging to a product of Nature may be preserved. This is shown by the ancient style of architecture. where every part or member is precisely suited to the purpose it is immediately meant to serve—a purpose thus naïvely brought into view, and where there is a total absence of anything that does not serve some purpose.

To this is opposed that Gothic style, which owes its mysterious appearance just to the multitude of aimless ornaments and accessories it displays, where we are obliged to ascribe to them some purpose which we cannot discern; and again, that quite degenerate style of architecture which affects originality by playing, in all sorts of unnecessary and roundabout ways, with the means used for producing artistic effect, dallying capriciously with them, and at the same time misunderstanding their aim.

The same remark holds good of ancient vessels and utensils, the beauty of which is due to the fact that they so naïvely express their nature, and the purpose they were meant to serve, and so of all other receptacles made by the ancients. You feel in looking at them that if Nature had produced vases, amphoræ, lamps, tables, stools, helmets, shields, armor and so on, they would be made in that style.

As regards the birth of a work of art in a man's mind, if he is only in a susceptible mood, almost any object that comes within his range of perception will begin to speak to him, in other words, will generate in him some lively, penetrating, original thought. So it is that a trivial event may become the seed of a great and glorious work. Jacob Böhme is said to have been enlightened upon some deep point of natural science by the sudden sight of a tin can.

In the end it all depends upon the power a man has in himself; and just as no food or medicine will bestow or take the place of vital energy, so no book or study can give a man a mind of his own.

THE ART OF LITERATURE.

THE ART OF LITERATURE.

ON AUTHORSHIP.

There are, first of all, two kinds of authors: those who write for the subject's sake, and those who write for writing's sake. While the one have had thoughts or experiences which seem to them worth communicating, the others want money, and so they write for money. Their thinking is part of the business of writing. They may be recognized by the way in which they spin out their thoughts to the greatest possible length; then, too, by the very nature of their thoughts, which are only half-true, perverse, forced, vacillating; again, by the aversion they generally show to saying anything straight out, so that they may seem other than they are. Hence their writing is deficient in clearness and definiteness, and it is not long before they betray that their only object in writing at all is to cover paper. This sometimes happens with the best authors: now and then, for example, with Lessing in his "Dramaturgie," and even in many of Jean Paul's romances. As soon as the reader perceives this, let him throw the book away; for time is precious. The truth is that when an author begins to write for the sake of covering paper he is cheating the reader; because he writes under the pretext that he has something to say.

Writing for money and reservation of copyright are, at bottom, the ruin of literature. No one writes anything that is worth writing, unless he writes entirely for the sake of his subject. What an inestimable boon it would be, if in every branch of literature there were only a few books, but those excellent! This can never happen, as long as money is to be made by writing. It seems as though the money lay under a curse; for every author degenerates as soon as he begins to put pen to paper in any way for the sake of gain. The best works of the greatest men all come from the time when they had to write for nothing or for very little. And here, too, that Spanish proverb holds good, which declares that honor and money are not to be found in the same purse—*honray provecho no caben en un saco.* The reason why literature is in such a bad plight nowadays is simply and solely that people write books to make money. A man who is in want sits down and writes a book, and the public is stupid enough to buy it. The secondary effect of this is the ruin of language.

A great many bad writers make their whole living by that foolish mania of the public for reading nothing but what has just been printed—journalists, I mean. Truly, a most appropriate name. In plain language it is journeymen, day-laborers!

Again, it may be said that there are three kinds of authors. First come those who write without thinking. They write from a full memory, from reminiscences; it may be, even straight out of other people's books. This class is the most numerous. Then come those who do their thinking whilst they are writing. They think in order to write; and there is no lack of them. Last of all come those authors who think before they begin to write. They are rare.

Authors of the second class, who put off their thinking until they come to write, are like a sportsman who goes forth at random and is not likely to bring very much home. On the other hand, when an author of the third or rare class writes, it is like a *battue.* Here the game has been previously captured and shut up within a very small space, from which it is afterward let out, so many at a time, into another space, also confined. The game cannot possibly escape the sportsman; he has nothing to do but aim and fire—in other words, write down his thoughts. This is a kind of sport from which a man has something to show.

But even though the number of those who really think seriously before they begin to write is small, extremely few of them think about the subject itself: the remainder think only about the books that have been written on the subject, and what has been said by others. In order to think at all, such writers need the more direct and powerful stimulus of having other people's thoughts before them. These become their immediate theme, and the result is that they are always under their influence, and so never, in any real sense of the word, original. But the former are roused to thought by the subject itself, to which their thinking is thus immediately directed. This is the only class that produces writers of abiding fame.

It must, of course, be understood that I am speaking here of writers who treat of great subjects; not of writers on the art of making brandy.

Unless an author takes the material on which he writes out of his own head, that is to say, from his own observation, he is not worth reading. Book-manufacturers, compilers, the common run of history-writers, and many others of the same class, take their material immediately out of books; and the material goes straight to their finger-tips without even paying freight or undergoing examination as it passes through their heads, to say nothing of elaboration or revision. How very learned many a man would be if he knew everything that was in his own books! The consequence of this is that these writers talk in such a loose and vague manner, that the reader puzzles his brains in vain to understand what it is of which they are really thinking. They are thinking of nothing. It may now and then be the case that the book from which they copy has been composed exactly in the same way; so that writing of this sort is like a plaster cast of a cast; and in the end, the bare outline of the face, and that, too, hardly recognizable, is all that is left of your Antinous. Let compilations be read as seldom as possible. It is difficult to avoid them altogether, since compilations also include those text-books which contain in a small space the accumulated knowledge of centuries.

There is no greater mistake than to suppose that the last work is always the more correct; that what is written later on is in every case an improvement on what was written before; and that change always means progress. Real thinkers, men of right judgment, people who are in earnest with their subject—these are all exceptions only. Vermin is the rule everywhere in the world: it is always on the alert, taking the mature opinions of the thinkers, and industriously seeking to improve upon them (save the mark!) in its own peculiar way.

If the reader wishes to study any subject, let him beware of rushing to the newest books upon it, and confining his attention to them alone, under the notion that science is always advancing, and that the old books have been drawn upon in the writing of the new. They have been drawn upon, it is true; but how? The writer of the new book often does not understand the old books thoroughly, and yet he is unwilling to take their exact words; so he bungles them, and says in his own bad way that which has been said very much better and more clearly by the old writers, who wrote from their own lively knowledge of the subject. The new writer frequently omits the best things they say, their most striking illustrations, their happiest remarks; because he does not see their value or feel how pregnant they are. The only thing that appeals to him is what is shallow and insipid.

It often happens that an old and excellent book is ousted by new and bad ones, which, written for money, appear with an air of great pretension and much puffing on the part of friends. In science a man tries to make his mark by bringing out something fresh. This often means nothing more than that he attacks some received theory which is quite correct, in order to make room for his own false notions. Sometimes the effort is successful for a time; and then a return is made to the old and true theory. These innovators are serious about nothing but their own precious self; it is this that they want to put forward, and the quick way of doing so, as they think, is to start a paradox. Their sterile heads take naturally to the path of negation; so they begin to deny truths that have long been admitted —the vital power, for example, the sympathetic nervous system, *generatio equivoca,* Bichat's distinction between the working of the passions and the working of intelligence; or else they want us to return to crass atomism, and the like. Hence it frequently happens that "the course of science is retrogressive."

To this class of writers belong those translators who not only translate their author but also correct and revise him; a proceeding which always seems to me impertinent. To such writers I say: Write books yourself which are worth translating, and leave other people's works as they are!

The reader should study, if he can, the real authors, the men who have founded and discovered things; or, at any rate, those who are recognized as the great masters in every branch of knowledge. Let him buy second-hand books rather than read their contents in new ones. To be sure, it is easy to add to any new discovery—*inventis aliquid addere facile est;* and, therefore, the student, after well mastering the rudiments of his subject, will have to make himself acquainted with the more recent additions to the knowledge of it. And, in general, the following rule may be laid down here as elsewhere; if a thing is new, it is seldom good; because if it is good, it is only for a short time new.

What the address is to a letter, the title should be to a book; in other words, its main object should be to bring the book to those among the public who will take an interest in its contents. It should, therefore, be expressive; and since by its very nature it must be short, it should be concise, laconic, pregnant, and if possible give the contents in one word. A prolix title is bad; and so is one that says nothing, or is obscure and ambiguous, or even, it may be, false and misleading; this last may possibly involve the book in the same fate as overtakes a wrongly addressed letter. The worst titles of all are those which have been stolen, those, I mean, which have already been borne by other books; for they are in the first place a plagiarism, and secondly the most convincing proof of a total lack of originality in the author. A man who has not enough originality to invent a new title for his book, will be still less able to give it new contents. Akin to these stolen titles are those which have been imitated, that is to say, stolen to the extent of one half; for instance, long after I had produced my treatise " On Will in Nature," Orested wrote a book entitled " On Mind in Nature."

A book can never be anything more than the impress of its author's thoughts; and the value of these will lie either " in the matter about which he has thought," or in the form which his thoughts take, in other words, " what it is that he has thought about it."

The matter of books is most various; and various also are the several excellences attaching to books on the score of their matter. By matter I mean everything that comes within the domain of actual experience; that is to say, the facts of history and the facts of nature, taken in and by themselves and in their widest sense. Here it is the thing treated of which gives its peculiar character to the book;

so that a book can be important, whoever it was that wrote it.

But in regard to the form, the peculiar character of a a book depends upon the person who wrote it. It may treat of matters which are accessible to every one and well known; but it is the way in which they are treated, what it is that is thought about them, that gives the book its value; and this comes from its author. If, then, from this point of view a book is excellent and beyond comparison, so is its author It follows that if a writer is worth reading his merit rises just in proportion as he owes little to his matter; therefore, the better known and the more hackneyed this is, the greater he will be. The three great tragedians of Greece, for example, all worked at the same subject-matter.

So when a book is celebrated, care should be taken to note whether it is so on account of its matter or its form; and a distinction should be made accordingly.

Books of great importance on account of their matter may proceed from very ordinary and shallow people, by the fact that they alone have had access to this matter; books, for instance, which describe journeys in distant lands, rare natural phenomena, or experiments; or historical occurrences of which the writers were witnesses, or in connection with which they have spent much time and trouble in the research and special study of original documents.

On the other hand where the matter is accessible to every one or very well known, everything will depend upon the form; and what it is that is thought about the matter will give the book all the value it possesses. Here only a really distinguished man will be able to produce anything worth reading; for the others will think nothing but what any one else can think. They will just produce an impress of their own minds; but this is a print of which every one possesses the original.

However, the public is very much more concerned to have matter than form; and for this very reason it is deficient in any high degree of culture. The public shows its preference in this respect in the most laughable way when it comes to deal with poetry; for there it devotes much trouble to the task of tracing out the actual events or personal circumstances in the life of the poet which served as the occasion of his various works; nay, these events and circumstances come in the end to be of greater importance than the works themselves; and rather than read Goethe himself, people prefer to read what has been written about him, and to study the legend of Faust more industriously than the drama of that name. And when Bürger declared that "people would write learned disquisitions on the question, who Leonora really was," we find this literally fulfilled in Goethe's case; for we now possess a great many learned disquisitions on Faust and the legend attaching to him. Study of this kind is, and remains, devoted to the material of the drama alone. To give such preference to the matter over the form, is as though a man were to take a fine Etruscan vase, not to admire its shape or coloring, but to make a chemical analysis of the clay and paint of which it is composed.

The attempt to produce an effect by means of the material employed—an attempt which panders to this evil tendency of the public—is most to be condemned in branches of literature where any merit there may be lies expressly in the form; I mean, in poetical work. For all that, it is not rare to find bad dramatists trying to fill the house by means of the matter about which they write. For example, authors of this kind do not shrink from putting on the stage any man who is in any way celebrated, no matter whether his life may have been entirely devoid of dramatic incident; and sometimes, even, they do not wait until the persons immediately connected with him are dead.

The distinction between matter and form to which I am here alluding, also holds good of conversation. The chief qualities which enable a man to converse well are intelligence, discernment, wit and vivacity: these supply the form of conversation. But it is not long before attention has to be paid to the matter of which he speaks; in other words, the subjects about which it is possible to converse with him—his knowledge. If this is very small, his conversation will not be worth anything, unless he possesses the above named formal qualities in a very exceptional degree: for he will have nothing to talk about but those facts of life and nature which everybody knows. It will be just the opposite, however, if a man is deficient in these formal qualities, but has an amount of knowledge which lends

value to what he says. This value will then depend
entirely upon the matter of his conversation; for, as
the Spanish proverb has it, *mas sabe el necio en su casa,
que el sabio en la ageno*—a fool knows more of his own business than a wise man of others'.

ON STYLE.

STYLE is the physiognomy of the mind, and a safer
index to character than the face. To imitate another
man's style is like wearing a mask, which, be it never so
fine, is not long in arousing disgust and abhorrence, because it is lifeless; so that even the ugliest living face is better. Hence those who write in Latin and copy the manner of ancient authors, may be said to speak through a
mask; the reader, it is true, hears what they say, but he
cannot observe their physiognomy too; he cannot see their
style. With the Latin works of writers who think for
themselves, the case is different, and their style is visible;
writers, I mean, who have not condescended to any sort of
imitation, such as Scotus Erigena, Petrarch, Bacon, Descartes, Spinoza, and many others. And affectation in
style is like making grimaces. Further, the language in
which a man writes is the physiognomy of the nation to
which he belongs; and here there are many hard and fast
differences, beginning from the language of the Greeks,
down to that of the Caribbean islanders.

To form a provisional estimate of the value of a writer's
productions, it is not directly necessary to know the subject
on which he has thought, or what it is that he has said
about it; that would imply a perusal of all his works. It
will be enough, in the main, to know how he has thought.
This, which means the essential temper or general quality
of his mind, may be precisely determined by his style. A
man's style shows the formal nature of all his thoughts—
the formal nature which can never change, be the subject
or the character of his thoughts what it may: it is, as it
were, the dough out of which all the contents of his mind
are kneaded. When Eulenspiegel was asked how long it
would take to walk to the next village, he gave the seemingly incongruous answer: Walk. He wanted to find out by

the man's pace the distance he would cover in a given time. In the same way, when I have read a few pages of an author, I know fairly well how far he can bring me.

Every mediocre writer tries to mask his own natural style, because in his heart he knows the truth of what I am saying. He is thus forced, at the outset, to give up any attempt at being frank or naïve—a privilege which is thereby reserved for superior minds, conscious of their own worth, and therefore sure of themselves. What I mean is that these everyday writers are absolutely unable to resolve upon writing just as they think; because they have a notion that, were they to do so, their work might possibly look very childish and simple. For all that, it would not be without its value. If they would only go honestly to work, and say, quite simply, the things they have really thought, and just as they have thought them, these writers would be readable, and, within their own proper sphere, even instructive.

But instead of that, they try to make the reader believe that their thoughts have gone much further and deeper than is really the case. They say what they have to say in long sentences that wind about in a forced and unnatural way: they coin new words and write prolix periods which go round and round the thought and wrap it up in a sort of disguise. They tremble between the two separate aims of communicating what they want to say and of concealing it. Their object is to dress it up so that it may look learned or deep, in order to give people the impression that there is very much more in it than for the moment meets the eye. They either jot down their thoughts bit by bit, in short, ambiguous, and paradoxical sentences, which apparently mean much more than they say, of this kind of writing Schelling's treatises on natural philosophy are a splendid instance; or else they hold forth with a deluge of words and the most intolerable diffusiveness, as though no end of fuss were necessary to make the reader understand the deep meaning of their sentences, whereas it is some quite simple if not actually trivial idea—examples of which may be found in plenty in the popular works of Fichte, and the philosophical manuals of a hundred other miserable dunces not worth mentioning; or, again, they try to write in some particular style which they have been pleased to take up and think very grand, a style, for example, *par excellence* profound and scientific, where the reader is tormented to death by the narcotic effect of long-spun periods without a single idea in them—such as are furnished in a special measure by those most impudent of all mortals, the Hegelians;* or it may be that it is an intellectual style they have striven after, where it seems as though their object were to go crazy altogether; and so on in many other cases. All these endeavors to put off the *nascetur ridiculus mus*—to avoid showing the funny little creature that is born after such mighty throes—often make it difficult to know what it is that they really mean. And then, too, they write down words, nay, even whole sentences, without attaching any meaning to them themselves but in the hope that some one else will get sense out of them.

And what is at the bottom of all this? Nothing but the untiring effort to sell words for thoughts; a mode of merchandise that is always trying to make fresh openings for itself, and by means of odd expressions, turns of phrase, and combinations of every sort, whether new or used in a new sense, to produce the appearance of intellect in order to make up for the very painfully felt lack of it.

It is amusing to see how writers with this object in view will attempt first one mannerism and then another, as though they were putting on the mask of intellect! This mask may possibly deceive the inexperienced for awhile, until it is seen to be a dead thing, with no life in it at all: it is then laughed at and exchanged for another. Such an author will at one moment write in a dithyrambic vein, as though he were tipsy; at another, nay, on the very next page, he will be pompous, severe, profoundly learned and prolix, stumbling on in the most cumbrous way and chopping up everything very small; like the late Christian Wolf, only in a modern dress. Longest of all lasts the mask of unintelligibility; but this is only in Germany, whither it was introduced by Fichte, perfected by Schelling, and carried to its highest pitch in Hegel—always with the best results.

And yet nothing is easier than to write so that no one can understand; just as, contrarily, nothing is more diffi-

---

* In their Hegel-gazette, commonly known as Jahrbucher der wissenschaftlichen Literatur.

cult than to express deep things in such a way that every one must necessarily grasp them. All the arts and tricks I have been mentioning are rendered superfluous if the author really has any brains; for that allows him to show himself as he is, and confirms to all time Horace's maxim that good sense is the source and origin of good style:

"Scribendi recte sapere est et principium et fons."

But those authors I have named are like certain workers in metal, who try a hundred different compounds to take the place of gold—the only metal which can never have any substitute. Rather than do that, there is nothing against which a writer should be more upon his guard than the manifest endeavor to exhibit more intellect than he really has; because this makes the reader suspect that he possesses very little; since it is always the case that if a man affects anything, whatever it may be, it is just there that he is deficient.

That is why it is praise to an author to say that he is naïve; it means that he need not shrink from showing himself as he is. Generally speaking, to be naïve is to be attractive; while lack of naturalness is everywhere repulsive. As a matter of fact we find that every really great writer tries to express his thoughts as purely, clearly, definitely and shortly as possible. Simplicity has always been held to be a mark of truth: it is also a mark of genius. Style receives its beauty from the thought it expresses; but with sham thinkers the thoughts are supposed to be fine because of the style. Style is nothing but the mere silhouette of thought; and an obscure or bad style means a dull or confused brain.

The first rule, then, for a good style is that the author should have something to say; nay, this is in itself almost all that is necessary. Ah, how much it means! The neglect of this rule is a fundamental trait in the philosophical writing, and, in fact, in all the reflective literature of my country, more especially since Fichte. These writers all let it be seen that they want to appear as though they had something to say; whereas they have nothing to say. Writing of this kind was brought in by the pseudo-philosophers at the universities, and now it is current everywhere, even among the first literary notabili-

ties of the age. It is the mother of that strained and
vague style, where there seem to be two or even more
meanings in the sentence; also of that prolix and cumbrous
manner of expression, called *le stile empesé;* again, of that
mere waste of words which consists in pouring them out
like a flood; finally, of that trick of concealing the direst
poverty of thought under a farrago of never-ending chatter,
which clacks away like a windmill and quite stupefies one
—stuff which a man may read for hours together without
getting hold of a single clearly expressed and definite idea. *
However, people are easy-going, and they have formed the
habit of reading page upon page of all sorts of such verbiage, without having any particular idea of what the author
really means. They fancy it is all as it should be, and fail
to discover that he is writing simply for writing's sake.

On the other hand, a good author, fertile in ideas, soon
wins his reader's confidence that, when he writes, he has
really and truly something to say; and this gives the
intelligent reader patience to follow him with attention.
Such an author, just because he really has something to
say, will never fail to express himself in the simplest and
most straightforward manner: because his object is to
awake the very same thought in the reader that he has in
himself, and no other. So he will be able to affirm with
Boileau that his thoughts are everywhere open to the light
of day, and that his verse always says something, whether
it says it well or ill:

> " Ma pensée au grand jour partout s'offre et s'expose,
>   Et mon vers, bien ou mal, dit toujours quelque chose."

while of the writers previously described it may be asserted,
in the words of the same poet, that they talk much and
never say anything at all—*qui parlant beaucoup ne disent
jamais rien.*

Another characteristic of such writers is that they always
avoid a positive assertion wherever they can possibly do so,
in order to leave a loophole for escape in case of need.
Hence they never fail to choose the more abstract way of
expressing themselves; whereas intelligent people use the
more concrete; because the latter brings things more within

---

* Select examples of the art of writing in this style are to be found
almost *passim* in the Jahrbücher, published in Halle, afterward
called the Deutschen Jahrbücher.

the range of actual demonstration, which is the source of all evidence.

There are many examples proving this preference for abstract expression; and a particularly ridiculous one is afforded by the use of the verb " to condition " in the sense of to cause or to produce. People say " to condition something " instead of to cause it, because being abstract and indefinite it says less; it affirms that A cannot happen without B, instead of that A is caused by B. A back door is always left open; and this suits people whose secret knowledge of their own incapacity inspires them with a perpetual terror of all positive assertion; while with other people it is merely the effect of that tendency by which everything that is stupid in literature or bad in life is immediately imitated—a fact proved in either case by the rapid way in which it spreads. The Englishman uses his own judgment in what he writes as well as in what he does; but there is no nation of which this eulogy is less true than of the Germans. The consequence of this state of things is that the word cause has of late almost disappeared from the language of literature, and people talk only of condition. The fact is worth mentioning because it is so characteristically ridiculous.

The very fact that these commonplace authors are never more than half-conscious when they write, would be enough to account for their dullness of mind and the tedious things they produce. I say they are only half-conscious, because they really do not themselves understand the meaning of the words they use; they take words ready-made and commit them to memory. Hence when they write, it is not so much words as whole phrases that they put together— *phrases banales.* This is the explanation of that palpable lack of clearly-expressed thought in what they say. The fact is that they do not possess the die to give this stamp to their writing; clear thought of their own is just what they have not got. And what do we not find in its place? —a vague, enigmatical intermixture of words, current phrases, hackneyed terms, and fashionable expressions. The result is that the foggy stuff they write is like a page printed with very old type.

On the other hand, an intelligent author really speaks to us when he writes, and that is why he is able to rouse our interest and commune with us. It is the intelligent

author alone who puts individual words together with a
full consciousness of their meaning, and chooses them
with deliberate design. Consequently, his discourse stands
to that of the writer described above, much as a picture
that has been really painted to one that has been produced
by the use of a stencil. In the one case, every word, every
touch of the brush, has a special purpose; in the other,
all is done mechanically. The same distinction may be
observed in music. For just as Lichtenberg says that
Garrick's soul seemed to be in every muscle in his body, so
it is the omnipresence of intellect that always and everywhere characterizes the work of genius.

I have alluded to the tediousness which marks the works
of these writers; and in this connection it is to be observed
generally, that tediousness is of two kinds: objective and
subjective. A work is objectively tedious when it contains
the defect in question; that is to say, when its author has
no perfectly clear thought or knowledge to communicate.
For if a man has any clear thought or knowledge his aim
will be to communicate it, and he will direct his energies
to this end; so that the ideas he furnishes are everywhere
clearly expressed. The result is that he is neither diffuse,
nor unmeaning, nor confused, and consequently not tedious.
In such a case, even though the author is at bottom in
error, the error is at any rate clearly worked out and well
thought over, so that it is at least formally correct; and
thus some value always attaches to the work. But for
the same reason a work that is objectively tedious is at all
times devoid of any value whatever.

The other kind of tediousness is only relative: a reader
may find a work dull because he has no interest in the
question treated of in it, and this means that his intellect
is restricted. The best work may, therefore, be tedious
subjectively, tedious, I mean to this or that particular
person: just as, contrarily, the worst work may be subjectively engrossing to this or that particular person who
has an interest in the question treated of, or in the writer
of the book.

It would generally serve writers in good stead if they
would see that, while a man should, if possible, think like
a great genius, he should talk the same language as
every one else. Authors should use common words to say
uncommon things. But they do just the opposite. We

find them trying to wrap up trivial ideas in grand words, and to clothe their very ordinary thoughts in the most extraordinary phrases, the most far-fetched, unnatural, and out-of-the-way expressions. Their sentences perpetually stalk about on stilts. They take so much pleasure in bombast, and write in such a high-flown, bloated, affected, hyperbolical and acrobatic style that their prototype is Ancient Pistol, whom his friend Falstaff once impatiently told to say what he had to say, "like a man of this world."*

There is no expression in any other language exactly answering to the French *sale empesé;* but the thing itself exists all the more often. When associated with affectation, it is in literature what assumption of dignity, grand airs and primness are in society; and equally intolerable. Dullness of mind is fond of donning this dress; just as in ordinary life it is stupid people who like being demure and formal.

An author who writes in the prim style resembles a man who dresses himself up in order to avoid being confounded or put on the same level with the mob—a risk never run by the gentleman, even in his worst clothes. The plebeian may be known by a certain showiness of attire, and a wish to have everything spick and span; and in the same way, the commonplace person is betrayed by his style.

Nevertheless, an author follows a false aim if he tries to write exactly as he speaks. There is no style of writing but should have a certain trace of kinship with the epigraphic or monumental style, which is, indeed, the ancestor of all styles. For an author to write as he speaks is just as reprehensible as the opposite fault, to speak as he writes; for this gives a pedantic effect to what he says, and at the same time makes him hardly intelligible.

An obscure and vague manner of expression is always and everywhere a very bad sign. In ninety-nine cases out of a hundred it comes from vagueness of thought; and this again almost always means that there is something radically wrong and incongruous about the thought itself—in a word, that it is incorrect. When a right thought springs up in the mind, it strives after expression and is not long in reaching it; for clear thought easily finds words to fit it. If a man is capable of thinking anything

---

* "King Henry IV.," Part II. Act v. Sc. 3.

at all, he is also always able to express it in clear, intelligible, and unambiguous terms. Those writers who construct difficult, obscure, involved, and equivocal sentences, most certainly do not know aright what it is that they want to say: they have only a dull consciousness of it, which is still in the stage of struggle to shape itself as thought. Often, indeed, their desire is to conceal from themselves and others that they really have nothing at all to say. They wish to appear to know what they do not know, to think what they do not think, to say what they do not say. If a man has some real communication to make, which will he choose—an indistinct or a clear way of expressing himself? Even Quintilian remarks that things which are said by a highly educated man are often easier to understand and much clearer: and that the less educated a man is, the more obscurely he will write— "*plerumque accidit ut faciliora sint ad intelligendum et lucidiora multo quæ a doctissimo quoque dicuntur . . . . Erit ergo etiam obscurior quo quisque deterior.*"

An author should avoid enigmatical phrases: he should know whether he wants to say a thing or does not want to say it. It is this indecision of style that makes so many writers insipid. The only case that offers an exception to this rule arises when it is necessary to make a remark that is in some way improper.

As exaggeration generally produces an effect the opposite of that aimed at, so words, it is true, serve to make thought intelligible—but only up to a certain point. If words are heaped up beyond it, the thought becomes more and more obscure again. To find where the point lies is the problem of style, and the business of the critical faculty; for a word too much always defeats its purpose. This is what Voltaire means when he says that "the adjective is the enemy of the substantive." But, as we have seen, many people try to conceal their poverty of thought under a flood of verbiage.

Accordingly, let all redundancy be avoided, all stringing together of remarks which have no meaning and are not worth perusal. A writer must make a sparing use of the reader's time, patience and attention; so as to lead him to believe that his author writes what is worth careful study, and will reward the time spent upon it. It is always better to omit something good than to add that which is not worth saying at all. This is the right application of Hesiod's maxim, πλέον ἥμισυ παντος*—the half is more than the whole. *Le secret pour étre ennuyeux, c'est de tout dire.* Therefore, if possible, the quintessence only! mere leading thoughts! nothing that the reader would think for himself. To use many words to communicate few thoughts is everywhere the unmistakable sign of mediocrity. To gather much thought into few words stamps the man of genius.

Truth is most beautiful undraped; and the impression it makes is deep in proportion as its expression has been simple. This is so, partly because it then takes unobstructed possession of the hearer's whole soul, and leaves him no by-thought to distract him: partly, also, because he feels that here he is not being corrupted or cheated by the arts of rhetoric, but that all the effect of what is said comes from the thing itself. For instance, what declamation on the vanity of human existence could ever be more telling than the words of Job?—"Man that is born of a woman hath but a short time to live and is full of misery. He cometh up, and is cut down, like a flower; he fleeth as it were a shadow, and never continueth in one stay."

For the same reason Goethe's naïve poetry is incomparably greater than Schiller's rhetoric. It is this, again, that makes many popular songs so affecting. As in architecture an excess of decoration is to be avoided, so in the art of literature a writer must guard against all rhetorical finery, all useless amplification, and all superfluity of expression in general: in a word, he must strive after chastity of style. Every word that can be spared is hurtful if it remains. The law of simplicity and naïvety holds good of all fine art; for it is quite possible to be at once simple and sublime.

True brevity of expression consists in everywhere saying only what is worth saying, and in avoiding tedious detail about things which every one can supply for himself. This involves correct discrimination between what is necessary and what is superfluous. A writer should never be brief at the expense of being clear, to say nothing of being grammatical. It shows lamentable want of judgment to weaken the expression of a thought or to stunt the mean-

---

* "Works and Days," 40.

ing of a period for the sake of using a few words less.
But this is the precise endeavor of that false brevity nowadays so much in vogue, which proceeds by leaving out
useful words and even by sacrificing grammar and logic.
It is not only that such writers spare a word by making a
single verb or adjective do duty for several different periods,
so that the reader, as it were, has to grope his way through
them in the dark; they also practice, in many other respects, an unseemly economy of speech, in the effort to
effect what they foolishly take to be brevity of expression
and conciseness of style. By omitting something that
might have thrown a light over the whole sentence, they
turn it into a conundrum, which the reader tries to solve
by going over it again and again.*

It is wealth and weight of thought, and nothing else,
that gives brevity to style, and makes it concise and pregnant. If a writer's ideas are important, luminous, and
generally worth communicating, they will necessarily furnish matter and substance enough to fill out the periods
which give them expression, and make these in all their
parts both grammatically and verbally complete; and so
much will this be the case that no one will ever find them
hollow, empty or feeble. The diction will everywhere be
brief and pregnant, and allow the thought to find intelligible and easy expression, and even unfold and move about
with grace.

Therefore instead of contracting his words and forms of
speech, let a writer enlarge his thoughts. If a man has
been thinned by illness and finds his clothes too big, it is
not by cutting them down, but by recovering his usual
bodily condition, that he ought to make them fit him again.

Let me here mention an error of style very prevalent
nowadays, and, in the degraded state of literature and the
neglect of ancient languages, always on the increase; I

---

* *Translator's Note.* In the original, Schopenhauer here enters
upon a lengthy examinaton of certain common errors in the writing
and speaking of German. His remarks are addressed to his own
countrymen, and would lose all point, even if they were intelligible,
in an English translation. But for those who practice their German
by conversing or corresponding with Germans, let me recommend
what he there says as a useful corrective to a slipshod style, such as
can easily be contracted if it is assumed that the natives of a country
always know their own language perfectly.

mean subjectivity. A writer commits this error when he thinks it enough if he himself knows what he means and wants to say, and takes no thought for the reader, who is left to get at the bottom of it as best he can. This is as though the author were holding a monologue, whereas it ought to be a dialogue; and a dialogue, too, in which he must express himself all the more clearly inasmuch as he cannot hear the questions of his interlocutor.

Style should for this very reason never be subjective, but objective; and it will not be objective unless the words are so set down that they directly force the reader to think precisely the same thing as the author thought when he wrote them. Nor will this result be obtained unless the author has always been careful to remember that thought so far follows the law of gravity that it travels from head to paper much more easily than from paper to head: so that he must assist the latter passage by every means in his power. If he does this, a writer's words will have a purely objective effect, like that of a finished picture in oils; while the subjective style is not much more certain in its working than spots on the wall, which look like figures only to one whose fantasy has been accidentally aroused by them; other people see nothing but spots and blurs. The difference in question applies to literary method as a a whole; but it is often established also in particular instances. For example, in a recently published work I found the following sentence: "I have not written in order to increase the number of existing books." This means just the opposite of what the writer wanted to say, and is nonsense as well.

He who writes carelessly confesses thereby at the very outset that he does not attach much importance to his own thoughts. For it is only where a man is convinced of the truth and importance of his thoughts, that he feels the enthusiasm necessary for an untiring and assiduous effort to find the clearest, finest, and strongest expression for them, just as for sacred relics or priceless works of art there are provided silvern or golden receptacles. It was this feeling that led ancient authors, whose thoughts, expressed in their own words, have lived thousands of years, and therefore bear the honored title of classics, always to write with care. Plato, indeed, is said to have written the introduction to his "Republic" seven times over in different ways.*

As neglect of dress betrays want of respect for the company a man meets, so a hasty, careless, bad style shows an outrageous lack of regard for the reader, who then rightly punishes it by refusing to read the book. It is especially amusing to see reviewers criticising the works of others in their own most careless style—the style of a hireling. It is as though a judge were to come into court in dressing-gown and slippers! If I see a man badly and dirtily dressed, I feel some hesitation, at first, in entering into conversation with him: and when, on taking up a book, I am struck at once by the negligence of its style, I put it away.

Good writing should be governed by the rule that a man can think only one thing clearly at a time; and therefore, that he should not be expected to think two or even more things in one and the same moment. But this is what is done when a writer breaks up his principal sentence into little pieces, for the purpose of pushing into the gaps thus made two or three other thoughts by way of parenthesis; thereby unnecessarily and wantonly confusing the reader. And here it is again my own countrymen who are chiefly in fault. That German lends itself to this way of writing, makes the thing possible, but does not justify it. No prose reads more easily or pleasantly than French, because, as a rule, it is free from the error in question. The Frenchman strings his thoughts together, as far as he can, in the most logical and natural order, and so lays them before his reader one after the other for convenient deliberation, so that every one of them may receive undivided attention. The German, on the other hand, weaves them together into a sentence which he twists and crosses, and crosses and twists again; because he wants to say six things all at once, instead of advancing them one by one. His aim should be to attract and hold the reader's attention; but, above and beyond neglect of this aim, he demands from the reader that he shall set the above mentioned rule at defiance, and think three or four different thoughts at one and the same time; or since that is impossible, that his thoughts shall

---

* *Translator's Note.*—It is a fact worth mentioning that the first twelve words of the "Republic" are placed in the exact order which would be natural in English.

succeed each other as quickly as the vibrations of a cord. In this way an author lays the foundation of his *stile empesé,* which is then carried to perfection by the use of high-flown, pompous expressions to communicate the simplest things, and other artifices of the same kind.

In those long sentences rich in involved parentheses, like a box of boxes one within another, and padded out like roast geese stuffed with apples, it is really the memory that is chiefly taxed; while it is the understanding and the judgment which should be called into play, instead of having their activity thereby actually hindered and weakened.* This kind of sentence furnishes the reader with mere half-phrases, which he is then called upon to collect carefully and store up in his memory, as though they were the pieces of a torn letter, afterward to be completed and made sense of by the other halves to which they respectively belong. He is expected to go on reading for a little without exercising any thought, nay, exerting only his memory, in the hope that, when he comes to the end of the sentence, he may see its meaning and so receive something to think about; and he is thus given a great deal to learn by heart before obtaining anything to understand. This is manifestly wrong and an abuse of the reader's patience.

The ordinary writer has an unmistakable preference for this style, because it causes the reader to spend time and trouble in understanding that which he would have understood in a moment without it; and this makes it look as though the writer had more depth and intelligence than the reader. This is, indeed, one of those artifices referred to above, by means of which mediocre authors unconsciously, and as it were by instinct, strive to conceal their poverty of thought and give an appearance of the opposite. Their ingenuity in this respect is really astounding.

It is manifestly against all sound reason to put one thought obliquely on top of another, as though both together formed a wooden cross. But this is what is done

---

* *Translator's Note.*—This sentence in the original is obviously meant to illustrate the fault of which it speaks. It does so by the use of a construction very common in German, but happily unknown in English ; where, however, the fault itself exists none the less, though in a different form.

where a writer interrupts what he has begun to say, for the purpose of inserting some quite alien matter; thus depositing with the reader a meaningless half-sentence, and bidding him keep it until the completion comes. It is much as though a man were to treat his guests by handing them an empty plate, in the hope of something appearing upon it. And commas used for a similar purpose belong to the same family as notes at the foot of the page and parentheses in the middle of the text; nay, all three differ only in degree. If Demosthenes and Cicero occasionally inserted words by way of parenthesis, they would have done better to have refrained.

But this style of writing becomes the height of absurdity when the parentheses are not even fitted into the frame of the sentence, but wedged in so as directly to shatter it. If, for instance, it is an impertinent thing to interrupt another person when he is speaking, it is no less impertinent to interrupt one's self. But all bad, careless, and hasty authors, who scribble with the bread actually before their eyes, use this style of writing six times on a page, and rejoice in it. It consists in—it is advisable to give rule and example together, wherever it is possible—breaking up one phrase in order to glue in another. Nor is it merely out of laziness that they write thus. They do it out of stupidity; they think there is a charming *légèreté* about it; that it gives life to what they say. No doubt there are a few rare cases where such a form of sentence may be pardonable.

Few write in the way in which an architect builds; who, before he sets to work, sketches out his plan, and thinks it over down to its smallest details. Nay, most people write only as though they were playing dominoes; and as in this game the pieces are arranged half by design, half by chance, so it is with the sequence and connection of their sentences. They only just have an idea of what the general shape of their work will be, and of the aim they set before themselves. Many are ignorant even of this, and write as the coral-insects build; period joins to period, and Lord knows what the author means.

Life now a days goes at a gallop; and the way in which this affects literature is to make it extremely superficial and slovenly.

ON THE STUDY OF LATIN.

The abolition of Latin as the universal language of learned men, together with the rise of that provincialism which attaches to national literatures, has been a real misfortune for the cause of knowledge in Europe. For it was chiefly through the medium of the Latin language that a learned public existed in Europe at all—a public to which every book as it came out directly appealed. The number of minds in the whole of Europe that are capable of thinking and judging is small, as it is; but when the audience is broken up and severed by differences of language, the good these minds can do is very much weakened. This is a great disadvantage; but a second and worse one will follow, namely, that the ancient languages will cease to be taught at all. The neglect of them is rapidly gaining ground both in France and Germany.

If it should really come to this, then farewell, humanity! farewell, noble taste and high thinking! The age of barbarism will return, in spite of railways, telegraphs and balloons. We shall thus in the end lose one more advantage possessed by all our ancestors. For Latin is not only a key to the knowledge of Roman antiquity; it also directly opens up to us the Middle Age in every country in Europe and modern times as well, down to about the year 1750. Erigena, for example, in the ninth century, John of Salisbury in the twelfth, Raimond Lully in the thirteenth, with a hundred others, speak straight to us in the very language that they naturally adopted in thinking of learned matters. They thus come quite close to us even at this distance of time: we are in direct contact with them, and really come to know them. How would it have been if every one of them spoke in the language that was peculiar to his time and country? We should not understand even the half of what they said. A real intellectual contact with them would be impossible. We should see them like shadows on the farthest horizon, or, maybe, through the translator's telescope.

It was with an eye to the advantage of writing in Latin that Bacon, as he himself expressly states, proceeded to translate his "Essays" into that language, under the title

" Sermones fideles; " at which work Hobbes assisted him.*

Here let me observe, by way of parenthesis, that when patriotism tries to urge its claims in the domain of knowledge, it commits an offense which should not be tolerated. For in those purely human questions which interest all men alike, where truth, insight, beauty, should be of sole account, what can be more impertinent than to let preference for the nation to which a man's precious self happens to belong, affect the balance of judgment, and thus supply a reason for doing violence to truth and being unjust to the great minds of a foreign country in order to make much of the smaller minds of one's own! Still, there are writers in every nation in Europe who afford examples of this vulgar feeling. It is this which led Yriarte to caricature them in the thirty-third of his charming " Literary Fables." †

In learning a language, the chief difficulty consists in making acquaintance with every idea which it expresses, even though it should use words for which there is no exact equivalent in the mother tongue; and this often happens. In learning a new language a man has, as it were, to mark out in his mind the boundaries of quite new spheres of ideas, with the result that spheres of ideas arise where none were before. Thus he not only learns words, he gains ideas too.

This is nowhere so much the case as in learning ancient

---

* Cf. Thomas Hobbes vita: "Carolopoli apud Eleutherium Anglicum, 1681, p. 22.

† Translator's Note.—Tomas de Yriarte (1750-91,) a Spanish poet, and keeper of archives in the war office at Madrid. His two best-known works are a didactic poem, entitled " La Musica " and the " Fables " here quoted, which satirise the peculiar foibles of literary men. They have been translated into many languages; into English by Rockcliffe (3d edition, 1866). The fable in question describes how, at a picnic of the animals, a discussion arose as to which of them carried off the palm for superiority of talent. The praises of the ant, the dog, the bee, and the parrot were sung in turn; but at last the ostrich stood up and declared for the dromedary. Whereupon the dromedary stood up and declared for the ostrich. No one could discover the reason for this mutual compliment. Was it because both were such uncouth beasts, or had such long necks, or were neither of them particularly clever or beautiful? or was it because each had a hump? " No ! " said the fox, " you are all wrong. Don't you see they are both foreigners?" Cannot the same be said of many men of learning?

languages, for the differences they present in their mode of expression as compared with modern languages is greater than can be found among modern languages as compared with one another. This is shown by the fact that in translating into Latin, recourse must be had to quite other turns of phrase than are in use in the original. The thought that is to be translated has to be melted down and recast; in other words, it must be analyzed and then recomposed. It is just this process which makes the study of the ancient languages contribute so much to the education of the mind.

It follows from this that a man's thought varies according to the language in which he speaks. His ideas undergo a fresh modification, a different shading, as it were, in the study of every new language. Hence an acquaintance with many languages is not only of much indirect advantage, but it is also a direct means of mental culture, in that it corrects and matures ideas by giving prominence to their many-sided nature and their different varieties of meaning, as also that it increases dexterity of thought; for in the process of learning many languages ideas become more and more independent of words. The ancient languages effect this to an incomparably greater degree than the modern, in virtue of the difference to which I have alluded.

From what I have said, it is obvious that to imitate the style of the ancients in their own language, which is so very much superior to ours in point of grammatical perfection, is the best way of preparing for a skillful and finished expression of thought in the mother-tongue. Nay, if a man wants to be a great writer, he must not omit to do this; just as, in the case of sculpture or painting, the student must educate himself by copying the great masterpieces of the past, before proceeding to original work. It is only by learning to write Latin that a man comes to treat diction as an art. The material in this art is language, which must therefore be handled with the greatest care and delicacy.

The result of such study is that a writer will pay keen attention to the meaning and value of words, their order and connection, their grammatical forms. He will learn how to weigh them with precision, and so become an expert in the use of that precious instrument which is meant not only to express valuable thought, but to preserve it as

well.   Further, he will learn to feel respect for the
language in which he writes, and thus be saved from any
attempt to remodel it by arbitrary and capricious treatment.   Without this schooling, a man's writing may easily
degenerate into mere chatter.

To be entirely ignorant of the Latin language is like
being in a fine country on a misty day. The horizon is
extremely limited.   Nothing can be seen clearly except
that which is quite close; a few steps beyond, everything is
buried in obscurity.   But the Latinist has a wide view,
embracing modern times, the Middle Age and Antiquity;
and his mental horizon is still further enlarged if he studies
Greek or even Sanscrit.

If a man knows no Latin, he belongs to the vulgar,
even though he be a great virtuoso on the electrical
machine and have the base of hydrofluoric acid in his
crucible.

There is no better recreation for the mind than the study
of the ancient classics.   Take any one of them into your
hand, be it only for half an hour, and you will feel yourself refreshed, relieved, purified, ennobled, strengthened;
just as though you had quenched your thirst at some pure
spring.   Is this the effect of the old language and its perfect expression, or is it the greatness of the minds whose
works remain unharmed and unweakened by the lapse of
a thousand years? Perhaps both together. But this I
know.   If the threatened calamity should ever come, and
the ancient languages cease to be taught, a new literature
will arise, of such barbarous, shallow and worthless stuff
as never was seen before.

ON MEN OF LEARNING.

When one sees the number and variety of institutions
which exist for the purposes of education, and the vast
throng of scholars and masters, one might fancy the human
race to be very much concerned about truth and wisdom.
But here, too, appearances are deceptive. The masters
teach in order to gain money, and strive, not after wisdom,
but the outward show and reputation of it ; and the scholars learn, not for the sake of knowledge and insight, but

to be able to chatter and give themselves airs. Every thirty years a new race comes into the world—a youngster that knows nothing about anything, and after summarily devouring in all haste the results of human knowledge as they have been accumulated for thousands of years, aspires to be thought cleverer than the whole of the past. For this purpose he goes to the university, and takes to reading books—new books, as being of his own age and standing. Everything he reads must be briefly put, must be new! he is new himself. Then he falls to and criticises. And here I am not taking the slightest account of studies pursued for the sole object of making a living.

Students, and learned persons of all sorts and every age, aim as a rule at acquiring information rather than insight. They pique themselves upon knowing about everything—stones, plants, battles, experiments, and all the books in existence. It never occurs to them that information is only a means of insight, and in itself of little or no value; that it is his way of thinking that makes a man a philosopher. When I hear of these portents of learning and their imposing erudition, I sometimes say to myself: Ah, how little they must have had to think about, to have been able to read so much! And when I actually find it reported of the elder Pliny that he was continually reading or being read to at table, on a journey, or in his bath, the question forces itself upon my mind, whether the man was so very lacking in thought of his own that he had to have alien thought incessantly instilled into him; as though he were a consumptive patient taking jellies to keep himself alive. And neither his undiscerning credulity nor his inexpressibly repulsive and barely intelligible style—which seems like that of a man taking notes, and very economical of paper—is of a kind to give me a high opinion of his power of independent thought.

We have seen that much reading and learning is prejudicial to thinking for one's self; and, in the same way, through much writing and teaching, a man loses the habit of being quite clear, and therefore thorough in regard to the things he knows and understands; simply because he has left himself no time to acquire clearness or thoroughness. And so, when clear knowledge fails him in his utterances, he is forced to fill out the gaps with words and phrases. It is this, and not the dryness of the subject-

matter, that makes most books such tedious reading.
There is a saying that a good cook can make a palatable
dish even out of an old shoe; and a good writer can make
the dryest things interesting.

With by far the largest number of learned men, knowledge is a means, not an end. That is why they will never
achieve any great work; because, to do that, he who pursues knowledge must pursue it as an end, and treat everything else, even existence itself, as only a means. For
everything which a man fails to pursue for its own sake is
but half pursued; and true excellence, no matter in what
sphere, can be attained only where the work has been produced for its own sake alone, and not as a means to
further ends.

And so, too, no one will ever succeed in doing anything
really great and original in the way of thought, who does
not seek to acquire knowledge for himself, and, making
this the immediate object of his studies, decline to trouble
himself about the knowledge of others. But the average
man of learning studies for the purpose of being able to
teach and write. His head is like a stomach and intestines
which let the food pass through them undigested. That is
just why his teaching and writing is of so little use. For
it is not upon undigested refuse that people can be nourished, but solely upon the milk which secretes from the
very blood itself.

The wig is the appropriate symbol of the man of learning, pure and simple. It adorns the head with a copious
quantity of false hair, in lack of one's own: just as erudition means endowing it with a great mass of alien thought.
This, to be sure, does not clothe the head so well and
naturally, nor is it so generally useful, nor so suited for all
purposes, nor so firmly rooted; nor when alien thought is
used up, can it be immediately replaced by more from the
same source. as is the case with that which springs from
soil of one's own. So we find Sterne, in his "Tristram
Shandy," boldly asserting that "an ounce of a man's own
wit is worth a ton of other people's."

And in fact the most profound erudition is no more akin
to genius than a collection of dried plants is like Nature,
with its constant flow of new life, ever fresh, ever young,
ever changing. There are no two things more opposed
than the childish naïvety of an ancient author and the
learning of his commentator.

Dilettanti, dilettanti! This is the slighting way in which those who pursue any branch of art or learning for the love and enjoyment of the thing—*per il loro diletto* are spoken of by those who have taken it up for the sake of gain, attracted solely by the prospect of money. This contempt of theirs comes from the base belief that no man will seriously devote himself to a subject, unless he is spurred on to it by want, hunger, or else some form of greed. The public is of the same way of thinking; and hence its general respect for professionals, and its distrust of *dilettanti*. But the truth is that the *dilettante* treats his subject as an end, whereas the professional, pure and simple, treats it merely as a means. He alone will be really in earnest about a matter, who has a direct interest therein, takes to it because he likes it, and pursues it *con amore*. It is these, and not hirelings, that have always done the greatest work.

In the republic of letters it is as in other republics; favor is shown to the plain man—he who goes on his way in silence and does not set up to be cleverer than others. But the abnormal man is looked upon as threatening danger; people band together against him, and have, oh! such a majority on their side.

The condition of this republic is much like that of a small state in America, where every man is intent only upon his own advantage, and seeks reputation and power for himself, quite heedless of the general weal, which then goes to ruin. So it is in the republic of letters; it is himself, and himself alone, that a man puts forward, because he wants to gain fame. The only thing in which all agree is in trying to keep down a really eminent man, if he should chance to show himself, as one who would be a common peril. From this it is easy to see how it fares with knowledge as a whole.

Between professors and independent men of learning there has always been from of old a certain antagonism, which may perhaps be likened to that existing between dogs and wolves. In virtue of their position, professors enjoy great facilities for becoming known to their contemporaries. Contrarily, independent men of learning enjoy, by their position, great facilities for becoming known to posterity; to which it is necessary that, among other and much rarer gifts, a man should have a certain leisure and

freedom.   As mankind takes a long time in finding out on
whom to bestow its attention, they may both work together side by side.

He who holds a professorship may be said to receive his
food in the stall; and this is the best way with ruminant animals.   But he who finds his food for himself at the hands
of nature is better off in the open field.

Of human knowledge as a whole and in every branch of
it, by far the largest part exists nowhere but on paper
—I mean, in books, that paper memory of mankind.
Only a small part of it is at any given period really active
in the minds of particular persons.   This is due in the
main, to the brevity and uncertainty of life ; but it also
comes from the fact that men are lazy and bent on pleasure.   Every generation attains, in its hasty passage
through existence, just so much of human knowledge as it
needs, and then soon disappears.   Most men of learning
are very superficial.   Then follows a new generation, full
of hope, but ignorant, and with everything to learn from
the beginning.   It seizes, in its turn, just so much as it
can grasp, or find useful on its brief journey, and then too
goes its way.   How badly it would fare with human
knowledge if it were not for the art of writing and print-
ing!   This it is that makes libraries the only sure and
lasting memory of the human race, for its individual members have all of them but a very limited and imperfect one.
Hence most men of learning are as loth to have their
knowledge examined as merchants to lay bare their
books.

Human knowledge extends on all sides farther than the
eye can reach; and of that which would be generally
worth knowing, no one man can possess even the thousandth part.

All branches of learning have thus been so much enlarged that he who would " do something " has to pursue
no more than one subject and disregard all others.   In his
own subject he will then, it is true, be superior to the vulgar; but in all else he will belong to it.   If we add to this
that neglect of the ancient languages, which is now-a-days
on the increase and is doing away with all general education in the humanities—for a mere smattering of Latin and
Greek is of no use—we shall come to have men of learning
who outside their own subject display an ignorance truly
bovine.

An exclusive specialist of this kind stands on a par with a workman in a factory, whose whole life is spent in making one particular kind of screw, or catch, or handle, for some particular instrument or machine, in which, indeed, he attains incredible dexterity. The specialist may also be likened to a man who lives in his own house and never leaves it. There he is perfectly familiar with everything, every little step, corner, or board; much as Quasimodo in Victor Hugo's "Notre Dame" knows the cathedral; but outside it, all is strange and unknown.

For true culture in the humanities it is absolutely necessary that a man should be many-sided and take large views; and for a man of learning in the higher sense of the word, an extensive acquaintance with history is needful. He, however, who wishes to be a complete philosopher, must gather into his head the remotest ends of human knowledge: for where else could they ever come together?

It is precisely minds of the first order that will never be specialists. For their very nature is to make the whole of existence their problem; and this is a subject upon which they will every one of them in some form provide mankind with a new revelation. For he alone can deserve the name of genius who takes the All, the Essential, the Universal, for the theme of his achievements; not he who spends his life in explaining some special relation of things one to another.

ON THINKING FOR ONE'S SELF.

A LIBRARY may be very large; but if it is in disorder, it is not so useful as one that is small but well arranged. In the same way, a man may have a great mass of knowledge, but if he has not worked it up by thinking it over for himself, it has much less value than a far smaller amount which he has thoroughly pondered. For it is only when a man looks at his knowledge from all sides, and combines the things he knows by comparing truth with truth, that he obtains a complete hold over it and gets it into his power. A man cannot turn over anything in his mind unless he knows it; he should therefore, learn something; but it is only when he has turned it over that he can be said to know it.

Reading and learning are things that any one can do of his own free will; but not so thinking. Thinking must be kindled, like a fire by a draught; it must be sustained by some interest in the matter in hand. This interest may be of purely objective kind, or merely subjective. The latter comes into play only in things that concern us personally. Objective interest is confined to heads that think by nature; to whom thinking is as natural as breathing; and they are very rare. This is why most men of learning show so little of it.

It is incredible what a different effect is produced upon the mind by thinking for one's self, as compared with reading. It carries on and intensifies that original difference in the nature of two minds which leads the one to think and the other to read. What I mean is that reading forces alien thoughts upon the mind—thoughts which are as foreign to the drift and temper in which it may be for the moment, as the seal is to the wax on which it stamps its imprint. The mind is thus entirely under compulsion from without; it is driven to think this or that, though for the moment it may not have the slightest impulse or inclination to do so.

But when a man thinks for himself, he follows the impulse of his own mind, which is determined for him at the time, either by his environment or some particular recollection. The visible world of a man's surroundings does not, as reading does, impress a single definite thought upon his mind, but merely gives the matter and occasion which lead him to think what is appropriate to his nature and present temper. So it is, that much reading deprives the mind of all elasticity; it is like keeping a spring continually under pressure. The safest way of having no thoughts of one's own is to take up a book every moment one has nothing else to do. It is this practice which explains why erudition makes most men more stupid and silly than they are by nature, and prevents their writings obtaining any measure of success. They remain, in Pope's words:

" Forever reading, never to be read!" *

Men of learning are those who have done their reading

---

* " Dunciad," iii. 194.

in the pages of a book. Thinkers and men of genius are those who have gone straight to the book of nature; it is they who have enlightened the world and carried humanity further on its way.

If a man's thoughts are to have truth and life in them, they must, after all be his own fundamental thoughts; for these are the only ones that he can fully and wholly understand. To read another's thoughts is like taking the leavings of a meal to which we have not been invited, or putting on the clothes which some unknown visitor has laid aside.

The thought we read is related to the thought which springs up in ourselves, as the fossil-impress of some pre-historic plant to a plant as it buds forth in springtime.

Reading is nothing more than a substitute for thought of one's own. It means putting the mind into leading-strings. The multitude of books serves only to show how many false paths there are, and how widely astray a man may wander if he follows any of them. But he who is guided by his genius, he who thinks for himself, who thinks spontaneously and exactly, possesses the only compass by which he can steer aright. A man should read only when his own thoughts stagnate at their source, which will happen often enough even with the best of minds. On the other hand, to take up a book for the purpose of scaring away one's own original thoughts is sin against the Holy Spirit. It is like running away from nature to look at a museum of dried plants or gaze at a landscape in copper-plate.

A man may have discovered some portion of truth or wisdom, after spending a great deal of time and trouble in thinking it over for himself and adding thought to thought; and it may sometimes happen that he could have found it all ready to hand in a book and spared himself the trouble. But even so, it is a hundred times more valuable if he has acquired it by thinking it out for himself. For it is only when we gain our knowledge in this way that it enters as an integral part, a living member into the whole system of our thought; that it stands in complete and firm relation with what we know; that it is understood with all that underlies it and follows from it; that it wears the color, the precise shade, the distinguishing mark of our own way of thinking; that it comes exactly at the right time, just as we felt the necessity for it; that it stands fast and cannot be forgotten. This is the perfect application, nay, the interpretation, of Goethe's advice to earn our inheritance for ourselves so that we may really possess it:

> " Was du ererbt von deinen Vätern hast,
>   Erwirb es, um es zu besitzen."*

The man who thinks for himself, forms his own opinions and learns the authorities for them only later on, when they serve but to strengthen his belief in them and in himself. But the book-philosopher starts from the authorities. He reads other people's books, collects their opinions, and so forms a whole for himself, which resembles an automaton made up of anything, but flesh and blood. Contrarily, he who thinks for himself creates a work like a living man as made by Nature. For the work comes into being as a man does; the thinking mind is impregnated from without and it then forms and bears its child! Truth that has been merely learned is like an artificial limb, a false tooth, a waxen nose; at best, like a nose made out of another's flesh; it adheres to us only because it is put on. But truth acquired by thinking of our own is like a natural limb; it alone really belongs to us. This is the fundamental difference between the thinker and the mere man of learning. The intellectual attainments of a man who thinks for himself resemble a fine painting, where the light and shade are correct, the tone sustained, the color perfectly harmonized; it is true to life. On the other hand, the intellectual attainments of the mere man of learning are like a large palette, full of all sorts of colors, which at most are systematically arranged, but devoid of harmony, connection and meaning.

Reading is thinking with some one else's head instead of one's own. To think with one's own head is always to aim at developing a coherent whole—a system, even though it be not a strictly complete one; and nothing hinders this so much as too strong a current of others' thoughts, such as comes of continual reading. These thoughts, springing every one of them from different minds, belonging to different systems, and tinged with different colors, never of themselves flow together into an intellectual whole;

---

*"Faust," 1. 329.

they never form a unity of knowledge, or insight, or conviction; but, rather, fill the head with a Babylonian confusion of tongues. The mind that is over-loaded with alien thought is thus deprived of all clear insight, and so well-nigh disorganized. This is a state of things observable in many men of learning; and it makes them inferior in sound sense, correct judgment and practical tact, to many illiterate persons who, after obtaining a little knowledge from without by means of experience, intercourse with others, and a small amount of reading, have always subordinated it to, and embodied it with, their own thought.

The really scientific thinker does the same thing as these illiterate persons, but on a larger scale. Although he has need of much knowledge, and so must read a great deal, his mind is nevertheless strong enough to master it all, to assimilate and incorporate it with the system of his thoughts, and so to make it fit in with the organic unity of his insight, which, though vast, is always growing. And in the process, his own thought, like the bass in an organ, always dominates everything, and is never drowned by other tones, as happens with minds which are full of mere antiquarian lore; where shreds of music, as it were, in every key, mingle confusedly, and no fundamental note is heard at all.

Those who have spent their lives in reading, and taken their wisdom from books, are like people who have obtained precise information about a country from the descriptions of many travelers. Such people can tell a great deal about it; but, after all, they have no connected, clear, and profound knowledge of its real condition. But those who have spent their lives in thinking resemble the travelers themselves; they alone really know what they are talking about; they are acquainted with the actual state of affairs, and are quite at home in the subject.

The thinker stands in the same relation to the ordinary book-philosopher as an eyewitness does to the historian; he speaks from direct knowledge of his own. That is why all those who think for themselves come, at bottom, to much the same conclusion. The differences they present are due to their different points of view; and when these do not affect the matter, they all speak alike. They merely express the result of their own objective perception of things. There are many passages in my works which I have given to the public only after some hesitation, because of their paradoxical nature; and afterward I have experienced a pleasant surprise in finding the same opinion recorded in the works of great men who lived long ago.

The book-philosopher merely reports what one person has said and another meant, or the objections raised by a third, and so on. He compares different opinions, ponders, criticises, and tries to get at the truth of the matter; herein on a par with the critical historian. For instance, he will set out to inquire whether Leibnitz was not for some time a follower of Spinoza, and questions of a like nature. The curious student of such matters may find conspicuous examples of what I mean in Herbart's "Analytical Elucidation of Morality and Natural Right," and in the same author's "Letters on Freedom." Surprise may be felt that a man of the kind should put himself to so much trouble; for, on the face of it, if he would only examine the matter for himself, he would speedily attain his object by the exercise of a little thought. But there is a small difficulty in the way. It does not depend upon his own will. A man can always sit down and read, but not—think. It is with thoughts as with men: they cannot always be summoned at pleasure; we must wait for them to come. Thought about a subject must appear of itself, by a happy and harmonious combination of external stimulus with mental temper and attention; and it is just that which never seems to come to these people.

This truth may be illustrated by what happens in the case of matters affecting our own personal interest. When it is necessary to come to some resolution in a matter of that kind, we cannot well sit down at any given moment and think over the merits of the case and make up our mind; for, if we try to do so, we often find ourselves unable, at that particular moment, to keep our mind fixed upon the subject; it wanders off to other things. Aversion to the matter in question is sometimes to blame for this. In such a case we should not use force, but wait for the proper frame of mind to come of itself. It often comes unexpectedly and returns again and again; and the variety of temper in which we approach it at different moments puts the matter always in a fresh light. It is this long process which is understood by the term" a ripe resolution."

For the work of coming to a resolution must be distributed; and in the process much that is overlooked at one moment occurs to us at another; and the repugnance vanishes when we find, as we usually do, on a closer inspection, that things are not so bad as they seemed.

This rule applies to the life of the intellect as well as to matters of practice. A man must wait for the right moment. Not even the greatest mind is capable of thinking for itself at all times. Hence a great mind does well to spend its leisure in reading, which, as I have said, is a substitute for thought: it brings stuff to the mind by letting another person do the thinking; although that is always done in a manner not our own. Therefore, a man should not read too much, in order that his mind may not become accustomed to the substitute and thereby forget the reality; that it may not form the habit of walking in well-worn paths; nor by following an alien course of thought grow a stranger to its own. Least of all should a man quite withdraw his gaze from the real world for the mere sake of reading; as the impulse and the temper which prompt to thought of one's own come far oftener from the world of reality than from the world of books. The real life that a man sees before him is the natural subject of thought; and in its strength as the primary element of existence, it can more easily than anything else rouse and influence the thinking mind.

After these considerations, it will not be matter for surprise that a man who thinks for himself can easily be distinguished from the book-philosopher by the very way in which he talks, by his marked earnestness, and the originality, directness, and personal conviction that stamp all his thoughts and expressions. The book-philosopher, on the other hand, lets it be seen that everything he has is second-hand; that his ideas are like the lumber and trash of old furniture-shop, collected together from all quarters. Mentally, he is dull and pointless—a copy of a copy. His literary style is made up of conventional, nay, vulgar phrases, and terms that happen to be current; in this respect much like a small state where all the money that circulates is foreign, because it has no coinage of its own.

Mere experience can as little as reading supply the place of thought. It stands to thinking in the same relation in which eating stands to digestion and assimilation. When experience boasts that to its discoveries alone is due the advancement of the human race, it is as though the mouth were to claim the whole credit of maintaining the body in health.

The works of all truly capable minds are distinguished by a character of decision and definiteness, which means that they are clear and free from obscurity. A truly capable mind always knows definitely and clearly what it is that it wants to express, whether its medium is prose, verse, or music. Other minds are not decisive and not definite; and by this they may be known for what they are.

The characteristic sign of a mind of the highest order is that it always judges at first hand. Everything it advances is the result of thinking for itself; and this is everywhere evident by the way in which it gives its thoughts utterance. Such a mind is like a prince. In the realm of intellect its authority is imperial, whereas the authority of minds of a lower order is delegated only; as may be seen in their style, which has no independent stamp of its own.

Every one who really thinks for himself is so far like a monarch. His position is undelegated and supreme. His judgments, like royal decrees, spring from his own sovereign power and proceed directly from himself. He acknowledges authority as little as a monarch admits a command; he subscribes to nothing but what he has himself authorized. The multitude of common minds, laboring under all sorts of current opinions, authorities, prejudices, is like the people, which silently obeys the law and accepts orders from above.

Those who are so zealous and eager to settle debated questions by citing authorities, are really glad when they are able to put the understanding and the insight of others into the field in place of their own, which are wanting. Their number is legion. For, as Seneca says, there is no man but prefers belief to the exercise of judgment—*unusquisque mavult credere quam judicare.* In their controversies such people make a promiscuous use of the weapon of authority, and strike out at one another with it. If any one chances to become involved in such a contest, he will do well not to try reason and argument as a mode of defense; for against a weapon of that kind these people are like Siegfrieds, with a skin of horn, and dipped in the flood of incapacity for thinking and judging. They will meet his attack by bringing up their authorities as a way of abashing him—*argumentum ad verecundiam*, and then cry out that they have won the battle.

In the real world, be it never so fair, favorable and pleasant, we always live subject to the law of gravity, which we have to be constantly overcoming. But in the world of intellect we are disembodied spirits, held in bondage to no such law, and free from penury and distress. Thus it is that there exists no happiness on earth like that which, at the auspicious moment, a fine and fruitful mind finds in itself.

The presence of a thought is like the presence of a woman we love. We fancy we shall never forget the thought nor become indifferent to the dear one. But out of sight, out of mind! The finest thought runs the risk of being irrevocably forgotten if we do not write it down, and the darling of being deserted if we do not marry her.

There are plenty of thoughts which are valuable to the man who thinks them; but only few of them which have enough strength to produce repercussive or reflex action— I mean, to win the reader's sympathy after they have been put on paper.

But still it must not be forgotten that a true value attaches only to what a man has thought in the first instance for his own case. Thinkers may be classed according as they think chiefly for their own case or for that of others. The former are the genuine independent thinkers; they really think and are really independent; they are the true philosophers; they alone are in earnest. The pleasure and the happiness of their existence consist in thinking. The others are the sophists; they want to seem that which they are not, and seek their happiness in what they hope to get from the world. They are in earnest about nothing else. To which of these two classes a man belongs may be seen by his whole style and manner. Lichtenberg is an example for the former class; Herder, there can be no doubt, belongs to the second.

When one considers how vast and how close to us is the problem of existence—this equivocal, tortured, fleeting, dream-like existence of ours—so vast and so close that a man no sooner discovers it than it overshadows and obscures all other problems and aims; and when one sees how all men, with few and rare exceptions, have no clear consciousness of the problem, nay, seem to be quite unaware of its presence, but busy themselves with everything rather than with this, and live on, taking no thought but for the passing day and the hardly longer span of their own personal future, either expressly discarding the problem or else over-ready to come to terms with it by adopting some system of popular metaphysics and letting it satisfy them; when, I say, one takes all this to heart, one may come to the opinion that man may be said to be a thinking being only in a very remote sense, and henceforth feel no special surprise at any trait of human thoughtlessnes or folly; but know, rather, that the normal man's intellectual range of vision does indeed extend beyond that of the brute, whose whole existence is, as it were, a continual present, with no consciousness of the past or the future, but not such an immeasurable distance as is generally supposed.

This is, in fact, corroborated by the way in which most men converse; where their thoughts are found to be chopped up fine, like chaff, so that for them to spin out a discourse of any length is impossible.

If this world were peopled by really thinking beings, it could never be that the noise of every kind would be allowed such generous limits, as in the case with the most horrible and at the same time aimless form of it.* If nature had meant man to think, she would not have given him ears: or, at any rate, she would have furnished them with air-tight flaps, such as are the enviable possession of the bat. But, in truth, man is a poor animal like the rest, and his powers are meant only to maintain him in the struggle for existence; so he must needs keep his ears always open, to announce of themselves, by night as by day, the approach of the pursuer.

ON SOME FORMS OF LITERATURE.

In the drama which is the most perfect reflection of human existence, there are three stages in the presentation of the subject, with a corresponding variety in the design and scope of the piece.

---

* Translator's note.—Schopenhauer refers to the cracking of whips. See the essay " On Noise " in " Studies in Pessimism."

At the first, which is also the most common stage, the drama is never anything more than merely interesting. The persons gain our attention by following their own aims which resemble ours; the action advances by means of intrigue and the play of character and incident; while wit and raillery season the whole.

At the second stage, the drama becomes sentimental. Sympathy is roused with the hero, and, indirectly, with ourselves. The action takes a pathetic turn; but the end is peaceful and satisfactory.

The climax is reached with the third stage, which is the most difficult. There the drama aims at being tragic. We are brought face to face with great suffering and the storm and stress of existence; and the outcome of it is to show the vanity of all human effort. Deeply moved, we are either directly prompted to disengage our will from the struggle of life, or else a chord is struck in us which echoes a similar feeling.

The beginning, it is said, is always difficult. In the drama it is just the contrary; for there the difficulty always lies in the end. This is proved by countless plays which promise very well for the first act or two, and then become muddled, stick or falter—notoriously so in the fourth act— and finally conclude in a way that is either forced or unsatisfactory or else long foreseen by every one. Sometimes, too, the end is positively revolting, as in Lessing's "Emilia Galotti," which sends the spectators home in a temper.

This difficulty in regard to the end of a play arises partly because it is everywhere easier to get things into a tangle than to get them out again; partly also because at the beginning we give the author *carte blanche* to do as he likes, but, at the end, make certain definite demands upon him. Thus we ask for a conclusion that shall be either quite happy or else quite tragic; whereas human affairs do not easily take so decided a turn; and then we expect that it shall be natural, fit and proper, unlabored, and at the same time foreseen by no one.

These remarks are also applicable to an epic and to a novel; but the more compact nature of the drama makes the difficulty plainer by increasing it.

E nihilo nihil fit. That nothing can come from nothing

is a maxim true in fine art as elsewhere. In composing an historical picture, a good artist will use living men as a model, and take the ground work of the faces from life; and then proceed to idealize them in point of beauty or expression. A similar method, I fancy, is adopted by good novelists. In drawing a character they take the general outline of it from some real person of their acquaintance, and then idealize and complete it to suit their purpose.

A novel will be of a high and noble order, the more it represents of inner, and the less it represents of outer, life; and the ratio between the two will supply a means of judging any novel, of whatever kind, from "Tristram Shandy" down to the crudest and most sensational tale of knight or robber. "Tristram Shandy" has, indeed, as good as no action at all; and there is not much in " La Nouvelle Heloise " and " Wilhelm Meister." Even " Don Quixote " has relatively little; and what there is, is very unimportant, and introduced merely for the sake of fun. And these four are the best of all existing novels.

Consider, further, the wonderful romances of Jean Paul, and how much inner life is shown on the narrowest basis of actual event. Even in Walter Scott's novels there is a great preponderance of inner over outer life, and incident is never brought in except for the purpose of giving play to thought and emotion; whereas, in bad novels, incident is there on its own account. Skill consists in setting the inner life in motion with the smallest possible array of circumstances, for it is this inner life that really excites our interest.

The business of the novelist is not to relate great events, but to make small ones interesting.

History, which I like to think of as the contrary of poetry ($i\sigma\tau o\rho o\nu\mu\epsilon\nu o\nu$—$\pi\epsilon\pi o\iota\eta\mu\epsilon\nu o\nu$), is for time what geography is for space; and it is no more to be called a science, in any strict sense of the word, than is geography, because it does not deal with universal truths, but only with particular details.* History has always been the favorite

---

* *Translator's Note.*—This line of argument is not likely to be popular nowadays, but if the reader is interested by it, he will find it more fully stated in " Die Welt als Wille und Vorstellung," Vol. II., c. 38.

study of those who wish to learn something, without having to face the effort demanded by any branch of real knowledge, which taxes the intelligence. In our time history is a favorite pursuit; as witness the numerous books upon the subject which appear every year.

If the reader cannot help thinking, with me, that history is merely the constant recurrence of similar things, just as in a kaleidoscope the same bits of glass are presented, but in different combinations, he will not be able to share all this lively interest; nor, however, will he censure it. But there is a ridiculous and absurd claim, made by many people, to regard history as a part of philosophy, nay, as philosophy itself; they imagine that history can take its place.

The preference shown for history by the greater public in all ages may be illustrated by the kind of conversation which is so much in vogue everywhere in society. It generally consists in one person relating something and then another person relating something else; so that in this way every one is sure of receiving attention. Both here and in the case of history it is plain that the mind is occupied with particular details. But as in science, so also in every worthy conversation, the mind rises to the consideration of some general truth.

This objection does not, however, deprive history of its value. Human life is short and fleeting, and many millions of individuals share in it, who are swallowed by that monster of oblivion which is waiting for them with ever-open jaws. It is thus a very thankworthy task to try to rescue something—the memory of interesting and important events, of the leading features and personages of some epoch—from the general shipwreck of the world.

From another point of view, we might look upon history as the sequel to zoology; for while with all other animals it is enough to observe the species, with man individuals, and therefore individual events, have to be studied; because every man possesses a character of an individual. And since individuals and events are without number or end, an essential imperfection attaches to history. In the study of it, all that a man learns never contributes to lessen that which he has still to learn. With any real science, a perfection of knowledge is, at any rate, conceivable.

When we gain access to the histories of China and of

India, the endlessness of the subject-matter will reveal to us the defects in the study, and force our historians to see that the object of science is to recognize the many in the one, to perceive the rules in any given example, and to apply to the life of nations a knowledge of mankind; not to go on counting up facts *ad infinitum*.

There are two kinds of history; the history of politics and the history of literature and art. The one is the history of the will; the other, that of the intellect. The first is a tale of woe, even of terror: it is a record of agony, struggle, fraud, and horrible murder *en masse*. The second is everywhere pleasing and serene, like the intellect when left to itself, even though its path be one of error. Its chief branch is the history of philosophy. This is, in fact, its fundamental base, and the notes of it are heard even in the other kind of history. These deep tones guide the formation of opinion, and opinion rules the world. Hence philosophy, rightly understood, is a material force of the most powerful kind, though very slow in its working. The philosophy of a period is thus the fundamental base of its history.

The newspaper is the second-hand in the clock of history; and it is not only made of baser metal than those which point to the minute and the hour, but it seldom goes right.

The so-called leading article is the chorus to the drama of passing events.

Exaggeration of every kind is as essential to journalism as it is to the dramatic art; for the object of journalism is to make events go as far as possible. Thus it is that all journalists are, in the very nature of their calling, alarmists; and this is their way of giving interest to what they write. Herein they are like little dogs; if anything stirs, they immediately set up a shrill bark.

Therefore, let us carefully regulate the attention to be paid to this trumpet of danger, so that it may not disturb our digestion. Let us recognize that a newspaper is at best but a magnifying-glass, and very often merely a shadow on the wall.

The pen is to thought what the stick is to walking; but you walk most easily when you have no stick, and you

think with the greatest perfection when you have no pen
in your hand. It is only when a man begins to be old that
he likes to use a stick and is glad to take up his pen.

When an hypothesis has once come to birth in the mind,
or gained a footing there, it leads a life so far comparable
with the life of an organism, as that it assimilates matter
from the outer world only when it is like in kind with it
and beneficial; and when, contrarily, such matter is not
like in kind but hurtful, the hypothesis, equally with the
organism, throws it off, or, if forced to take it, gets rid of
it again entire.

To gain immortality an author must possess so many
excellences that, while it will not be easy to find any one
to understand and appreciate them all, there will be men
in every age who are able to recognize and value some of
them. In this way the credit of his book will be maintained throughout the long course of centuries, in spite of
the fact that human interests are always changing.

An author like this, who has a claim to the continuance
of his life even with posterity, can only be a man who,
over the wide earth, will seek his like in vain, and offer a
palpable contrast with every one else in virtue of his unmistakable distinction. Nay more: were he, like the wandering Jew, to live through several generations, he would
still remain in the same superior position. If this were
not so, it would be difficult to see why his thoughts should
not perish like those of other men.

Metaphors and similes are of great value, in so far as
they explain an unknown relation by a known one. Even
the more detailed smile which grows into a parable or an
allegory, is nothing more than the exhibition of some relation in its simplest, most visible and palpable form.
The growth of ideas rests, at bottom, upon similes; because ideas arise by a process of combining the similarities
and neglecting the differences between things. Further,
intelligence, in the strict sense of the word, ultimately
consists in a seizing of relations; and a clear and pure
grasp of relations is all the more often attained when the
comparison is made between cases that lie wide apart from
one another, and between things of quite different nature.
As long as a relation is known to me as existing only in a

single case, I have none but an individual idea of it—in other words, only an intuitive or perceptive knowledge of it; but as soon as I see the same relation in two different cases, I have a general idea of its whole nature, and this is a deeper and more perfect knowledge.

Since, then, similes and metaphors are such a powerful engine of knowledge, it is a sign of great intelligence in a writer if his similes are unusual and, at the same time, to the point. Aristotle also observes that by far the most important thing to a writer is to have this power of metaphor; for it is a gift which cannot be acquired, and it is a mark of genius.*

As regards reading, to require that a man shall retain everything he has ever read, is like asking him to carry about with him all he has ever eaten. The one kind of food has given him bodily, and the other mental nourishment; and it is through these two means that he has grown to be what he is. The body assimilates only that which is like it; and so a man retains in his mind only that which interests him, in other words, that which suits his system of thought or his purposes in life. Every one has purposes, no doubt; but very few have anything like a system of thought. Few people take an objective interest in anything, and so their reading does them no good; they retain nothing.

If a man wants to read good books, he must make a point of avoiding bad ones; for life is short, and time and energy limited.

Repetitio est mater studiorum. Any book that is at all important ought to be at once read through twice; partly because, on a second reading, the connection of the different portions of the book will be better understood, and the beginning comprehended only when the end is known; and partly because we are not in the same temper and disposition on both readings. On the second perusal we get a new view of every passage and a different impression of the whole book, which then appears in another light.

It would be a good thing to buy books if one could also buy the time in which to read them; but generally the pur-

---

* "Poetics." c. 22.

chase of a book is mistaken for the acquisition of its contents.

A man's works are the quintessence of his mind, and even though he may possess very great capacity they will always be incomparably more valuable than his conversation. Nay, in all essential matters his works will not only make up for the lack of personal intercourse with him, but they will far surpass it in solid advantages. The writings even of a man of moderate genius may be edifying, worth reading and instructive, because they are his quintessence—the result and fruit of all his thought and study; while conversation with him may be unsatisfactory.

So it is that we can read books by men in whose company we find nothing to please, and that a high degree of culture leads us to seek entertainment almost wholly from books and not from men.

ON CRITICISM.

THE following brief remarks on the critical faculty are chiefly intended to show that, for the most part, there is no such thing. It is a *rara avis;* almost as rare, indeed, as the phœnix, which appears only once in five hundred years.

When we speak of taste—an expression not chosen with any regard for it—we mean the discovery, or, it may be only the recognition, of what is right æsthetically, apart from the guidance of any rule; and this, either because no rule has as yet been extended to the matter in question, or else because, if existing, it is unknown to the artist, or the critic, as the case may be. Instead of taste, we might use the expression æsthetic sense, if this were not tautological.

The perceptive critical taste is, so to speak, the female analogue to the male quality of productive talent or genius. Not capable of begetting great work itself, it consists in a capacity of reception, that is to say, of recognizing as such what is right, fit, beautiful, or the reverse; in other words, of discriminating the good from the bad, of discovering and appreciating the one and condemning the other.

In appreciating a genius, criticism should not deal with

the errors in his productions or with the poorer of his works, and then proceed to rate him low; it should attend only to the qualities in which he most excels. For in the sphere of intellect, as in other spheres, weakness and perversity cleave so firmly to human nature that even the most brilliant mind is not wholly and at all times free from them. Hence the great errors to be found even in the works of the greatest men; or as Horace puts it, *quandoque bonus dormitat Homerus*.

That which distinguishes genius, and should be the standard for judging it, is the height to which it is able to soar when it is in the proper mood and finds a fitting occasion—a height always out of the reach of ordinary talent. And, in like manner, it is a very dangerous thing to compare two great men of the same class; for instance, two great poets, or musicians, or philosophers, or artists; because injustice to the one or the other, at least for the moment, can hardly be avoided. For in making a comparison of the kind the critic looks to some particular merit of the one and at once discovers that it is absent in the other, who is thereby disparaged. And then if the process is reversed, and the critic begins with the latter and discovers his peculiar merit, which is quite of a different order from that presented by the former, with whom it may be looked for in vain, the result is that both of them suffer undue depreciation.

There are critics who severally think that it rests with each one of them what shall be accounted good, and what bad. They all mistake their own toy-trumpets for the trombones of fame.

A drug does not effect its purpose if the dose is too large; and it is the same with censure and adverse criticism when it exceeds the measure of justice.

The disastrous thing for intellectual merit is that it must wait for those to praise the good who have themselves produced nothing but what is bad; nay, it is a primary misfortune that it has to receive its crown at the hands of the critical power of mankind—a quality of which most men possess only the weak and impotent semblance, so that the reality may be numbered among the rarest gifts of nature. Hence La Bruyère's remark is, unhappily, as true as it is neat. *"Apres l'esprit de discernement,"* he says, *" ce qu'il y a au monde de plus rare, ce sont*

les diamans et les perles." The spirit of discernment! the
critical faculty! it is these that are lacking. Men do not
know how to distinguish the genuine from the false, the
corn from the chaff, gold from copper; or to perceive the
wide gulf that separates a genius from an ordinary man.
Thus we have that bad state of things described in an old-
fashioned verse, which gives it as the lot of the great ones
here on earth to be recognized only when they are gone:

> " Es ist nun das Geschick der Grossen hier auf Erden,
>   Erst wann sie nicht mehr sind, von uns erkannt zu werden."

When any genuine and excellent work makes its appearance, the chief difficulty in its way is the amount of
bad work it finds already in possession of the field, and
accepted as though it were good. And then if, after a
long time, the new-comer really succeeds, by a hard
struggle, in vindicating his place for himself and winning
reputation, he will soon encounter fresh difficulty from
some affected, dull, awkward imitator, whom people drag
in, with the object of calmly setting him up on the altar
beside the genius, not seeing the difference and really
thinking that here they have to do with another great man.
This is what Yriarte means by the first lines of his 28th
Fable, where he declares that the ignorant rabble always
sets equal value on the good and the bad:

> " Siempre acostumbra hacer el vulgo necio
>   De lo bueno y lo malo igual aprecio."

So even Shakespeare's dramas had, immediately after his
death, to give place to those of Ben Jonson, Massinger,
Beaumont and Fletcher, and to yield the supremacy for a
hundred years. So Kant's serious philosophy was crowded
out by the nonsense of Fichte, Schelling, Jacobi, Hegel.
And even in a sphere accessible to all, we have seen unworthy imitators quickly diverting public attention from
the incomparable Walter Scott. For, say what you will,
the public has no sense for excellence, and therefore no
notion how very rare it is to find men really capable of
doing anything great in poetry, philosophy, or art, or that
their works are alone worthy of exclusive attention. The
dabblers, whether in verse or in any other high sphere,

should be every day unsparingly reminded that neither
gods, nor men, nor booksellers have pardoned their mediocrity:

> "Mediocribus esse poetis
> Non homines, non Dî, non concessere columnæ." *

Are they not the weeds that prevent the corn coming up,
so that they may cover all the ground themselves? And
then there happens that which has been well and freshly
described by the lamented Feuchtersleben,† who died so
young: how people cry out in their haste that nothing is
being done, while all the while great work is quietly
growing to maturity; and then, when it appears, it is not
seen or heard in the clamor, but goes its way silently, in
modest grief:

> "Ist doch"—rufun sie vermessen—
> "Nichts im Werke, nichts gethan!"
>   Und das Grosse, reift indessen
>   Still heran.

> "Es erscheint nun: niemand sieht es,
>   Niemand hört es im Geschrei.
>   Mit bescheid'ner Trauer zieht es
>   Still vorbei."

This lamentable dearth of the critical faculty is not less
obvious in the case of science, as is shown by the tenacious
life of false and disproved theories. If they are once accepted, they may go on bidding defiance to truth for fifty
or even a hundred years and more, as stable as an iron pier
in the midst of the waves. The Ptolemaic system was
still held a century after Copernicus had promulgated his
theory. Bacon, Descartes and Locke made their way extremely slowly and only after a long time; as the reader
may see by D'Alembert's celebrated Preface to the "En-
cyclopædia." Newton was not more successful; and this
is sufficiently proved by the bitterness and contempt with

---

* Horace, "Ars Poetica," 372.

† *Translator's Note* Ernst Freiherr von Feuchtersleben (1806–49),
an Austrian physician, philosopher, and poet, and a specialist
in medical psychology. The best known of his songs is that
beginning "Es ist bestimmt in Gottes Rath," to which Mendelssohn
composed one of his finest melodies.

which Leibnitz attacked his theory of gravitation in the controversy with Clarke.* Although Newton lived for almost forty years after the appearance of the "Principia," his teaching was, when he died, only to some extent accepted in his own country, while outside England he counted scarcely twenty adherents; if we may believe the introductory note to Voltaire's exposition of his theory. It was, indeed, chiefly owing to this treatise of Voltaire's that the system became known in France nearly twenty years after Newton's death. Until then a firm, resolute, and patriotic stand was made by the Cartesian "Vortices;" while only forty years previously, this same Cartesian philosophy had been forbidden in the French schools; and now in turn d'Agnesseau, the chancellor, refused Voltaire the "Imprimatur" for his treatise on the Newtonian doctrine. On the other hand, in our day Newton's absurd theory of color still completely holds the field, forty years after the publication of Goethe's. Hume, too, was disregarded up to his fiftieth year, though he began very early and wrote in a thoroughly popular style. And Kant, in spite of having written and talked all his life long, did not become a famous man until he was sixty.

Artists and poets have, to be sure, more chance than thinkers, because their public is at least a hundred times as large. Still, what was thought of Beethoven and Mozart during their lives? what of Dante? what even of Shakespeare? If the latter's contemporaries had in any way recognized his worth, at least one good and accredited portrait of him would have come down to us from an age when the art of painting flourished; whereas we possess only some very doubtful pictures, a bad copperplate, and a still worse bust on his tomb.* And in like manner, if he had been duly honored, specimens of his handwriting would have been preserved to us by the hundred, instead of being confined, as is the case, to the signatures to a few legal documents. The Portuguese are still proud of their only poet Camoëns. He lived, however, on alms collected every evening in the street by a black slave whom he had

---

* See especially §§ 35, 113, 118, 120, 122, 128.

* A. Wivell: "An Inquiry into the History, Authenticity, and Characteristics of Shakespeare's Portraits;" with 21 engravings. London, 1836.

brought with him from the Indies. In time, no doubt, justice will be done to every one; *tempo é galant' uomo;* but it as late and slow in arriving as in a court of law, and the secret condition of it is that the recipient shall be no longer alive. The precept of Jesus the son of Sirach is faithfully followed: "Judge none blessed before his death." * He, then, who has produced immortal works, must find comfort by applying to them the words of the Indian myth, that the minutes of life among the immortals seem like years of earthly existence; and so, too, that years upon earth are only as the minutes of the immortals.

This lack of critical insight is also shown by the fact that, while in every century the excellent work of earlier time is held in honor, that of its own is misunderstood, and the attention which is its due is given to bad work, such as every decade carries with it only to be the sport of the next. That men are slow to recognize genuine merit when it appears in their own age, also proves that they do not understand or enjoy or really value the long-acknowledged works of genius, which they honor only on the score of authority. The crucial test is the fact that bad work—Fichte's philosophy, for example—if it wins any reputation, also maintains it for one or two generations; and only when its public is very large does its fall follow sooner.

Now, just as the sun cannot shed its light but to the eye that sees it, nor music sound but to the hearing ear, so the value of all masterly work in art and science is conditioned by the kinship and capacity of the mind to which it speaks. It is only such a mind as this that possesses the magic word to stir and call forth the spirits that lie hidden in great work. To the ordinary mind a masterpiece is a sealed cabinet of mystery, an unfamiliar musical instrument from which the player, however much he may flatter himself, can draw none but confused tones. How different a painting looks when seen in a good light, instead of in some dark corner! Just in the same way, the impression made by a masterpiece varies with the capacity of the mind to understand it.

A fine work, then, requires a mind sensitive to its beauty; a thoughtful work, a mind that can really think, if it is to

---

* Ecclesiasticus, xi. 28.

exist and live at all. But alas! it may happen only too often that he who gives a fine work to the world afterward feels like a maker of fireworks, who displays with enthusiasm the wonders that have taken him so much time and trouble to prepare, and then learns that he has come to the wrong place, and that the fancied spectators were one and all inmates of an asylum for the blind. Still, even that is better than if his public had consisted entirely of men who made fireworks themselves; as in this case, if his display had been extraordinarily good, it might possibly have cost him his head.

The source of all pleasure and delight is the feeling of kinship. Even with the sense of beauty it is unquestionably our own species in the animal world, and then again our own race, that appears to us the fairest. So too in intercourse with others, every man shows a decided preference for those who resemble him: and a blockhead will find the society of another blockhead incomparably more pleasant than that of any number of great minds put together. Every man must necessarily take his chief pleasure in his own work, because it is the mirror of his own mind, the echo of his own thought; and next in order will come the work of people like him; that is to say, a dull, shallow and perverse man, a dealer in mere words, will give his sincere and hearty applause only to that which is dull, shallow, perverse or merely verbose. On the other hand, he will allow merit to the work of great minds only on the score of authority, in other words because he is ashamed to speak his opinion; for in reality they give him no pleasure at all. They do not appeal to him; nay, they repel him; and he will not confess this even to himself. The works of genius cannot be fully enjoyed except by those who are themselves of the privileged order. The first recognition of them, however, when they exist without authority to support them, demands considerable superiority of mind.

When the reader takes all this into consideration, he should be surprised, not that great work is so late in winning reputation but that it wins it at all. And as a matter of fact, fame comes only by a slow and complex process. The stupid person is by degrees forced, and as it were tamed, into recognizing the superiority of one who stands immediately above him: this one in his turn bows before some one else; and so it goes on until the weight of the votes gradually prevail over their number; and this is just the condition of all genuine, in other words, deserved fame. But until then, the greatest genius, even after he has passed his time of trial, stands like a king amid a crowd of his own subjects, who do not know him by sight and therefore will not do his behests; unless, indeed, his chief ministers of state are in his train. For no subordinate official can be the direct recipient of the royal commands, as he knows only the signature of his immediate superior; and this is repeated all the way up into the highest ranks, where the under-secretary attests the minister's signature, and the minister that of the king. There are analogous stages to be passed before a genius can attain widespread fame. This is why his reputation most easily comes to a standstill at the very outset; because the highest authorities, of whom there can be but few, are most frequently not to be found; but the further down he goes in the scale the more numerous are those who take the word from above, so that his fame is no more arrested.

We must console ourselves for this state of things by reflecting that it is really fortunate that the greater number of men do not form a judgment on their own responsibility but merely take it on authority. For what sort of criticism should we have on Plato and Kant, Homer, Shakespeare and Goethe, if every man were to form his opinion by what he really has and enjoys of these writers, instead of being forced by authority to speak of them in a fit and proper way, however little he may really feel what he says. Unless something of this kind took place, it would be impossible for true merit, in any high sphere, to attain fame at all. At the same time it is also fortunate that every man has just so much critical power of his own as is necessary for recognizing the superiority of those who are placed immediately over him, and for following their lead. This means that the many come in the end to submit to the authority of the few; and there results that hierarchy of critical judgments on which is based the possibility of a steady, and eventually wide-reaching fame.

The lowest class in the community is quite impervious to the merits of a great genius; and for these people there is nothing left but the monument raised to him, which, by the impression it produces on their senses, awakes in them a dim idea of the man's greatness.

Literary journals should be a dam against the unconscionable scribbling of the age, and the ever-increasing deluge of bad and useless books. Their judgments should be uncorrupted, just and rigorous; and every piece of bad work done by an incapable person; every device by which the empty head tries to come to the assistance of the empty purse, that is to say, about nine-tenths of all existing books, should be mercilessly scourged. Literary journals would then perform their duty, which is to keep down the craving for writing and put a check upon the deception of the public, instead of furthering these evils by a miserable toleration, which plays into the hands of author and publisher, and robs the reader of his time and his money.

If there was such a paper as I mean, every bad writer, every brainless compiler, every plagiarist from others' books, every hollow and incapable place-hunter, every sham-philosopher, every vain and languishing poetaster, would shudder at the prospect of the pillory in which his bad work would inevitably have to stand soon after publication. This would paralyze his twitching fingers, to the true welfare of literature, in which what is bad is not only useless but positively pernicious. Now, most books are bad and ought to have remained unwritten. Consequently praise should be as rare as is now the case with blame, which is withheld under the influence of personal consideration, coupled with the maxim "*accedas socius, laudes lauderis ut absens.*"

It is quite wrong to try to introduce into literature the same toleration as must necessarily prevail in society toward those stupid, brainless people who everywhere swarm in it. In literature such people are impudent intruders; and to disparage the bad is here duty toward the good; for he who thinks nothing bad will think nothing good either. Politeness, which has its source in social relations, is in literature an alien, and often injurious, element; because it exacts that bad work shall be called good. In this way the very aim of science and art is directly frustrated.

This ideal journal could, to be sure, be written only by people who joined incorruptible honesty with rare knowledge and still rarer power of judgment; so that perhaps there could, at the very most, be one, and even hardly one,

in the whole country; but there it would stand, like a just
Areopagus, every member of which would have to be
elected by all the others.   Under the system that prevails
at present literary journals are carried on by a clique, and
secretly perhaps also by booksellers for the good of the
trade; and they are often nothing but coalitions of bad
heads to prevent the good ones succeeding.   As Goethe
once remarked to me, nowhere is there so much dishonesty
as in literature.

But, above all, anonymity, that shield of all literary
rascality, would have to disappear It was introduced
under the pretext of protecting the honest critic, who
warned the public, against the resentment of the author
and his friends.   But where there is one case of this sort,
there will be a hundred where it merely serves to take all
responsibility from the man who cannot stand by what he
has said, or possibly to conceal the shame of one who has
been cowardly and base enough to recommend a book to
the public for the purpose of putting money into his own
pocket.   Often enough it is only a cloak for covering the
obscurity, incompetence and insignificance of the critic.
It is incredible what impudence these fellows will show,
and what literary trickery they will venture to commit, as
soon as they know they are safe under the shadow of
anonymity.   Let me recommend a general anticriticism, a
universal medicine or panacea, to put a stop to all anonymous reviewing, whether it praises the bad or blames the
good: Rascal ! your name! For a man to wrap himself up
and draw his hat over his face, and then fall upon people
who are walking about without any disguise—this is not
the part of a gentleman, it is the part of a scoundrel and a
knave.

An anonymous review has no more authority than an
anonymous letter: and one should be received with the
same mistrust as the other.   Or shall we take the name of
the man who consents to preside over what is, in the
strict sense of the word, *une société anonyme* as a guarantee
for the veracity of his colleagues.

Even Rousseau, in the preface to the Nouvelle " Heloïse"
declares *tout honnête homme doit avouer les livres qu'il
publie;* which in plain language means that every honorable
man ought to sign his articles, and that no one is honorable
who does not do so.   How much truer this is of polemical

writing, which is the general character of reviews! Riemer was quite right in the opinion he gives in his " Reminis- scences of Goethe:" * " An overt enemy," he says, " an en- emy who meets you face to face, is an honorable man, who will treat you fairly, and with whom you can come to terms and be reconciled: but an enemy who conceals himself " is a base, cowardly scoundrel, " who has not courage enough to avow his own judgment: it is not his opinion that he cares about, but only the secret pleasure of wreaking his anger without being found out or punished." This will also have been Goethe's opinion, as he was generally the source from which Riemer drew his observations. And, indeed, Rousseau's maxim applies to every line that is printed. Would a man in a mask ever be allowed to harangue a mob, or speak in any assembly: and that, too, when he was going to attack others and overwhelm them with abuse?

Anonymity is the refuge for all literary and journalistic rascality. It is a practice which must be completely stopped. Every article, even in a newspaper, should be accompanied by the name of its author; and the editor should be made strictly responsible for the accuracy of the signature. The freedom of the press should be thus far restricted; so that what a man publicly proclaims through the far sounding trumpet of the newspaper, he should be answerable for, at any rate with his honor, if he has any; and if he has none, let his name neutralize the effect of his words. And since even the most insignificant person is known in his own circle, the result of such a measure would be to put an end to two-thirds of the newspaper lies, and to restrain the audacity of many a poisonous tongue.

ON REPUTATION.

Writers may be classified as meteors, planets and fixed stars. A meteor makes a striking effect for a moment. You look up and cry There! and it is gone forever. Planets and wandering stars last a much longer time. They often outshine the fixed stars and are confounded with them by the inexperienced; but this is only because they

---

* Preface, p. xxix.

are near. It is not long before they too must yield their place; nay, the light they give is reflected only, and the sphere of their influence is confined to their own orbit—their contemporaries. Their path is one of change and movement, and with the circuit of a few years their tale is told. Fixed stars are the only ones that are constant; their position in the firmament is secure; they shine with a light of their own; their effect to-day is the same as it was yesterday, because, having no parallax, their appearance does not alter with a difference in our standpoint. They belong not to one system, one nation only, but to the universe. And just because they are so very far away, it is usually many years before their light is visible to the inhabitants of this earth.

We have seen in the previous chapter that where a man's merits are of a high order, it is difficult for him to win reputation, because the public is uncritical and lacks discernment. But another and no less serious hindrance to fame comes from the envy it has to encounter. For even in the lowest kind of work, envy balks even the beginnings of a reputation, and never ceases to cleave to it up to the last. How great a part is played by envy in the wicked ways of the world! Ariosto is right in saying that the dark side of our mortal life predominates, so full it is of this evil:

> "questa assai piú oscura che serena
> Vita mortal, tutta d'invidia piena."

For envy is the moving spirit of that secret and informal, though flourishing, alliance everywhere made by mediocrity against individual eminence, no matter of what kind. In his own sphere of work no one will allow another to be distinguished: he is an intruder who cannot be tolerated. *Si quelqu'un excelle parmi nous, qu'il aille exceller ailleurs!* this is the universal password of the second-rate. In addition, then, to the rarity of true merit and the difficulty it has in being understood and recognized, there is the envy of thousands to be reckoned with, all of them bent on surpressing, nay, on smothering it altogether. No one is taken for what he is, but for what others make of him; and this is the handle used by mediocrity to keep down distinction, by not letting it come up as long as that can possibly be prevented.

There are two ways of behaving in regard to merit: either to have fame of one's own, or to refuse any to others. The latter method is more convenient, and so it is generally adopted. As envy is a mere sign of of deficiency, so to envy merit argues the lack of it. My excellent Balthazar Gracian has given a very fine account of this relation between envy and merit in a lengthy fable, which may be found in his " Discreto " under the heading " Hombre de ostentation." He describes all the birds as meeting together and conspiring against the peacock, because of his magnificent feathers: "If," said the magpie, "we could only manage to put a stop to the cursed parading of his tail, there would soon be an end of his beauty; for what is not seen is as good as what does not exist."

This explains how modesty came to be a virtue. It was invented only as a protection against envy. That there have always been rascals to urge this virtue, and to rejoice heartily over the bashfulness of a man of merit, has been shown at length in my chief work.* In Lichtenberg's " Miscellaneous Writings," I find this sentence quoted: "Modesty should be the virtue of those who possess no other." Goethe has a well-known saying, which offends many people: " It is only knaves who are modest! "—*Nur die Lumpen sind bescheiden!* but it has its prototype in Cervantes, who includes in his "Journey up Parnassus," certain rules of conduct for poets, and among them the following: " Every one whose verse shows him to be a poet should have a high opinion of himself, relying on the proverb that he is a knave who thinks himself one." And Shakespeare, in many of his Sonnets, which gave him the only opportunity he had of speaking of himself, declares, with a confidence equal to his ingenuousness, that what he writes is immortal.†

---

* "Welt als Wille," Vol. II. c. 37.

† Collier, one of his critical editors, in his "Introduction to the Sonnets," remarks upon this point : "In many of them are be found most remarkable indications of self-confidence and of assurance in the immortality of his verses, and in this respect the author's opinion was constant and uniform. He never scruples to express it . . . and perhaps there is no writer of ancient or modern times who, for the quantity of such writings left behind him, has so frequently or so strongly declared that what he had produced in this department of poetry 'the world would not willingly let die.'"

A method of underrating good work often used by envy —in reality, however, only the obverse side of it—consists in the dishonorable and unscrupulous laudation of the bad; for no sooner does bad work gain currency than it draws attention from the good. But however effective this method may be for awhile, especially if it is applied on a large scale, the day of reckoning comes at last, and the fleeting credit given to bad work is paid off by the lasting discredit which overtakes those who abjectly praised it. Hence these critics prefer to remain anonymous.

A like fate threatens, though more remotely, those who depreciate and censure good work: and consequently many are too prudent to attempt it. But there is another way; and when a man of eminent merit appears, the first effect he produces is often only to pique all his rivals, just as the peacock's tail offended the birds. This reduces them to a deep silence; and their silence is so unanimous that it savors of preconcertion. Their tongues are all paralyzed. It is the *silentium livoris* described by Seneca. This malicious silence, which is technically known as ignoring, may for a long time interfere with the growth of reputation; if, as happens in the higher walks of learning, where a man's immediate audience is wholly composed of rival workers and professed students, who then form the channel of his fame, the greater public is obliged to use its suffrage without being able to examine the matter for itself. And if, in the end, that malicious silence is broken in upon by the voice of praise, it will be but seldom that this happens entirely apart from some ulterior aim, pursued by those who thus manipulate justice. For, as Goethe says in the " West-östlicher Divan," a man can get no recognition, either from many persons or from only one, unless it is to publish abroad the critic's own discernment:

> " Denn es ist kein Anerkennen,
>   Weder Vieler, noch des Einen,
>   Wenn es nicht am Tagoe frdert,
>   Wo man selbst was mochte scheinen."

The credit you allow to another man engaged in work similar to your own or akin to it, must at bottom be withdrawn from yourself; and you can praise him only at the expense of your own claims.

Accordingly, mankind is in itself not at all inclined to

award praise and reputation; it is more disposed to blame and find fault, whereby it indirectly praises itself. If, notwithstanding this, praise is won from mankind, some extraneous motive must prevail. I am not here referring to the disgraceful way in which mutual friends will puff one another into a reputation; outside of that, an effectual motive is supplied by the feeling that next to the merit of doing something one's self, comes that of correctly appreciating and recognizing what others have done. This accords with the three-fold division of heads drawn up by Hesiod,* and afterward by Machiavelli.† "There are," says the latter," in the capacities of mankind, three varieties: one man will understand a thing by himself; another so far as it is explained to him; a third, neither of himself nor when it is put clearly before him." He, then, who abandons hope of making good his claims to the first class, will be glad to seize the opportunity of taking a place in the second. It is almost wholly owing to this state of things that merit may always rest assured of ultimately meeting with recognition,

To this also is due the fact that when the value of a work has once been recognized and may no longer be concealed or denied, all men vie in praising and honoring it; simply because they are conscious of thereby doing themselves an honor. They act in the spirit of Xenophon's remark: "he must be a wise man who knows what is wise." So when they see that the prize of original merit is forever out of their reach, they hasten to possess themselves of that which comes second best—the correct appreciation of it. Here it happens as with an army which has been forced to yield; when, just as previously every man wanted to be foremost in the fight, so now every man tries to be foremost in running away. They all hurry forward to offer their applause to one who is now recognized to be worthy of praise, in virtue of a recognition, as a rule unconscious, of that law of homogeneity which I mentioned in the last chapter; so that it may seem as though their way of thinking and looking at things were homogeneous with that of the celebrated man, and that they may at least save the honor of their literary taste, since nothing else is left them.

---

* "Works and Days, 293".　　　　† "The Prince, ch. 22."

From this it is plain that, whereas it is very difficult to win fame, it is not hard to keep it when once attained; and also that 'a reputation which comes quickly does not last very long; for here too, *quod cito fit, cito perit.* It is obvious that if the ordinary, average man can easily recognize, and the rival workers willingly acknowledge, the value of any performance, it will not stand very much above the capacity of either of them to achieve it for themselves. *Tantum quisque laudat, quantum se posse sperat imitari*—a man will praise a thing only so far as he hopes to be able to imitate it himself. Further, it is a suspicious sign if a reputation comes quickly; for an application of the laws of homogeneity will show that such a reputation is nothing but the direct applause of the multitude. What this means may be seen by a remark once made by Phocion, when he was interrupted in a speech by the loud cheers of the mob. Turning to his friends who were standing close by, he asked: " Have I made a mistake and said something stupid? " *

Contrarily, a reputation that is to last a long time must be slow in maturing, and the centuries of its duration have generally to be bought at the cost of contemporary praise. For that which is to keep its position so long, must be of a perfection difficult to attain; and even to recognize this perfection requires men who are not always to be found, and never in numbers sufficiently great to make themselves heard; whereas envy is always on the watch and doing its best to smother their voice. But with moderate talent, which soon meets with recognition, there is the danger that those who possess it will outlive both it and themselves; so that a youth of fame may be followed by an old age of obscurity. In the case of great merit, on the other hand, a man may remain unknown for many years, but make up for it later on by attaining a brilliant reputation. And if it should be that this comes only after he is no more, well! he is to be reckoned among those of whom Jean Paul says that extreme unction is their baptism. He may console himself by thinking of the saints, who also are canonized only after they are dead.

Thus what Mahlmann† has said so well in " Herodes "

---

* Plutarch; " Apothegms."

† *Translator's Note.*—August Mahlmann (1771-1826), journalist.

holds good; in this world truly great work never pleases at once, and the god set up by the multitude keeps his place on the altar but a short time:

> " Ich denke, das wahre Grosse in der Welt
> Ist immer nur Das was nicht gleich gefällt
> Und wen der Pobel zum Gotte weiht
> Der steht auf dem Altar nur kurze Zeit."

It is worth mention that this rule is most directly confirmed in the case of pictures, where, as connoisseurs well know, the greatest masterpieces are not the first to attract attention. If they make a deep impression, it is not after one, but only after repeated, inspections; but then they excite more and more admiration every time they are seen.

Moreover, the chances that any given work will be quickly and rightly appreciated, depend upon two conditions: firstly, the character of the work, whether high or low, in other words, easy or difficult to understand; and, secondly, the kind of public it attracts, whether large or small. This latter condition is, no doubt, in most instances a corollary of the former; but it also partly depends upon whether the work in question admits, like books and musical compositions, of being reproduced in great numbers. By the compound action of these two conditions, achievements which serve no materially useful end—and these alone are under consideration here—will vary in regard to the chances they have of meeting with timely recognition and due appreciation; and the order of precedence, beginning with those who have the greatest chance, will be somewhat as follows: acrobats, circus-riders, ballet-dancers, jugglers, actors, singers, musicians, composers, poets (both the last on account of the multiplication of their works), architects, painters, sculptors, philosophers.

The last place of all is unquestionably taken by philosophers, because their works are meant not for entertainment but for instruction, and because they presume some knowledge on the part of the reader, and require him to make an effort of his own to understand them. This makes their public extremely small and causes their fame to be

---

poet and story-writer. His " Herodes vor Bethlehem," is a parody of Kotzebue's "Hussiten vor Naumburg."

more remarkable for its length than for its breadth. And, in general, it may be said that the possibility of a man's fame lasting a long time, stands in almost inverse ratio with the chance that it will be early in making its appearance; so that, as regards length of fame, the above order of precedence may be reversed. But, then, the poet and the composer will come in the end to stand on the same level as the philosopher; since, when once a work is committed to writing, it is possible to preserve it to all time. However, the first place still belongs by right to the philosopher, because of the much greater scarcity of good work in this sphere, and the high importance of it; and also because of the possibility it offers of an almost perfect translation into any language. Sometimes, indeed it happens that a philosopher's fame outlives even his works themselves; as has happened with Thales, Empedocles, Heraclitus, Democitus, Parmenides, Epicurus, and many others.

My remarks are, as I have said, confined to achievements that are not of any material use. Work that serves some practical end, or ministers directly to some pleasure of the senses; will never have any difficulty in being duly appreciated. No first-rate pastry-cook could long remain obscure in any town, to say nothing of having to appeal to posterity.

Under fame of rapid growth is also to be reckoned fame of a false and artificial kind; where, for instance, a book is worked into a reputation by means of unjust praise, the help of friends, corrupt criticism, prompting from above and collusion from below. All this tells upon the multitude, which is rightly presumed to have no power of judging for itself. This sort of fame is like a swimming-bladder; by its aid a heavy body may keep afloat. It bears up for a certain time, long or short according as the bladder is well sewed up and blown; but still the air comes out gradually, and the body sinks. This is the inevitable fate of all works which are famous by reason of something outside of themselves. False praise dies away; collusion comes to an end; critics declare the reputation ungrounded; it vanishes, and is replaced by so much the greater contempt. Contrarily, a genuine work, which, having the source of its fame in itself, can kindle admiration afresh in every age, resembles a body of low specific gravity, which always keeps up of its own accord, and so goes floating down the stream of time.*

Men of great genius, whether their work be in poetry, philosophy or art, stand in all ages like isolated heroes, keeping up single-handed a desperate struggle against the onslaught of an army of opponents. Is not this character-istic of the miserable nature of mankind? The dullness, grossness, perversity, silliness and brutality of by far the greater part of the race, are always an obstacle to the efforts of the genius, whatever be the method of his art; they so form that hostile army to which at last he has to succumb. Let the isolated champion achieve what he may: it is slow to be acknowledged; it is late in being appreci-ated, and then only on the score of authority; it may easily fall into neglect again, at any rate for awhile. Ever afresh it finds itself opposed by false, shallow, and insipid ideas, which are better suited to that large majority, and so generally hold the field. Though the critic may step forth and say, like Hamlet when he held up the two portraits to his wretched mother, " Have you eyes? Have you eyes? " alas! they have none. When I watch the be-haviour of a crowd of people in the presence of some great master's work, and mark the manner of their applause, they often remind me of trained monkeys in a show. The monkeys' gestures are, no doubt, much like those of men; but now and again they betray that the real inward spirit of those gestures is not in them. Their irrational nature peeps out.

It is often said of a man that " he is in advance of his age;" and it follows from the above remarks that this must be taken to mean that he is in advance of humanity in general. Just because of this fact, a genius makes no direct appeal except to those who are themselves consid-erably above the average in capacity; and these are too rare to allow of their ever forming a numerous body at any one period. If he is in this respect not particularly fa-

---

Translator's note.—At this point Schopenhauer interrupts the thread of his discourse to speak at length upon an example of false fame. Those who are at all acquainted with the philosopher's views will not be surprised to find that the writer thus held up to scorn is Hegel; and readers of the other volumes in this series will, with the translator, have had by now quite enough of the subject. The pas-sage is therefore omitted-

vored by fortune, he will be misunderstood by his own age; in other words, he will remain unaccepted until time gradually brings together the voices of those few persons who are capable of judging a work of such high character. Then posterity will say: "This man was in advance of his age," instead of "in advance of humanity;" because humanity will be glad to lay the burden of its own faults upon a single epoch.

Hence if a man has been superior to his own age, he would also have been superior to any other; provided that, in that age, by some rare and happy chance, a few just men, capable of judging in the sphere of his achievements, had been born at the same time with him; just as when, according to a beautiful Indian myth, Vishnu becomes incarnate as a hero, so, too, Brahma at the same time appears as the singer of his deeds; and hence Valmiki, Vyasa and Kalidasa are incarnations of Brahma.

In this sense, then, it may be said that every immortal work puts its age to the proof, whether or no it will be able to recognize the merit of it. As a rule, the men of any age stand such a test no better than neighbors of Philemon and Baucis, who expelled the deities they failed to recognize. Accordingly, the right standard for judging the intellectual worth of any generation is supplied, not by the great minds that make their appearance in it—for their capacities are the work of Nature, and the possibility of cultivating them a matter of chance circumstance—but by the way in which contemporaries receive their works; whether, I mean, they give their applause soon and with a will, or late and in niggardly fashion, or leave it to be bestowed altogether by posterity.

This last fate will be specially reserved for works of a high character. For the happy chance mentioned above will be all the more certain not to come, in proportion as there are few to appreciate the kind of work done by great minds. Herein lies the immeasurable advantage possessed by poets in respect of reputation; because their work is accessible to almost every one. If it had been possible for Sir Walter Scott to be read and criticised by only some hundred persons, perhaps in his lifetime any common scribbler would have been preferred to him; and afterward, when he had taken his proper place, it would also have been said in his honor that he was "in advance of his age."

But if envy, dishonesty and the pursuit of personal aims are added to the incapacity of those hundred persons who, in the name of their generation, are called upon to pass judgment on a work, then indeed it meets with the same sad fate as attends a suitor who pleads before a tribunal of judges one and all corrupt.

In corroboration of this, we find that the history of literature generally shows all those who made knowledge and insight their goal to have remained unrecognized and neglected, while those who paraded with the vain show of it received the admiration of their contemporaries, together with the emoluments.

The effectiveness of an author turns chiefly upon his getting the reputation that he should be read. But by practicing various arts, by the operation of chance, and by certain natural affinities, this reputation is quickly won by a hundred worthless people; while a worthy writer may come by it very slowly and tardily. The former possess friends to help them; for the rabble is always a numerous body which holds well together. The latter has nothing but enemies; because intellectual superiority is everywhere and under all circumstances the most hateful thing in the world, and especially to bunglers in the same line of work, who want to pass for something themselves.*

This being so, it is a prime condition for doing any great work—any work which is to outlive its own age, that a man pay no heed to his contemporaries, their views and opinions, and the praise or blame which they bestow. This condition is, however, fulfilled of itself when a man really does anything great, and it is fortunate that it is so. For if, in producing such a work, he were to look to the general opinion or the judgment of his colleagues, they would lead him astray at every step. Hence, if a man wants to go down to posterity, he must withdraw from the influence of his own age. This will, of course generally mean that he must also renounce any influence upon it, and be ready to buy centuries of fame by foregoing the applause of his contemporaries.

For when any new and wide-reaching truth comes into

---

* If the professors of philosophy should chance to think that I am here hinting at them and the tactics they have for more than thirty years pursued toward my works, they have hit the nail upon the head.

the world—and if it is new, it must be paradoxical—an
obstinate stand will be made against it as long as possible;
nay, people will continue to deny it even after they slacken
their opposition and are almost convinced of its truth.
Meanwhile it goes on quietly working its way, and, like an
acid, undermining everything around it. From time to
time a crash is heard; the old error comes tottering to the
ground, and suddenly the new fabric of thought stands
revealed, as though it were a monument just uncovered.
Every one recognizes and admires it. To be sure, this all
comes to pass for the most part very slowly. As a rule,
people discover a man to be worth listening to only after
he is gone; their "hear, hear!" resounds when the orator
has left the platform.

Works of the ordinary type meet with a better fate.
Arising as they do in the course of, and in connection
with, the general advance in contemporary culture, they
are in close alliance with the spirit of their age—in other
words, just those opinions which happen to be prevalent at
the time. They aim at suiting the needs of the moment.
If they have any merit, it is soon recognized; and they gain
currency as books which reflect the latest ideas. Justice,
nay, more than justice, is done to them. They afford
little scope for envy; since, as was said above, a man will
praise a thing only so far as he hopes to be able to imitate
it himself.

But those rare works which are destined to become the
property of all mankind and to live for centuries, are, at
their origin, too far in advance of the point at which
culture happens to stand, and on that very account foreign
to it and the spirit of their own time. They neither
belong to it nor are they in any connection with it, and
hence they excite no interest in those who are dominated
by it. They belong to another, a higher stage of culture,
and a time that is still far off. Their course is related to
that of ordinary works as the orbit of Uranus to the orbit
of Mercury. For the moment they get no justice done to
them. People are at a loss how to treat them; so they
leave them alone, and go their own snails' pace for themselves. Does the worm see the eagle as it soars aloft?

Of the number of books written in any language, about
one in 100,000 forms a part of its real and permanent literature. What a fate this one book has to endure before it

outstrips those 100,000 and gains its due place of honor!
Such a book is the work of an extraordinary and eminent
mind, and therefore it is specifically different from the
others; a fact which sooner or later becomes manifest.

Let no one fancy that things will ever improve in this
respect. No! the miserable constitution of humanity
never changes, though it may, to be sure, take somewhat
varying forms with every generation. A distinguished
mind seldom has its full effect in the lifetime of its possessor; because, at bottom, it is completely and properly understood only by minds already akin to it.

As it is a rare thing for even one man out of many millions to tread the path that leads to immortality, he must
of necessity be very lonely. The journey to posterity lies
through a horribly dreary region, like the Lybian desert.
of which, as is well known, no one has any idea who has
not seen it himself. Meanwhile let me before all things
recommend the traveler to take light baggage with him;
otherwise he will have to throw away too much on the
road. Let him never forget the words of Balthazar Gracian;
lo bueno, si breve, dos vezes bueno—good work is doubly
good if it is short. This advice is specially applicable to
my own countrymen.

Compared with the short span of time they live, men of
great intellect are like huge buildings, standing on a small
plot of ground. The size of the building cannot be seen
by anyone just in front of it; nor, for an analogous reason,
can the greatness of a genius be estimated while he lives.
But when a century has passed, the world recognizes it and
wishes him back again.

If the perishable son of time has produced an imperish-
ble work, how short his own life seems compared with that
of his child! He is like Semele or Maia—a mortal mother
who gave birth to an immortal son; or, contrarily, like
Achilles in regard to Thetis. What a contrast there is
between what is fleeting and what is permanent! The
short span of man's life, his necessitous, afflicted, unstable
existence, will seldom allow of his seeing even the beginning of his immortal child's brilliant career: nor will the
father himself be taken for that which he really is. It
may be said, indeed, that a man whose fame comes after
him is the reverse of a nobleman, who is preceded by it.

However, the only difference that it ultimately makes to a

man to receive his fame at the hands of contemporaries
rather than from posterity is that in the former case his
admirers are separated from him by space, and in the latter
by time. For even in the case of contemporary fame, a
man does not, as a rule, see his admirers actually before
him. Reverence cannot endure close proximity; it almost
always dwells at some distance from its object; and in the
presence of the person revered it melts like butter in the
sun. Accordingly, if a man is celebrated with his contemporaries, nine-tenths of those among whom he lives
will let their esteem be guided by his rank and fortune;
and the remaining tenth may perhaps have a dull consciousness of his high qualities, because they have heard about
him from remote quarters. There is a fine Latin letter of
Petrarch's on this incompatibility between reverence and
the presence of the person, and between fame and life. It
comes second in his " Epistolæ familiares "* and it is
addressed to Thomas Messanensis. He there observes,
among other things, that the learned men of his age all
made it a rule to think little of a man's writings if they
had even once seen him.

Since distance, then, is essential if a famous man is to be
recognized and revered, it does not matter whether it is
distance of space or of time It is true that he may sometimes hear of his fame in the one case, but never in the
other; but still, genuine and great merit may make up for
this by confidently anticipating its posthumous fame.
Nay, he who produces some really great thought is conscious of his connection with coming generations at the
very moment he conceives it; so that he feels the extension
of his existence through centuries and thus lives with posterity as well as for it. And when, after enjoying a great
man's work, we are seized with admiration for him, and
wish him back, so that we might see and speak with him,
and have him in our possession, this desire of ours is not un-
requited, for he, too, has had his longing for that posterity
which will grant the recognition, honor, gratitude and love
denied by envious contemporaries.

If intellectual works of the highest order are not allowed
their due until they come before the tribunal of posterity,
a contrary fate is prepared for certain brilliant errors which

* In the Venetian edition of 1492.

proceed from men of talent, and appear with an air of being well grounded. These errors are defended with so much acumen and learning that they actually become famous with their own age, and maintain their position at least during their author's lifetime. Of this sort are many false theories and wrong criticisms; also poems and works of art, which exhibit some false taste or mannerism favored by contemporary prejudice. They gain reputation and currency simply because no one is yet forthcoming who knows how to refute them or otherwise prove their falsity; and when he appears, as he usually does, in the next generation, the glory of these works is brought to an end. Posthumous judges, be their decision favorable to the appellant or not, form the proper court for quashing the verdict of contemporaries. That is why it is so difficult and so rare to be victorious alike in both tribunals.

The unfailing tendency of time to correct knowledge and judgment should always be kept in view as a means of allaying anxiety, whenever any grievous error appears, whether in art, or science, or practical life, and gains ground; or when some false and thoroughly perverse policy or movement is undertaken and receives applause at the hands of men. No one should be angry, or, still less, despondent; but simply imagine that the world has already abandoned the error in question, and now only requires time and experience to recognize of its own accord that which a clear vision detected at the first glance.

When the facts themselves are eloquent of a truth, there is no need to rush to its aid with words: for time will give it a thousand tongues. How long it may be before they speak, will of course depend upon the difficulty of the subject and the plausibility of the error; but come they will, and often it would be of no avail to try to anticipate them. In the worst cases it will happen with theories as it happens with affairs in practical life; where sham and deception emboldened by success, advance to greater and greater lengths, until discovery is made almost inevitable. It is just so with theories; through the blind confidence of the blockheads who broach them, their absurdity reaches such a pitch that at last it is obvious even to the dullest eye. We may thus say to such people: "the wilder your statements the better."

There is also some comfort to be found in reflecting upon

all the whims and crotchets which had their day and have now utterly vanished. In style, in grammar, in spelling, there are false notions of this sort which last only three or four years. But when the errors are on a large scale, while we lament the brevity of human life, we shall, in any case do well to lag behind our own age when we see it on a downward path. For there are two ways of not keeping on a level with the times. A man may be below it; or he may be above it.

ON GENIUS.

No DIFFERENCE of rank, position, or birth, is so great as the gulf that separates the countless millions who use their head only in the service of their belly, in other words look upon it as an instrument of the will, and those very few and rare persons who have the courage to say: No it is too good for that; my head shall be active only in its own service; it shall try to comprehend the wondrous and varied spectacle of this world, and then reproduce it in some form whether as art or as literature, that may answer to my character as an individual. These are the truly noble, the real *noblesse* of the world. The others are serfs and go with the soil—*glebæ adscripti.* Of course, I am here referring to those who have not only the courage, but also the call, and therefore the right, to order the head to quit the service of the will; with a result that proves the sacrifice to have been worth the making. In the case of those to whom all this can only partially apply, the gulf is not so wide; but even though their talent be small, so long as it is real, there will always be a sharp line of demarcation between them and the millions.*

---

* The correct scale for adjusting the hierarchy of intelligences is furnished by the degree in which the mind takes merely individual or approaches universal views of things. The brute recognizes only the individual as such ; its comprehension does not extend beyond the limits of the individual. But man reduces the individual to the general; herein lies the exercise of his reason; and the higher his intelligence reaches, the nearer do his general ideas approach the point at which they become universal. If his grasp of the universal is so deep as to be intuitive, and to apply not only to general ideas, but to an individual object by itself, then there arises a knowledge of

The works of fine art, poetry and philosophy produced by a nation are the outcome of the superfluous intellect existing in it.

For him who can understand aright—*cum grano salis*—the relation between the genius and the normal man may, perhaps, be best expressed as follows: A genius has a double intellect, one for himself and the service of his will; the other for the world, of which he becomes the mirror, in virtue of his purely objective attitude toward it. The work of art or poetry or philosophy produced by the genius is simply the result, or quintessence, of this contemplative attitude, elaborated according to certain technical rules.

The normal man, on the other hand, has only a single intellect, which may be called subjective by contrast with the objective intellect of genius. However acute this subjective intellect may be—and it exists in very various degrees of perfection—it is never on the same level with the double intellect of genius; just as the open chest notes of the human voice, however high, are essentially different from the falsetto notes. These, like the two upper octaves of the flute and the harmonics of the violin, are produced by the column of air dividing itself into two vibrating halves, with a node between them: while the open chest notes of the human voice and the lower octave of the flute are produced by the undivided column of air vibrating as a whole. This illustration may help the reader to understand that specific peculiarity of genius which is unmistakably stamped on the works, and even on the physiognomy, of him who is gifted with it. At the same time it is obvious that a double intellect like this must, as a rule, obstruct the service of the will; and this explains the poor capacity often shown by genius in the conduct of life. And what specially characterizes genius is that it has none

the Ideas in the sense used by Plato. This knowledge is of an æsthetic character; when it is self-active, it rises to genius, and reaches the highest degree of intensity when it becomes philosophic; for then the whole of life and existence as it passes away, the world and all it contains, are grasped in their true nature by an act of intuition, and appear in a form which forces itself upon consciousness as an object of meditation. Here reflection attains its highest point. Between it and the merely animal perception there are countless stages, which differ according to the approach made to a universal view of things.

of that sobriety of temper which is always to be found in the ordinary simple intellect, be it acute or dull.

The brain may be likened to a parasite which is nourished as a part of the human frame without contributing directly to its inner economy; it is securely housed in the topmost story, and there leads a self-sufficient and independent life. In the same way it may be said that a man endowed with great mental gifts leads, apart from the individual life common to all, a second life, purely of the intellect. He devotes himself to the constant increase, rectification and extension, not of mere learning, but of real systematic knowledge and insight; and remains untouched by the fate that overtakes him personally, so long as it does not disturb him in his work. It is thus a life which raises a man and sets him above fate and its changes. Always thinking, learning, experimenting, practicing his knowledge, the man soon comes to look upon this second life as the chief mode of existence, and his merely personal life as something subordinate, serving only to advance ends higher than itself.

An example of this independent, separate existence is furnished by Goethe. During the war in the Champagne, and amid all the bustle of the camp, he made observations for his theory of color; and as soon as the numberless calamities of that war allowed of his retiring for a short time to the fortress of Luxembourg, he took up the manuscript of his " Farbenlehre." This is an example which we, the salt of the earth, should endeavor to follow, by never letting anything disturb us in the pursuit of our intellectual life, however much the storm of the world may invade and agitate our personal environment; always remembering that we are the sons, not of the bondwoman, but of the free. As our emblem and coat of arms, I propose a tree mightily shaken by the wind, but still bearing its ruddy fruit on every branch; with the motto *Dum convellor mitescunt,* or *Conquassata sed ferax.*

That purely intellectual life of the individual has its counterpart in humanity as a whole. For there, too, the real life is the life of the will, both in the empirical and in the transcendental meaning of the word. The purely intellectual life of humanity lies in its effort to increase knowledge by means of the sciences, and its desire to perfect the arts. Both science and art thus advance slowly from one generation to another, and grow with the centuries, every race as it hurries by furnishing its contribution. This intellectual life, like some gift from heaven, hovers over the stir and movement of the world; or it is, as it were, a sweet-scented air developed out of the ferment itself—the real life of mankind, dominated by will; and side by side with the history of nations, the history of philosophy, science and art takes its innocent and bloodless way.

The difference between the genius and the ordinary man is, no doubt, a quantitative one, in so far as it is a difference of degree; but I am tempted to regard it also as qualitative, in view of the fact that ordinary minds, notwithstanding individual variation, have a certain tendency to think alike. Thus on similar occasions their thoughts at once all take a similar direction, and run on the same lines; and this explains why their judgments constantly agree—not, however, because they are based on truth. To such lengths does this go that certain fundamental views obtain among mankind at all times, and are always being repeated and brought forward anew, while the great minds of all ages are in open or secret opposition to them.

A genius is a man in whose mind the world is presented as an object is presented in a mirror, but with a degree more of clearness and a greater distinction of outline than is attained by ordinary people. It is from him that humanity may look for most instruction; for the deepest insight into the most important matters is to be acquired, not by an observant attention to detail, but by a close study of things as a whole. And if his mind reaches maturity, the instruction he gives will be conveyed now in one form, now in another. Thus genius may be defined as an eminently clear consciousness of things in general, and therefore, also of that which is opposed to them, namely, one's own self.

The world looks up to a man thus endowed, and expects to learn something about life and its real nature. But several highly favorable circumstances must combine to produce genius, and this is a very rare event. It happens only now and then, let us say once in a century, that a man is born whose intellect so perceptibly surpasses the normal measure as to amount to that second faculty which seems to be accidental, as it is out of all relation to the will. He may remain a long time without being recognized or appreciated, stupidity preventing the one and envy the other. But should this once come to pass, mankind will crowd round him and his works, in the hope that he may be able to enlighten some of the darkness of their existence or inform them about it. His message is, to some extent, a revelation, and he himself a higher being, even though he may be but little above the ordinary standard.

Like the ordinary man, the genius is what he is chiefly for himself. This is essential to his nature, a fact which can neither be avoided nor altered. What he may be for others remains a matter of chance and secondary importance. In no case can people receive from his mind more than a reflection, and then only when he joins with them in the attempt to get his thought into their heads; where, however, it is never anything but an exotic plant, stunted and frail.

In order to have original, uncommon, and perhaps even immortal thoughts, it is enough to estrange one's self so fully from the world of things for a few moments, that the most ordinary objects and events appear quite new and unfamiliar. In this way their true nature is disclosed. What is here demanded cannot, perhaps, be said to be difficult; it is not in our power at all, but is just the province of genius.

By itself, genius can produce original thoughts just as little as a woman by herself can bear children. Outward circumstances must come to fructify genius, and be, as it were, a father to its progeny.

The mind of genius is among other minds what the carbuncle is among precious stones: it sends forth light of its own, while the others reflect only that which they have received. The relation of the genius to the ordinary mind may also be described as that of an idio-electrical body to one which merely is a conductor of electricity.

The mere man of learning, who spends his life in teaching what he has learned, is not strictly to be called a man of genius; just as idio-electrical bodies are not conductors. Nay, genius stands to mere learning as the words to the music in a song. A man of learning is a man who has learned a great deal; a man of genius, one from whom we learn something which the genius has learned from nobody. Great minds, of which there is scarcely one in a hundred millions, are thus the lighthouses of humanity; and without them mankind would lose itself in the boundless sea of monstrous error and bewilderment.

And so the simple man of learning, in the strict sense of the word—the ordinary professor, for instance—looks upon the genius much as we look upon a hare, which is good to eat after it has been killed and dressed up. So long as it is alive, it is only good to shoot at.

He who wishes to experience gratitude from his contemporaries, must adjust his pace to theirs. But great things are never produced in this way. And he who wants to do great things must direct his gaze to posterity, and in firm confidence elaborate his work for coming generations. No doubt, the result may be that he will quite remain quite unknown to his contemporaries, and comparable to a man who, compelled to spend his life upon a lonely island, with great effort sets up a monument there, to transmit to future seafarers the knowledge of his existence. If he thinks it a hard fate, let him console himself with the reflection that the ordinary man who lives for practical aims only, often suffers a like fate, without having any compensation to hope for; inasmuch as he may, under favorable conditions, spend a life of material production, earning, buying, building fertilizing, laying out, founding, establishing, beautifying, with daily effort and unflagging zeal, and all the time think that he is working for himself; and yet in the end it is his descendants who reap the benefit of it all, and sometimes not even his descendants. It is the same with the man of genius; he, too hopes for his reward and for honor at least; and at last finds that he has worked for posterity alone. Both, to be sure, have inherited a great deal from their ancestors.

The compensation I have mentioned as the privilege of genius lies, not in what it is to others, but in what it is to itself. What man has in any real sense lived more than he whose moments of thought make their echoes heard through the tumult of centuries? Perhaps, after all, it would be the best thing for a genius to attain undisturbed possession of himself, by spending his life in enjoying the pleasure of his own thoughts, his own works, and by admitting the world only as the heir of his ample existence.

Then the world would find the mark of his existence only after his death, like the marks in the Ichnolith.*

Nor is it only in the activity of his highest powers that the genius surpasses ordinary people. A man who is unusually well-knit, supple and agile, will perform all his movements with exceptional ease, even with comfort, because he takes a direct pleasure in an activity for which he is particularly well-equipped; and therefore often exercises it without any object. Further, if he is an acrobat or a dancer, not only does he take leaps which other people cannot execute, but he also betrays rare elasticity and agility in those easier steps which others can also perform, and even in ordinary walking. In the same way a man of superior mind will not only produce thoughts and works which could never have come from another; it will not be here alone that he will show his greatness; but as knowledge and thought form a mode of activity natural and easy to him, he will also delight himself in them at all times, and so apprehend small matters which are within the range of other minds, more easily, quickly and correctly than they. Thus he will take a direct and lively pleasure in every increase of knowledge, every problem solved, every witty thought, whether of his own or another's; and so his mind will have no further aim than to be constantly active. This will be an inexhaustible spring of delight; and boredom, that specter which haunts the ordinary man, can never come near him.

Then, too, the masterpieces of past and contemporary men of genius exist in their fullness for him alone. If a great product of genius is recommended to the ordinary, simple mind, it will take as much pleasure in it as the victim of gout receives in being invited to a ball. The one goes for the sake of formality, and the other reads the book so as not to be in arrear. For La Bruyère was quite right when he said: "All the wit in the world is lost upon him who has none." The whole range of thought of a man of talent, or of a genius, compared with the thoughts of the common man, is, even when directed to objects essentially the same, like a brilliant oil-painting, full of

---

* *Translator's Note.*—For an illustration of this feeling in poetry, Schopenhauer refers the reader to Byron's " Prophecy of Dante:" introd. to C. 4.

life, compared with a mere outline or a weak sketch in water-color.

All this is part of the reward of genius, and compensates him for a lonely existence in a world with which he has nothing in common and no sympathies. But since size is relative, it comes to the same thing whether I say, Caius was a great man, or Caius has to live among wretchedly small people; for Brobdingnag and Lilliput vary only in the point from which they start. However great, then, however admirable and instructive, a long posterity may think the author of immortal works, during his lifetime he will appear to his contemporaries small, wretched, and insipid in proportion. This is what I mean by saying that as there are three hundred degrees from the base of a tower to the summit, so there are exactly three hundred from the summit to the base. Great minds thus owe little ones some indulgence; for it is only in virtue of these little minds that they themselves are great.

Let us, then, not be surprised if we find men of genius generally unsociable and repellent. It is not their want of sociability that is to blame. Their path through the world is like that of a man who goes for a walk on a bright summer morning. He gazes with delight on the beauty and freshness of nature, but he has to rely wholly on that for entertainment; for he can find no society but the peasants as they bend over the earth and cultivate the soil. It is often the case that a great mind prefers soliloquy to the dialogue he may have in this world. If he condescends to it now and then, the hollowness of it may possibly drive him back to his soliloquy; for in forgetfulness of his interlocutor, or caring little whether he understands or not, he talks to him as a child talks to a doll.

Modesty in a great mind would, no doubt, be pleasing to the world; but, unluckily, it is a *contradictio in adjecto.* It would compel a genius to give the thoughts and opinions, nay, even the method and style, of the million preference over his own; to set a higher value upon them; and, wide apart as they are, to bring his views into harmony with theirs, or even suppress them altogether, so as to let the others hold the field. In that case, however, he would either produce nothing at all, or else his achievements would be just upon a level with theirs. Great, genuine and extraordinary work can be done only in so far as its author disregards the method, the thoughts, the opinions of his contemporaries, and quietly works on, in spite of their criticism, on his side despising what they praise. No one becomes great without arrogance of this sort. Should his life and work fall upon a time which cannot recognize and appreciate him, he is at any rate true to himself; like some noble traveler forced to pass the night in a miserable inn; when morning comes, he contentedly goes his way.

A poet or philosopher should have no fault to find with his age if it only permits him to do his work undisturbed in his own corner; nor with his fate if the corner granted him allows of his following his vocation without having to think about other people.

For the brain to be a mere laborer in the service of the belly, is indeed the common lot of almost all those who do not live on the work of their hands; and they are far from being discontented with their lot. But it strikes despair into a man of great mind, whose brain-power goes beyond the measure necessary for the service of the will; and he prefers, if need be, to live in the narrowest circumstances, so long as they afford him the free use of his time for the development and application of his faculties; in other words, if they give him the leisure which is invaluable to him. It is otherwise with ordinary people; for them leisure has no value in itself, nor is it, indeed, without its dangers, as these people seem to know. The technical work of our time, which is done to an unprecedented perfection, has, by increasing and multiplying objects of luxury, given the favorites of fortune a choice between more leisure and culture upon one side, and additional luxury and good living, but with increased activity, upon the other; and, true to their character, they choose the latter, and prefer champagne to freedom. And they are consistent in their choice; for, to them, every exertion of the mind which does not serve the aims of the will is folly. Intellectual effort for its own sake, they call eccentricity. Therefore, persistence in the aims of the will and the belly will be concentricity; and, to be sure, the will is the center, the kernel of the world.

But in general it is very seldom that any such alternative is presented. For as with money, most men have no superfluity, but only just enough for their needs, so with intelligence; they possess just what will suffice for the service of the will, that is, for the carrying on of their business. Having made their fortune, they are content to gape or to indulge in sensual pleasures or childish amusements, cards or dice; or they will talk in the dullest way, or dress up and make obeisance to one another. And how few are those who have even a little superfluity of intellectual power! Like the others they too make themselves a pleasure; but it is a pleasure of the intellect. Either they will pursue some liberal study which brings them in nothing, or they will practice some art; and, in general, they will be capable of taking an objective interest in things, so that it will be possible to converse with them. But with the others it is better not to enter into any relations at all; for, except when they tell the results of their own experience or give an account of their special vocation, or at any rate impart what they have learned from someone else, their conversation will not be worth listening to; and if anything is said to them, they will rarely grasp or understand it aright, and it will in most cases be opposed to their own opinions. Balthazar Gracian describes them very strikingly as men who are not men—*hombres che non lo son*. And Giordano Bruno says the same thing: "What a difference there is in having to do with men compared with those who are only made in their image and likeness!* And how wonderfully this passage agrees with that remark in the Kurral: The common people look like men, but I have never seen anything quite like them." If the reader will consider the extent to which these ideas agree in thought and even in expression, and the wide difference between them in point of date and nationality, he cannot doubt but that they are at one with the facts of life. It was certainly not under the influence of those passages that, about twenty years ago, I tried to get a snuff-box made the lid of which should have two fine chestnuts represented upon it, if possible in mosaic; together with a leaf which was to show that they were horse-chestnuts. This symbol was meant to keep the thought constantly before my mind. If any one wishes for entertainment, such as will prevent him feeling solitary even when he is alone, let me recommend the company of dogs, whose moral and

---

* Opera: ed. Wagner, I. 224.

intellectual qualities may almost always afford delight and gratification.

Still, we should always be careful to avoid being unjust. I am often surprised by the cleverness, and now and again by the stupidity, of my dog; and I have similar experiences with mankind. Countless times, in indignation at their incapacity, their total lack of discernment, their bestiality, I have been forced to echo the old complaint that folly is the mother and the nurse of the human race:

"Humani generis mater nutrixque profecto
    Stultitia est."

But at other times I have been astounded that from such a race there could have gone forth so many arts and sciences, abounding in so much use and beauty, even though it has always been the few that produce them. Yet these arts and sciences have struck root, established and perfected themselves; and the race has with persistent fidelity preserved Homer, Plato, Horace and others for thousands of years, by copying and treasuring their writings, thus saving them from oblivion, in spite of all the evils and atrocities that have happened in the world. Thus the race has proved that it appreciates the value of these things, and at the same time it can form a correct view of special achievements or estimate signs of judgment and intelligence. When this takes place among those who belong to the great multitude, it is by a kind of inspiration. Sometimes a correct opinion will be formed by the multitude itself; but this is only when the chorus of praise has grown full and complete. It is then like the sound of untrained voices; where there are enough of them, it is always harmonious.

Those who emerge from the multitude, those who are called men of genius, are merely the *lucida intervalla* of the whole human race. They achieve that which others could not possibly achieve. Their originality is so great that not only is their divergence from others obvious, but their individuality is expressed with such force, that all the men of genius who have ever existed show, every one of them, peculiarities of character and mind; so that the gift of his works is one which he alone of all men could ever have presented to the world. This is what makes

that simile of Ariosto's so true and so justly celebrated:
Natura lo fece e poi ruppe lo stampo. After Nature stamps
a man of genius, she breaks the die.

But there is always a limit to human capacity; and no
one can be a great genius without having some decidedly
weak side, it may even be some intellectual narrowness.
In other words, there will be some faculty in which he is
now and then inferior to men of moderate endowments.
It will be a faculty which, if strong, might have been an
obstacle to the exercise of the qualities in which he excels.
What this weak point is, it will always be hard to define
with any accuracy even in a given case. It may be better
expressed indirectly; thus Plato's weak point is exactly
that in which Aristotle is strong, and *vice versâ;* and so,
too, Kant is deficient just where Goethe is great.

Now, mankind is fond of venerating something; but its
veneration is generally directed to the wrong object, and it
remains so directed until posterity comes to set it right.
But the educated public is no sooner set right in this, than
the honor which is due to genius degenerates; just as the
honor which the faithful pay to their saints easily passes
into a frivolous worship of relics. Thousands of Christians
adore the relics of a saint whose life and doctrine are unknown to them; and the religion of thousands of Buddhists
lies more in veneration of the Holy Tooth or some such
object, or the vessel that contains it, or the Holy Bowl,
or the fossil foosteps, or the Holy Tree which Buddha
planted, than in the thorough knowledge and faithful
practice of his high teaching. Petrarch's house in Arqua;
Tasso's supposed prison in Ferrara; Shakespeare's house in
Stratford, with his chair; Goethe's house in Weimar, with
its furniture; Kant's old hat; the autographs of great
men; these things are gaped at with interest and awe by
many who have never read their works. They cannot do
anything more than just gape.

The intelligent among them are moved by the wish to
see the objects which the great man habitually had before
his eyes; and by a strange illusion, these produce the mistaken notion that with the objects they are bringing back
the man himself, or that something of him must cling to
them. Akin to such people are those who earnestly strive
to acquaint themselves with the subject matter of a poet's
works, or to unravel the personal circumstances and events

in his life which have suggested particular passages. This is as though the audience in a theater were to admire a fine scene, and then rush upon the stage to look at the scaffolding that supports it. There are in our day enough instances of these critical investigators, and they prove the truth of the saying that mankind is interested, not in the form of a work, that is, in its manner of treatment, but in its actual matter. All it cares for is the theme. To read a philosopher's biography, instead of studying his thoughts, is like neglecting a picture and attending only to the style of its frame, debating whether it is carved well or ill, and how much it cost to gild it.

This is all very well. However, there is another class of persons whose interest is also directed to material and personal considerations, but they go much further and carry it to a point where it becomes absolutely futile. Because a great man has opened up to them the treasures of his inmost being, and, by a supreme effort of his faculties, produced works which not only redound to their elevation and enlightenment, but will also benefit their posterity to the tenth and twentieth generation; because he has presented mankind with a matchless gift, these varlets think themselves justified in sitting in judgment upon his personal morality, and trying if they cannot discover here or there some spot in him which will soothe the pain they feel at the sight of so great a mind, compared with the overwhelming feeling of their own nothingness.

This is the real source of all those prolix discussions, carried on in countless books and reviews, on the moral aspect of Goethe's life and whether he ought not to have married one or other of the girls with whom he fell in love in his young days; whether, again, instead of honestly devoting himself to the service of his master, he should not have been a man of the people, a German patriot, worthy of a seat in the Paulskirche, and so on. Such crying ingratitude and malicious detraction prove that these self-constituted judges are as great knaves morally as they are intellectually, which is saying a great deal.

A man of talent will strive for money and reputation; but the spring that moves genius to the production of its works is not so easy to name. Wealth is seldom its reward. Nor is it reputation or glory; only a Frenchman could mean that. Glory is such an uncertain thing, and, if you look at it closely, of so little value. Besides it never corresponds to the effort you have made:

" Responsura tuo nunquam est par fama labori."

Nor, again, is it exactly the pleasure it gives you; for this is almost outweighed by the greatness of the effort. It is rather a peculiar kind of instinct, which drives the man of genius to give permanent form to what he sees and feels, without being conscious of any further motive. It works, in the main, by a necessity similar to that which makes a tree bear its fruit; and no external condition is needed but the ground upon which it is to thrive.

On a closer examination, it seems as though, in the case of a genius, the will to live, which is the spirit of the human species, were conscious of having by some rare chance, and for a brief period, attained a greater clearness of vision, and were now trying to secure it, or at least the outcome of it, for the whole species, to which the individual genius in his inmost being belongs; so that the light which he sheds about him may pierce the darkness and dullness of ordinary human consciousness and there produce some good effect.

Arising in some such way, this instinct drives the genius to carry his work to completion, without thinking of reward or applause or sympathy; to leave all care for his own personal welfare; to make his life one of industrious solitude, and to strain his faculties to the utmost. He thus comes to think more about posterity than about contemporaries; because, while the latter can only lead him astray, posterity forms the majority of the species, and time will gradually bring the discerning few who can appreciate him. Meanwhile it is with him as with the artist described by Goethe; he has no princely patron to prize his talents, no friend to rejoice with him:

> "Ein Fürst der die Talente schätzt,
> Ein Freund der sich mit mir ergötzt,
> Die haben leider mir gefehlt."

His work is, as it were, a sacred object and the true fruit of his life, and his aim in storing it away for a more discerning posterity will be to make it the property of mankind. An aim like this far surpasses all others, and for it he wears the crown of thorns which is one day to bloom into a wreath of laurel. All his powers are concentrated in the effort to complete and secure his work; just as the insect, in the last stage of its development, uses its whole strength on behalf of a brood it will never live to see; it puts its eggs in some place of safety, where, as it well knows, the young will one day find life and nourishment, and then dies in confidence.

STUDIES IN PESSIMISM.

NOTE.

The essays here presented form a further selection from Schopenhauer's "Parerga," brought together under a title which is not to be found in the original, and does not claim to apply to every chapter in the volume. The first essay is, in the main, a rendering of the philosopher's remarks under the heading of "Nachträge zur Lehre vom Leiden der Welt," together with certain parts of another section entitled "Nachträge zur Lehre von der Bejahung und Verneinung des Willens zum Leben." Such omissions as I have made are directed chiefly by the desire to avoid repeating arguments already familiar to the readers of the other volumes in this series. The "Dialogue on Immortality" sums up views expressed at length in the philosopher's chief work, and treated again in the "Parerga." The psychological observations in this and the previous volume practically exhaust the chapter of the original which bears this title.

The essay on "Women" must not be taken in jest. It expresses Schopenhauer's serious convictions; and, as a penetrating observer of the faults of humanity, he may be allowed a hearing on a question which is just now receiving a good deal of attention among us.

T. B. S.

STUDIES IN PESSIMISM.

ON THE SUFFERINGS OF THE WORLD.

Unless suffering is the direct and immediate object of life, our existence must entirely fail of its aim. It is absurd to look upon the enormous amount of pain that abounds everywhere in the world, and originates in needs and necessities inseparable from life itself, as serving no purpose at all and the result of mere chance. Each separate misfortune, as it comes, seems, no doubt, to be something exceptional; but misfortune in general is the rule.

I know of no greater absurdity than that propounded by most systems of philosophy in declaring evil to be negative in its character. Evil is just what is positive; it makes its own existence felt. Leibnitz is particularly concerned to defend this absurdity; and he seeks to strengthen his position by using a palpable and paltry sophism.* It is the good which is negative: in other words, happiness and satisfaction always imply some desire fulfilled, some state of pain brought to an end.

This explains the fact that we generally find pleasure to be not nearly so pleasant as we expected, and pain very much more painful.

The pleasure in this world, it has been said, outweighs the pain; or, at any rate, there is an even balance between the two. If the reader wishes to see shortly whether this

---

Translator's Note cf. *Théod*; §153. Leibnitz argued that evil is a negative quality—*i.e.*, the absence of good: and that its active and seemingly positive character is an incidental and not an essential part of its nature. Cold, he said, is only the absence of the power of heat, and the active power of expansion in freezing water is an incidental and not an essential part of the nature of cold. The fact is, that the power of expansion in freezing water is really an increase of repulsion among its molecules; and Schopenhauer is quite right in calling the whole argument a sophism.

statement is true, let him compare the respective feelings of two animals, one of which is engaged in eating the other.

The best consolation in misfortune or affliction of any kind will be thought of other people who are in a still worse plight than yourself; and this is a form of consolation open to every one. But what an awful fate this means for mankind as a whole!

We are like lambs in a field, disporting themselves under the eye of the butcher, who chooses out first one and then another for his prey. So it is that in our good days we are all unconscious of the evil fate may have presently in store for us—sickness, poverty, mutilation, loss of sight or reason.

No little part of the torment of existence lies in this, that Time is continually pressing upon us, never letting us take breath, but always coming after us, like a taskmaster with a whip. If at any moment Time stays his hand, it is only when we are delivered over to the misery of boredom.

But misfortune has its uses; for, as our bodily frame would burst asunder if the pressure of the atmosphere were removed, so, if the lives of men were relieved of all need, hardship and adversity; if everything they took in hand were successful, they would be so swollen with arrogance that, though they might not burst, they would present the spectacle of unbridled folly—nay, they would go mad. And I may say, further, that a certain amount of care or pain or trouble is necessary for every man at all times. A ship without ballast is unstable and will not go straight.

Certain it is that work, worry, labor and trouble, form the lot of almost all men their whole life long. But if all wishes were fulfilled as soon as they arose, how would men occupy their lives? what would they do with their time? If the world were a paradise of luxury and ease, a land flowing with milk and honey, where every Jack obtained his Jill at once and without any difficulty, men would either die of boredom or hang themselves; or there would be wars, massacres, and murders; so that in the end mankind would inflict more suffering on itself than it has now to accept at the hands of Nature.

In early youth, as we contemplate our coming life, we are like children in a theater before the curtain is raised, sitting there in high spirits and eagerly waiting for the play to begin. It is a blessing that we do not know what is really going to happen. Could we foresee it, there are times when children might seem like innocent prisoners, condemned not to death, but to life, and as yet all unconscious of what their sentence means. Nevertheless, every man desires to reach old age; in other words, a state of life of which it may be said: "It is bad to-day, and it will be worse to-morrow; and so on till the worst of all."

If you try to imagine, as nearly as you can, what an amount of misery, pain and suffering of every kind the sun shines upon in its course, you will admit that it would be much better if on the earth as little as on the moon the sun were able to call forth the phenomena of life; and if, here as there the surface were still in a crystalline state.

Again, you may look upon life as an unprofitable episode, disturbing the blessed calm of non-existence. And, in any case, even though things have gone with you tolerably well, the longer you live the more clearly you will feel that, on the whole, life is a disappointment, nay, a cheat.

If two men who were friends in their youth meet again when they are old, after being separated for a lifetime, the chief feeling they will have at the sight of each other will be one of complete disappointment at life as a whole; because their thoughts will be carried back to that earlier time when life seemed so fair as it lay spread out before them in the rosy light of dawn, promised so much—and then performed so little. This feeling will so completely predominate over every other that they will not even consider it necessary to give it words; but on either side it will be silently assumed, and form the ground-work of all they have to talk about.

He who lives to see two or three generations is like a man who sits some time in the conjurer's booth at a fair, and witnesses the performance twice or thrice in succession. The tricks were meant to be seen only once; and when they are no longer a novelty and cease to deceive, their effect is gone.

While no man is much to be envied for his lot, there are countless numbers whose fate is to be deplored.

Life is a task to be done. It is a fine thing to say *defunctus est;* it means that the man has done his task.

If children were brought into the world by an act of pure reason alone, would the human race continue to exist? Would not a man rather have so much sympathy with the coming generation as to spare it the burden of existence? or at any rate not take it upon himself to impose that burden upon it in cold blood.

I shall be told, I suppose, that my philosophy is comfortless—because I speak the truth; and people prefer to be assured that everything the Lord has made is good. Go to the priests, then, and leave philosophers in peace. At any rate, do not ask us to accommodate our doctrines to the lessons you have been taught. That is what those rascals of sham philosophers will do for you. Ask them for any doctrine you please, and you will get it. Your University professors are bound to preach optimism; and it is an easy and agreeable task to upset their theories.

I have reminded the reader that every state of welfare, every feeling of satisfaction, is negative in its character; that is to say, it consists in freedom from pain, which is the positive element of existence. It follows, therefore, that the happiness of any given life is to be measured, not by its joys and pleasures, but by the extent to which it has been free from suffering—from positive evil. If this is the true standpoint, the lower animals appear to enjoy a happier destiny than man. Let us examine the matter a little more closely.

However varied the forms that human happiness and misery may take, leading a man to seek the one and shun the other, the material basis of it all is bodily pleasure or bodily pain. This basis is very restricted: it is simply health, food, protection from wet and cold, the satisfaction of the sexual instinct; or else the absence of these things. Consequently, as far as real physical pleasure is concerned, the man is not better off than the brute, except in so far as the higher possibilities of his nervous system make him more sensitive to every kind of pleasure, but also, it must be remembered, to every kind of pain. But then compared with the brute, how much stronger are the passions aroused in him! what an immeasurable difference there is in the depth and vehemence of his emotions!—and yet, in the one case, as in the other, all to produce the same result in the end: namely, health, food, clothing, and so on.

The chief source of all this passion is that thought for what is absent and future, which, with man, exercises such a powerful influence upon all he does. It is this that is the real origin of his cares, his hopes, his fears—emotions which affect him more deeply than could ever be the case with those present joys and sufferings to which the brute is confined. In his powers of reflection, memory and fore-sight, man possesses, as it were, a machine for condensing and storing up his pleasures and his sorrows. But the brute has nothing of the kind; whenever it is in pain, it is as though it were suffering for the first time, even though the same thing should have previously happened to it times out of number. It has no power of summing up its feel-ings. Hence its careless and placid temper, how much it is to be envied. But in man reflection comes in, with all the emotions to which it gives rise; and taking up the same elements of pleasure and pain which are common to him and the brute, it develops his susceptibility to happi-ness and misery to such a degree that, at one moment the man is brought in an instant to a state of delight that may even prove fatal, at another to the depths of despair and suicide.

If we carry our analysis a step farther, we shall find that, in order to increase his pleasures, man has intentionally added to the number and pressure of his needs, which in their original state were not much more difficult to satisfy than those of the brute. Hence luxury in all its forms; delicate food, the use of tobacco and opium, spirituous liquors, fine clothes and the thousand and one things that he considers necessary to his existence.

And above and beyond all this, there is a separate and peculiar source of pleasure, and consequently of pain, which man has established for himself, also as the result of using his powers of reflection; and this occupies him out of all proportion to its value, nay, almost more than all his other interests put together—I mean ambition and the feeling of honor and shame; in plain words, what he thinks about the opinion other people have of him. Tak-ing a thousand forms, often very strange ones, this becomes the goal of almost all the efforts he makes that are not rooted in physical pleasure or pain. It is true that besides the sources of pleasure which he has in common with the brute, man has the pleasures of the mind as well. These admit of many gradations, from the most innocent trifling or the merest talk up to the highest intellectual achievements; but there is the accompanying boredom to be set against them on the side of suffering. Boredom is a form of suffering unknown to brutes, at any rate in their natural state; it is only the very cleverest of them who show faint traces of it when they are domesticated; whereas in the case of man it has become a downright scourge. The crowd of miserable wretches whose one aim in life is to fill their purses but never to put anything into their heads, offers a singular instance of this torment of boredom. Their wealth becomes a punishment by delivering them up to the misery of having nothing to do; for, to escape it, they will rush about in all directions, traveling here, there and everywhere. No sooner do they arrive in a place than they are anxious to know what amusements it affords: just as though they were beggars asking where they could receive a dole! Of a truth, need and boredom are the two poles of human life. Finally, I may mention that as regards the sexual relation, man is committed to a peculiar arrangement which drives him obstinately to choose one person. This feeling grows, now and then, into a more or less passionate love, * which is the source of little pleasure and much suffering.

It is, however, a wonderful thing that the mere addition of thought should serve to raise such a vast and lofty structure of human happiness and misery: resting, too, on the same narrow basis of joy and sorrow as man holds in common with the brute, and exposing him to such violent emotions, to so many storms of passion, so much convulsion of feeling, that what he has suffered stands written and may be read in the lines on his face. And yet, when all is told, he has been struggling ultimately for the very same things as the brute has attained, and with an incomparably smaller expenditure of passion and pain.

But all this contributes to increase the measure of suffering in human life out of all proportion to its pleasures; and the pains of life are made much worse for man by the fact that death is something very real to him. The brute flies from death instinctively without really knowing what

---

* I have treated this subject at length in a special chapter of the second volume of my chief work

it is, and therefore without ever contemplating it in the
way natural to a man, who has this prospect always before
his eyes. So that even if only a few brutes die a natural
death, and most of them live only just long enough to
transmit their species, and then, if not earlier, become the
prey of some other animal—while man, on the other hand,
manages to make so-called natural death the rule, to
which, however, there are a good many exceptions—the
advantage is on the side of the brute, for the reason stated
above. But the fact is that man attains the natural term
of years just as seldom as the brute; because the unnatural
way in which he lives, and the strain of work and emotion,
lead to a degeneration of the race; and so his goal is not
often reached.

The brute is much more content with mere existence
than man; the plant is wholly so; and man finds satisfaction in it just in proportion as he is dull and obtuse. Accordingly, the life of the brute carries less of sorrow with
it, but also less of joy, when compared with the life of man;
and while this may be traced, on the one side, to freedom
from the torment of care and anxiety, it is also due to the
fact that hope, in any real sense, is unknown to the brute.
It is thus deprived of any share in that which gives us the
most and the best of our joys and pleasures, the mental
anticipation of a happy future, and the inspiriting play of
fantasy, both of which we owe to our power of imagination. If the brute is free from care, it is also, in this
sense, without hope; in either case because its consciousness is limited to the present moment, to what it can
actually see before it. The brute is an embodiment of
present impulses, and hence what elements of fear and
hope exist in its nature—and they do not go very far—
arise only in relation to objects that lie before it and within reach of those impulses: whereas a man's range of
vision embraces the whole of his life, and extends far into
the past and the future.

Following upon this, there is one respect in which brutes
show real wisdom when compared with us—I mean, their
quiet, placid enjoyment of the present moment. The
tranquillity of mind which this seems to give them often
puts us to shame for the many times we allow our thoughts
and our cares to make us restless and discontented. And,
in fact, those pleasures of hope and anticipation which I

have been mentioning are not to be had for nothing. The delight which a man has in hoping for and looking forward to some special satisfaction is a part of the real pleasure attaching to it enjoyed in advance. This is afterward deducted; for the more we look forward to anything, the less satisfaction we find in it when it comes. But the brute's enjoyment is not anticipated and therefore suffers no deduction; so that the actual pleasure of the moment comes to it whole and unimpaired. In the same way, too, evil presses upon the brute only with its own intrinsic weight; whereas with us the fear of its coming often makes its burden ten times more grievous.

It is just this characteristic way in which the brute gives itself up entirely to the present moment that contributes so much to the delight we take in our domestic pets. They are the present moment personified, and in some respects they make us feel the value of every hour that is free from trouble and annoyance, which we, with our thoughts and preoccupations, mostly disregard. But man, that selfish and heartless creature, misuses this quality of the brute to be more content than we are with mere existence, and often works it to such an extent that he allows the brute absolutely nothing more than mere, bare life. The bird which was made so that it might rove over half the world, he shuts up into the space of a cubic foot, there to die a slow death in longing and crying for freedom; for in a cage it does not sing for the pleasure of it. And when I see how man misuses the dog, his best friend; how he ties up this intelligent animal with a chain, I feel the deepest sympathy with the brute and burning indignation against its master.

We shall see later that by taking a very high standpoint it is possible to justify the sufferings of mankind. But this justification cannot apply to animals, whose sufferings, while in a great measure brought about by men, are often considerable even apart from their agency.* And so we are forced to ask, Why and for what purpose does all this torment and agony exist? There is nothing here to give the will pause; it is not free to deny itself and so obtain redemption. There is only one consideration that may serve to explain the sufferings of animals. It is this: that

---

* Cf. "Welt als Wille und Vorstellung," vol. ii. p. 404.·

the will to live, which underlies the whole world of phenomena, must in their case satisfy its cravings by feeding
upon itself. This it does by forming a gradation of phenomena, every one of which exists at the expense of another.
I have shown, however, that the capacity for suffering is
less in animals than in man. Any further explanation
that may be given of their fate will be in the nature of
hypothesis, if not actually mythical in its character; and
I may leave the reader to speculate upon the matter for
himself.

Brahma is said to have produced the world by a kind of
fall or mistake; and in order to atone for his folly, he is
bound to remain in it himself until he works out his redemption. As an account of the origin of things, that is
admirable! According to the doctrines of Buddhism, the
world came into being as the result of some inexplicable
disturbance in the heavenly calm of Nirvana, that blessed
state obtained by expiation, which had endured so long a
time—the change taking place by a kind of fatality. This
explanation must be understood as having at bottom some
moral bearing; although it is illustrated by an exactly parallel theory in the domain of physical science, which places
the origin of the sun in a primitive streak of mist, formed
one knows not how. Subsequently, by a series of moral
errors, the world became gradually worse and worse—true
of the physical orders as well—until it assumed the dismal
aspect it wears to-day. Excellent! The Greeks looked
upon the world and the gods as the work of an inscrutable
necessity. A passable explanation: we may be content
with it until we can get a better. Again, Ormuzd and
Ahriman are rival powers, continually at war. That is
not bad. But that a God like Jehovah should have created
this world of misery and woe, out of pure caprice, and because he enjoyed doing it, and should then have clapped
his hands in praise of his own work, and declared everything to be very good—that will not do at all! In its explanation of the origin of the world, Judaism is inferior to
any other form of religious doctrine professed by a civilized nation; and it is quite in keeping with this that it is
the only one which presents no trace whatever of any belief in the immortality of the soul.*

---

* See " Parerga," vol. i. pp. 136 et seq.

Even though Leibnitz' contention, that this is the best of all possible worlds, were correct, that would not justify God in having created it. For he is the Creator not of the world only, but of possibility itself; and, therefore, he ought to have so ordered possibility as that it would admit of something better.

There are two things which make it impossible to believe that this world is the successful work of an all-wise, all-good, and, at the same time, all-powerful being; firstly, the misery which abounds in it everywhere; and secondly the obvious imperfection of its highest product, man, who is a burlesque of what he should be. These things cannot be reconciled with any such belief. On the contrary, they are just the facts which support what I have been saying; they are our authority for viewing the world as the outcome of our own misdeeds, and therefore, as something that had better not have been. While, under the former hypothesis, they amount to a bitter accusation against the Creator, and supply material for sarcasm; under the latter they form an indictment against our own nature, our own will, and teach us a lesson of humility. They lead us to see that, like the children of a libertine, we come into the world with the burden of sin upon us; and that it is only through having continually to atone for this sin that our existence is so miserable, and that its end is death.

There is nothing more certain than the general truth that it is the grievous sin of the world which has produced the grievous suffering of the world. I am not referring here to the physical connection between these two things lying in the realm of experience; my meaning is metaphysical. Accordingly, the sole thing that reconciles me to the Old Testament is the story of the fall. In my eyes, it is the only metaphysical truth in that book, even though it appears in the form of an allegory. There seems to me no better explanation of our existence than that it is the result of some false step, some sin of which we are paying the penalty. I cannot refrain from recommending the thoughtful reader a popular, but, at the same time, profound treatise on this subject by Claudius * which exhibits

---

* *Translator's Note.*—Matthias Claudius (1740–1815), a popular poet, and friend of Klopstock, Herder and Lessing. He edited the " Wandsbecker Bote," in the fourth part of which appeared the treatise mentioned above. He generally wrote under the pseudonym of " Asmus," and Schopenhauer often refers to him by this name.

the essentially pessimistic spirit of Christianity. It is entitled: " Cursed is the ground for thy sake."

Between the ethics of the Greeks and the ethics of the Hindoos, there is a glaring contrast. In the one case (with the exception, it must be confessed, of Plato), the object of ethics is to enable a man to lead a happy life; in the other, it is to free and redeem him from life altogether—as is directly stated in the very first words of the " Sankhya Karika."

Allied with this is the contrast between the Greek and the Christian idea of death. It is strikingly presented in a visible form on a fine antique sarcophagus in the gallery at Florence, which exhibits, in relief, the whole series of ceremonies attending a wedding in ancient times, from the formal offer to the evening when Hymen's torch lights the happy couple home. Compare with that the Christian coffin, draped in a mournful black and surmounted with a crucifix! How much significance there is in these two ways of finding comfort in death. They are opposed to each other, but each is right. The one points to the affirmation of the will to live, which remains sure of life for all time, however rapidly its forms may change. The other, in the symbol of suffering and death, points to the denial of the will to live, to redemption from this world, the domain of death and devil. And in the question between the affirmation and the denial of the will to live, Christianity is in the last resort right.

The contrast which the New Testament presents when compared with the Old, according to the ecclesiastical view of the matter, is just that existing between my ethical system and the moral philosophy of Europe. The Old Testament represents man as under the dominion of law, in which, however, there is no redemption. The New Testament declares law to have failed, frees man from its dominion,* and in its stead preaches the kingdom of grace, to be won by faith, love of neighbor and entire sacrifice of self. This is the path of redemption from the evil of the world. The spirit of the New Testament is undoubtedly asceticism, however your protestants and rationalists may twist it to suit their purpose. Asceticism is the denial of the will to live; and the transition from the Old Testament

---

* Cf. Romans vii: Galatians ii. iii.

to the New, from the dominion of law to that of faith, from justification by works to redemption through the mediator, from the domain of sin and death to eternal life in Christ, means, when taken in its real sense, the transition from the merely moral virtues to the denial of the will to live. My philosophy shows the metaphysical foundation of justice and the love of mankind, and points to the goal to which these virtues necessarily lead, if they are practiced in perfection. At the same time it is candid in confessing that a man must turn his back upon the world, and that the denial of the will to live is the way of redemption. It is therefore really at one with the spirit of the New Testament, while all other systems are couched in the spirit of the Old; that is to say, theoretically as well as practically, their result is Judaism— mere despotic theism. In this sense, then, my doctrine might be called the only true Christian philosophy—however paradoxical a statement this may seem to people who take superficial views instead of penetrating to the heart of the matter.

If you want a safe compass to guide you through life, and to banish all doubt as to the right way of looking at it, you cannot do better than accustom yourself to regard this world as a penitentiary, a sort of penal colony or ἐργαστήριον, as the earliest philosophers called it.* Among the Christian Fathers, Origen, with praiseworthy courage, took this view,† which is further justified by certain objective theories of life. I refer, not to my own philosophy alone, but to the wisdom of all ages, as expressed in Brahmanism and Buddhism, and in the sayings of Greek philosophers like Empedocles and Pythagoras; as also by Cicero, in his remark that the wise men of old used to teach that we come into this world to pay the penalty of crime committed in another state of existence—a doctrine which formed part of the initiation into the mysteries.‡ And Vanini—whom his contemporaries burned, finding that an easier task than to confute him—puts the same thing in a very forcible way. " Man," he says, " is so full of every kind of misery that, were it not repugnant to the Christian religion, I should venture to affirm that if evil spirits exist

---

* Cf. Clem. Alex. Strom. L. iii., c. 3, p. 399.

† Augustine de civitate Dei., L. xi. c. 23.

‡ Cf. " Fragmenta de philosophia."

at all, they have passed into human form and are now atoning for their crimes." *   And true Christianity—using the word in its right sense—also regards our existence as the consequence of sin and error.

If you accustom yourself to this view of life you will regulate your expectations accordingly, and cease to look upon all its disagreeable incidents, great and small, its sufferings, its worries, its misery, as anything unusual or irregular ; nay, you will find that everything is as it should be, in a world where each of us pays the penalty of existence in his own peculiar way.   Among the evils of a penal colony is the society of those who form it; and if the reader is worthy of better company, he will need no words from me to remind him of what he has to put up with at present.   If he has a soul above the common, or if he is a man of genius, he will occasionally feel like some noble prisoner of state, condemned to work in the galleys with common criminals; and he will follow his example and try to isolate himself.

In general, however, it should be said that this view of life will enable us to contemplate the so-called imperfections of the great majority of men, their moral and intellectual deficiencies, and the resulting base type of countenance, without any surprise, to say nothing of indignation; for we shall never cease to reflect where we are, and that the men about us are beings conceived and born in sin, and living to atone for it.   That is what Christianity means in speaking of the sinful nature of men.

" Pardon's the word to all." †   Whatever folly men commit, be their shortcomings or their vices what they may, let us exercise forbearance; remembering that when these faults appear in others, it is our follies and vices that we behold. They are the shortcomings of humanity, to which we belong; whose faults, one and all, we share; yes, even those very faults at which we now wax so indignant, merely because they have not yet appeared in ourselves. They are faults that do not lie on the surface.   But they exist down there in the depths of our nature; and should anything call them forth, they will come and show them-

---

* " De admirandis naturæ arcanis; " dial L. p. 35.

† "Cymbeline," Act v. Sc. 5.

selves, just as we now see them in others. One man, it is true, may have faults that are absent in his fellow; and it is undeniable that the sum total of bad qualities is in some cases very large; for the difference of individuality between man and man passes all measure.

In fact, the conviction that the world and man is something that had better not have been, is of a kind to fill us with indulgence toward one another. Nay, from this point of view, we might well consider the proper form of address to be, not "Monsieur, Sir, mein Herr," but "my fellow-sufferer," *Soci malorum, compagnon de misères!* This may perhaps sound strange, but it is in keeping with the facts; it puts others in a right light; and it reminds us of that which is after all the most necessary thing in life—the tolerance, patience, regard and love of neighbor, of which every one stands in need, and which, therefore, every man owes to his fellow.

THE VANITY OF EXISTENCE.

THIS vanity finds expression in the whole way in which things exist: in the infinite nature of Time and Space, as opposed to the finite nature of the individual in both; in the ever-passing present moment as the only mode of actual existence; in the interdependence and relativity of all things; in continual becoming without ever being; in constant wishing and never being satisfied; in the long battle which forms the history of life, where every effort is checked by difficulties, and stopped until they are overcome. Time is that in which all things pass away; it is merely the form under which the will to live—the thing in itself and therefore imperishable—has revealed to it that its efforts are in vain; it is that agent by which at every moment all things in our hands become as nothing, and lose any real value they possess.

That which has been exists no more; it exists as little as that which has never been. But of everything that exists you must say, in the next moment, that it has been. Hence something of great importance now past is inferior to something of little importance now present, in that the latter is a reality, and related to the former as something to nothing.

A man finds himself, to his great astonishment, suddenly existing, after thousands and thousands of years of non-existence: he lives for a little while; and then, again, comes an equally long period when he must exist no more. The heart rebels against this, and feels that it cannot be true. The crudest intellect cannot speculate on such a subject without having a presentiment that Time is something ideal in its nature. This ideality of Time and Space is the key to every true system of metaphysics; because it provides for quite another order of things than is to be met with in the domain of nature. This is why Kant is so great.

Of every event in our life we can say only for one moment that it is; forever after, that it was. Every evening we are poorer by a day. It might, perhaps, make us mad to see how rapidly our short span of time ebbs away, if it were not that in the furthest depths of our being we are secretly conscious of our share in the inexhaustible spring of eternity, so that we can always hope to find life in it again.

Considerations of the kind touched on above might, indeed, lead us to embrace the belief that the greatest wisdom is to make the enjoyment of the present the supreme object of life; because that is the only reality, all else being merely the play of thought. On the other hand, such a course might just as well be called the greatest folly: for that which in the next moment exists no more, and vanishes utterly, like a dream, can never be worth a serious effort.

The whole foundation on which our existence rests is the present—the ever-fleeting present. It lies, then, in the very nature of our existence to take the form of constant motion, and to offer no possibility of our ever attaining the rest for which we are always striving. We are like a man running downhill, who cannot keep on his legs unless he runs on, and will inevitably fall if he stops; or, again, like a pole balanced on the tip of one's finger: or like a planet, which would fall into its sun the moment it ceased to hurry forward on its way. Unrest is the mark of existence.

In a world where all is unstable, and nought can endure, but is swept onward at once in the hurrying whirlpool of change; where a man, if he is to keep erect at all, must always be advancing and moving, like an acrobat on a rope —in such a world, happiness is inconceivable. How can it dwell where, as Plato says, "continual Becoming and never Being" is the sole form of existence? In the first place, a man never is happy, but spends his whole life in striving after something which he thinks will make him so; he seldom attains his goal, and when he does, it is only to be disappointed; he is mostly shipwrecked in the end, and comes into harbor with masts and rigging gone. And then, it is all one whether he has been happy or miserable; for his life was never anything more than a present moment always vanishing; and now it is over.

At the same time it is a wonderful thing that, in the world of human beings as in that of animals in general, this manifold restless motion is produced and kept up by the agency of two simple impulses—hunger and the sexual instinct; aided a little, perhaps, by the influence of boredom, but by nothing else; and that, in the theater of life, these suffice to form the *primum mobile* of how complicated a machinery, setting in motion how strange and varied a scene!

On looking a little closer, we find that inorganic matter presents a constant conflict between chemical forces, which eventually works dissolution; and on the other hand, that organic life is impossible without continual change of matter, and cannot exist if it does not receive perpetual help from without. This is the realm of finality; and its opposite would be an infinite existence, exposed to no attack from without, and needing nothing to support it; ἀεὶ ὡσαύτως ὄν, the realm of eternal peace; οὔτε γιγνόμενον οὔτε ἀπολλύμενον. some timeless changeless state, one and undiversified; the negative knowledge of which forms the dominant note of the Platonic philosophy. It is to some such state as this that the denial of the will to live opens up the way.

The scenes of our life are like pictures done in rough mosaic. Looked at close, they produce no effect. There is nothing beautiful to be found in them, unless you stand some distance off. So, to gain anything we have longed for is only to discover how vain and empty it is; and even though we are always living in expectation of better things, at the same time we often repent and long to have the past back again. We look upon the present as something to be put up with while it lasts, and serving only as the way toward our goal. Hence most people, if they glance back when they come to the end of life, will find that all along they have been living *ad interim:* they will be surprised to find that the very thing they disregarded and let slip by unenjoyed, was just the life in the expectation of which they passed all their time. Of how many a man may it not be said that hope made a fool of him until he danced into the arms of death!

Then again, how insatiable a creature is man. Every satisfaction he attains lays the seeds of some new desire, so that there is no end to the wishes of each individual will. And why is this? The real reason is simply that, taken in itself, Will is the lord of all worlds; everything belongs to it, and therefore no one single thing can ever give it satisfaction, but only the whole, which is endless. For all that, it must rouse our sympathy to think how very little the Will, this lord of the world, really gets when it takes the form of an individual; usually only just enough to keep the body together. This is why man is so very miserable.

Life presents itself chiefly as a task—the task, I mean, of subsisting at all, *ganger sa vie.* If this is accomplished, life is a burden, and then there comes the second task of doing something with that which has been won—of warding off boredom, which, like a bird of prey, hovers over us, ready to fall wherever it sees a life secure from need. The first task is to win something; the second, to banish the feeling that it has been won; otherwise it is a burden.

Human life must be some kind of mistake. The truth of this will be sufficiently obvious if we only remember that man is a compound of needs and necessities hard to satisfy; and that even when they are satisfied, all he obtains is a state of painlessness, where nothing remains to him but abandonment to boredom. This is direct proof that existence has no real value in itself; for what is boredom but the feeling of the emptiness of life? If life—the craving for which is the very essence of our being—were possessed of any positive intrinsic value, there would be no such thing as boredom at all: mere existence would satisfy us in itself, and we should want for nothing. But as it is, we take no delight in existence except when we are struggling for something; and then distance and difficulties to be

overcome make our goal look as though it would satisfy us
—an illusion which vanishes when we reach it; or else
when we are occupied with some purely intellectual interest
—where in reality we have stepped forth from life to look
upon it from the outside, much after the manner of spectators at a play. And even sensual pleasure itself means
nothing but a struggle and aspiration, ceasing the moment
its aim is attained. Whenever we are not occupied in one
of these ways, but cast upon existence itself, its vain and
worthless nature is brought home to us; and this is what
we mean by boredom. The hankering after what is strange
and uncommon—an innate and ineradicable tendency of
human nature—shows how glad we are at any interruption
of that natural course of affairs which is so very tedious.

That this most perfect manifestation of the will to live,
the human organism, with the cunning and complex working of its machinery, must fall to dust and yield up itself
and all its strivings to extinction—this is the naïve way in
which Nature, who is always so true and sincere in what
she says, proclaims the whole struggle of this will as in its
very essence barren and unprofitable. Were it of any value
in itself, anything unconditioned and absolute, it could
not thus end in mere nothing.

If we turn from contemplating the world as a whole,
and, in particular, the generations of men as they live their
little hour of mock-existence and then are swept away in
rapid succession; if we turn from this, and look at life in
its small details, as presented, say, in a comedy, how ridiculous it all seems! It is like a drop of water seen through
a microscope, a single drop teeming with *infusoria* or a
speck of cheese full of mites invisible to the naked eye.
How we laugh as they bustle about so eagerly, and struggle
with one another in so tiny a space! And whether here,
or in the little span of human life, this terrible activity
produces a comic effect.

It is only in the microscope that our life looks so big.
It is an indivisible point, drawn out and magnified by the
powerful lenses of Time and Space.

ON SUICIDE.

As far as I know, none but the votaries of monotheistic, that is to say, Jewish religions, look upon suicide as a crime. This is all the more striking, inasmuch as neither in the Old nor in the New Testament is there to be found any prohibition or positive disapproval of it; so that religious teachers are forced to base their condemnation of suicide on philosophical grounds of their own invention. These are so very bad that writers of this kind endeavor to make up for the weakness of their arguments by the strong terms in which they express their abhorrence of the practice; in other words, they declaim against it. They tell us that suicide is the greatest piece of cowardice; that only a madman could be guilty of it; and other insipidities of the same kind; or else they make the nonsensical remark that suicide is wrong; when it is quite obvious that there is nothing in the world to which every man has a more unassailable title than to his own life and person.

Suicide, as I have said, is actually accounted a crime; and a crime which, especially under the vulgar bigotry that prevails in England, is followed by an ignominious burial and the seizure of the man's property; and for that reason, in a case of suicide, the jury almost always bring in a verdict of insanity. Now let the reader's own moral feelings decide as to whether or not suicide is a criminal act. Think of the impression that would be made upon you by the news that some one you know had committed the crime, say, of murder or theft, or been guilty of some act of cruelty or deception; and compare it with your feelings when you hear that he has met a voluntary death. While in the one case a lively sense of indignation and extreme resentment will be aroused, and you will call loudly for punishment or revenge, in the other you will be moved to grief and sympathy; and mingled with your thoughts will be admiration for his courage, rather than the moral disapproval which follows upon a wicked action. Who has not had acquaintances, friends, relations, who of their own free will have left this world; and are these to be thought of with horror as criminals? Most emphatically, No! I am rather of opinion that the clergy should be challenged to explain what right they have to go into the pulpit, or take up their pens, and stamp as a crime an action which many men whom we hold in affection and honor have committed: and to refuse an honorable burial to those who relinquish this world voluntarily. They have no Biblical authority to boast of, as justifying their condemnation of suicide; nay, not even any philosophical arguments that will hold water; and it must be understood that it is arguments we want, and that we will not be put off with mere phrases or words of abuse. If the criminal law forbids suicide, that is not an argument valid in the Church; and besides, the prohibition is ridiculous; for what penalty can frighten a man who is not afraid of death itself? If the law punishes people for trying to commit suicide, it is punishing the want of skill that makes the attempt a failure.

The ancients, moreover, were very far from regarding the matter in that light. Pliny says: "Life is not so desirable a thing as to be protracted at any cost. Whoever you are, you are sure to die, even though your life has been full of abomination and crime. The chief of all remedies for a troubled mind is the feeling that among the blessings which Nature gives to man, there is none greater than an opportune death; and the best of it is that every one can avail himself of it."* And elsewhere the same writer declares: "Not even to God are all things possible; for he could not compass his own death, if he willed to die, and yet in all the miseries of our earthly life, this is the best of his gifts to man."† Nay, in Messilia and on the isle of Ceos, the man who could give valid reasons for relinquishing his life, was handed the cup of hemlock by the magistrate; and that, too, in public.‡ And in ancient times, how many heroes and wise men died a voluntary death. Aristotle,§ it is true, declared suicide to be an offense against the state, although not against the person; but in Stobæus' exposition of the Peripatetic philosophy there is the following remark: "The good man should flee life when his misfortunes become too great; the bad

---

* Hist. Nat. Lib. xxviii., 1.

† Loc. cit. Lib ii c. 7.

‡ Valerius Maximus; hist. Lib. ii., c. 6,§ 7 et 8. Heraclides Ponticus; fragmenta de rebus publicus, ix. Aeliani variæ historiæ, iii 36 Scrabo; Lib. x., c. 5, 6.

§ *Eth. Nichom.*, v. 15.

man, also, when he is too prosperous. And similarly: So he will marry and beget children and take part in the affairs of the state, and generally, practice virtue and continue to live; and then, again, if need be, at any time necessity compels him, he will depart to his place of refuge in the tomb."* And we find that the Stoics actually praised suicide as a noble and heroic action, as hundreds of passages show; above all in the works of Seneca, who expresses the strongest approval of it. As is well known, the Hindoos look upon suicide as a religious act, especially when it takes the form of self-immolation by widows; but also when it consists in casting one's self under the wheels of the chariot of the god at Juggernaut, or being eaten by crocodiles in the Ganges, or being drowned in the holy tanks in the temples, and so on. The same thing occurs on the stage—that mirror of life. For example, in "L'orphelin de la Chine,"† a celebrated Chinese play, almost all the noble characters end by suicide; without the slightest hint anywhere, or any impression being produced on the spectator, that they are committing a crime. And in our own theater it is much the same—Palmira, for instance, in "Mahomet," or Mortimer in "Maria Stuart," Othello, Countess Terzky.‡ Is Hamlet's monologue the meditation of a criminal? He merely declares that if we had any certainty of being annihilated by it, death would be infinitely preferable to the world as it is. But there lies the rub!

The reasons advanced against suicide by the clergy of monotheistic, that is to say, Jewish religions, and by those philosophers who adapt themselves hitherto, are weak sophisms which can easily be refuted.§ The most thoroughgoing refutation of them is given by Hume in his "Essay on Suicide." This did not appear until after his death, when it was immediately suppressed, owing to the scandalous bigotry and outrageous ecclesiastical tyranny that prevailed in England; and hence only a very few copies of it

---

* Stobæus. *Ecl. Eth.* ii., c. 7, pp. 286, 312,

† Traduit par St. Julien, 1834.

‡ *Translator's Note*—Palmira: a female slave in Goethe's play of "Mahomet." Mortimer: a would-be lover and rescuer of Mary in Schiller's "Maria Stuart." Countess Terzky: a leading character in Schiller's "Wallenstein's Tod."

§ See my treatise on the "Foundation of Morals," § 5.

were sold under cover of secrecy and at a high price. This and another treatise by that great man have come to us from Basle, and we may be thankful for the reprint.* It is a great disgrace to the English nation that a purely philosophical treatise, which, proceeding from one of the first thinkers and writers in England, aimed at refuting the current arguments against suicide by the light of cold reason, should be forced to sneak about in that country, as though it were some rascally production, until at last it found refuge on the continent. At the same time it shows what a good conscience the Church has in such matters.

In my chief work I have explained the only valid reason existing against suicide on the score of morality. It is this: that suicide thwarts the attainment of the highest moral aim by the fact that, for a real release from this world of misery, it substitutes one that is merely apparent.† But from a mistake to a crime is a far cry; and it is as a crime that the clergy of Christendom wish us to regard suicide.

The inmost kernel of Christianity is the truth that suffering—the Cross—is the real end and object of life. Hence Christianity condemns suicide as thwarting this end; while the ancient world, taking a lower point of view, held it in approval, nay, in honor. but if that is to be accounted a valid reason against suicide, it involves the recognition of asceticism; that is to say, it is valid only from a much higher ethical standpoint than has ever been adopted by moral philosophers in Europe. If we abandon that high standpoint, there is no tenable reason left, on the score of morality, for condemning suicide. The extraordinary energy and

---

* "Essays on Suicide" and the "Immortality of the Soul," by the late David Hume, Basle, 1799, sold by James Decker.

† *Translator's Note.*—Schopenhauer refers to "Die Welt als Wille und Vorstellung," vol. i., § 69, where the reader may find the same argument stated at somewhat greater length. According to Schopen-. hauer, moral freedom—the highest ethical aim—is to be obtained only by a denial of the will to live. Far from being a denial, suicide is an emphatic assertion of this will. For it is in fleeing from the pleasures, not from the sufferings of life, that this denial consists. When a man destroys his existence as an individual, he is not by any means destroying his will to live. On the contrary, he would like to live if he could do so with satisfaction to himself; if he could assert his will against the power of circumstance; but circumstance is too strong for him.

zeal with which the clergy of monotheistic religions attack suicide is not supported either by any passages in the Bible or by any considerations of weight; so that it looks as though they must have some secret reason for their contention. May it not be this—that the voluntary surrender of life is a bad compliment for him who said that "all things were very good?" If this is so, it offers another instance of the crass optimism of these religions, denouncing suicide to escape being denounced by it.

It will generally be found that, as soon as the terrors of life reach the point at which they outweigh the terrors of death, a man will put an end to his life. But the terrors of death offer considerable resistance; they stand like a sentinel at the gate leading out of this world. Perhaps there is no man alive who would not have already put an end to his life, if this end had been of a purely negative character, a sudden stoppage of existence. There is something positive about it; it is the destruction of the body; and a man shrinks from that because his body is the manifestation of the will to live.

However, the struggle with that sentinel is, as a rule, not so hard as it may seem from a long way off, mainly in consequence of the antagonism between the ills of the body and the ills of the mind. If we are in great bodily pain, or the pain lasts a long time, we become indifferent to other troubles; all we think about is to get well. In the same way great mental suffering makes us insensible to bodily pain; we despise it; nay, if it should outweigh the other, it distracts our thoughts, and we welcome it as a pause in mental suffering. It is this feeling that makes suicide easy; for the bodily pain that accompanies it loses all significance in the eyes of one who is tortured by an excess of mental suffering. This is especially evident in the case of those who are driven to suicide by some purely morbid and exaggerated ill-humor. No special effort to overcome their feelings is necessary, nor do such people require to be worked up in order to take the step; but as soon as the keeper into whose charge they are given leaves them for a couple of minutes, they quickly bring their life to an end.

When, in some dreadful and ghastly dream, we reach the moment of greatest horror, it awakes us; thereby banishing all the hideous shapes that were born of the night. And life is a dream: when the moment of greatest horror compels us to break it off, the same thing happens.

Suicide may also be regarded as an experiment—a question which man puts to Nature, trying to force her to an answer. The question is this: What change will death produce in a man's existence and in his insight into the nature of things? It is a clumsy experiment to make; for it involves the destruction of the very consciousness which puts the question and awaits the answer.

IMMORTALITY:* A DIALOGUE.

THRASYMACHOS—PHILALETHES.

THRASYMACHOS.—Tell me now, in one word, what shall I be after my death? And mind you be clear and precise.

PHILALETHES.—All and nothing.

THRASYMACHUS.—I thought so! I gave you a problem and you solve it by a contradiction. That's a very stale trick.

PHILALETHES. Yes, but you raise transcendental questions, and you expect me to answer them in language that is only made for immanent knowledge. It's no wonder that a contradiction ensues.

THRASYMACHOS.—What do you mean by transcendental questions and immanent knowledge? I've heard these expressions before, of course; they are not new to me. The professor was fond of using them, but only as predicates of the Deity, and he never talked of anything else; which was all quite right and proper. He argued thus: if the Deity

------

* *Translator's Note.*—The word immortality—" Unsterblichkeit " —does not occur in the original; nor would it, in its usual application find a place in Schopenhauer's vocabulary. The word he uses is " Unzerstorbarkeit "—indestructibility. But I have preferred immortality, because that word is commonly associated with the subject touched upon in this little debate. If any critic doubts the wisdom of this preference, let me ask him to try his hand at a short, concise, and, at the same time, popularly intelligible rendering of the German original, which runs thus: " Zur Lehre von der Unzerstörbarkeit unseres wahren Wesens durch den Tod: kleine dialogische Schlussbelustigung."

was in the world itself, he was immanent; if he was somewhere outside it, he was transcendent. Nothing could be clearer and more obvious. You knew where you were. But this Kantian rigmarole won't do any more: it's antiquated and no longer applicable to modern ideas. Why, we've had a whole row of eminent men in the metropolis of German learning——

PHILALETHES (aside).—German humbug, he means.

THRASYMACHOS.—The mighty Schleiermacher, for instance, and that gigantic intellect, Hegel; and at this time of day we've abandoned that nonsense. I should rather say we're so far beyond it that we can't put up with it any more. What's the use of it then? What does it all mean?

PHILALETHES.—Transcendental knowledge is knowledge which passes beyond the bounds of possible experience, and strives to determine the nature of things as they are in themselves. Immanent knowledge, on the other hand, is knowledge which confines itself entirely within those bounds; so that it cannot apply to anything but actual phenomena. As far as you are an individual, death will be the end of you. But your individuality is not your true and inmost being: it is only the outward manifestation of it. It is not the thing in-itself, but only the phenomenon presented in the form of time; and therefore with a beginning and an end. But your real being knows neither time nor beginning nor end, nor yet the limits of any given individual. It is everywhere present in every individual, and no individual can exist apart from it. So when death comes, on the one hand you are annihilated as an individual; on the other, you are and remain everything. That is what I meant when I said that after your death you would be all and nothing. It is difficult to find a more precise answer to your question and at the same time be brief. The answer is contradictory, I admit; but it is so simply because your life is in time, and the immortal part of you in eternity. You may put the matter thus: Your immortal part is something that does not last in time and yet is indestructible; but there you have another contradiction. You see what happened by trying to bring the transcendental within the limits of immanent knowledge. It is in some sort doing violence to the latter by misusing it for ends it was never meant to serve.

THRASYMACHOS.—Look here, I sha'n't give twopence for your immortality unless I'm to remain an individual.

PHILALETHES.—Well, perhaps I may be able to satisfy you on this point.   Suppose I guarantee that after death you shall remain an individual, but only on condition that you first spend three months of complete unconsciousness.

THRASYMACHOS.—I shall have no objection to that.

PHILALETHES.—But remember, if people are completely unconscious, they take no account of time.   So, when you are dead, it's all the same to you whether three months pass in the world of unconsciousness, or ten thousand years. In one case as in the other, it is simply a matter of believing what is told you when you awake.   So far, then you can afford to be indifferent whether it is three months or ten thousand years that pass before you recover your individuality.

THRASYMACHOS.—Yes, if it comes to that, I suppose you're right.

PHILALETHES.—And if by chance, after those ten thousand years have gone by, no one ever thinks of awaking you, I fancy it would be no great misfortune.   You would have become quite accustomed to non-existence after so long a spell of it—following upon such a very few years of life.   At any rate you may be sure you would be perfectly ignorant of the whole thing.   Further, if you knew that the mysterious power which keeps you in your present state of life had never once ceased in those ten thousand years to bring forth other phenomena like yourself, and to endow them with life, it would fully console you.

THRASYMACHOS.—Indeed!   So you think you're quietly going to do me out of my individuality with all this fine talk.   But I'm up to your tricks.   I tell you I won't exist unless I can have my individuality.   I'm not going to put off with " mysterious powers," and what you call " phenomena."   I can't do without my individuality, and I won't give it up.

PHILALETHES.—You mean, I suppose, that your individuality is such a delightful thing—so splendid, so perfect, and beyond compare—that you can't imagine anything better.   Aren't you ready to exchange your present state for one which, if we can judge by what is told us, may possibly be superior and more endurable?

THRASYMACHOS.—Don't you see that my individuality,

be it what it may, is my very self? To me it is the most important thing in the world,

> " For God is God and I am I."

I want to exist, *I, I.* That's the main thing. I don't care about an existence which has to be proved to be mine, before I can believe it.

PHILALETHES.—Think what you're doing! When you say *I, I, I* want to exist, it is not you alone that says this. Everything says it, absolutely everything that has the faintest trace of consciousness. It follows then, that this desire of yours is just the part of you that is not individual—the part that is common to all things without distinction. It is the cry, not of the individual, but of existence itself; it is the intrinsic element in everything that exists, nay, it is the cause of anything existing at all. This desire craves for and so is satisfied with nothing less than existence in general—not any definite individual existence. No! that is not its aim. It seems to be so only because this desire—this will—attains consciousness only in the individual, and therefore looks as though it were concerned with nothing but the individual. There lies the illusion, an illusion it is true, in which the individual is held fast: but, if he reflects, he can break the fetters and set himself free. It is only indirectly, I say, that the individual has this violent craving for existence. It is the will to live which is the real and direct aspirant—alike and identical in all things. Since then, existence is the free work, nay, the mere reflection of the will, where existence is, there too, must be will: and for the moment, the will finds its satisfaction in existence itself; so far, I mean, as that which never rests, but presses forward eternally, can ever find any satisfaction at all. The will is careless of the individual: the individual is not its business; although, as I have said, this seems to be the case, because the individual has no direct consciousness of will except in himself. The effect of this is to make the individual careful to maintain his own existence; and if this were not so, there would be no surety for the preservation of the species. From all this it is clear that individuality is not a form of perfection, but rather of limitation; and so to be freed from it is not loss but gain. Trouble yourself no more about the matter. Once thoroughly recognize what you are, what your existence really is, namely, the universal will to live and the whole question will seem to you childish and most ridiculous!

THRASYMACHOS.—You're childish yourself and most ridiculous, like all philosophers! and if a man of my age lets himself in for a quarter-of-an-hour's talk with such fools, it is only because it amuses me and passes the time. I've more important business to attend to, so good-by.

FURTHER PSYCHOLOGICAL OBSERVATIONS.

THERE is an unconscious propriety in the way in which, in all European languages, the word person is commonly used to denote a human being. The real meaning of *persona* is a mask, such as actors were accustomed to wear on the ancient stage; and it is quite true that no one shows himself as he is, but wears his mask and plays his part. Indeed, the whole of our social arrangements may be likened to a perpetual comedy; and this is why a man who is worth anything finds society so insipid, while a block-head is quite at home in it.

Reason deserves to be called a prophet; for in showing us the consequence and effect of our actions in the present, does it not tell us what the future will be? This is precisely why reason is such an excellent power of restraint in moments when we are possessed by some base passion, some fit of anger, some covetous desire, that will lead us to do things whereof we must presently repent.

Hatred comes from the heart; contempt from the head; and neither feeling is quite within our control. For we cannot alter our heart; its bias is determined by motives; and our head deals with objective facts and applies to them rules which are immutable. Any given individual is the union of a particular heart with a particular head.

Hatred and contempt are diametrically opposed and mutually exclusive. There are even not a few cases where hatred of a person is rooted in nothing but forced esteem for his qualities. And besides, if a man sets out to hate all the miserable creatures he meets, he will not have much energy left for anything else; whereas he can despise them, one and all, with the greatest ease. True, genuine contempt is just the reverse of true, genuine pride; it keeps quite quiet and gives no sign of its existence. For if a man shows that he despises you, he signifies at least this much regard for you, that he wants to let you know how little he appreciates you; and his wish is dictated by hatred, which cannot exist with real contempt. On the contrary, if it is genuine, it is simply the conviction that the object of it is a man of no value at all. Contempt is not incompatible with indulgent and kindly treatment, and for the sake of one's own peace and safety, this should not be omitted; it will prevent irritation; and there is no one who cannot do harm if he is roused to it. But if this pure, cold, sincere contempt ever shows itself, it will be met with the most truculent hatred; for the despised person is not in a position to fight contempt with its own weapons.

Melancholy is a very different thing from bad humor, and of the two, it is not nearly so far removed from a gay and happy temperament. Melancholy attracts, while bad humor repels.

Hypochondria is a species of torment which not only makes us unreasonably cross with the things of the present; not only fills us with groundless anxiety on the score of future misfortunes entirely of our own manufacture; but also leads to unmerited self-reproach for what we have done in the past.

Hypochondria shows itself in a perpetual hunting after things that vex and annoy, and then brooding over them. The cause of it is an inward morbid discontent, often coexisting with a naturally restless temperament. In their extreme form, this discontent and this unrest lead to suicide.

Any incident, however trivial, that rouses disagreeable emotion, leaves an after-effect in our mind, which, for the time it lasts, prevents our taking a clear objective view of the things about us, and tinges all our thoughts: just as a small object held close to the eye limits and distorts our field of vision.

What makes people hard-hearted is this, that each man has, or fancies he has, as much as he can bear in his own troubles.   Hence if a man suddenly finds himself in an unusually happy position, it will in most cases result in his being sympathetic and kind.   But if he has never been in any other than a happy position, or this becomes his permanent state, the effect of it is often just the contrary: it so far removes him from suffering that he is incapable of feeling any more sympathy with it.   So it is that the poor often show themselves more ready to help than the rich.

At times it seems as though we both wanted and did not want the same thing, and felt at once glad and sorry about it.   For instance, if on some fixed date we are going to be put to a decisive test about anything in which it would be a great advantage to us to come off victorious, we shall be anxious for it to take place at once, and at the same time we shall tremble at the thought of its approach.   And if, in the meantime, we hear that, for once in a way, the date has been postponed, we shall experience a feeling both of pleasure and of annoyance; for the news is disappointing, but nevertheless it affords us momentary relief.   It is just the same thing if we are expecting some important letter carrying a definite decision, and it fails to arrive.

In such cases there are really two different motives at work in us; the stronger but more distant of the two being the desire to stand the test and to have the decision given in our favor; and the weaker, which touches us more nearly, the wish to be left for the present in peace and quiet, and accordingly in further enjoyment of the advantage which at any rate attaches to a state of hopeful uncertainty, compared with the possibility that the issue may be unfavorable.

In my head there is a permanent opposition party; and whenever I take any step or come to any decision—though I may have given the matter mature consideration—it afterward attacks what I have done, without, however, being each time necessarily in the right. This is, I suppose, only a form of rectification on the part of the spirit of scrutiny; but it often reproaches me when I do not deserve it. The same thing, no doubt, happens to many others as well; for where is the man who can help thinking that, after all, it were better not to have done something that he did with every hope of success:

> "Quid tam dextro pede concipis ut te
> Conatus non poeniteat votique peracti?"

Why is it that common is an expression of contempt? and that uncommon, extraordinary, distinguished, denote approbation? Why is everything that is common contemptible?

Common in its original meaning denotes that which is peculiar to all men, *i. e.*, shared equally by the whole species, and therefore an inherent part of its nature. Accordingly, if an individual possesses no qualities beyond those which attach to mankind in general, he is a common man. Ordinary is a much milder word, and refers rather to intellectual character; whereas common has more of a moral application.

What value can a creature have that is not a whit different from millions of its kind? Millions, do I say? nay, an infinitude of creatures which, century after century, in never-ending flow, nature sends bubbling up from her inexhaustible springs; as generous with them as the smith with the useless sparks that fly around his anvil.

It is obviously quite right that a creature which has no qualities except those of the species, should have to confine its claim to an existence entirely within the limits of the species, and live a life conditioned by those limits.

In various passages of my works,* I have argued that while a lower animal possesses nothing more than the generic character of its species, man is the only being which can lay claim to possess an individual character. But in most men this individual character comes to very little in reality; and they may be almost all ranged under

---

* " Grundprobleme der Ethik," p. 48; " Welt als Wille und Vorstellung," vol. i. p. 338.

certain classes: *ce sont des espèces*. Their thoughts and desires, like their faces, are those of the species, or at any rate, those of the class to which they belong: and accordingly, they are of a trivial, every-day, common character, and exist by the thousand. You can usually tell beforehand what they are likely to do and say. They have no special stamp or mark to distinguish them; they are like manufactured goods, all of a piece.

If, then, their nature is merged in that of the species, how shall their existence go beyond it? The curse of vulgarity puts men on a par with the lower animals, by allowing them none but a generic nature, a generic form of existence.

Anything that is high or great or noble must then, as a matter of course, and by its very nature, stand alone in a world where no better expression can be found to denote what is base and contemptible than that which I have mentioned as in general use, namely, common.

Will, as the thing-in-itself, is the foundation of all being; it is part and parcel of every creature, and the permanent element in everything. Will, then, is that which we possess in common with all men, nay, with all animals, and even with lower forms of existence; and in so far we are akin to everything—so far, that is, as everything is filled to overflowing with will. On the other hand, that which places one being over another, and sets differences between man and man, is intellect and knowledge; therefore in every manifestation of self we should, as far as possible, give play to the intellect alone; for, as we have seen, the will is the common part of us. Every violent exhibition of will is common and vulgar; in other words, it reduces us to the level of the species, and makes us a mere type and example of it; in that it is just the character of the species that we are showing. So every fit of anger is something common—every unrestrained display of joy, or of hate, or fear—in short, every form of emotion; in other words, every movement of the will, if it is so strong as decidedly to outweigh the intellectual element in consciousness, and to make the man appear as a being that wills rather than knows.

In giving way to emotion of this violent kind, the

greatest genius puts himself on a level with the commonest
son of earth. Contrarily, if a man desires to be absolutely
uncommon, in other words, great, he should never allow
his consciousness to be taken possession of and dominated
by the movement of his will, however much he may be
solicited thereto. For example, he must be able to observe
that other people are badly disposed toward him, without
feeling any hatred toward them himself; nay, there is no
surer sign of a great mind than that it refuses to notice
annoying and insulting expressions, but straightway
ascribes them, as it ascribes countless other mistakes, to
the defective knowledge of the speaker, and so merely
observes without feeling them. This is the meaning of
that remark of Gracian, that nothing is more unworthy of
a man than to let it be seen that he is one—*el mayor des-
doro de un hombre es dar muestras de que es hombre.*

And even in the drama, which is the peculiar province
of the passions and emotions, it is easy for them to appear
common and vulgar. And this is specially observable in
the works of the French tragic writers, who set no other
aim before themselves but the delineation of the passions;
and by indulging at one moment in a vaporous kind of
pathos which makes them ridiculous, at another in epigrammatic witticisms, endeavor to conceal the vulgarity of their
subject. I remember seeing the celebrated Mademoiselle
Rachel as Maria Stuart; and when she burst out in fury
against Elizabeth—though she did it very well—I could
not help thinking of a washerwoman. She played the
final parting in such a way as to deprive it of all true
tragic feeling, of which, indeed, the French have no notion
at all. The same part was incomparably better played by
the Italian Ristori; and, in fact, the Italian nature, though
in many respects very different from the German, shares
its appreciation for what is deep, serious, and true in Art;
herein opposed to the French, which everywhere betrays
that it possesses none of this feeling whatever.

The noble, in other words, the uncommon, element in
the drama—nay, what is sublime in it—is not reached
until the intellect is set to work, as opposed to the will;
until it takes a free flight over all those passionate movements of that will, and makes them the subject of its contemplation. Shakespeare, in particular, shows that this
is his general method, more especially in Hamlet. And

only when intellect rises to the point where the vanity of all effort is manifest, and the will proceeds to an act of self-annulment, is the drama tragic in the true sense of the word: it is then that it reaches its highest aim in becoming really sublime.

Every man takes the limits of his own field of vision for the limits of the world. This is an error of the intellect as inevitable as that error of the eye which lets us fancy that on the horizon heaven and earth meet. This explains many things, and among them the fact that every one measures us with his own standard—generally about as long as a tailor's tape, and we have to put up with it: as also that no one will allow us to be taller than himself—a supposition which is once for all taken for granted.

There is no doubt that many a man owes his good fortune in life solely to the circumstance that he has a pleasant way of smiling, and so wins the heart in his favor.

However, the heart would do better to be careful, and to remember what Hamlet put down in his tablets—" that one may smile, and smile, and be a villain."

Everything that is really fundamental in a man, and therefore genuine, works, as such, unconsciously; in this respect like the power of nature. That which has passed through the domain of consciousness is thereby transformed into an idea or picture; and so if it comes to be uttered, it is only an idea or picture which passes from one person to another.

Accordingly, any quality of mind or character that is genuine and lasting, is originally unconscious; and it is only when unconsciously brought into play that it makes a profound impression. If any like quality is consciously exercised, it means that it has been worked up; it becomes intentional, and therefore a matter of affectation, in other words, of deception.

If a man does a thing unconsciously, it costs him no trouble; but if he tries to do it by taking trouble, he fails.

This applies to the origin of those fundamental ideas which form the pith and marrow of all genuine work. Only that which is innate is genuine and will hold water; and every man who wants to achieve something, whether in practical life, in literature, or in art, must "follow the rules without knowing them."

Men of very great capacity will, as a rule, find the company of very stupid people preferable to that of the common run; for the same reason that the tyrant and the mob, the grandfather and the grandchildren, are natural allies.

That line of Ovid's,

"Pronaque cum spectent animalia cetera terram,"

can be applied in its true physical sense to the lower animals alone; but in a metaphorical and spiritual sense it is, alas! true of nearly all men as well. All their plans and projects are merged in the desire of physical enjoyment, physical well-being. They may, indeed, have personal interests, often embracing a very varied sphere; but still these latter receive their importance entirely from the relation in which they stand to the former. This is not only proved by their manner of life and the things they say, but it even shows itself in the way they look, the expression of their physiognomy, their gait and gesticulations. Everything about them cries out: *in terram prona!* It is not to them, it is only to the nobler and more highly endowed natures—men who really think and look about them in the world, and form exceptional specimens of humanity—that the next lines are applicable:

"Os homini sublime dedit coelumque tueri
Jussit et erectos ad sidera tollere voltus."

No one knows what capacities for doing and suffering he has in himself, until something comes to rouse them to activity: just as in a pond of still water, lying there like a mirror, there is no sign of the roar and thunder with which it can leap from the precipice, and yet remain what it is;

or again, rise high in the air as a fountain. When water is as cold as ice, you can have no idea of the latent warmth contained in it.

———

Why is it that in spite of all the mirrors in the world, no one really knows what he looks like?

A man may call to mind the face of his friend, but not his own. Here, then, is an initial difficulty in the way of applying the maxim, " Know thyself."

This is partly, no doubt, to be explained by the fact that it is physically impossible for a man to see himself in the glass except with face turned straight toward it and perfectly motionless; where the expression of the eye, which counts for so much, and really gives its whole character to the face, is to a great extent lost. But co-existing with this physical impossibility, there seems to me to be an ethical impossibility of an analogous nature, and producing the same effect. A man cannot look upon his own reflection as though the person presented there were a stranger to him; and yet this is necessary if he is to take an objective view. In the last resort, an objective view means a deep-rooted feeling on the part of the individual, as a moral being, that that which he is contemplating is not himself; * and unless he can take this point of view, he will not see things in a really true light, which is possible only if he is alive to their actual defects, exactly as they are. Instead of that, when a man sees himself in the glass, something out of his own egoistic nature whispers to him to take care to remember that it is no stranger, but himself, that he is looking at; and this operates as a *noli me tangere*, and prevents him taking an objective view. It seems, indeed, as if without the leaven of a grain of malice, such a view were impossible.

———

According as a man's mental energy is exerted or relaxed, will life appear to him either so short, and petty, and fleeting, that nothing can possibly happen over which it is worth his while to spend emotion; that nothing really

---

* Cf. "Grundprobleme der Ethik." p. 275.

matters, whether it is pleasure or riches, or even fame, and that in whatever way a man may have failed, he cannot have lost much—or, on the other hand, life will seem so long, so important, so all in all, so momentous and so full of difficulty that we have to plunge into it with our whole soul if we are to obtain a share of its goods, make sure of its prizes, and carry out our plans. This latter is the immanent and common view of life; it is what Gracian means when he speaks of the serious way of looking at things—*tomar muy de veras el vivir.* The former is the transcendental view, which is well expressed in Ovid's *non est tanti*—it is not worth so much trouble; still better, however, by Plato's remark that nothing in human affairs is worth any great anxiety—οὔτε τι τῶν ἀνθρωπίνων ἄξιον ἐστὶ μεγάλης σπουδῆς. This condition of mind is due to the intellect having got the upper hand in the domain of consciousness, where, freed from the mere service of the will, it looks upon the phenomena of life objectively, and so cannot fail to gain a clear insight into its vain and futile character. But in the other condition of mind, will predominates; and the intellect exists only to light it on its way to the attainment of its desires.

A man is great or small according as he leans to the one or the other of these views of life.

People of very brilliant ability think little of admitting their errors and weaknesses, or of letting others see them. They look upon them as something for which they have duly paid; and instead of fancying that these weaknesses are a disgrace to them, they consider they are doing them an honor. This is especially the case when the errors are of the kind that hang together with their qualities—*conditiones sine quibus non*—or as George Sand said, *les défauts de ses vertus.*

Contrarily, these are people of good character and irreproachable intellectual capacity, who, far from admitting the few little weaknesses they have, conceal them with care, and show themselves very sensitive to any suggestion of their existence; and this, just because their whole merit consists in being free from error and infirmity. If these people are found to have done anything wrong, their reputation immediately suffers.

With people of only moderate ability, modesty is mere honesty; but with those who possess great talent, it is hypocrisy. Hence it is just as becoming in the latter to make no secret of the respect they bear themselves and no disguise of the fact that they are conscious of unusual power, as it is in the former to be modest. Valerius Maximus gives some very neat examples of this in his chapter on self-confidence, *de fiducia sui.*

Not to go to the theater is like making one's toilet without a mirror. But it is still worse to take a decision without consulting a friend. For a man may have the most excellent judgment in all other matters, and yet go wrong in those which concern himself; because here the will comes in and deranges the intellect at once. Therefore let a man take counsel of a friend. A doctor can cure every one but himself; if he falls ill, he sends for a colleague.

In all that we do, we wish, more or less, to come to the end; we are impatient to finish and glad to be done. But the last scene of all, the general end, is something that, as a rule, we wish as far off as may be.

Every parting gives a foretaste of death; every coming together again a foretaste of the resurrection. This is why even people who were indifferent to each other, rejoice so much if they come together again after twenty or thirty years' separation.

Intellects differ from one another in a very real and fundamental way; but no comparison can well be made by merely general observations. It is necessary to come close, and to go into details; for the difference that exists cannot be seen from afar; and it is not easy to judge by outward appearances, as in the several cases of education, leisure and occupation. But even judging by these alone, it must be admitted that many a man has a degree of existence at least ten times as high as another—in other words, exists ten times as much.

I am not speaking here of savages whose life is often only one degree above that of the apes in their woods. Consider, for instance, a porter in Naples or Venice (in the north of Europe solicitude for the winter months makes people more thoughtful and therefore reflective); look at the life he leads, from its beginning to its end—driven by poverty; living on his physical strength; meeting the needs of every day, nay, of every hour, by hard work, great effort, constant tumult, want in all its forms, no care for the morrow; his only comfort, rest after exhaustion; continuous quarreling; not a moment free for reflection; such sensual delights as a mild climate and only just sufficient food will permit of; and then, finally, as the metaphysical element, the crass superstition of his church; the whole forming a manner of life with only a low degree of consciousness, where a man hustles, or rather is hustled, through his existence. This restless and confused dream forms the life of how many millions!

Such men think only just so much as is necessary to carry out their will for the moment. They never reflect upon their life as a connected whole, let alone, then, upon existence in general; to a certain extent they may be said to exist without really knowing it. The existence of the mobsman or the slave who lives on in this unthinking way, stands very much nearer than ours to that of the brute, which is confined entirely to the present moment; but, for that very reason, it has also less of pain in it than ours. Nay, since all pleasure is in its nature negative, that is to say, consists in freedom from some form of misery or need, the constant and rapid interchange between setting about something and getting it done, which is the permanent accompaniment of the work they do, and then again the augmented form which this takes when they go from work to rest and the satisfaction of their needs—all this gives them a constant source of enjoyment; and the fact that it is much commoner to see happy faces among the poor than among the rich, is a sure proof that it is used to good advantage.

Passing from this kind of man, consider, next, the sober, sensible merchant, who leads a life of speculation, thinks long over his plans and carries them out with great care, founds a house, and provides for his wife, his children and descendants; takes his share, too, in the life of the community. It is obvious that a man like this has a much higher degree of consciousness than the former, and so his existence has a higher degree of reality.

Then look at the man of learning, who investigates, it may be, the history of the past. He will have reached the point at which a man becomes conscious of existence as a whole, sees beyond the period of his own life, beyond his own personal interests, thinking over the whole course of the world's history.

Then, finally, look at the poet or the philosopher, in whom reflection has reached such a height, that, instead of being drawn on to investigate any one particular phenomenon of existence, he stands in amazement before existence itself, this great sphinx, and makes it his problem. In him consciousness has reached the degree of clearness at which it embraces the world itself: his intellect has completely abandoned its function as the servant of his will, and now holds the world before him; and the world calls upon him much more to examine and consider it, than to play a part in it himself. If, then, the degree of consciousness is the degree of reality, such a man will be sure to exist most of all, and there will be sense and significance in so describing him.

Between the two extremes here sketched, and the intervening stages, every one will be able to find the place at which he himself stands.

We know that man is in general superior to all other animals, and this is also the case in his capacity for being trained. Mohammedans are trained to pray with their faces turned toward Mecca, five times a day; and they never fail to do it. Christians are trained to cross themselves on certain occasions, to bow, and so on. Indeed, it may be said that religion is the *chef d'œuvre* of the art of training, because it trains people in the way they shall think· and, as is well known, you cannot begin the process too early. There is no absurdity so palpable but that it may be firmly planted in the human head if you only begin to inculcate it before the age of five, by constantly repeating it with an air of great solemnity. For as in the case of animals, so in that of men, training is successsful only when you begin in early youth.

Noblemen and gentlemen are trained to hold nothing sacred but their word of honor—to maintain a zealous, rigid, and unshaken belief in the ridiculous code of chivalry; and if they are called upon to do so, to seal their belief by dying for it, and seriously to regard a king as a being of a higher order.

Again, our expressions of politeness, the compliments we make, in particular, the respectful attentions we pay to ladies, are a matter of training; as also our esteem for good birth, rank, titles, and so on. Of the same character is the resentment we feel at any insult directed against us; and the measure of this resentment may be exactly determined by the nature of the insult. An Englishman, for instance, thinks it a deadly insult to be told that he is no gentleman, or, still worse, that he is a liar; a Frenchman has the same feeling if you call him a coward, and a German if you say he is stupid.

There are many persons who are trained to be strictly honorable in regard to one particular matter, while they have little honor to boast of in anything else. Many a man, for instance, will not steal your money; but he will lay hands on everything of yours that he can enjoy without having to pay for it. A man of business will often deceive you without the slightest scruple, but he will absolutely refuse to commit a theft.

Imagination is strong in a man when that particular function of the brain which enables him to observe is roused to activity without any necessary excitement of the senses. Accordingly, we find that imagination is active just in proportion as our senses are not excited by external objects. A long period of solitude, whether in prison or in a sick room; quiet, twilight, darkness—these are the things that promote its activity; and under their influence it comes into play of itself. On the other hand, when a

great deal of material is presented to our faculties of observation, as happens on a journey, or in the hurly-burly of
the world, or, again, in broad daylight, the imagination is
idle, and, even though call may be made upon it, refuses
to become active, as though it understood that that was not
its proper time.

However, if the imagination is to yield any real product,
it must have received a great deal of material from the
external world. This is the only way in which its store-
house can be filled. The fantasy is nourished much in
the same way as the body, which is least capable of any
work and enjoys doing nothing, just in the very moment
when it receives its food, which it has to digest. And yet
it is to this very food that it owes the power which it afterward puts forth at the right time.

Opinion is like a pendulum and obeys the same law. If
it goes past the center of gravity on one side, it must go a
like distance on the other; and it is only after a certain
time that it finds the true point at which it can remain at
rest.

By a process of contraction, distance in space makes
things look small, and therefore free from defect. This is
why a landscape looks so much better in a contracting
mirror or in a *camera obscura*, than it is in reality. The
same effect is produced by distance in time. The scenes
and events of long ago and the persons who took part in
them, wear a charming aspect to the eye of memory, which
sees only the outlines and takes no note of disagreeable
details. The present enjoys no such advantage, and so it
always seems defective.

And again as regards space, small objects close to us look
big. and if they are very close, we may be able to see nothing else, but when we go a little way off, they become
minute and invisible. It is the same again, as regards
time. The little incidents and accidents of every day fill
us with emotion, anxiety, annoyance, passion, as long as
they are close to us, when they appear so big, so important,
so serious; but as soon as they are borne down the restless
stream of time, they lose what significance they had; we

think no more of them and soon forget them altogether. They were big only because they were near.

___

Joy and sorrow are not ideas of the mind, but affections of the will, and so they do not lie in the domain of memory. We cannot recall our joys and sorrows; by which I mean that we cannot renew them. We can recall only the ideas that accompanied them; and, in particular, the things we were led to say; and these form a gauge of our feelings at the time. Hence our memory of joys and sorrows is always imperfect, and they become a matter of indifference to us as soon as they are over. This explains the vanity of the attempt, which we sometimes make, to revive the pleasures and the pains of the past. Pleasure and pain are essentially an affair of the will, and the will, as such, is not possessed of memory, which is a function of the intellect; and this in its turn gives out and takes in nothing but thoughts and ideas, which are not here in question.

It is a curious fact that in bad days we can very vividly recall the good time that is now no more; but that in good days, we have only a very cold and imperfect memory of the bad.

___

We have a much better memory for actual objects or pictures than for mere ideas. Hence a good imagination makes it easier to learn languages; for by its aid, the new word is at once united with the actual object to which it refers; whereas, if there is no imagination, it is simply put on a parallel with the equivalent word in the mother tongue.

Mnemonics should not only mean the art of keeping something indirectly in the memory by the use of some direct pun or witticism; it should, rather, be applied to a systematic theory of memory, and explain its several attributes by reference both to its real nature, and to the relation in which these attributes stand to one another.

___

There are moments in life when our senses obtain a higher and rarer degree of clearness, apart from any particular occasion for it in the nature of our surroundings;

and explicable, rather, on physiological grounds alone, as the result of some enhanced state of susceptibility, working from within outward. Such moments remain indelibly impressed upon the memory and preserve themselves in their individuality entire. We can assign no reason for it, nor explain why this among so many thousand moments like it should be specially remembered. It seems as much a matter of chance as when single specimens of a whole race of animals now extinct are discovered in the layers of a rock; or when, on opening a book, we light upon an insect accidentally crushed within the leaves. Memories of that kind are always sweet and pleasant.

———

It occasionally happens that, for no particular reason, long-forgotten scenes suddenly start up in the memory. This may in many cases be due to the action of some hardly perceptible odor, which accompanied those scenes and now recurs exactly the same as before. For it is well known that the sense of smell is specially effective in awaking memories, and that in general it does not require much to rouse a train of ideas. And I may say, in passing, that the sense of sight is connected with the understanding,[*] the sense of hearing with the reason,[†] and, as we see in the present case, the sense of smell with the memory. Touch and taste are more material and dependent upon contact. They have no ideal side.

———

It must also be reckoned among the peculiar attributes of memory that a slight state of intoxication often so greatly enhances the recollection of past times and scenes, that all the circumstances connected with them come back much more clearly than would be possible in a state of sobriety; but that, on the other hand, the recollection of what one said or did while the intoxication lasted, is more than usually imperfect; nay, that if one has been absolutely tipsy, it is gone altogether. We may say, then, that while intoxication enhances the memory for what is past, it allows it to remember little of the present.

———

[*] " Vierfache Wurzel," § 21.

[†] " Parerga," vol. ii., § 311.

Men need some kind of external activity, because they are inactive within. Contrarily, if they are active within, they do not care to be dragged out of themselves; it disturbs and impedes their thoughts in a way that is often most ruinous to them.

I am not surprised that some people are bored when they find themselves alone; for they cannot laugh if they are quite by themselves. The very idea of it seems folly to them.

Are we, then to look upon laughter as merely a signal for others—a mere sign, like a word? What makes it impossible for people to laugh when they are alone is nothing but want of imagination, dullness of mind generally— ἀναισθησία καὶ βραδυτὴς ψυχῆς, as Theophrastus has it.* The lower animals never laugh, either alone or in company. Myson, the misanthropist, was once surprised by one of these people as he was laughing to himself. "Why do you laugh?" he asked; "there is no one with you." That is just why I am laughing," said Myson.

Natural gesticulation, such as commonly accompanies any lively talk, is a language of its own, more widespread, even, than the language of words—so far, I mean, as it is independent of words and alike in all nations. It is true that nations make use of it in proportion as they are vivacious, and that in particular cases, among the Italians, for, instance, it is supplemented by certain peculiar gestures which are merely conventional, and therefore possessed of nothing more than a local value.

In the universal use made of it, gesticulation has some analogy with logic and grammar, in that it has to do with the form, rather than with the matter, of conversation; but on the other hand it is distinguishable from them by the fact that it has more of a moral than of an intellectual bearing; in other words, it reflects the movements of the will. As an accompaniment of conversation it is like the bass of a melody; and if, as in music, it keeps true to the progress of the treble, it serves to heighten the effect.

---

* "Characters," c. 27.

In a conversation, the gesture depends upon the form in which the subject-matter is conveyed; and it is interesting to observe that, whatever that subject-matter may be, with a recurrence of the form, the very same gesture is repeated. So if I happen to see—from my window, say—two persons carrying on a lively conversation, without my being able to catch a word, I can, nevertheless, understand the general nature of it perfectly well; I mean, the kind of thing that is being said and the form it takes. There is no mistake about it. The speaker is arguing about something, advancing his reasons, then limiting their application, then driving them home and drawing the conclusion in triumph; or he is recounting his experiences, proving perhaps, beyond the shadow of a doubt, how much he has been injured, but bringing the clearest and most damning evidence to show that his opponents were foolish and obstinate people who would not be convinced or else he is telling of the splendid plan he laid, and how he carried it to a successful issue, or perhaps failed because the luck was against him; or, it may be, he is saying that he was completely at a loss to know what to do, or that he was quick in seeing through some trap set for him; and that by insisting on his rights or by applying a little force, he succeeded in frustrating and punishing his enemies; and so on in hundreds of cases of a similar kind.

Strictly speaking, however, what I get from gesticulation alone is an abstract notion of the essential drift of what is being said, and that, too, whether I judge from a moral or an intellectual point of view. It is the quintessence, the true substance of the conversation, and this remains identical, no matter what may have given rise to the conversation, or what it may be about; the relation between the two being that of a general idea or class-name to the individuals which it covers.

As I have said, the most interesting and amusing part of the matter is the complete identity and solidarity of the gestures used to denote the same set of circumstances, even though by people of every different temperament; so that the gestures become exactly like words of a language, alike for every one, and subject only to such small modifications as depend upon variety of accent and education. And yet there can be no doubt but that these standing gestures which every one uses are the result of no convention or collusion. They are original and innate—a true language of nature; consolidated, it may be, by imitation and the influence of custom.

It is well known that it is part of an actor's duty to make a careful study of gesture; and the same thing is true, to a somewhat smaller degree, of a public speaker. This study must consist chiefly in watching others and imitating their movements, for there are no abstract rules fairly applicable to the matter, with the exception of some very general leading principles, such as—to take an example—that the gesture must not follow the word, but rather come immediately before it, by way of announcing its approach and attracting the hearer's attention.

Englishmen entertain a peculiar contempt for gesticulation, and look upon it as something vulgar and undignified. This seems to me a silly prejudice on their part, and the outcome of their general prudery. For here we have a language which nature has given to every one, and which every one understands; and to do away with and forbid it for no better reason than that it is opposed to that much-lauded thing, gentlemanly feeling, is a very questionable proceeding.

ON EDUCATION.

THE human intellect is said to be so constituted that general ideas arise by abstraction from particular observations, and therefore come after them in point of time. If this is what actually occurs, as happens in the case of a man who has to depend solely upon his own experience for what he learns—who has no teacher and no book—such a man knows quite well which of his particular observations belong to and are represented by each of his general ideas. He has a perfect acquaintance with both sides of his experience, and accordingly, he treats everything that comes in his way from a right standpoint. This might be called the natural method of education.

Contrarily, the artificial method is to hear what other people say, to learn and to read, and so to get your head crammed full of general ideas before you have any sort of extended acquaintance with the world as it is, and as you may see it for yourself. You will be told that the particular observations which go to make these general ideas will come to you later on in the course of experience; but until that time arrives, you apply your general ideas wrongly, you judge men and things from a wrong standpoint, you see them in a wrong light, and treat them in a wrong way. So it is that education perverts the mind.

This explains why it so frequently happens that, after a long course of learning and reading, we enter upon the world in our youth, partly with an artless ignorance of things, partly with wrong notions about them; so that our demeanor savors at one moment of a nervous anxiety, at another of a mistaken confidence. The reason of this is simply that our head is full of general ideas which we are now trying to turn to some use, but which we hardly ever apply rightly. This is the result of acting in direct opposition to the natural development of the mind by obtaining general ideas first, and particular observations last: it is putting the cart before the horse. Instead of developing the child's own faculties of discernment, and teaching it to judge and think for itself, the teacher uses all his energies to stuff its head full of the ready-made thoughts of other people. The mistaken views of life, which spring from a false application of general ideas, have afterward to be corrected by long years of experience; and it is seldom that they are wholly corrected. This is why so few men of learning are possessed of common-sense, such as is often to be met with in people who have had no instruction at all.

To acquire a knowledge of the world might be defined as the aim of all education; and it follows from what I have said that special stress should be laid upon beginning to acquire this knowledge at the right end. As I have shown, this means, in the main, that the particular observation of a thing shall precede the general idea of it; further, that narrow and circumscribed ideas shall come before ideas of a wide range. It means, therefore, that the whole system of education shall follow in the steps that must have been taken by the ideas themselves in the course of their formation. But whenever any of these steps are skipped or left out, the instruction is defective, and the ideas obtained are false; and, finally, a distorted view of the world arises.

peculiar to the individual himself—a view such as almost every one entertains for some time, and most men for as long as they live. No one can look into his own mind without seeing that it was only after reaching a very mature age, and in some cases when he least expected it, that he came to a right understanding or a clear view of many matters in his life that, after all, were not very difficult or complicated. Up till then, they were points in his knowledge of the world which were still obscure, due to his having skipped some particular lesson in those early days of his education, whatever it may have been like— whether artificial and conventional or of that natural kind which is based upon individual experience.

It follows that an attempt should be made to find out the strictly natural course of knowledge, so that education may proceed methodically by keeping to it, and that children may become acquainted with the ways of the world, without getting wrong ideas into their heads, which very often cannot be got out again. If this plan were adopted, special care would have to be taken to prevent children from using words without clearly understanding their meaning and application. The fatal tendency to be satisfied with words instead of trying to understand things —to learn phrases by heart, so that they may prove a refuge in time of need, exists, as a rule, even in children; and the tendency lasts on into manhood, making the knowledge of many learned persons to consist in mere verbiage.

However, the main endeavor must always be to let particular observations precede general ideas, and not *vice versâ*, as is usually and unfortunately the case; as though a child should come feet foremost into the world, or a verse be begun by writing down the rhyme! The ordinary method is to imprint ideas and opinions, in the strict sense of the word, prejudices, on the mind of the child, before it has had any but a very few particular observations. It is thus that he afterward comes to view the world and gather experience through the medium of those ready-made ideas, rather than to let his ideas be formed for him out of his own experience of life, as they ought to be.

A man sees a great many things when he looks at the world for himself, and he sees them from many sides; but this method of learning is not nearly so short or so quick as the method which employs abstract ideas and makes hasty generalizations about everything. Experience, therefore, will be a long time in correcting preconceived ideas, or perhaps never bring its task to an end: for wherever a man finds that the aspect of things seems to contradict the general ideas he has formed, he will begin by rejecting the evidence it offers as partial and one-sided; nay, he will shut his eyes to it altogether and deny that it stands in any contradiction at all with his preconceived notions, in order that he may thus preserve them uninjured. So it is that many a man carries about a burden of wrong notions all his life long—crotchets, whims, fancies, prejudices, which at last become fixed ideas. The fact is that he has never tried to form his fundamental ideas for himself out of his own experience of life, his own way of looking at the world, because he has taken over his ideas ready-made from other people; and this it is that makes him—as it makes how many others!—so shallow and superficial.

Instead of that method of instruction, care should be taken to educate children on the natural lines. No idea should ever be established in a child's mind otherwise than by what the child can see for itself, or at any rate it should be verified by the same means; and the result of this would be that the child's ideas, if few, would be well-grounded and accurate. It would learn how to measure things by its own standard rather than by another's; and so it would escape a thousand strange fancies and prejudices, and not need to have them eradicated by the lessons it will subsequently be taught in the school of life. The child would, in this way, have its mind once for all habituated to clear views and thorough-going knowledge: it would use its own judgment and take an unbiased estimate of things.

And, in general, children should not form their notions of what life is like from the copy before they have learned it from the original, to whatever aspect of it their attention may be directed. Instead, therefore, of hastening to place books, and books alone, in their hands, let them be made acquainted, step by step, with things—with the actual circumstances of human life. And above all let care be taken to bring them to a clear and objective view of the world as it is, to educate them always to derive their ideas directly from real life, and to shape them in conformity with it—not to fetch them from other sources, such as books, fairy tales, or what people say—than to apply them ready-made to real life. For this will mean that their heads are full of wrong notions, and that they will either see things in a false light or try in vain to remodel the world to suit their views, and so enter upon false paths; and that, too, whether they are only constructing theories of life or engaged in the actual business of it. It is incredible how much harm is done when the seeds of wrong notions are laid in the mind in those early years, later on to bear a crop of prejudice; for the subsequent lessons which are learned from real life in the world have to be devoted mainly to their extirpation. "To unlearn the evil" was the answer which, according to Diogenes Laertius,* Antisthenes gave, when he was asked what branch of knowledge was most necessary; and we can see what he meant.

No child under the age of fifteen should receive instruction in subjects which may possibly be the vehicle of serious error, such as philosophy, religion, or any other branch of knowledge where it is necessary to take large views; because wrong notions imbibed early can seldom be rooted out, and of all the intellectual faculties, judgment is the last to arrive at maturity. The child should give its attention either to subjects where no error is possible at all, such as mathematics, or to those in which there is no particular danger in making a mistake, such as languages, natural science, history, and so on. And in general, the branches of knowledge which are to be studied at any period of life should be such as the mind is equal to at that period and can perfectly understand. Childhood and youth form the time for collecting materials, for getting a special and thorough knowledge of individual and particular things. In those years it is too early to form views on a large scale; and ultimate explanations must be put off to a later date. The faculty of judgment, which cannot come into play without mature experience, should be left to itself; and care should be taken not to anticipate its action by inculcating prejudice, which will paralyze it forever.

On the other hand, the memory should be specially taxed in youth, since it is then that it is strongest and most tenacious. But in choosing the things that should be com-

* vi. 7.

mitted to memory the utmost care and forethought must
be exercised; as lessons well learned in youth are never forgotten. This precious soil must therefore be cultivated so
as to bear as much fruit as possible. If you think how
deeply rooted in your memory are those persons whom you
knew in the first twelve years of your life, how indelible the
impression made upon you by the events of those years,
how clear your recollection of most of the things that
happened to you then, most of what was told or taught you,
it will seem a natural thing to take the susceptibility and
tenacity of the mind at that period as the groundwork of
education. This may be done by a strict observance of
method, and a systematic regulation of the impressions
which the mind is to receive.

But the years of youth alloted to man are short, and
memory is, in general, bound within narrow limits; still more
so, the memory of any one individual. Since this is the
case, it is all-important to fill the memory with what is
essential and material in any branch of knowledge, to the
exclusion of everything else. This decision as to what is
essential and material should rest with the master-minds in
every department of thought; their choice should be made
after the most mature deliberation, and the outcome of it
fixed and determined. Such a choice would have to proceed by sifting the things which it is necessary and important for a man to know in general, and then, necessary and
important for him to know in any particular business or
calling. Knowledge of the first kind would have to be
classified, after an encyclopedic fashion, in graduated
courses, adapted to the degree of general culture which a
man may be expected to have in the circumstances in
which he is placed; beginning with a course limited to the
necessary requirements of primary education, and extending upward to the subjects treated of in all the branches
of philosophical thought. The regulation of the second
kind of knowledge would be left to those who had shown
genuine mastery in the several departments into which it
is divided; and the whole system would provide an elabo-
ate rule or canon for intellectual education, which would,
of course, have to be revised every ten years. Some such
arrangement as this would employ the youthful power of
the memory to best advantage, and supply excellent working material to the faculty of judgment, when it made its
appearance later on.

A man's knowledge may be said to be mature, in other words, it has reached the most complete state of perfection to which he, as an individual, is capable of bringing it, when an exact correspondence is established between the whole of his abstract ideas and the things he has actually perceived for himself. This will mean that each of his abstract ideas rests, directly or indirectly, upon a basis of observation, which alone endows it with any real value; and also that he is able to place every observation he makes under the right abstract idea which belongs to it. Maturity is the work of experience alone; and therefore it requires time. The knowledge we derive from our own observation is usually distinct from that which we acquire through the medium of abstract ideas; the one coming to us in the natural way, the other by what people tell us, and the course of instruction we receive, whether it is good or bad. The result is, that in youth there is generally very little agreement or correspondence between our abstract ideas, which are merely phrases fixed in the mind, and that real knowledge which we have obtained by our own observation. It is only later on that a gradual approach takes place between these two kinds of knowledge, accompanied by a mutual correction of error; and knowledge is not mature until this coalition is accomplished. This maturity or perfection of knowledge is something quite independent of another kind of perfection, which may be of a high or a low order—the perfection, I mean, to which a man may bring his own individual faculties; which is measured, not by any correspondence between the two kinds of knowledge, but by the degree of intensity which each kind attains.

For the practical man the most needful thing is to acquire an accurate and profound knowledge of the ways of the world. But this, though the most needful, is also the most wearisome of all studies, as a man may reach a great age without coming to the end of his task; whereas, in the domain of the sciences, he masters the more important facts when he is still young. In acquiring that knowledge of the world, it is while he is a novice, namely, in boyhood and in youth, that the first and hardest lessons are put before him; but it often happens that even in later years there is still a great deal to be learned.

The study is difficult enough in itself; but the difficulty

is doubled by novels, which represent a state of things in life and the world, such as, in fact, does not exist. Youth is credulous, and accepts these views of life, which then become part and parcel of the mind; so that, instead of a merely negative condition of ignorance, you have positive error—a whole tissue of false notions to start with; and at a later date these actually spoil the schooling of experience, and put a wrong construction on the lessons it teaches. If, before this, the youth had no light at all to guide him, he is now misled by a will-o-the-wisp; still more often is this the case with a girl. They have both had a false view of things foisted on to them by reading novels; and expectations have been aroused which can never be fulfilled. This generally exercises a baneful influence on their whole life. In this respect those whose youth has allowed them no time or opportunity for reading novels—those who work with their hands and the like—are in a position of decided advantage There are a few novels to which this reproach cannot be addressed—nay, which have an effect the contrary of bad. First and foremost, to give an example, "Gil Blas," and the other works of Le Sage (or rather their Spanish originals); further, "The Vicar of Wakefield," and, to some extent, Sir Walter Scott's novels. "Don Quixote" may be regarded as a satirical exhibition of the error to which I am referring.

ON WOMEN.

SCHILLER'S poem in honor of women, "Würde der Frauen," is the result of much careful thought, and it appeals to the reader by its antithetic style and its use of contrast; but as an expression of the true praise which should be accorded to them, it is, I think, inferior to these few words of Jouy's: "Without women, the beginning of our life would be helpless; the middle, devoid of pleasure; and the end, of consolation." The same thing is more feelingly expressed by Byron in "Sardanapalus:"

> "The very first
> Of human life must spring from woman's breast,
> Your first small words are taught you from her lips,
> Your first tears quench'd by her, and your last sighs

Too often breathed out in a woman's hearing,
When men have shrunk from the ignoble care
Of watching the last hour of him who led them."
(Act I. Scene 2.)

These two passages indicate the right standpoint for the appreciation of women.

You need only look at the way in which she is formed, to see that woman is not meant to undergo great labor, whether of the mind or of the body. She pays the debt of life not by what she does, but by what she suffers; by the pains of child-bearing and care for the child, and by submission to her husband, to whom she should be a patient and cheering companion. The keenest sorrows and joys are not for her, nor is she called upon to display a great deal of strength. The current of her life should be more gentle, peaceful and trivial than man's, without being essentially happier or unhappier.

Women are directly fitted for acting as the nurses and teachers of our early childhood by the fact that they are themselves childish, frivolous and short-sighted; in a word, they are big children all their life long—a kind of intermediate stage between the child and the full-grown man, who is man in the strict sense of the word. See how a girl will fondle a child for days together, dance with it and sing to it; and then think what a man, with the best will in the world, could do if he were put in her place.

With young girls nature seems to have had in view what, in the language of the drama, is called a striking effect; as for a few years she dowers them with a wealth of beauty and is lavish in her gift of charm, at the expense of all the rest of their life; so that during those years they may capture the fantasy of some man to such a degree, that he is hurried away into undertaking the honorable care of them, in some form or other, as long as they live—a step for which there would not appear to be any sufficient warranty if reason only directed his thoughts. Accordingly, Nature has equipped woman, as she does all her creatures, with the weapons and implements requisite for the safeguarding of her existence, and for just as long as it is necessary for her to have them. Here, as elsewhere, Nature proceeds with her usual economy; for just as the female ant, after fecundation, loses her wings, which are then superfluous, nay, actually a danger to the business of breeding; so, after giving birth to one or two children, a woman generally loses her beauty; probably, indeed, for similar reasons.

And so we find that young girls, in their hearts, look upon domestic affairs or work of any kind as of secondary importance, if not actually as a mere jest. The only business that really claims their earnest attention is love, making conquests, and everything connected with this—dress, dancing, and so on.

The nobler and more perfect a thing is, the later and slower it is in arriving at maturity. A man reaches the maturity of his reasoning powers and mental faculties hardly before the age of twenty-eight; a woman, at eighteen. And then, too, in the case of woman, it is only reason of a sort—very niggard in its dimensions. That is why women remain children their whole life long; never seeing anything but what is quite close to them, cleaving to the present moment, taking appearance for reality, and preferring trifles to matters of the first importance. For it is by virtue of his reasoning faculty that man does not live in the present only, like the brute, but looks about him and considers the past and the future; and this is the origin of prudence, as well as of that care and anxiety which so many people exhibit. Both the advantages and the disadvantages which this involves, are shared in by the woman to a smaller extent because of her weaker power of reasoning. She may, in fact, be described as intellectually shortsighted, because, while she has an intuitive understanding of what lies quite close to her, her field of vision is narrow and does not reach to what is remote: so that things which are absent, or past, or to come, have much less effect upon women than upon men. This is the reason why women are more often inclined to be extravagant, and sometimes carry their inclination to a length that borders upon madness. In their hearts women think that it is men's business to earn money and theirs to spend it—if possible during their husband's life, but, at any rate, after his death. The very fact that their husband hands them over his earnings for purposes of housekeeping, strengthens them in this belief.

However many disadvantages all this may involve, there is at least this to be said in its favor; that the woman lives more in the present than the man, and that, if the present is at all tolerable, she enjoys it more eagerly. This is the source of that cheerfulness which is peculiar to woman, fitting her to amuse man in his hours of recreation, and, in case of need, to console him when he is borne down by the weight of his cares.

It is by no means a bad plan to consult women in matters of difficulty, as the Germans used to do in ancient times; for their way of looking at things is quite different from ours, chiefly in the fact that they like to take the shortest way to their goal, and, in general, manage to fix their eyes upon what lies before them; while we, as a rule, see far beyond it, just because it is in front of our noses. In cases like this, we need to be brought back to the right standpoint, so as to recover the near and simple view.

Then, again, women are decidedly more sober in their judgment than we are, so that they do not see more in things than is really there; while, if our passions are aroused, we are apt to see things in an exaggerated way, or imagine what does not exist.

The weakness of their reasoning faculty also explains why it is that women show more sympathy for the unfortunate than men do, and so treat them with more kindness and interest; and why it is that, on the contrary, they are inferior to men in point of justice, and less honorable and conscientious. For it is just because their reasoning power is weak that present circumstances have such a hold over them, and those concrete things which lie directly before their eyes exercise a power which is seldom counteracted to any extent by abstract principles of thought, by fixed rules of conduct, firm resolutions, or, in general, by consideration for the past and the future, or regard for what is absent and remote. Accordingly, they possess the first and main elements that go to make a virtuous character, but they are deficient in those secondary qualities which are often a necessary instrument in the formation of it. *

Hence it will be found that the fundamental fault of the female character is that it has no sense of justice. This is mainly due to the fact, already mentioned, that women are defective in the powers of reasoning and

---

* In this respect they may be compared to an animal organism which contains a liver but no gall-bladder. Here let me refer to what I have said in my treatise on "The Foundation of Morals," § 17.

deliberation; but it is also traceable to the position which Nature has assigned to them as the weaker sex. They are dependent, not upon strength, but upon craft; and hence their instinctive capacity for cunning, and their ineradicable tendency to say what is not true. For as lions are provided with claws and teeth, and elephants and boars with tusks, bulls with horns, and the cuttle fish with its cloud of inky fluid, so Nature has equipped woman, for her defense and protection, with the arts of dissimulation; and all the power which Nature has conferred upon man in the shape of physical strength and reason, has been bestowed upon women in this form. Hence dissimulation is innate in woman, and almost as much a quality of the stupid as of the clever. It is as natural for them to make use of it on every occasion as it is for those animals to employ their means of defense when they are attacked; they have a feeling that in doing so they are only within their rights. Therefore a woman who is perfectly truthful and not given to dissimulation is perhaps an impossibility, and for this very reason they are so quick at seeing through dissimulation in others that it is not a wise thing to attempt it with them. But this fundamental defect which I have stated, with all that it entails, gives rise to falsity, faithlessness, treachery, ingratitude, and so on. Perjury in a court of justice is more often committed by women than by men. It may, indeed, be generally questioned whether women ought to be sworn at all. From time to time one finds repeated cases everywhere of ladies, who want for nothing, taking things from shop-counters, when no one is looking, and making off with them.

Nature has appointed that the propagation of the species shall be the business of men who are young, strong and handsome; so that the race may not degenerate. This is the firm will and purpose of Nature in regard to the species, and it finds its expression in the passions of women. There is no law that is older or more powerful than this. Woe, then, to the man who sets up claims and interests that will conflict with it; whatever he may say and do, they will be unmercifully crushed at the first serious encounter. For the innate rule that governs women's conduct, though it is secret and unformulated, nay, unconscious in its working, is this: " We are justified in deceiving those who think they have acquired rights over the species by paying little attention to the individual, that is, to us. The constitution and, therefore, the welfare of the species have been placed in our hands and committed to our care, through the control we obtain over the next generation, which proceeds from us; let us discharge our duties conscientiously." But women have no abstract knowledge of this leading principle; they are conscious of it only as a concrete fact; and they have no other method of giving expression to it than the way in which they act when the opportunity arrives. And then their conscience does not trouble them so much as we fancy; for in the darkest recesses of their heart, they are aware that in committing a breach of their duty toward the individual, they have all the better fulfilled their duty towards the species, which is infinitely greater.*

And since women exist in the main solely for the propagation of the species, and are not destined for anything else, they live, as a rule, more for the species than for the individual, and in their hearts take the affairs of the species more seriously than those of the individual. This gives their whole life and being a certain levity; the general bent of their character is in a direction fundamentally different from that of man; and it is this which produces that discord in married life which is so frequent, and almost the normal state.

The natural feeling between men is mere indifference, but between women it is actual enmity. The reason of this is that trade-jealousy—*odium figulinum*—which, in the case of men, does not go beyond the confines of their own particular pursuit; but, with women, embraces the whole sex; since they have only one kind of business. Even when they meet in the street, women look at one another like Guelphs and Ghibellines. And it is a patent fact that when two women make first acquaintance with each other, they behave with more constraint and dissimulation than two men would show in a like case; and hence it is that an exchange of compliments between two women is a much more ridiculous proceeding than between two men. Further, while a man will, as a general rule, always

---

* A more detailed discussion of the matter in question may be found in my chief work, "Die Welt als Wille und Vorstellung," vol. ii., ch. 44.

preserve a certain amount of consideration and humanity in speaking to others, even to those who are in a very inferior position, it is intolerable to see how proudly and disdainfully a fine lady will generally behave toward one who is in a lower social rank (I do not mean a woman who is in her service), whenever she speaks to her. The reason of this may be that, with women, differences of rank are much more precarious than with us; because, while a hundred considerations carry weight in our case, in theirs there is only one, namely, with which man they have found favor; as also that they stand in much nearer relations with one another than men do, in consequence of the one-sided nature of their calling. This makes them endeavor to lay stress upon differences of rank.

It is only the man whose intellect is clouded by his sexual impulses that could give the name of the fair sex to that undersized, narrow-shouldered, broad-hipped, and short-legged race; for the whole beauty of the sex is bound up with this impulse. Instead of calling them beautiful, there would be more warrant for describing women as the unæsthetic sex. Neither for music, nor for poetry, nor for fine art, have they really and truly any sense or susceptibility; it is a mere mockery if they make a pretense of it in order to assist their endeavor to please. Hence, as a result of this, they are incapable of taking a purely objective interest in everything; and the reason of it seems to me to be as follows. A man tries to acquire direct mastery over things, either by understanding them, or by forcing them to do his will. But a woman is always and everywhere reduced to obtaining this mastery indirectly, namely through a man; and whatever direct mastery she may have is entirely confined to him. And so it lies in woman's nature to look upon everything only as a means for conquering man; and if she takes an interest in anything else, it is simulated—a mere roundabout way of gaining her ends by coquetry, and feigning what she does not feel. Hence even Rousseau declared: "Women have, in general, no love of any art; they have no proper knowledge of any; and they have no genius." *

No one who sees at all below the surface can have failed to remark the same thing. You need only observe the

---

* Lettre à d'Alembert. Note xx.

kind of attention women bestow upon a concert, an opera, or a play—the childish simplicity, for example, with which they keep on chattering during the finest passages in the greatest masterpieces. If it is true that the Greeks excluded women from their theaters, they were quite right in what they did; at any rate you would have been able to hear what was said upon the stage. In our day, besides, or in lieu of saying, "Let a woman keep silence in the church," it would be much to the point to say, "Let a woman keep silence in the theater." This might, perhaps, be put up in big letters on the curtain.

And you cannot expect anything else of women if you consider that the most distinguished intellects among the whole sex have never managed to produce a single achievement in the fine arts that is really great, genuine, and original, or given to the world any work of permanent value in any sphere. This is most strikingly shown in regard to painting, where mastery of technique is at least as much within their power as within ours—and hence they are diligent in cultivating it; but still, they have not a single great painting to boast of, just because they are deficient in that objectivity of mind which is so directly indispensable in painting. They never get beyond a subjective point of view. It is quite in keeping with this that ordinary women have no real susceptibility for art at all; for nature proceeds in strict sequence—*non facit saltum.* And Huarte * in his "Examen de ingenios para las scienzias"—a book which has been famous for three hundred years—denies women the possession of all the higher faculties. The case is not altered by particular and partial exceptions; taken as a whole, women are, and remain, thorough-going Philistines, and quite incurable. Hence, with that absurd arrangement which allows them to share the rank and title of their husbands, they are a constant stimulus to his ignoble ambitions. And, further, it is just because they are Philistines that modern society, where they take the lead and set the tone, is in such a bad way. Napoleon's saying—that "women have no rank"— should be adopted as the right standpoint in determining

---

* *Translator's Note.*—Juan Huarte (1520?–1590) practiced as a physician at Madrid. The work cited by Schopenhauer is well known, and has been translated into many languages.

their position in society; and as regards their other qualities, Chamfort * makes the very true remark: "They are made to trade with our own weaknesses and our follies, but not with our reason. The sympathies that exist between them and men are skin-deep only, and do not touch the mind or the feelings or the character."

They form the *sexus sequior*—the second sex, inferior in every respect to the first; their infirmities should be treated with consideration; but to show them great reverence is extremely ridiculous, and lowers us in their eyes. When nature made two divisions of the human race, she did not draw the line exactly through the middle. These divisions are polar and opposed to each other, it is true; but the difference between them is not qualitative merely, it is also quantitative.

This is just the view which the ancients took of woman, and the view which people in the East take now; and their judgment as to her proper position is much more correct than ours, with our old French notions of gallantry and our preposterous system of reverence—that highest product of Teutonico-Christian stupidity. These notions have served only to make women more arrogant and overbearing: so that one is occasionally reminded of the holy apes in Benares, who in the consciousness of their sanctity and inviolable position, think they can do exactly as they please.

But in the West, the women, and especially the "lady," finds herself in a false position; for woman, rightly called by the ancients *sexus sequior* is by no means fit to be the object of our honor and veneration, or to hold her head higher than man and be on equal terms with him. The consequences of this false position are sufficiently obvious. Accordingly, it would be a very desirable thing if this Number Two of the human race were in Europe also relegated to her natural place, and an end put to that lady-nuisance, which not only moves all Asia to laughter, but would have been ridiculed by Greece and Rome as well. It is impossible to calculate the good effects which such a change would bring about in our social, civil and political arrangements. There would be no necessity for the Salic law: it would be a superfluous truism. In Europe the "lady"

---

* *Translator's Note.*—See "Counsels and Maxims," p. 12, note.

strictly so-called, is a being who should not exist all all; she should be either a housewife or a girl who hopes to become one; and she should be brought up, not to be arrogant, but to be thrifty and submissive. It is just because there are such people as "ladies" in Europe that the women of the lower classes, that is to say, the great majority of the sex, are much more unhappy than they are in the East. And even Lord Byron says: "Thought of the state of women under the ancient Greeks—convenient enough. Present state, a remnant of the barbarism of the chivalric and the feudal ages—artificial and unnatural. They ought to mind home—and be well fed and clothed—but not mixed in society. Well educated, too, in religion—but to read neither poetry nor politics—nothing but books of piety and cookery. Music—drawing—dancing—also a little gardening and plowing now and then. I have seen them mending the roads in Epirus with good success. Why not, as well as hay-making and milking?"

The laws of marriage prevailing in Europe consider the woman as the equivalent of the man—start, that is to say, from a wrong position. In our part of the world where monogamy is the rule, to marry means to have one's rights and double one's duties. Now, when the laws gave women equal rights with man, they ought to have also endowed her with a masculine intellect. But the fact is, that just in proportion as the honors and privileges which the laws accord to women, exceed the amount which Nature gives, is there a diminution in the number of women who really participate in these privileges; and all the remainder are deprived of their natural rights by just so much as is given to the others over and above their share. For the institution of monogamy, and the laws of marriage which it entails, bestow upon the woman an unnatural position of privilege, by considering her throughout as the full equivalent of the man, which is by no means the case; and seeing this, men who are shrewd and prudent very often scruple to make so great a sacrifice and to acquiesce in so unfair an arrangement.

Consequently, while among polygamous nations every woman is provided for, where monogamy prevails the number of married women is limited; and there remains over a large number of women without stay or support, who, in the upper classes, vegetate as useless old maids and in the lower succumb to hard work for which they are not suited; or else become *filles de joie*, whose life is as destitute of joy as it is of honor. But under the circumstances they become a necessity; and their position is openly recognized as serving the special end of warding off temptation from those women favored by fate, who have found, or may hope to find, husbands. In London alone there are eighty thousand prostitutes. What are they but the women, who, under the institution of monogamy, have come off worst? Theirs is a direful fate: they are human sacrifices offered up on the altar of monogamy. The women whose wretched position is here described are the inevitable set-off to the European lady with her arrogance and pretension. Polygamy is therefore a real benefit to the female sex if it is taken as a whole. And, from another point of view, there is no true reason why a man whose wife suffers from chronic illness, or remains barren, or has gradually become too old for him, should not take a second. The motives which induce so many people to become converts to Mormonism * appear to be just those which militate against the unnatural institution of monogamy.

Moreover, the bestowal of unnatural rights upon women has imposed upon them unnatural duties, and, nevertheless, a breach of these duties makes them unhappy. Let me explain. A man may often think that his social or financial position will suffer if he marries, unless he makes some brilliant alliance. His desire will then be to win a woman of his own choice under conditions other than those of marriage, such as will secure her position and that of the children. However fair, reasonable, fit and proper these conditions may be, and the woman consents by foregoing that undue amount of privilege which marriage alone can bestow, she to some extent loses her honor, because marriage is the basis of civic society; and she will lead an unhappy life, since human nature is so constituted that we pay an attention to the opinion of other people which is out of all proportionate to its value. On the other hand, if she does not consent, she runs the risk either of having to be given in marriage to a man whom she does not like, or of being landed high and dry as an old maid;

---

* *Translator's Note.*—The Mormons have recently given up polygamy, and received the American franchise in its stead.

for the period during which she has a chance of being settled for life is very short. And in view of this aspect of the institution of monogamy, Thomasius' profoundly learned treatise, "de Concubinatu," is well worth reading; for it shows that, among all nations and in all ages, down to the Lutheran Reformation, concubinage was permitted; nay, that it was an institution which was to a certain extent actually recognized by law, and attended with no dishonor. It was only the Lutheran Reformation that degraded it from this position. It was seen to be a further justification for the marriage of the clergy; and then, after that the Catholic Church did not dare to remain behindhand in the matter.

There is no use arguing about polygamy; it must be taken as *de facto* existing everywhere, and the only question is as to how it shall be regulated. Where are there, then, any real monogamists? We all live, at any rate, for a time, and most of us, always, in polygamy. And so, since every man needs many women, there is nothing fairer than to allow him, nay, to make it incumbent upon him, to provide for many women. This will reduce woman to her true and natural position as a subordinate being; and the lady—that monster of European civilization and Teutonico-Christian stupidity—will disappear from the world, leaving only women, but no more unhappy women, of whom Europe is now full.

In India no woman is ever independent, but in accordance with the law of Manu,* she stands under the control of her father, her husband, her brother or her son. It is, to be sure, a revolting thing that a widow should immolate herself upon her husband's funeral pyre; but it is also revolting that she should spend her husband's money with her paramours—the money for which he toiled his whole life long, in the consoling belief that he was providing for his children. Happy are those who have kept the middle course—*medium tenuere beati.*

The first love of a mother for her child is, with the lower animals as with men, of a purely instinctive character, and so it ceases when the child is no longer in a physically helpless condition. After that, the first love should give way to one that is based on habit and reason; but this

---

* Ch. V., v. 148.

often fails to make its appearance, especially where the mother did not love the father. The love of a father for his child is of a different order, and more likely to last; because it has its foundation in the fact that in the child he recognizes his own inner self; that is to say, his love for it is metaphysical in its origin.

In almost all nations, whether of the ancient or the modern world, even among the Hottentots, * property is inherited by the male descendants alone; it is only in Europe that a departure has taken place; but not among the nobility, however. That the property which has cost men long years of toil and effort, and been won with so much difficulty, should afterward come into the hands of women, who then, in their lack of reason, squander it in a short time, or otherwise fool it away, is a grievance and a wrong, as serious as it is common, which should be prevented by limiting the right of women to inherit. In my opinion, the best arrangement would be that by which women, whether widows or daughters, should never receive anything beyond the interest for life on property secured by mortgage, and in no case the property itself, or the capital, except where all male descendants fail. The people who make money are men, not women; and it follows from this that women are neither justified in having unconditional possession of it, nor fit persons to be entrusted with its administration. When wealth, in any true sense of the word, that is to say, funds, houses or land, is to go to them as an inheritance, they should never be allowed the free disposition of it. In their case a guardian should always be appointed; and hence they should never be given the free control of their own children, wherever it can be avoided. The vanity of women, even though it should not prove to be greater than that of men, has this much danger in it, that it takes an entirely material direction. They are vain, I mean, of their personal beauty, and then of finery, show and magnificence. That is just why they are so much in their element in society. It is this, too which makes them so inclined to be extravagant, all the more as their reasoning power is low. Accordingly we find

---

* Leroy. " Lettres philosophiques sur l'intelligence et la perfectibilité des animaux, avec quelques lettres sur l'homme," p. 298, Paris. 1802.

an ancient writer describing women as in general of an extravagant nature—Γυνὴ τὸ σύνολον ἔστι δαπανηρὸν φύσει.*
But with men vanity often takes the direction of non-material advantages, such as intellect, learning, courage.

In the Politics † Aristotle explains the great disadvantage which accrued to the Spartans from the fact that they conceded too much to their women, by giving them the right of inheritance and dower, and a great amount of independence; and he shows how much this contributed to Sparta's fall. May it not be the case in France that the influence of women, which went on increasing steadily from the time of Louis XIII., was to blame for that gradual corruption of the court and the government, which brought about the revolution of 1789, of which all subsequent disturbances have been the fruit? However that may be, the false position which women occupy, demonstrated as it is, in the most glaring way, by the institution of the lady, is a fundamental defect in our social scheme, and this defect, proceeding from the very heart of it, must spread its baneful influence in all directions.

That woman is by nature meant to obey may be seen by the fact that every woman who is placed in the unnatural position of complete independence, immediately attaches herself to some man, by whom she allows herself to be guided and ruled. It is because she needs a lord and master. If she is young, it will be a lover; if she is old, a priest.

ON NOISE.

KANT wrote a treatise on "The Vital Powers." I should prefer to write a dirge for them. The superabundant display of vitality, which takes the form of knocking, hammering, and tumbling things about, has proved a daily torment to me all my life long. There are people, it is true—nay, a great many people—who smile at such things, because they are not sensitive to noise; but they are just the very people who are also not sensitive to argument, or thought, or poetry, or art, in a word, to any kind of intel-

---

* Brunck's "Gnomici poetae graeci," v. 115.

† Bk. I., ch. 9.

lectual influence. The reason of it is that the tissue of
their brains is of a very rough and coarse quality. On the
other hand, noise is a torture to intellectual people. In
the biographies of almost all great writers, or wherever
else their personal utterances are recorded, I find complaints
about it; in the case of Kant, for instance, Goethe, Lichtenberg, Jean Paul; and if it should happen that any
writer has omitted to express himself on the matter, it is
only for want of an opportunity.

This aversion to noise I should explain as follows: If
you cut up a large diamond into little bits, it will entirely
lose the value it had as a whole; and an army divided up
into small bodies of soldiers, loses all its strength. So a great
intellect sinks to the level of an ordinary one, as soon as
it is interrupted and disturbed, its attention distracted and
drawn off from the matter in hand; for its superiority depends upon its power of concentration—of bringing all its
strength to bear upon one theme, in the same way as a
concave mirror collects into one point all the rays of light
that strike upon it. Noisy interruption is a hindrance to
this concentration. That is why distinguished minds have
always shown such an extreme dislike to disturbance in
any form, as something that breaks in upon and distracts
their thoughts. Above all have they been averse to that
violent interruption that comes from noise. Ordinary
people are not much put out by anything of the sort. The
most sensible and intelligent of all the nations in Europe
lays down the rule, "Never interrupt!" as the eleventh com-
mandment. Noise is the most impertinent of all forms of
interruption. It is not only an interruption, but also a
disruption of thought. Of course, where there is nothing
to interrupt, noise will not be so particularly painful.
Occasionally it happens that some slight but constant
noise continues to bother, and distract me for a time before I become distinctly conscious of it. All I feel is a
steady increase in the labor of thinking—just as though I
were trying to walk with a weight on my foot. At last I
find out what it is.

Let me now, however, pass from genus to species. The
most inexcusable and disgraceful of all noises is the crack
ing of whips—a truly infernal thing when it is done in the
narrow resounding streets of a town. I denounce it as
making a peaceful life impossible; it puts an end to all

quiet thought. That this cracking of whips should be allowed at all seems to me to show in the clearest way how senseless and thoughtless is the nature of mankind. No one with anything like an idea in his head can avoid a feeling of actual pain at this sudden, sharp crack, which paralyzes the brain, rends the thread of reflection, and murders thought. Every time this noise is made, it must disturb a hundred people who are applying their minds to business of some sort, no matter how trivial it may be; while on the thinker its effect is woeful and disastrous, cutting his thoughts asunder, much as the executioner's axe severs the head from the body. No sound, be it ever so shrill, cuts so sharply into the brain as this cursed cracking of whips; you feel the sting of the lash right inside your head; and it affects the brain in the same way as touch affects a sensitive plant, and for the same length of time.

With all due respect for the most holy doctrine of utility, I really cannot see why a fellow who is taking away a wagon-load of gravel or dung should thereby obtain the right to kill in the bud the thoughts which may happen to be springing up in ten thousand heads—the number he will disturb one after another in half an hour's drive through the town. Hammering, the barking of dogs, and the crying of children are horrible to hear; but your only genuine assassin of thought is the crack of a whip; it exists for the purpose of destroying every pleasant moment of quiet thought that any one may now and then enjoy. If the driver had no other way of urging on his horse than by making this most abominable of all noises, it would be excusable; but quite the contrary is the case. This cursed cracking of whips is not only unnecessary, but even useless. Its aim is to produce an effect upon the intelligence of the horse; but through the constant abuse of it, the animal becomes habituated to the sound, which falls upon blunted feelings and produces no effect at all. The horse does not go any the faster for it. You have a remarkable example of this in the ceaseless cracking of his whip on the part of a cab-driver, while he is proceeding at a slow pace on the look-out for a fare. If he were to give his horse the slightest touch with the whip, it would have much more effect. Supposing, however, that it were absolutely necessary to crack the whip in order to keep the horse constantly in mind of its presence, it would be enough to make the hundredth part of the noise. For it is a well-known fact that, in regard to sight and hearing, animals are sensitive to even the faintest indications; they are alive to things that we can scarcely perceive. The most surprising instances of this are furnished by trained dogs and canary-birds.

It is obvious, therefore, that here we have to do with an act of pure wantonness; nay, with an impudent defiance offered to those members of the community who work with their heads by those who work with their hands. That such infamy should be tolerated in a town is a piece of barbarity and iniquity, all the more as it could easily be remedied by a police-notice to the effect that every lash shall have a knot at the end of it. There can be no harm in drawing the attention of the mob to the fact that the classes above them work with their heads, for any kind of headwork is mortal anguish to the man in the street. A fellow who rides through the narrow alleys of a populous town with unemployed post-horses or cart-horses, and keeps on cracking a whip several yards long with all his might, deserves there and then to stand down and receive five really good blows with a stick. All the philanthropists in the world, and all the legislators, meeting to advocate and decree the total abolition of corporal punishment, will never persuade me to the contrary. There is something even more disgraceful than what I have just mentioned. Often enough you may see a carter walking along the street quite alone, without any horses, and still cracking away incessantly; so accustomed has the wretch become to it in consequence of the unwarrantable toleration of this practice. A man's body and the needs of his body are now everywhere treated with a tender indulgence. Is the thinking mind then, to be the only thing that is never to obtain the slightest measure of consideration or protection, to say nothing of respect? Carters, porters, messengers—these are the beasts of burden among mankind; by all means let them be treated justly, fairly, indulgently, and with forethought; but they must not be permitted to stand in the way of the higher endeavors of humanity by wantonly making a noise. How many great and splendid thoughts, I should like to know, have been lost to the world by the crack of a whip? If I had the upper hand,

I should soon produce in the heads of these people an indissoluble association of ideas between cracking a whip and getting a whipping.

Let us hope that the more intelligent and refined among the nations will make a beginning in this matter, and then that the Germans may take example by it and follow suit.* Meanwhile, I may quote what Thomas Hood says of them: † " For a musical nation, they are the most noisy I ever met with". That they are so is due to the fact, not that they are more fond of making a noise than other people—they would deny it if you asked them—but that their senses are obtuse; consequently, when they hear a noise, it does not affect them much. It does not disturb them in reading or thinking, simply because they do not think; they only smoke, which is their substitute for thought. The general toleration of unnecessary noise—the slamming of doors, for instance, a very unmannerly and ill-bred thing— is direct evidence that the prevailing habit of mind is dullness and lack of thought. In Germany it seems as though care were taken that no one should ever think for mere noise—to mention one form of it, the way in which drumming goes on for no purpose at all.

Finally, as regards the literature of the subject treated of in this chapter, I have only one work to recommend, but it is a good one. I refer to a poetical epistle in *terzo rimo* by the famous painter Bronzino: entitled " De Romori, a Messer Luca Martini." It gives a detailed description of the torture to which people are put by the various noises of a small Italian town. Written in a tragi-comic style, it is very amusing. The epistle may be found in " Opere burlesche del Berni, Aretino et altri." Vol. II. p. 258; apparently published in Utrecht in 1771.

---

* According to a notice issued by the Society for the Protection of Animals in Munich the superfluous whipping and the cracking of whips were, in December, 1858, positively forbidden in Nuremburg.

† In " Up the Rhine."

A FEW PARABLES.

IN A FIELD of ripening corn I came to a place which had been trampled down by some ruthless foot; and as I glanced among the countless stalks, every one of them alike, standing there so erect and bearing the full weight of the ear, I saw a multitude of different flowers, red and blue and violet. How pretty they looked as they grew there so naturally with their little foliage! But, thought I, they are quite useless; they bear no fruit; they are mere weeds. suffered to remain only because there is no getting rid of them. And yet, but for these flowers, there would be nothing to charm the eye in that wilderness of stalks. They are emblematic of poetry and art, which, in civic life—so severe, but still useful and not without its fruit—play the same part as flowers in the corn.

There are some really beautiful landscapes in the world, but the human figures in them are poor, and you had not better look at them.

The fly should be used as the symbol of impertinence and audacity; for while all other animals shun man more than anything else, and run away even before he comes near them, the fly lights upon his very nose.

Two Chinamen traveling in Europe went to the theater for the first time. One of them did nothing but study the machinery, and he succeeded in finding out how it was worked. The other tried to get at the meaning of the piece in spite of his ignorance of the language. Here you have the astronomer and the philosopher.

Wisdom which is only theoretical and never put into practice, is like a double rose; its color and its perfume are delightful, but it withers away and leaves no seed.

No rose without a thorn. Yes, but many a thorn without a rose.

A widespreading apple tree stood in full bloom, and behind it a straight fir raised its dark and tapering head. " Look at the thousands of gay blossoms which cover me everywhere," said the apple tree; " what have you to show in comparison? Dark green needles!" "That is true," replied the fir, "but when winter comes, you will be bared of your glory; and I shall be as I am now."

Once, as I was botanizing under an oak, I found among a number of other plants of similar height one that was dark in color, with tightly closed leaves and a stalk that was very straight and stiff. When I touched it, it said to me in firm tones: " Let me alone; I am not for your collection, like these plants to which Nature has given only a single year of life. I am a little oak."

So it is with a man whose influence is to last for hundreds of years. As a child, as a youth, often even as a full-grown man, nay, his whole life long, he goes about among his fellows, looking like them and seemingly as unimportant. But let him alone; he will not die. Time will come and bring those who know how to value him.

The man who goes up in a balloon does not feel as though he were ascending; he only sees the earth sinking deeper and deeper under him.

This is a mystery which only those will understand who feel the truth of it.

Your estimation of a man's size will be affected by the distance at which you stand from him, but in two entirely opposite ways according as it is his physical or his mental stature that you are considering. The one will seem smaller, the farther off you move; the other, greater.

Nature covers all her works with a varnish of beauty, like the tender bloom that is breathed, as it were, on the surface of a peach or plum. Painters and poets lay themselves out to take off this varnish, to store it up, and give it us to be enjoyed at our leisure. We drink deep of this beauty long before we enter upon life itself; and when afterward we come to see the works of nature for ourselves, the varnish is gone: the artists have used it up and we have enjoyed it in advance. Thus it is that the world so often appears harsh and devoid of charm, nay, actually repulsive. It were better to leave us to discover the varnish for ourselves. This would mean that we should not enjoy it all at once and in large quantities; we should have no finished pictures, no perfect poems; but we should look at all things in the genial and pleasing light in which even now a child of nature sometimes sees them—some one who has not anticipated his æsthetic pleasures by the help of art, or taken the charms of life too early.

The cathedral in Mayence is so shut in by the houses that are built round about it, that there is no one spot from which you can see it as a whole. This is symbolic of everything great or beautiful in the world. It ought to exist for its own sake alone, but before very long it is misused to serve alien ends. People come from all directions wanting to find in it support and maintenance for themselves; they stand in the way and spoil its effect. To be sure, there is nothing surprising in this, for in a world of need and imperfection everything is seized upon which can be used to satisfy want. Nothing is exempt from this service, no, not even those very things which arise only when need and want are for a moment lost sight of—the beautiful and the true, sought for their own sakes.

This is especially illustrated and corroborated in the case of institutions—whether great or small, wealthy or poor, founded, no matter in what century or in what land, to maintain and advance human knowledge, and generally to afford help to those intellectual efforts which ennoble the race. Wherever these institutions may be, it is not long before people sneak up to them under the pretense of wishing to further those special ends, while they are really led on by the desire to secure the emoluments which have been left for their furtherance, and thus to satisfy certain coarse and brutal instincts of their own. Thus it is that we come to have so many charlatans in every branch of knowledge. The charlatan takes very different shapes according to circumstances; but at bottom he is a man who cares nothing about knowledge for his own sake, and only strives to gain the semblance of it that he may use it for his own personal ends, which are always selfish and material.

Every hero is a Samson. The strong man succumbs to the intrigues of the weak and the many; and if in the end he loses all patience he crushes both them and himself. Or he is like Gulliver at Lilliput, overwhelmed by an enormous number of little men.

A mother gave her children Æsop's fables to read, in the hope of educating and improving their minds; but they very soon brought the book back, and the eldest, wise beyond his years, delivered himself as follows: "This is no book for us; it's much too childish and stupid. You can't make us believe that foxes and wolves and ravens are able to talk; we've got beyond stories of that kind!"

In these young hopefuls you have the enlightened Rationalists of the future.

A number of porcupines huddled together for warmth on a cold day in winter; but, as they began to prick one another with their quills, they were obliged to disperse. However the cold drove them together again, when just the same thing happened. At last, after many turns of huddling and dispersing, they discovered that they would be best off by remaining at a little distance from one another. In the same way the need of society drives the human porcupines together, only to be mutually repelled by the many prickly and disagreeable qualities of their nature. The moderate distance which they at last discover to be the only tolerable condition of intercourse, in the code of politeness and fine manners; and those who transgress it are roughly told—in the English phrase—"to keep their distance." By this arrangement the mutual need of warmth is only very moderately satisfied; but then people do not get pricked. A man who has some heat in himself prefers to remain outside, where he will neither prick other people nor get pricked himself.

THE END.